A WOMAN'S PLACE

HOUSE CHURCHES IN EARLIEST CHRISTIANITY

▫▯▫ ▫▯▫ ▫▯▫

CAROLYN OSIEK

AND

MARGARET Y. MACDONALD

WITH JANET H. TULLOCH

FORTRESS PRESS

▫▯▫ MINNEAPOLIS ▫▯▫

Cover image: Detail from a meal scene from room 45 at Peter and Marcellinus catacomb, Pontificia Commissione di Archeologia Sacra, Rome. Used by permission.
Cover design: Zan Ceeley
Interior design: Beth Wright

Scripture quotations marked NRSV are from the New Revised Standard Version Bible, copyright © 1989 by the Division of Christian Education of the National Council of the Churches of Christ in the USA and used by permission. Otherwise, scripture quotations are authors' own translation.

Library of Congress Cataloging-in-Publication Data
Osiek, Carolyn.
   A woman's place : house churches in earliest Christianity / Carolyn Osiek and Margaret Y. MacDonald with Janet H. Tulloch.
      p. cm.
   Includes bibliographical references and index.
   ISBN 0-8006-3690-2 (hardcover : alk. paper) — ISBN 0-8006-3777-1 (pbk. : alk. paper)
      1. House churches. 2. Sex role—Religious aspects—Christianity. 3. Women in church work. 4. Women in Christianity. 5. Church history —Primitive and early church, ca. 30-600.   I. MacDonald, Margaret Y. II. Tulloch, Janet H. III. Title.
   BV601.85.O85 2005
   270.1'082—dc22   2005024274

The paper used in this publication meets the minimum requirements of American National Standard for Information Sciences—Permanence of Paper for Printed Library Materials, ANSI Z329.48-1984.

Manufactured in the U.S.A.
10   09   08   07   06   2   3   4   5   6   7   8   9   10

CONTENTS

ACKNOWLEDGMENTS

▣▣▣ ▣▣▣ ▣▣▣

The idea for this book arose from a conversation between the two authors at the annual meeting of the Studiorum Novi Testamenti Societas in Montreal in the summer of 2001. The collaboration in the writing project has been mutually stimulating in a way that solitary writing can never be. The authors are pleased to include the chapter contribution by Janet Tulloch, whose expertise in visual arts has been an important complement to their own textual studies.

While writing this book the two authors have each, in turn, served as the cochair with Halvor Moxnes (University of Oslo) of the Early Christian Families Group at the Society of Biblical Literature. We would like to thank the members of this group for enriching us with so many excellent papers, and we extend special appreciation to Halvor Moxnes for his ongoing interest in our work.

Carolyn Osiek is especially grateful to her administrative assistant, Lucy Rodriguez, and her student assistants, Sean Allen and Jason Merritt, for their considerable time and attention to the proofreading and editing of these chapters.

Margaret MacDonald would like to thank the Social Sciences and Humanities Research Council of Canada (SSHRC) for supporting her collaborative research with Carolyn Osiek. She is grateful to Steven Fai, whose architectural expertise has enriched her appreciation of Rome, Ostia, and Pompeii immensely. She is also grateful to her research assistant, Gillian

Pink, for her meticulous work during the summer of 2004. To Margaret's husband, Duncan, and children, Delia and Jake, thank you for your patience and understanding.

An earlier version of chapter 1 appeared as "Women in House Churches," in *Common Life in the Early Church: Essays Honoring Graydon F. Snyder*, edited by Julian V. Hills (Harrisburg, Pa.: Trinity Press International, 1998), 300–315. We are grateful to Trinity for permission to use a revised version of this chapter.

Earlier versions of chapters 5 and 10 appeared as "Female Slaves and the Limits of *Porneia*," and "Was Celsus Right? The Role of Women in the Expansion of Early Christianity," in *Early Christian Families in Context: An Interdisciplinary Dialogue*, edited by David L. Balch and Carolyn Osiek (Grand Rapids: Eerdmans, 2003), 157–84, 255–74. We are grateful to Eerdmans for permission to use revised versions of these chapters.

CHAPTER ONE

INTRODUCTION

The subject of the house church raises most of the questions about early Christian life, and the bibliography on women in the early church continues to multiply exponentially. What we propose to do in this book is to bring these two topics together.

In this introduction, we identify three polarities that have pervaded the study of women in the early church: patriarchy versus the discipleship of equals, public versus private, and ascetic versus domestic lifestyle. After rendering some judgment about each of these, we lay out three working assumptions that must inform our investigation: about masculine language, about the honor/shame system, and about how house churches functioned.

Three Polarities

The first polarity is *patriarchy versus the discipleship of equals*. Scholarship on the position of women in Greco-Roman antiquity and early Christianity has tended to fall into two camps. On the one hand, legal and social historians and social-science interpreters have portrayed the social structures of the culture, in which the Roman father[1] had legal authority of life and death over everyone in his *familia* (household) and women could not act as legal persons without a male *tutor* or legal guardian, as patriarchal.

Social-science analysis has shown the prevalence of the sexual double standard, the emphasis on female purity and exclusiveness and the obligation of males to defend their women's honor.[2]

On the other hand, feminist and liberation writers, based on a different reading of the sources, have argued for a new spark of insight in earliest Christianity, especially in the teaching of Jesus, a vision of a new way of relating as female and male in the church. According to this reading, the model of discipleship offered by Jesus broke through the barriers of social discrimination to a vision of true equality. But also according to the model, later disciples did not maintain this liberative tendency. The "fall from primal grace" occurred at different moments, depending on one's point of view: with Paul, with Deutero-Paul, or just after the New Testament. Thus this model becomes a new version of the "early catholicism" argument, whereby the pristine origins degenerated at some point into accommodation with the world.

A variation on this model is the suggestion that there were indeed moderate liberative tendencies at work in the period, but they did not originate with Christianity. Rather, we can see the movement toward greater social freedom for women already happening in the Roman Empire independent of the influence of Christianity, which simply rode the wave of social development and followed these tendencies to a certain extent.[3] In this scenario, not much of the credit goes to the early church. Christianity was not the only game in town contributing to a transformation of patriarchy, but it was *one* of the games.

Jewish feminist scholars have made us quite aware of the implicit anti-Judaism that can lie behind the argument that Christianity created a discipleship of equals: Jesus liberated women from the oppression of Judaism.[4] So there are problems all around: if Jesus liberated women, he was unfair to his own Judaism; if he did and the church could not keep up with him, it has failed him in a major way; if patriarchy really held sway all along, then from the perspective of modern sympathies, Jesus may have been a failure.

We find ourselves most convinced by the position that identifies a movement toward greater social freedom for women (not toward "liberation" in the modern sense) that was happening already in Roman society and in which Christianity partially participated. Indeed, we can trace in Roman society of the first century such a movement for women in a number of ways: the virtual disappearance of marriage by *manus* (transfer of the bride from the family and authority of her father to that of her husband); Augustus's incentive of freedom from *tutela* (legal guardianship) to women who bore a certain number of children (three for a freeborn woman, four for a freedwoman); evidence mentioned by several authors that respectable women were beginning to recline at public banquets alongside their husbands; evidence of women administering their property, conducting business, and owning businesses.[5] Some strains of Christianity seem to have picked up on this movement and given it a religious motivation. Others represented a continuity of more traditional patterns. Both tendencies were probably at work simultaneously.

The second polarity: *public versus private*. Much work has been done on the analysis, one could almost say creation, of these social structures for Greco-Roman antiquity. According to ancient texts as well as modern anthropological theories, the public domain of temples, theatre, forum, assemblies, and law courts or, in the countryside among peasants, the town square and the fields is the world of men in which women do not mix, while the domain of house and garden, domestic production, and childcare is the private domain of women. In some earlier thinking, the two categories remained as rigidly fixed and separated as if the way they functioned today in the most conservative Islamic society were the way they functioned everywhere.

The model is not all wrong, of course. The *social* invisibility of women in public life in Greco-Roman antiquity is striking compared to many other cultures. But social invisibility is conceptual; it exists in the minds of those who articulate the ideal and may bear no resemblance to what is really going on. The fact that women may not be addressed in public settings does not mean that they were not there. The evidence for women in business and professions demonstrates that social invisibility is not actual invisibility.[6]

Moreover, the categories are overdrawn and often too rigidly applied. The Roman *paterfamilias*[7] conducted much if not most of his business and political activities—the two intrinsically interwoven through the patronage system—at home, in the front part of the house, to which Roman women, in contrast to Greek women, were not denied access. Here the stated differences between Greek and Roman use of domestic space must be taken seriously into account. The elite Greek house, according to Vitruvius and others, segregated women in the back of the house, while the Roman house did not (Vitruvius, *On architecture* 6.10.1–5).[8] To the extent that Roman customs penetrated the Greek East, Romanizing changes can be presumed eventually in the East as well, at least for the relatively elite. Of course, an author like Vitruvius—and indeed most of the non-Christian ancient sources—does not envision dwellings of the lower classes and the poor, where lack of adequate space would have made any kind of sexual segregation virtually impossible.

There has sometimes been an assumption that the house church, because it most often met in a domestic structure, also met under the rules of the private sphere, in which women are thought to have had greater freedom within the circle of the immediate family. But most often a house-church meeting was not that of the immediate family, and this notion of "private rules" for it has been ably challenged by an analysis of Paul's expectations in 1 Corinthians.[9] Rather than thinking of the house church as a private haven, we should probably think of it as the crossroads between public and private, and the old Roman idea that as goes the household, so goes the state, was equally applicable in the Christian community. First Timothy 3:4-5 specifies that an overseer (*episkopos*) of the community must give evidence of governing his own household well, for if he cannot do that, the text asks rhetorically, how can he govern the church?

Again, we are warned that an implicit bias can lurk beneath the assumption that the synagogue was a public meeting, therefore more restrictive of women than the private Christian meeting in the house. The use and even renovation of private houses for public meetings were common to Jews, Christians, and others, and nothing can be construed about social behavior by the use of domestic space, much less comparisons made between the relative freedom of Jewish and Christian women on this basis.[10]

The third polarity to discuss briefly is *ascetic versus domestic lifestyle*. How early did the ascetic lifestyle begin in Christianity, including the permanent embrace of prayer, fasting, and especially celibacy? Are we to assume that most of the women we hear about are ascetics or living normal family lives? Already in 1 Corinthians 7, Paul seems to advocate a certain asceticism for eschatological motives, especially the discouraging of marriage and remarriage. Since women's chastity already bore great symbolic weight, it is reasonable to expect that celibacy as an ideal would be applied especially to women and eventually would appeal strongly to them as an alternative to marriage.[11] In 1 Cor. 7:36-38, Paul speaks of a decision to be made by a man about a woman's marital status, and it is frequently interpreted as an indication that "celibate marriages" have already begun, at least in Corinth, where several kinds of unusual behavior seem to have been indigenous. Officially enrolled widows are not allowed to remarry in the church of Timothy, but younger widows are in fact encouraged to remarry (1 Tim. 5:9, 14). This latter gathering would have been a highly volatile group when they came together, just the kind that aroused unconscious fears of anarchy. They were young and not directly under male control, hence the advice to Timothy to get them remarried as soon as possible. Ignatius (*Smyrn.* 13.1) suggests the existence of an identifiable group of "virgins called widows" in at least one community of Asia Minor in the early second century. Bonnie Bowman Thurston has made the plausible suggestion that the term *parthenos* be taken here in its broader sense of women of marriageable age and that the reference refers to these "nonenrolled" widows young enough to remarry (see 1 Tim. 5:11-14).[12] Acceptable "safe" older widows as an identifiable group who did not remarry, however, flourished in the church for several centuries, not only as objects of charity but as a recognized service organization.[13]

Celibacy for the kingdom appealed not only to women. Hermas is told that his wife will "from now on be to you as a sister," presumably meaning that his new identity as a seer required sexual continence (Herm. *Vis.* 2.2.3). In the middle of the second century Justin boasts that both men and women have been celibate from their youth into old age (1 *Apology* 15, 29). Yet there can be no doubt that as time advanced, the ethos of consecrated female virgins formed a strong characteristic in early Christianity, for a variety of reasons that cannot be examined here but that have everything to do with the female body as symbol of political, social, and theological integrity.

The idealization of virginity and female celibacy has so overshadowed the rest of the evidence that there has been a tendency to assume that women singled out as engaged in ministry were members of this ascetic group. It is only in recent years that we have begun to look at the accumulation of evidence on the other side, for example, the married evangelists Prisca and Junia, Mary mother of John Mark (Acts 12:12), the mother of Rufus (Rom. 16:13), the wife of Epitropos (Ignatius, *Pol.* 8.2), the married martyr Perpetua and her pregnant companion Felicitas (as a slave, not legally married),[14] to name only a few. In light of that culture's obsession with classifying women by sexual status, it is striking that so many women are named in the Pauline and Ignatian letters and elsewhere without such designation: Phoebe, Mary, Tryphaena, Tryphosa, Persis, Julia, and the unnamed sister of Nereus (Rom. 16:1, 6, 12, 15); Euodia and Syntyche (Phil. 4:2); Grapte (Herm. *Vis.* 2.4.3), Tavia (Ignatius, *Smyrn.* 13.2), Alke (Ignatius, *Pol.* 8.3; *Smyrn.* 13.2; *Mart. Pol.* 17.2), and Blandina (*Martyrs of Lyons and Vienne*), to name only a few. It is highly unlikely that all or most of them were ascetics. Rather, women in ministerial roles in the first centuries were more likely married or widowed than celibate ascetic, in spite of some evidence of a growing custom of consecrated celibacy.

Three Assumptions

We turn now to an overview of the three assumptions that are basic to the rest of the book. The first is that masculine plural titles should not always presume men to the exclusion of women. The second is that the cultural values of honor and shame were at work, but differently in different situations. The third assumption is that women participated in all the principal activities of the house church: worship, hospitality, patronage, education, communication, social services, evangelization, and missionary initiatives.

The first assumption, that *masculine plural titles should not always presume men to the exclusion of women*, should be obvious according to grammatical and social custom. In both domains, women were considered to be included with, and embedded in, men, as they still are in many languages and cultures. Yet discussions of the literature have not completely abandoned the assumption that masculine references refer exclusively to men when it comes to positions of leadership, in spite of the *diakonos* Phoebe (Rom. 16:1); the apostle Junia (Rom. 16:7); teachers of women like Grapte and the public Gnostic teacher Marcellina in the mid-second century in Rome, so effective, according to Irenaeus, that she "exterminated many" (Irenaeus, *Against Heresies* 1.25.6; see Epiphanius, *Panarion* 27.6); and a number of known women prophets (including "Jezebel," Rev. 2:20). Rationally, we assent to the principle and perhaps do not see a problem. However, consider what we may assume when passages roll off our lips such as 1 Cor. 12:28 ("God has established in the church first apostles, second prophets, third teachers"), Phil. 1:1 ("to all the holy ones in Philippi with *episkopoi* and *diakonoi*"), Eph. 4:11 (God provided "some to be apostles, some prophets, some evangelists, some pastors and teachers"), and Eph. 2:20 (the church is "built upon the foundation of the apostles and prophets with Christ Jesus as cornerstone"). Even if we have acknowledged in that last one that the prophets referred to are Christian rather than ancient Israelite prophets, most of us imagine groups of men, and one can be quite certain that the general Bible-reading population does the same. We need continually to remind others and especially ourselves to readjust the mental picture.

The second assumption concerns *the function of the cultural values of honor and shame*, often considered the "pivotal values" of ancient Mediterranean culture. There has been a tendency in scholarship to adopt general formulations uncritically into any ancient situation and assume that the dynamic works in the same way from ancient Israel to Augustine, and from Spain to Babylonia, in spite of anthropologists' careful documentation and adaptation of cultural generalities to given situations.[15] Indeed, some anthropologists have questioned the existence of a single system of honor and shame across Mediterranean civilization, preferring instead to link the culture patterns in a north/south direction, taking in southern and northern Europe, rather than in an east/west direction, from Spain to the Middle East.[16]

There is no agreement on the exact way that honor and shame function within a given cultural context. Some would claim that in traditional Mediterranean cultures the only real honor for a woman is that of her family and its dominant males, while for her there is only appropriate sensitivity to shame, expressed in shyness and sexual exclusivity. For others, women bear the responsibility for guarding not only family but national honor, and the honor of women is that of the family. In this case, the entire weight of corporate honor is projected onto the bodies of women.

In a society clearly divided along gender lines in its structures of work, leisure, and friendship, male anthropologists have access only to the male world of meaning and therefore derive their interpretations from it. Women anthropologists with access to the private world of women usually suggest that women in honor/shame cultures adapt to the more public male honor system, in which women are something like commodities to be guarded, raided, and traded, but privately such women operate on a different kind of honor system based not on competition for honor but on mutual confidence.[17] Still others argue that the honor/shame system has more to do with political ideologies or the presuppositions of the interpreter than it does with what is really happening in the culture.[18]

In the ancient Mediterranean world, as today, the honor/shame code was actualized with significant variations according to time and place, and much of the difference by the first century depended on the degree of Roman influence. If Vitruvius (first century BCE) is correct that the Greek house was built to segregate the family's women from the business and entertaining conducted by the adult male members of the family, that is one system. If the Roman house was designed not to segregate but to display social status in which women participated, that is another. Both are honor/shame systems. The difference lies in the specific content of what constitutes honor and shame. It would seem that the strict segregation of women such as that described by Philo, in which married women were not to venture beyond the front door and unmarried women not even to get that far (*Special Laws* 3.169), was based on the most conservative upper-class male ideal of classical Athens. By Philo's time, it was pretty much a male fantasy.

The veiling of women in public, still a custom in Islamic countries, is meant to symbolize shame or sensitivity to honorable chastity by concealing beauty and sexuality—though the veil can certainly be worn in such a way that it augments those very qualities. Considerable evidence indicates that covering a woman's head with a veil was once customary throughout both Greek and Roman spheres of influence, but that it was much less prevalent in western Roman areas by the middle of the first century. Many official portraits of women continued to feature the suggestion of a veil, but it was more symbolic than concealing.[19]

One of the practices of a strictly segregated honor/shame society is that respectable women's names should never be spoken in public because such women should draw the attention of no one beyond the immediate family. If it is necessary to mention them in public, they should be referred to only by their relationship with a relevant male: the wife of A, the mother of B, the daughter of C, and so on. On the contrary, Roman aristocratic women were patrons of public associations, with their names inscribed and their dedicatory statues on display.[20] Paul's direct naming of women friends, collaborators, and benefactors, in most cases without giving their marital or familial status, contradicts this rule as well. It may not be coincidental, however, that the largest number of women whom Paul greets is in his letter to the church at Rome, which was probably the place with the most rapid social change.[21]

All of this is not to say that there was no operative honor/shame code or that it did not affect women in a different way from men. Roman society remained highly patriarchal and passed on this characteristic to

Judaism and Christianity. Early Christianity created its own adaptations of the honor/shame code by proposing an alternate standard for honorable conduct based on its moral system and the inversion of values that accompanied a theology of the cross. Consequently, a different standard of shameful behavior consisted of failure to live according to those standards. But even apart from a different set of religious expectations, the standards for female chastity and passive virtue were undoubtedly higher than those for male sexual containment.[22]

The third assumption proposes that *women participated in all the activities of the house church in the first generations of the Christian era and that the house church was the center for worship, hospitality, patronage, education, communication, social services, evangelization, and mission.* Several questions need to be entertained in order to discuss this assumption. These are questions to which scholars wish they knew the answers. First, what kinds of houses are we envisioning when we talk about the "house church"? Second, where were women, and how did they function at the common meals of the gathered community? Third, some of the best evidence for women heads of households in the ancient Mediterranean world comes from the New Testament. How were women both patrons and heads of house churches in a culture in which male headship of the house was the norm?

We need first to talk about what kinds of houses are envisioned. While the household terminology of *oikos*, *oikia*, *domus*, and *familia* is not clear in social use, in Roman law a *domus* was any place in which a *paterfamilias*, that is, a property owner, resided.[23] Some Christian groups must certainly have met in more modest accommodations, even in some of the grimier apartment houses (*insulae*) or "tenement churches," as Robert Jewett has called them.[24] But there is no reason, given the ample evidence of the ownership of some rather spacious houses at Pompeii by persons of modest social status but less modest wealth,[25] why groups of worshipping Christians, like their Jewish or Mithraist neighbors, could not have met in a peristyled *domus* (a building featuring a colonnade). It seems best to leave open the possibility of a variety of different configurations for house-church meetings, in the earliest years at least. The households of Stephanas and of Prisca and Aquila in Corinth (1 Cor. 16:15, 19) are likely to have been a *domus*, even if ever so modest. "Those from Chloe" (1 Cor. 1:11) may be messengers to Paul in Ephesus, therefore away from home in Corinth, but they may also be members of a gathering in more modest circumstances, since no household (*oikos*) of Chloe is mentioned. In the case of this group, however, it is also possible that Chloe herself is not a Christian, but a large number of her household are.

The relevant question here is: Would the position of women in the assembly have been any different whether it took place in a spacious and luxurious house, a more modest peristyled house, or a rented room in the corner of an *insula*? It is sometimes assumed that the larger and more imposing the *domus*, the more hierarchical and patriarchal the social structure, so that in less formal meeting situations, more flexibility of leadership structures could be presumed. Perhaps this was true, but most of the evidence of various voluntary associations and private cults suggests rather highly organized leadership structures, with less evidence of women as actual leaders than of women as patrons. We do not yet know enough about how patronage functioned in private associations, much less how women patrons functioned.

There is also the question of whether all who attended such meals reclined. In a gathering in a *domus*, the room designated as dining room would have most likely been arranged as a *triclinium* (three-couch arrangement, usually for nine persons) or *stibadium* (semicircular seating arrangement), the latter a slightly more flexible arrangement that was already appearing in the first century but only became common much later,[26] with hosts and most important guests reclining. What about everyone else? We are simply lacking the information, but probably the more solemn the occasion, the more likely that temporary couches would be set up to include at least all males in the formal position and that the dining room of most houses would not have been large enough to contain the whole membership.[27]

The possible options for women at the common meal of a house church, then, are, first, absence of women and children, leaving the ritual meal to be eaten by men alone; second, separate dining rooms for men and women, children either excluded or brought in with the women; third, women and children seated next to their reclining male relatives; fourth, women and children seated in a separate place from the reclining men; or fifth, women and men reclining together, children either seated near them or together in a separate place. The first option, complete absence of women from the ritual meal, is unlikely, given the large number of women who were active in various kinds of ministry. The second option, separate dining rooms, is also unlikely if all were supposed to share from the same table and hear the word read and preached. The third through the fifth options, however, are all possibilities, depending on time and place, namely: women and children seated next to men's couches, women and children seated separately but in the same area, and men and women reclining together. The persistent accusation of suspicious outsiders and authorities against private associations, including Christian ones, that they indiscriminately mixed both sexes and all social ranks, probably had a basis in just such things as seating or reclining arrangements at official gatherings.

Given what we know about Roman colonies like Philippi and Corinth, we can conclude that reclining together was more likely the style there than perhaps in some other Pauline churches. Eventually, of course, the couches and chairs disappeared, and everyone stood, probably men on one side of the room and women on the other, but that was to take at least another century.[28] A wider question is the role of women in the patronage system, specifically as patrons in Christian communities. Patronage was the backbone of the informal social system of cohesion among men, providing means for political and social advancement as well as economic benefits.[29] Ample evidence suggests that women, too, exercised patronage, though it must have been in a somewhat different way. Elite women were actively, though indirectly, involved in politics.[30] There is no reason to assume that something analogous did not operate at other social levels. Women were public patrons of guilds, clubs, synagogues, and other types of private associations. By the third century, we know of the tendency of Christian benefaction to be centered on giving at the ritual assembly so that all resources would be channeled through the hands of the bishop and his deacons.[31] But it was not always so. We must read in the light of patronage the stories and references to Phoebe, Lydia, the mother of John Mark in Jerusalem, and others, bearing in mind that in the traditional Roman patronage system, it was customary for clients to maintain a relationship of *obsequium*, compliance and submission. Did Paul give suitable tribute to his patrons Phoebe and Lydia and perhaps give them private instruction or repair leatherwork around the house in exchange for the hospitality and financial assistance he received from them?

Patronage is one thing; managing a household is another. The literature on household management never raises the question of a female manager without at least in the background the presence of a male *paterfamilias*, and autonomous female leadership of a household is so contrary to the ideals of the conservative theorists that they never discuss it. Yet we know it happened frequently. Some historians will assume that a reference to a house church meeting "in the house of" a woman refers merely to the name of the *owner* of the house—and women did own property on their own—and that it says nothing about who presided at social activities of the household.

Activities in House Churches

We turn now to a closer look at women's involvement in house churches in terms of the churches' functions: worship, hospitality, patronage, education, communication, social services, evangelization, and mission. As discussed above, women were present for the principal act of worship, the ritual meal of the assembly, perhaps in background locations in some circumstances but in the foreground in others. They were, after all, half or more of the membership.

Some of the best examples of houses led by women, probably in most cases widows, is from the New Testament: Mary mother of John Mark in Jerusalem (Acts 12:12), Lydia (Acts 16:14, 40), Nympha (Col. 4:15), and perhaps Chloe (1 Cor. 1:11). This does not mean that the first generation of Christians was different in this regard but that here we have unbiased social information from nonelite sources. It is probably correct to surmise that in such cases, these women hosted formal dinners and presided at them, including the assembly of the *ekklēsia*. The sources would understandably be silent about this, not wanting to encourage more of it. In the absence of definite evidence, we will probably never know, but in the context of the slender evidence that we do have, it makes sense.

Women have traditionally been chiefly responsible for hospitality. The ancient Greco-Roman world is full of evidence of households that take in family members or friends of family members who require a place to live commensurate with their status, or even those in immediate need of safe housing. In similar situations in the Christian community, the same kind of hospitality was undoubtedly practiced, and, as always, women would have to have been in the forefront of making the practice effective. This would include reception of passing Christian visitors, especially itinerant missionaries like the wandering apostles and prophets of the *Didache* or the founder of a church. A general pattern was probably to host such dignitaries in the house in which a house church assembled. Soon, however, this was a ministry entrusted particularly to those widows who would have the capacity to receive guests (1 Tim. 5:10). Of course, in some cases, the widow's house might also be the meeting place of the assembly, and she would be its patron. One wonders, for instance, about Ignatius's fondness for Tavia and Alke. As a prisoner, Ignatius may not have been allowed out overnight, but perhaps he was. These women must have performed some special service for him, and the most likely scenario is that they were widows who provided hospitality. It is highly unlikely that Ignatius would have referred to them alone by name if they had husbands.

These women's houses thus became important centers of education, not only initial instruction but also ongoing education in faith. Those who qualified for advanced instruction, for a "graduate degree" such as that provided by professional teachers like Justin in mid-second-century Rome, must first have been through the regular instruction based in houses, at meetings other than that of the weekly assembly. Whatever instruction could be given through preaching at the weekly assembly could not have borne the entire weight of a program of religious formation. One is reminded of Pliny's account of Christians who meet very early in the morning to bind themselves by oath not to commit crimes, then hold a prayer service with singing (Pliny, *Ep.* 10.96.7).

The character of the culture makes it unlikely that all such religious instruction took place in mixed groups. Some, perhaps much, of it was gender-specific, with instruction oriented to the particular roles of women and men in the family. It is here that we have ample evidence of the special role of women teachers, a role often neglected because scholarly interest remains at the public, predominantly male, level. Every cultural and religious tradition that practices any kind of gender separation develops distinctive teaching traditions for men and women. The three religions of the book, Judaism, Christianity, and Islam, do so still today.

Allusions to the teaching of women by women tell us of a continuing custom of whose content we know very little: older women are to form character in younger women while male teachers do the same for young men (Titus 2:3-8). While Hermas delivers his revelatory message to the presbyters in the assembly, an otherwise unknown Grapte receives her own copy of the text to give special instruction to widows and their children, implying some kind of regular assembly of persons in that category (Herm. *Vis.* 2.4.3).[32] Widows form a more or less distinctive group as the church grows, sometimes objects of charity but also a group of women on whom church leaders come to depend for a variety of services, one of them being instruction of other women. Later, in the Eastern churches, deaconesses will take over much of that work. It has been suggested that since much teaching in oral cultures is done by storytelling, instructional stories told in these circles eventually emerged into the "malestream" as the apocryphal Gospels and Acts.[33]

Communication was also an important activity centered on the house church. News from visitors (perhaps Chloe's people, in Ephesus from Corinth in 1 Cor. 1:11), reception and sending of letters from one city to another (for example, Paul's letters, 2 and 3 John, *1 Clement*), and warnings of persecution and accounts of persecutions experienced (for example, the letter from the churches of Lyons and Vienne) were all important types of information that passed through the house churches, disseminated then to all associated with them. Women's social networks were especially valuable for their ability to spread information through already organized structures.

Another function of the house church was as a center of social services for those members of the church who were in need. Again, young widows and their children from families who could not support them come immediately to mind. Apparently, there were some attempts by families to sidestep their own responsibility in this regard and have their widow freeload on the church (see, for example, 1 Tim. 5:4, 5, 8, 16), just as some slaves began to expect from the church not only moral encouragement but funding for their manumission (Ignatius, *Pol.* 4.3). Justin speaks of a common collection for orphans and widows, the sick, the imprisoned, and visiting strangers (*1 Apology* 67). Tertullian speaks of the monthly contribution for works of charity: food and burial for the poor and support of orphans, old slaves and sailors, and those imprisoned (*Apology* 39.5–6). Already by the middle of the second century, therefore, a common collection for relief of the needy was in place. This custom, eventually to be centralized in church leadership, did not, however, immediately replace private deeds of patronage and benefaction, in which Greco-Roman women in general were known to be active participants. Just as women were patrons of clubs and synagogues, so they were of house churches as well. But Christian women's private patronage of the poor and needy will never be adequately documented. We catch fleeting glimpses, for instance, of the "enrolled" widow of 1 Tim. 5:10, who is expected not only to have shown hospitality and washed the feet of visitors but to have relieved the afflicted and done other kinds of good works, too.

Visiting the sick and the imprisoned was also included in the kinds of charitable activity expected of Christians (Matt. 25:36, 39). Much of this fell to the deacons once their position was in place. Deacons visit Perpetua and her companions in prison (*Acts of Perpetua and Felicitas*

2.7), yet in Lucian's account of the imprisonment of the then-Christian Peregrinus, widows and orphans come in droves to visit him (*Death of Peregrinus* 12). Tertullian expects that among the duties of a Christian woman, even one married to a non-Christian, is visitation of both the sick and those in prison, duties that an unbelieving husband will be reluctant to let her do (*To His Wife* 2.4).

Finally, the house church was a center for evangelization and mission. Each family unit was a locus for evangelization, including—perhaps especially—the mixed marriage. Paul considers the presence of the believer in the family to render it holy (1 Cor. 7:14). The writer of 1 Peter sees the submission of Christian wives to their non-Christian husbands as a means of converting them (1 Pet. 3:1-2). Later, Tertullian would take a much dimmer view and try to discourage mixed marriages (*To His Wife* 2.4–7). There was as yet no "missionary school." Those who would be sent as missionaries by local churches got their training and encouragement in local assemblies that would then commission them for their mission. Paul claims the right, which he did not use, to bring a wife with him as the other apostles do (1 Cor. 9:5). Missionary couples like Prisca and Aquila and Andronicus and Junia were able to put not only their houses but their assets and their lives at the service of the gospel. Countless others did the same, either singly or in pairs. For all we know, traveling missionary couples may have been more the norm than the exception.

One question worth asking in this context is: How would early Christian women have heard and received the household codes and related expressions of their role as that of submission? Already accustomed to the rhetoric of submission, such women might have seen in Eph. 5:21-33, which likens wife and husband to the church and Christ, a bestowal of new identity. Already used to bearing the symbolic weight of house, family, chastity, and the honor of family and city-state, they may have been filled with an appropriate sense of their own importance as representatives of the church itself, that is to say, the whole gathered community before Christ.[34]

The Discussion to Come:
An Overview

These, then, are the issues that we probe in the following pages. Chapter 2 examines the lives of wives who are specifically mentioned in early Christian texts in light of recent research on the Roman family. The texts include not only presentations of dutiful wives but also several examples of less than dutiful wives by Roman or Christian standards. Chapter 3 discusses the real lives of most early Christian women, who were both faithful attendants at the weekly assembly and mothers of infants who had to be birthed, nursed, and raised. Chapter 4 continues the discussion of the raising and education of those children with a special focus on early Christian girls.

But there were other female members of these households: slaves, whose lives were much more difficult and much more vulnerable to forces beyond their control. Chapter 5 considers aspects of their fate. Offering a detailed analysis of Eph. 5:22-33, chapter 6 moves away from a specific focus on the daily lives of female participants in house churches to consider how their lives were increasingly becoming the subject of ideological discourse. Chapter 7 moves to the consideration of women's responsibilities in the management of households, the transition in Christian groups from ruling the house to hosting the house church, and what was likely to have happened in a house church hosted by a woman.

In chapter 8 Janet Tulloch examines the figures of women in the meal scenes of the Catacomb of Marcellinus and Peter in Rome, with new suggestions that present these women as actual participants and leaders in family funerary banquets; the scenes, from the late third and early fourth centuries, depict family rituals that no doubt go back to the first Christian practices and earlier still. Chapter 9 extends the influence of early Christian women beyond their own house churches to their place within the wider patronage system of the Greco-Roman world. Finally, chapter 10 depicts the participation of women in the missionary mainstream of early Christianity, paying particular attention to marriages between Christian women and pagan men.

In a society in which greater social freedom for women was increasing to some limited extent, within a new faith system that was still working out its identity vis-à-vis its parent religion and the cultural origins of its members, women actively contributed to the formation of a new movement that was to change the Mediterranean world and bring profound new challenges to male-female relationships, changes whose effects are still with us today.

CHAPTER TWO

DUTIFUL AND LESS THAN DUTIFUL WIVES

In books on women and Christian origins, wives do not usually have a starring role. The idealized bride who surfaces in prescriptive texts such as the household codes (for example, Col. 3:18-4:1; Eph. 5:21—6:9; 1 Pet. 2:18—3:7) or the nameless woman who is part of the extended household of a prominent male believer (for example, 1 Cor. 1:16) seems to lead such a conventional life that it generates little information or interest. Not only do we know very little about the lives of early Christian wives, but what little we do know is of questionable value for understanding the distinctiveness of early Christianity or for finding evidence for ancient emancipatory trends. As a general rule, in describing the lives of single and ascetic women, the texts are far more forthcoming. It is not surprising that such named New Testament women as Phoebe, the deacon of Cenchrae who has frequently been understood to be a widow (Rom. 16:1-2), and the powerful (but probably imaginary) virgin Thecla (from the second-century *Acts of [Paul and] Thecla*) have attracted so much attention, especially from scholars intent on investigating the leadership of early Christian women. But the deliberate focus on the house-church setting of this book may cause us to see the contribution of wives in a new light.

By considering recent research on the lives of wives in the Roman world and analyzing in detail early church texts in which particular wives are mentioned (sometimes without giving their names), we will show that collectively the wives of early Christianity played an important role in guaranteeing the survival of a fledgling new religious movement. However, we will also see that evidence for the less than dutiful wife (by Roman or Christian standards or both) becomes predominant.

An Imaginary Scene:
Testing Our Assumptions

We begin our study of the lives of wives with an ironic scene: a gathering in the house of Nympha, where the hierarchical household code is being proclaimed (Col. 3:18—4:1).[1] The irony lies in the fact that Nympha is clearly a woman leader of a house church, yet the epistle that is being read in her house recommends the subjugation of wife to husband in a manner that makes the endorsement of Nympha's role in Col. 4:15-16 surprising. The apparent contradiction has frequently been dismissed on account of the fact that Nympha appears to be single, perhaps a widow, and thereby free to offer her services to the church and to act as a leader in a way that was not typical of married women (see Acts 16:14-15; Rom. 16:1-2).[2] But even if Nympha's role was made possible by her life as a single woman in charge of a household (a fact that cannot be established conclusively), it is surprising to find the explicit reference to her leadership of a house church in a document that marks the beginning of a trend in early church literature of the latter half of the first century CE: the tendency to instruct subordinate members of the household to be subject to the *paterfamilias* (the husband, father, and master of slaves) and to instruct him to be benevolent in ruling his household as is appropriate for life in the Lord.[3]

On the basis of Col. 4:15-16, it seems quite likely that Nympha's house was in Laodicea. It is also not entirely clear whether the house church associated with Nympha was part of a larger community that included other house churches or whether Nympha hosted meetings of the city's entire community.[4] In either case, however, the intention of Col. 4:16 is plain: there is to be a public proclamation of Paul's letter to the Colossians in Nympha's house. It is valuable to imagine the impact of the epistle in a house ruled by a woman. We need to imagine members of extended households entering the house and being greeted by Nympha, who was most likely well-known in the neighborhood: wives and husbands who were believers accompanied by their children and slaves, but in all likelihood also wives and children who lived in the household of a pagan man. Near the end of the epistle, read aloud in Nympha's house, each group would be addressed directly, with the members who were traditionally subordinate in the house being told to submit to the *paterfamilias* "in the Lord" as well.

The scene raises many questions: Would the wives who entered, many with children in tow (or accompanied by slaves who looked after the master's children in addition to their own), have understood their lives as being substantially different from Nympha's life? To what extent were expectations tied to social status? Would Nympha have interpreted the call for wives to be subject to their husbands to have any bearing on her circumstances at all? Would the hierarchical marriage teaching have been so familiar to all in the room as to seem banal, or would it have resonated with powerful cultural codes linking household behavior with broader social expectations? Should we assume that the code proclaimed in a house setting was inevitably viewed by Nympha, the other women, or even others present as having implications for the leadership of women—married or celibate?

It is impossible to come up with conclusive answers to these questions, but our imagined encounter between Nympha and the nameless married women whom the author of Colossians addresses in Col. 3:18—4:1 can nevertheless raise methodological cautions to guide our discussion. First, we must be ready to examine our assumptions about differing patterns of behavior between married and unmarried early church women. Second, we must remember that hierarchical teaching concerning married women such as that found in the household codes was prescriptive and not descriptive. We must be open to the possibility that it may sometimes have had little impact on the social realm because it was either ignored or circumvented by women; conversely, we must also look for signs of its impact, including indications that marriage teaching was being used to restrict women in a variety of ways. Finally, we must keep in mind the existence of a world of women about which the texts remain silent—a world of sisterhood, conversation, and exchange among women on issues of hospitality, childcare, service, and allegiance to Christ under the authority of a (sometimes pagan) *paterfamilias* as a wife, daughter, or slave, a world where distinctions among various categories of women possibly broke down.

The Roman Family

Recent work on the Roman family confirms the probability that the picture of the ideal Christian house (and house church) under the dominion of the *paterfamilias* reflected in the household codes nevertheless offered some latitude to the influence of women and stood in tension with family circumstances that were often quite complex. Teaching concerning wives in the household codes constitutes a type of ideological discourse, with Eph. 5:22-33 offering the most important example of theological reflection on the significance of early Christian wives in the literature from the period of house churches—the period extending to the middle of the second century CE. It is best, therefore, to examine Eph. 5:22-33 within the context of a separate chapter (chapter 6); there we will explore the points of contact between this text and idealizations of marriage serving moral and political purposes in the empire. Untangling the complicated relationship between textual idealization and reality is an extraordinarily difficult task. But careful consideration of how women figure in rhetorical constructions in light of what we know of their daily lives can lead to cautious suggestions about how the world of wives served to foster the boundaries of early Christian identity. In order to lay the groundwork for this later discussion and for the examination of references to specific married women in this chapter, we will set forth some of the most important aspects of the lives of wives in this era.

The Roman sources exhibit considerable interest in married couples and their children, but it is also clear that marriages were often impermanent and remarriages very common. In a society in which women were frequently much younger than their husbands at the age of marriage—in our terms really only adolescent girls—it is not surprising that they sometimes were widowed at a very young age and subsequently remarried. Upper-class girls were usually married by the time they were sixteen. While the evidence for lower classes is not conclusive, there are some indications that they married later in their teens.[5] The chances that women would reach old age, however, were dependent on whether they survived their child-bearing years. In antiquity, giving birth was by far the greatest threat to a young woman's life.

For those who survived the hazardous business of giving birth, there was a high probability that they would soon be caring for the children of both first and subsequent marriages and, if they had married a widower or divorced man, his children as well. If the woman herself had been divorced (and in some cases even widowed and remarried), she would need to maintain contact with children living in the house of her previous husband or his family (the children remained under the *potestas* [legal authority] of the *paterfamilias* after divorce). In other words, the relations within families often involved quite complicated relations among parents, siblings, half-siblings, and step-siblings, not always living in the same house. The complexity of the situation was compounded by the likelihood of significant gaps in the ages of children because of childhood mortality and remarriages with frequent overlaps (quite rare in our times) between the ages of children and grandchildren—once again perhaps not all living in the same house.

In describing the features of the Roman family, Keith Bradley has spoken in terms of "the creation through serial marriage of networks of marital relationships which extended beyond the immediate household."[6] What might this mean for the use of familial metaphors to describe church groups in this era? Scholars have long recognized that a network of house churches existed in the cities of the eastern Mediterranean from New Testament times. But by linking the life of the church so closely to the life of the family, this network could build upon already existing networks of marital relationships. The wife who served as a missionary partner (see Acts 18:26) or as an apt image for the *ekklēsia* (Eph. 5:22-33) had familial points of contact and influence beyond those who lived with her in her house. The child, for example, who was instructed to obey his or her parents in the Lord might just as easily owe such respect to his or her divorced mother who was a believer married to a nonbelieving mate as to his or her father and stepmother whether they were believers or not. What this might mean for the role of women in the expansion of church groups requires further exploration.

In a very important sense, the early Christian household codes hold out an image of the mutually faithful, permanently unified Christian couple, perhaps implicitly encoding the early church teaching against divorce (see Ignatius, *Pol.* 5.1–2). But what might this idealization mean in relation to the practicalities of family life in the empire? Lofty ideals can certainly be found in the writings of the times, including the highly praised state of being *univira*—having only one husband within one's lifetime. Perhaps the most frequently quoted passages expressing these ideals is the so-called *Laudatio Turiae* (dating from the last decade of the first century BCE), an unusually long funerary inscription from Rome written for a woman named Turia whose speaker is the devoted and bereft husband. Although the marriage produced no children, the husband extolled the harmony of the union, highlighting at the same time the rarity of a marriage that had lasted for forty years without being prematurely ended by death or broken by divorce. He praised his wife for displaying a myriad of traditional domestic virtues, including industry in wool-working, being religious without being superstitious, and being modest, obedient, kind, and generous. Her devotion to family was as equally visible in her treatment of his mother as in the care she offered to her own parents.[7]

The *Laudatio Turiae* offers a particularly vivid example of the overlap among duty, public respectability, and domestic virtues that was so typical of the marriage ethics in the society of this time and that was largely absorbed in early church teaching.[8] But with respect to the Roman world, at least, the consensus among scholars is that these ideals need to be read against evidence for a very different reality. The *univira* seems to be have been comparatively rare, and specifically with respect to sexual exclusivity between spouses, one ancient historian has gone so far as to state: "the very ways in which the ideal is expressed suggest that it did not enjoy widespread support, and the very texts that subscribe to the ideal often undercut it at the same time."[9] Despite Juvenal's caricature of the accusatory wife who is herself guilty of infidelity (Juvenal, *Satires* 6.268–72), it seems that societal norms were designed to protect the sexual adventures of married men. The Augustan legislation on adultery clearly reflects a double standard on fidelity within marriage and was designed largely to protect a woman's chastity within marriage. A husband incurred no legal punishment at all for infidelity unless the woman was married.[10]

We can probably be fairly confident that the wives belonging to early church communities, especially those who came from Gentile backgrounds, would have experienced infidelity and would even, as Plutarch's advice suggests (*Advice to the Bride and Groom* 140B), have been subject to societal expectations to look the other way.[11] Although married women who sought sexual relations with their male slaves could be charged with adultery, it was generally accepted that husbands would make use of slaves both male and female for sexual purposes.[12] This sexual exploitation was rooted in the notion of slaves as property that could be used or disposed of at the whim of the master. As has recently been argued so forcefully by Jennifer Glancy, the sexual use of slaves was such a dominant expectation in the Roman world that its presence in early Christian communities can by no means be ruled out, especially given the silence on the matter in early Christian texts.[13] It is impossible to know for sure how the household code teaching would have affected the behavior of believers who were masters of slaves accustomed to such liberties, but the exhortation to treat slaves "justly" (Eph. 6:9; compare Col. 4:1; Ignatius, *Pol.* 4.3—5.1) might extend to protecting the stability of slave families and respecting their marriages.[14]

Whether marriages were considered licit in terms of Roman law probably had little impact on perceptions of marriage within church groups. Even in the case of slaves, for whom no legal capacity for marriage existed, there is evidence for the use of marriage terminology to describe their unions in the Roman world.[15] Moreover, within the Jewish community marriages between Jews would be considered licit regardless of the legal status of Jews within the various cities of the Roman Empire.[16] But things were rendered more complicated by the fact that many members of the congregations probably did not belong to the harmonious believing household idealized in the household codes. Some of the women exhorted in the codes were undoubtedly the slaves and former slaves of pagan masters. Many wives who had stable relations with a pagan man would technically be concubines and not true wives; they would be subject to some legal limitations and perhaps some social stigma associated with their lower social status or an unsavory past (for example, freeborn persons could not contract legal marriages with persons associated with dishonorable occupations such as prostitution and acting or with women convicted of adultery).[17] But there is also evidence that on a practical level concubinage sometimes functioned as the equivalent of marriage, was recognized in the law code as a position similar to that of a legal wife, and could be public and honorable[18]—though it could potentially quickly be rendered dishonorable upon the discovery of the woman's adherence to what was considered a superstition, such as Christianity.

Thus far we have concentrated on recent research that has highlighted the vulnerability of women in various marital relationships. But our picture would be incomplete without an awareness of research revealing the influence of wives in the Roman world. Contemporary scholars show a growing appreciation of the "new woman" who emerged on the scene beginning in the first century BCE. As a wife, but also frequently as a widow, her independence and public visibility were increasingly being demonstrated not only in Rome but in the eastern provinces, where many early church communities would take root.[19] Women acting as patrons and creating networks of relationships are part of this picture, and this fact has a particular importance for the life of house churches, as we will argue in chapter 9.

Even if we concentrate more specifically on familial relationships, there are strong indications that the traditional hierarchical understanding of the relationship between husband and wife was subject to competing forces. There was considerable tension, for example, between the authority of husbands and the influence of fathers (or a guardian appointed by the wife's family). In the most extreme cases this could mean that a woman's marriage was dissolved against her wishes on account of the interests of her *paterfamilias*. As a result of the desire to keep family fortunes intact, marriages without *manus* (literally, "hand"), in which women remained under the legal and economic authority (*potestas*) of their fathers or another family-appointed guardian, were the norm in the empire (in contrast to earlier times when *manus* was transferred to the husbands).[20] The extent to which fathers interfered with their daughters' affairs must have varied considerably, but at the very least it is clear that society sanctioned ongoing connections between wives and their own families. In fact, these connections should be considered as one more link in a familial chain that was in place prior to the conversion of any household or member of the household to early Christianity. In *The Martyrdom of Perpetua and Felicitas* discussed in detail below, for example, the strong role played by Perpetua's father (her husband is conspicuously absent from the ordeal) may bear witness to the strength of the connection between fathers and daughters in the empire.

That the power of the husband was not as all-pervasive as the hierarchical household code implies is also suggested by the significant attention given to mothers in the Roman world and to their role as household managers.[21] In her impressive study of the role of the Roman mother, Suzanne Dixon has argued that the weighty authority of the Roman *paterfamilias* (so clearly reinforced by the household codes) should not be taken at face value. While mothers clearly lacked this kind of formal, legal authority, they nevertheless had considerable influence based on convention:

> In principle, then, a Roman woman was always under some form of masculine control, even if independent of her husband and father. In this sense she resembled the women of classical Athens. In prac-

tice, however, the term "guardianship" was quite inapplicable to her. A Roman matron, whether legally in the power of her husband or father or *in tutela*, had a certain status of respectability as mistress of the household which was enhanced if she became a mother and further elevated if she became a widowed mother.[22]

Among the examples given by Dixon of the autonomy and influence of Roman women, the role of mothers in arranging marriages for their children is particularly revealing in comparison with the early Christian evidence. The legal right of life and death of the *paterfamilias* over his children extended to the right to select marriage partners. The mother's permission was not legally required in such cases, but Dixon cites several examples from Roman literature (including the letters of Cicero and Pliny) that indicate that women played a part in arranging matches and that some were particularly active in this regard.[23] It is interesting here to consider the role of the mother Theocleia in the legendary *Acts of [Paul and] Thecla*: her communication with the rejected fiancé Thamyris and her strong voice of protest against the influence of Paul on young virgins of the city. Where one might expect to hear of the outrage of a *paterfamilias*, it is the mother's loss and negotiations that occupy center stage.[24]

In discussing the spheres of influence of Roman women, Dixon has also pointed to the growing tendency for women to assume power to administer the affairs of their children. Young children rendered *sui iuris* (legally independent) by the death of their father seem to have continued to live with their mother unless she remarried. Technically, such children were required to remain under male *tutela*, but in reality it seems that many women were involved in managing their children's affairs. Moreover, some forms of husband-wife inheritance seem to have given mothers considerable rights in practice to look after their children's finances. The main condition that seems to have ensured that they continued to do so was that the mother remain unmarried and therefore removed from the self-interest of a stepfather.[25]

Some of Dixon's observations are particularly valuable in light of early church evidence. The general prominence of widows in early Christianity may have created a powerful venue for influencing children (see chapter 4) and contributed to the expansion of early church groups. The Pastoral Epistles, for example, speak of Timothy's faith being kindled by his grandmother Lois and his mother, Eunice (2 Tim. 1:5), perhaps on account of the special influence of widows in managing the affairs of their children—assuming here that autonomy in arrangement of the affairs of children could have included religious guidance and formation. In light of Dixon's observations, however, the author's insistence that young widows remarry (1 Tim. 5:14) stands out. While commentators have usually assumed that the determination to remain unmarried on the part of these women was inspired by asceticism, we should also keep in mind that they may have been motivated by a desire to maintain control over the affairs of their children.

Missionary Partners in the Letters of Paul

As we now consider early church texts in which specific married women are mentioned, we should keep in mind the central features of the lives of wives that have emerged within the broad enterprise of research on the Roman family. It is perhaps not surprising that each of these key aspects has a bearing on some piece of the early Christian evidence.

Some of the earliest evidence for the life and influence of married women in house churches is found in Paul's letters. Wives are within the purview of Paul's instructions in 1 Corinthians 7, but the text reveals much more about the aspirations of ascetic women than of wives. The passages 1 Cor. 11:2-16 and 1 Cor. 14:34-36 may reveal something about the activities of wives in church meetings, but the problems of interpretation of these texts are notorious. With respect to 1 Cor. 11:2-16, in the opinion of some we are dealing once again with activities largely inspired by asceticism.[26] The most tangible evidence for the contribution of wives to the life of house churches in Paul's letters is probably found in the references to missionary partners that included such notable women as Prisca and Junia, but even these references raise many problems of interpretation.

In working together, the missionary partners mentioned in Paul's letters were likely continuing the practices of the Jesus movement (see Mark 6:7; Luke 10:1—though here not presented as male-female pairs). As has frequently been observed, these partnerships did not always involve a man and a woman (such as Prisca and Aquila [Rom. 16:3; 1 Cor. 16:19], Andronicus and Junia [Rom. 16:7], Philogus and Julia, Nereus and his "sister" [Rom. 16:15], and Rufus and his mother [Rom. 16:13]), but sometimes involved teams of two women (such as Euodia and Syntyche [Phil. 4:2-3],

Tryphaena and Tryphosa [Rom. 16:12]). The nature of the arrangements between these couples was not limited to husband and wife.

Before we discuss the specific circumstances of the wives who were involved in these partnerships, we should consider some of the cautions scholars have raised concerning the textual evidence. First, the symbolic role of familial language in Pauline literature makes it impossible always to be certain about the meaning of designations. A key text to consider here is Paul's reference to the right of an apostle to be accompanied by "a sister as wife" (*adelphēn gynaika*) in 1 Cor. 9:5. This text should probably be taken as an acknowledgment of the importance of missionary partnerships to the success of the movement, rather than simply as a reference to a "domestic" supporter of the husband's missionary work as has traditionally been assumed from the patristic era to the modern day.[27] Although it can sometimes simply refer to membership in the believing group (see 1 Cor. 7:15), brotherhood and sisterhood language is also used in a special way to refer to leadership in Paul's letters. "Brother" (*adelphos*) and "sister" (*adelphē*) are two of a variety of terms sometimes designating special leadership roles and including such other familiar Pauline ministerial labels as "deacon" (*diakonos*; Rom. 16:1-2) and "coworker" (*synergos*; Rom. 16:3; Phil. 4:2-3). As is supported by the detailed examination of the life of Prisc(ill)a below, there is much to suggest that the "sister wives" were as valued in the Pauline movement as their "brother husbands."

Commentators have also raised questions about the precise nature of the relationships between male and female missionary partners on textual and legal grounds. As is frequently noted, the term for "wife" in Greek (*gynē*) in 1 Cor. 9:5 can also be translated simply as "woman" and therefore leaves open a variety of possibilities for the nature of the sexual or legal relationship. Some have read this text, as Clement of Alexandria did (*Miscellanies* 3.6.53.3), as a reference to "spiritual marriage" (couples living together without physical union), which may be a topic of concern in 1 Cor. 7:36-38.[28] It has also been pointed out that we should not assume that male-female pairs were legally married. Legal capacity for marriage in the Roman Empire existed between two free citizens and was ruled out completely for slaves.[29] For the slaves and freedpersons who were members of early church groups we cannot assume the existence of stable, ongoing family relationships. Moreover, it is important to note that none of the women singled out by name in Paul's letters is explicitly said to be married. Prisca (called Priscilla in Acts) is specifically identified as Aquila's wife only in Acts (see Acts 18:2, 18, 26), a fact that should be balanced against Luke's tendency to highlight the respectability of women associated with the new religious movement.[30]

Feminist scholarship on the missionary partners has highlighted the need for a nuanced reading of the evidence and has accurately warned against drawing unjustified conclusions about the nature of the partnerships based on assumptions about marriage that have more to do with modern arrangements than first-century realities. On balance, however, it seems most likely that Prisca and Aquila (Rom. 16:3; 1 Cor. 16:19), Andronicus and Junia (Rom. 16:7), and Philogus and Julia (Rom. 16:15) understood themselves and were understood by others in the Pauline movement as married.[31] As noted previously, whether marriages were considered licit in terms of Roman law probably had little impact on perceptions of marriage within church groups. Conclusive evidence for spiritual marriage comes from considerably later, and it is difficult to harmonize the "spiritual marriage" interpretation of these couples with Paul's strong rejection of perpetual celibacy within marriage in 1 Cor. 7:2-5. The reference in 1 Cor. 7:36-38 may be to cohabitation in marriages that had never been consummated, and it is possible that these couples were living out such arrangements.[32] But there is also a good chance that these couples were together before they came in contact with the Pauline movement and simply continued to live as a married couple after their new allegiances. Although it is not frequently considered to be a significant feature of the Pauline mission, we must also keep in mind the possibility, indeed the probability, that at least some of the missionary pairs of men and women conducted their work as parents of children.

It must be admitted, however, that Paul's preference for celibacy, which emerges so clearly in 1 Corinthians 7, does raise questions about the male-female pairs who are singled out in his letters, in terms of both their own sexual relations and their status in the movement, including their relationship with Paul. Antoinette Clark Wire has raised some interesting questions about the practical problems associated with offering hospitality to these itinerant couples[33] and to matters that would need to be worked out between the wives and the Corinthian women prophets, whom she understands to be unmarried:

> For the Corinthian women prophets who apparently are not married,
> nor—at least in their local capacities—itinerant, the impact of the

itinerant wives would be at least twofold. In the first place, as Corinthian women the prophets might be made physically responsible for the work involved in caring for the couples. . . . Second, because Paul sees the rights of support to belong to itinerant male apostles and by extension to their wives regardless of the wives' contribution, this puts in question the relative rights of single women, of local residents, and of those whose authority is based on spiritual gifts—three characteristics of the Corinthian women prophets.[34]

Wire's comments alert us to the kind of issues that would need to be worked out on the ground, between women. Paul's rhetoric in 1 Corinthians takes little account of many concrete realities facing women in a household setting. Even the association of marriage with worldly anxiety and distraction—so carefully applied to both men and women (1 Cor. 7:32-35)—must have had little application to the lives of once-married women (widowed, separated, or divorced) who had their own children to care for or who were looking after orphaned or abandoned children.[35]

Prisca: Moving and Setting Up House

Of the wives in the Pauline movement, we possess most information about Prisc(ill)a. In evaluating her role in the house church, however, we must deal with many of the issues that characterize the study of early Christian women generally. For example, we must confront the interplay between the history of real women and the shaping of women's identity to suit the literary purposes and ideological agendas of male authors.

Prisc(ill)a's role was clearly so important that her influence along with that of her partner is attested by three different church authors writing from the middle of the first century to (as late as) the early second century: Paul, Luke-Acts, and the author of the Pastoral Epistles. In the undisputed letters of Paul the evidence for Prisc(ill)a's role is found in 1 Cor. 16:19 (Paul sends greetings from Ephesus) and Rom. 16:3-5 (Paul sends greetings from Corinth). Both texts refer to church groups meeting in the house of Prisc(ill)a and Aquila. References to the couple in Acts are found at Acts 18:1-3 and Acts 18:18—19:1, with the couple depicted as offering hospitality to Paul and later teaching Apollos, apparently also in their house. In addition to the instructing of Apollos, Acts refers to many biographical details about the couple not mentioned by Paul, including their identity as a Jewish married couple, their expulsion from Rome, and their involvement in the same tent-making craft as Paul.

The difficulty with evaluating the evidence from Acts concerning Prisc(ill)a is that there is a growing consensus among scholars that the depiction of women in Acts cannot be taken at face value. The author of Acts sometimes downplays the leadership role of women.[36] There is also a tendency to stress the association of prominent women with earliest Christianity and to highlight the respectability of the domestic arrangements, all seemingly in an effort to demonstrate the legitimacy of the group within the empire. Even the repeated theme of household conversions (following the initial conversion of prominent householders, both men and women [see Acts 16:14-15, 40]) has sometimes been viewed as largely fictional—part of the author's apologetic agenda of presenting a movement that accepts traditional household arrangements and is thereby inoffensive.[37] The recent work of scholars on Acts reminds us that we cannot take the historicity of the presentation of the role of Prisc(ill)a for granted (does the author seek to emphasize her role as a legitimately married woman?) and raises questions about whether such scenes as the "in-house" instruction of Apollos contain real historical details (or only a reconstruction of what might generally have occurred). But in many ways the recent work of scholars on women in Acts allows the presentation of Prisc(ill)a to stand out as all the more striking.[38] Her contribution as a teacher and missionary wife was so important that it could not be circumscribed beyond the recounting of the traditions with as much decorum as possible. In fact, her legacy was remembered as so significant that she appears one final time at the dawn of the patristic era in the greetings found at the end of 2 Timothy (2 Tim. 4:19).

With respect to geographical locations and movements of the couple from place to place, scholars have had little difficulty in harmonizing the material in Acts with what is known from Paul's letters and more generally about the circumstances in the Roman Empire at this period. In fact, in his recent study of the situation of foreigners at Rome, David Noy has described Prisc(ill)a and Aquila as having "one of the most complete surviving migration histories of any individuals of similar status" and as revealing "the distances it was possible for migrants to travel and the range of contacts they could make."[39] When evidence from Paul's letters is combined with evidence from Acts, we arrive at the following chronology of events: having been exiled from Rome, Prisc(ill)a and Aquila offered hospitality to Paul in Corinth (Acts 18:2-3). Paul eventually left Corinth and headed for Ephesus, accompanied by the couple. In Ephesus the missionary pair instructed Apollos, who in turn left for Corinth (Acts 18:18—19:1). They apparently eventually left Ephesus and returned to Rome, for they occupy a prominent place in Paul's list of greetings at the end of Romans.[40] In short, their migration histories (all probably within less than a decade) indicate that they traveled between and took up residence in three major cities of the Roman Empire (Rome, Ephesus, and Corinth). From Paul's letters, it is clear that they were hosts to house churches in Ephesus and in Rome (1 Cor. 16:19 and Rom. 16:3-5). The reference to them offering hospitality to Paul in Corinth (Acts 18:2-3; 18:18—9:1) suggests that this may have been the case in Corinth as well.

Noy's work, which focuses particularly on the circumstances of foreigners in the city of Rome, alerts us to the challenges facing Prisc(ill)a and Aquila as they arrived in the city and eventually sought to host church groups there. Above all else, there would be the challenge of finding work and a place to stay. The description of Paul staying with the couple and sharing their craft offers a glimpse into the realities of travel and work for itinerant artisans in the empire (Acts 18:1-3). But where would Prisc(ill)a and Aquila find accommodation upon arrival, and where would they eventually have settled and hosted a church in their house? The city of Rome seems to have provided a variety of levels of temporary rental accommodation, ranging from a room in an inn, which could be rented simply overnight or on a more long-term basis, to lodging houses and guesthouses occupied by the more well-to-do.[41] At the lowest end of the spectrum, there is some evidence to suggest the building of huts or shanties within the city or just outside and the imposition of penalties on account of fire risk. Desperate foreigners may have joined the resident poor and made their way to such places.[42] It is doubtful that Prisc(ill)a and Aquila would fall under that category, but the itinerancy associated with this missionary couple leaves open the possibility of temporary accommodation. Although it is not usually discussed in relation to house churches, might some of the earliest meeting places for believers have been rooms in inns that had been rented by itinerant leaders?

Of course, as Jews, Prisc(ill)a and Aquila may have initially sought accommodation in an establishment or house owned by a fellow Jew (or eventually a fellow believer in Jesus or both), with arrangements in place before their arrival (compare Acts 28:15).[43] Hospitality emerges early as a

key virtue in early Christian groups, as is demonstrated by the very hospitality offered by the missionary couple to Paul himself (Acts 18:1-3;
see Rom. 12:13; Heb. 13:2; *1 Clem.* 10.7). As prescriptions for the lives
of women develop, hospitality becomes an important virtue for women
(1 Tim. 5:10), and, as discussed further below, Prisc(ill)a may have had a
special role to play here. The ability to offer hospitality is linked to a certain
extent with social status. In his detailed study of the social level of Pauline
Christians, Wayne Meeks offers a profile of the pair that includes a combination of high- (for example, relative wealth) and low-status indicators (for
example, Jewish "foreigners" from the East). The fact that Prisc(ill)a's name
is mentioned before her husband's name by Paul and two out of three times
in Acts has intrigued commentators and has led to the suggestion that she
had a higher status than her husband.[44] It may well be the case that it was
her patronage in particular that believers, including Paul himself, sought
out.[45] All of this raises questions about the type of accommodation offered
by Prisc(ill)a and Aquila to those who came to the church in their house.
We should not be too quick to assume that early Christians met only in
very modest houses or crowded *insulae* (large, multi-unit housing com-
plexes). Evidence from Pompeii includes the ownership of quite spacious
houses—the peristyled *domus*—by people of considerable wealth but overall modest social status, including freedmen and women.[46] Whether rented
or owned, the typical house of Prisc(ill)a and Aquila is most likely to have
been a *domus* (even if fairly modest) and similar to the houses owned by
such prominent male householders as Stephanas (1 Cor. 1:16; 16:16-18) or
Gaius of Corinth (Rom. 16:23; 1 Cor. 1:14), whose house was apparently
large enough to hold the whole of the Corinthian community.

Prisc(ill)a and Aquila were movers and shakers in Pauline circles. As
missionaries, teachers, collaborators of Paul and others, and patrons of
house churches in three different cities, they helped people get where they
wanted to go and obtain needed information, and they created spaces that
offered vital infrastructure for the expansion and support of the movement—taking risks in the process. In thinking about how the arena of
business and existing networks of communication between Eastern cities
and Rome may have supported the growth of early Christian communities, we encounter a vital point of intersection between the mission of Paul
himself and that of Prisc(ill)a and Aquila, who shared his craft. But the
mission of Prisc(ill)a and Aquila differed from Paul in two important ways,
perhaps indicating a certain independence. First and most obvious, they
conducted their work as a partnership of husband and wife, while Paul

chose to work without a partner (having renounced his right to be accompanied by "a sister as wife" [1 Cor. 9:5]). Second, the house-church setting was vital to their mission; to the best of our knowledge Paul did not stay in one place long enough to set up a church in his house.

One of the most fascinating features of the description of Prisc(ill)a and Aquila's activities in Acts and presentation of their contribution by Paul in his letters is that they combined aspects of an itinerant existence with the more settled existence of hosting a house church; their lives may, therefore, offer very important insight into how the Jesus movement managed to establish itself in the Greco-Roman city. Their missionary pattern was literally one of moving and setting up house. In the work of Prisc(ill)a and Aquila, the in situ leadership of the local community obviously played a larger role than in Paul's missionary strategies, but it is by no means clear that this more "settled" life actually was less successful in winning new members. In one of the few places where Paul tells us how new members might be won, he speaks of outsiders witnessing an early church meeting, presumably in a house church (see 1 Cor. 14:23-25). But could the household base of the mission of Prisc(ill)a and Aquila have meant that Prisc(ill)a actually was more successful at winning new members than her partner? As noted above, the fact that Prisc(ill)a's name appears before that of Aquila in Acts 18:18, 26 and Rom. 16:3 is usually taken as a sign that she was of higher status than her partner, but could it not also mean that she was the more successful missioner?

Consideration of Prisc(ill)a's life raises one of the most important areas for investigation in the study of women and house churches: whether the physical meeting of church groups in the house may have enhanced women's leadership and missionary opportunities. Common sense would seem to indicate that this would have been the case. Women were traditionally associated with the house and viewed as natural household managers (for example, 1 Tim. 5:14; Titus 2:5) and thereby already in a position to have considerable influence in a house church. Yet our sources remain largely silent on the matter. As discussed in the introduction to this volume, one of the main factors affecting our understanding of women's roles in the house church is the question of the gendered division of space (the use of women's quarters, separate dining arrangements for men and women, and so forth). Although there is literary evidence (which deals largely with elite houses) to support the segregation of women from men, especially in the Greek East, the architectural evidence is not conclusive.[47] Allowing for variations in local custom and degrees of Romanization, we could say that there might have been more of a tendency to segregate women from male company in the East than in the West, but we cannot be absolutely certain. What is clear, however, is that when male authors wished to illustrate the propriety of certain arrangements or when women were viewed as being in danger of violating boundaries, there was a tendency to call for a return to more traditional values, including less public visibility for women.[48]

As a wife, artisan, missionary, and foreign immigrant, Prisc(ill)a lived on the crossroads of the public (and traditionally viewed as male) sphere and the private (and traditionally viewed as female) sphere, exerting her influence through a broad spectrum of activities. But Prisc(ill)a may also have used traditional cultural expectations concerning her behavior as a woman and wife to her advantage. Anthropologists working on women and gender have documented instances in which women have found avenues to exercise power by submitting to traditional authority structures actually designed to limit their power.[49] Meeting cultural expectations for wifely behavior may well have offered Prisc(ill)a the opportunity to pass on

Fig. 2.1: Traditional banquet arrangement of reclining males and seated female. Funeral stele, Antioch. Photo by C. Osiek.

and gain information and to help people to get where they wanted to go. It is easy to imagine that Prisc(ill)a's role as wife of Aquila and collaborator of Paul would contribute to her leadership among women and, more specifically, to her facilitation of several detailed conversations among women (see chapter 7).

Although it is not frequently discussed, we might also consider the role of a wife like Prisc(ill)a in evangelizing very young women, commonly known today as adolescents but very much of a marriageable age in Roman times (see chapter 4). Where would such teaching have taken place? Did adolescent girls in ancient times gather in their bedrooms (which would not have been very large, even in an upscale *domus*) as they do today, and were such women's spaces a place of teaching and evangelization? The special focus on virgins in 1 Corinthians 7 suggests that sexual asceticism was an attractive option for some young women; in the context of the ancient world, it seems natural to assume that women played a large role in the teaching of these young, impressionable, and vulnerable women.[50] It is also easy to imagine wives and mothers acting as advocates for young women who were in danger of having their virtue compromised. Could it have been such women who were responsible for raising the issue of improper behavior toward a virgin as a serious community concern in Corinth (1 Cor. 7:36-38)?

A final intriguing question concerning the role of wives in the growth and support of the movement has to do with the presence in the communities of the wives of unbelievers (discussed further below and in chapter 10). Was the appearance of female believers as respectable wives key to the ability to make contact with these women, who turn up in communities as early as Paul's day (1 Cor. 7:12-16; see also 1 Pet. 3:1-2)?[51] Did women like Prisc(ill)a, hostesses of house churches and household managers (see chapter 7), provide the necessary cover for women to attend meetings when it might otherwise not have been possible? Were they the ones who comforted women whose association with the new movement had led to household strife?

Less Than Dutiful?
Marriages of the Second Generation and Beyond

From the time of the composition of the household codes in the latter decades of the first century CE, we hear very little about specific married couples in early Christian texts. The ones we do hear about often seem to bear very little resemblance to the ideal couple of Eph. 5:22-33. It is difficult to know why this is so. We might surmise that only couples who were in trouble or subject to unusual circumstances would come to the surface in texts, when in reality many marital partnerships were stable and, by making their various resources available (including their domestic dwellings), contributed to the development of a fledgling new movement. In that case, the history of early Christian marriages would have much in common with the history of early Christian women, whose comparative invisibility in the literature masks what recent scholars have uncovered to be a significant contribution to the success of the movement. But it is also possible that the tendency in the literature to present less than ideal marriages reflects to some extent the fact that quite frequently the married lives of believers departed significantly from the Ephesians ideal. Once again, a direct focus on the house-church setting can shed light upon the subject as we survey the marriages about which we have any significant information in this era.

Ananias and Sapphira, Valens and His Wife, and Hermas and His Wife: Wives and Failure

Among the scant evidence for named married couples, three couples are notable for their association with sin. The first couple, Ananias and Sapphira, is mentioned early in the Acts of the Apostles (Acts 5:1-11) as part of the author's description of the first church community. We have seen that the explicit presentation of Prisc(ill)a and Aquila as a married couple in Acts (Acts 18:18, 26) may well have been inspired by the need to bolster the community's image of respectability. But if as a married couple Prisc(ill)a and Aquila are Paul's apostolic or missionary allies par excellence, Ananias and Sapphira are their rather tragic antithesis. In the initial formation of the community, believers are said to have sold property and placed the proceeds at the feet of the apostles (Acts 4:34-35). The sin of Ananias and Sapphira lies in greed, concealment, and implicit lack of recognition of the apostles' authority: they collude and "hold back something of their own." Ananias places only a portion of the proceeds at the apostles' feet (Acts 5:2). Confronted by Peter about their actions, they fall down dead. Both Ananias and Sapphira are presented as equally culpable in their guilt—both are interrogated separately by Peter.[52] Similar mutual responsibility is implied by Polycarp, bishop of Smyrna, in the middle of the second century to refer of the sins of Valens (probably avarice; Poly-carp, *Phil.* 11.2) and his wife: "I am deeply sorry for him [that is, Valens] and for his wife, and 'may the Lord grant them true repentance.'"[53]

It is notable that each of these cases involves some form of greed. Given the close association of the economy with the household in antiquity and that the church community is based in the house church, it is important to recognize that the transgressions of these couples are understood by the early church authors as involving the very foundation of the community. In the case of Ananias and Sapphira this is made explicit by the contrast between the symbolic action that brings the community together—the placing of funds at the feet of the apostles (Acts 4:35, 36; 5:2)—and the act that expels the member from the community permanently—the falling down dead at the feet of the apostles (in this case Peter; Acts 5:10). Used extensively within this passage and Luke-Acts in general (for example, Acts 10:25; 22:3), "being at the feet" is a biblical idiom that symbolizes submission and obedience (for example, Josh. 10:24; 1 Sam. 25:24, 41; 2 Sam. 22:39; Ps. 8:7) and ultimately the acknowledgment of the apostles' authority over the collection and the dispersal of goods—the use, manage-ment, and dispersal of property including housing (Acts 4:34-35).[54]

In the case of Valens and his wife, that the sin is perceived as involving the very basis of community life is suggested by the association of avarice with idolatry (Polycarp, *Phil.* 4.2). The true magnitude of the guilt, how-ever, comes into sharper relief when one considers the fact that Valens was once made presbyter among the Philippians (Polycarp, *Phil.* 4.1). The close association of the office of elder or presbyter with house ownership and management is suggested by the manner in which household code ethics (Polycarp, *Phil.* 4.1—6.1; compare Ignatius, *Pol.* 4.1—5.2) concern-ing behavior of various members of the family (wives, children, and so on) merges with references to church offices (for example, widows, dea-cons, presbyters). It is even difficult at times to determine whether the exhortation refers primarily to behavior within family units or to broader leadership roles within the house church (for example, younger men, vir-gins).[55] There is a high degree of probability that Valens's greed involved some type of action related to household and house-church management. Various scenarios come to mind, including refusal to distribute goods as required by his role as patron or unequal distribution of goods reminiscent of the division caused during celebrations of the Lord's supper in Paul's day (1 Cor. 11:17-34).

In a house-church setting, there is good reason to believe that as a presbyter's wife, the wife of Valens would have participated in his leadership role
in significant ways. She would have been an important wife and mother in
the community and at times may even have been viewed as a woman "presbyter" herself.[56] In his teaching on wives, Polycarp makes specific reference
to the role of wives in the education of children and to the importance of
loving not only their husbands, but all others equally (Polycarp, *Phil.* 4.2).
One wonders if the wife of Valens failed in her responsibilities somehow.
Did her husband's avarice reinforce divisions in status that meant that the
children of the *ekklēsia* were not all treated equally?

In seeking to recover the lives of wives in house churches, it is valuable
to think as concretely as possible about what familial tensions and divisions might have arisen from day to day. But it must be admitted that, in
contrast to the case of Ananias and Sapphira, in which the two are clearly
represented as co-conspirators, the reference to Valens and his wife leaves
open the possibility that she may in fact not have been directly involved in
the wrongdoing (although she shares in the consequences and responsibility for the wrongdoing). Modern notions of the autonomy of individuals
within the household are inconsistent with ancient views in which relationships appear to have been far more symbiotic than is usually the case
in our context. Such considerations should be kept in mind when seeking
to understand the relationship between church leaders and their wives—
whether such relations be depicted as positive or negative.

Notions of collective punishment that seem so abhorrent in a modern
context are clearly evident in a work from the first part of the second century that takes the form of a series of revelations: *The Shepherd of Hermas*.[57]
Perhaps more than any other writing from this era, *The Shepherd of Hermas*
capitalizes on the close association between the family and the *ekklēsia* in
order to teach and admonish. The exhortations shift from direct focus on
the individual family unit (the main character, Hermas, a wealthy freedman,
his wife, and their children) to the broader community of God's children,
but it is ultimately impossible to clearly distinguish between the two. In
reflecting upon the historical reliability of the work, it is important to keep
in mind that "the text contains a mixture of biography and literary reworking, so that the family becomes a literary mirror of the whole community."[58]
We see this mixture at play in the manner in which Hermas's wife and
children are portrayed as participating in his sinful past—they are a family
that has acted "lawlessly against God." In keeping with Roman legal cus-

tom, Hermas is ultimately responsible for the financial state and conduct of his children, including adult sons and daughters (at least those married without *manus*, as was usually the case in this era).[59] Hermas is to take care in admonishing his children who, if sincerely converted, will participate in eternal life (Herm. *Vis.* 1.3.1–2). Explanations of his family's guilt and his responsibilities in this regard do not, however, stop Hermas from protesting against the punishments he himself must endure on their behalf. During a vision the angel of punishment explains: only if he is afflicted as the head of the house can his family receive the required affliction. While he prospers, their punishment is ruled out entirely (Herm. *Sim.* 7).

Hermas's children are depicted generally as "betrayers of parents," but his wife's wrongdoing is named more explicitly: she "does not hold her tongue, with which she does evil" (Herm. *Vis.* 2.2.3). Inappropriate speech is certainly a vice that both men and women may demonstrate in early Christian literature (for example, Col. 4:5; Eph. 4:29-31), but the manner in which the wife's sin is singled out from the rest of the family suggests that the text reflects a stereotypical tendency to depict women as inclined to gossip or speak at inopportune times.[60] Considered within a house-church setting, the sin of Hermas's wife takes on new significance and points to the symbolic value of the behavior of wives. Anthropologists of modern Mediterranean societies have noted a tendency for women's domestic comportment to be seen as an especially important sign of the stability of the household and society more generally. Like suspicious absences from the home and neglect of household duties, gossiping in effect amounts to careless neglect or release of household commodities that should be carefully guarded—much as a woman guards her own chastity. Even in cases where no real sexual activity has taken place, there is a tendency to associate the vices of women with women's sexuality and basic moral nature.[61]

These dynamics are probably at work in the proclamation that from now on Hermas's wife will be to him as a "sister" (Herm. *Vis.* 2.2.3; compare *Sim.* 9.11.3). Other exhortations (for example, Herm. *Mand.* 4.1) make it clear that the directive should not be taken as a reference to the need for the whole community to take up "spiritual marriage" (a man and woman cohabitating while remaining celibate). Nevertheless, the references to sexual abstinence between Hermas and his wife probably serve a broad catechetical purpose.[62] The wife's conversion is being represented with reference to reaching a higher level of purity than she had before. Instead of being loose-tongued and out of control, she will now "hold back," and her body will become "the symbol of family integrity and purity" and of the church community as a whole.[63]

In addition to offering a window into the less-than-ideal family unit (although admittedly to some extent using the family as a mirror for community division and harmony), *Hermas* offers insight into the variety of possible male-female alliances that touched early Christian life. The text in fact opens with a reference to an alliance associated with Hermas's previous life as a slave: his relationship with Rhoda. In the opening biographical section of the work, we hear of the one who raised Hermas—probably a reference to the fact that Hermas was adopted as a foundling and raised as a slave. The text then refers to Hermas having been eventually sold to Rhoda; the fact that he only meets up with her again after many years probably means that he had been sold again to another owner before becoming manumitted (otherwise, we would expect the kind of contact and obligations that slaves continued to owe to their former owners).[64] Hermas states that he eventually saw Rhoda bathing in the River Tiber and describes a scene that reveals the literary conventions and erotic overtones of many bathing scenes found in ancient literature (for example, 2 Sam. 11:2).[65] But despite these conventional overtones, Hermas's heartfelt desire is intriguing, especially considering both the weakness of his own wife and the manner in which the church is later presented as a woman in the text: "How happy I would be if I had such a wife, both in regard to beauty and manner" (Herm. *Vis.* 1.1.2).

Throughout the narrative, Hermas is insistent that he harbors no adulterous or inappropriate thoughts in relation to Rhoda (Herm. *Vis* 1.1.2, 6–7). But the ancient recipients of this work must surely have identified with the possibility of a sexual encounter between an owner and a slave. As discussed previously, the sexual availability of slaves to their owners was generally accepted in the Roman world. Moreover, the manumission of female slaves in order to marry their male owners was quite common. The reverse (as is suggested by the scene in *Hermas*) was generally considered socially unacceptable, even though the inscriptional evidence indicates that it sometimes did occur.[66] Therefore, Hermas's heartfelt wish to have a wife such as Rhoda might well reflect ambitions that were within the realm of possibility. The opening scene of *The Shepherd of Hermas* reveals the very real possibility that early church members might meet up again with former owners (sometimes even as fellow believers), and it shows that sexual encounters between slaves and their owners were part of a shared past. Many questions would arise as a result concerning the parameters of the relations among slaves, former slaves, and householders who were believers. Were former social taboos still in place concerning sexual partnerships? Did the sexual availability of slaves come to an end with the conversion of a master? These questions and others lie just under the surface of *The Shepherd of Hermas* and will be discussed further in chapter 5.

Eventually, the beautiful slave owner Rhoda is transformed within the narrative to become the heavenly revelatory Rhoda. Despite his protests, the heavenly Rhoda is insistent that "the desire of wickedness" entered his heart (Herm. *Vis.* 1.1.8). As the narrative unfolds, readers receive several indications that the scope of desire in the work includes not only lust but the desire to amass riches as well. Throughout the encounter with Rhoda—as biography becomes interwoven with literary composition—there is tension not only between the earthly and heavenly characters, but also between individual family circumstances and that of the house-church community. The scene culminates in the appeal to "pray to God, who will heal your sins and those of your whole household and of all the holy ones" (Herm. *Vis.* 1.1.9).

If it were not for the very strong suggestion that Hermas and his family are being scripted as a reflection of the whole community, it would be very difficult to understand the basis for the heavenly Rhoda's accusation. Hermas's desire for Rhoda seems to be more one of admiration than one of lust (Herm. *Vis.* 1.1.4), and he vigorously defends his own intentions. It might be argued, however, that since Hermas receives his vision of Rhoda as a married man, his admiration comes dangerously close to desiring another as his wife—an impression that is heightened by the description of the weakness of his own wife and by the fact that desire for "someone else's wife" is explicitly singled out as a great sin (Herm. *Mand.* 4.1.1). Such desire might have been experienced fairly widely in the familial atmosphere of house-church communities! But be that as it may, the more predominant impression that one gains by setting the Rhoda episode within the context of the work as a whole is that Hermas's desire is a symptom of a far more serious and far-reaching problem: "But those who intend evil in their hearts draw down upon themselves death and imprisonment, especially those who acquire the things this world has to offer and rejoice in their riches and do not take part in the goods of the world to come" (Herm. *Sim.* 1.1.8).

Hermas, his family, and the church seem to be caught up in a very difficult situation that transcends the acts of any one individual. From the perspective of this book, it is valuable to note how female partners—both Rhoda (whom he admires as perfect wifely candidate) and his own wife (whose sins are at the heart of his trouble)—figure in descriptions of sinfulness and remedies for overcoming sin. Moreover, the vision of the heavenly Rhoda moves immediately into a vision of the main revealer in the *The Visions*: the woman church (Herm. *Vis.* 1-4). She is introduced initially as an older woman (*gynē presbytis*; Herm. *Vis.* 1.2.2), but she is later identified as the church (Herm. *Vis.* 2.4.1). To state that the woman church, as has sometimes been suggested, is simply Rhoda in another form would be to overstate the case, since each of these female characters seems to play somewhat different roles and have different relationships with Hermas himself.[67] But the fact that both Rhoda and the woman church draw upon ideals associated with the Roman matron should not be overlooked. Rhoda, a woman whom Hermas knows from the past and admires—in fact desires—prepares the way for him to listen to the woman church. It is not beyond the realm of possibility that women emerge as revealers in the text precisely because women like them—older, stately, handsome, well-respected matrons (who sometimes may have been widows)—were important patrons of house churches (see chapter 7). Nympha of Laodicea was clearly such a woman (Col. 4:15). The instructions for spreading the message that Hermas receives from the woman church in fact include a reference to the woman Grapte, who may well be the patron of a house-church community (Herm. *Vis.* 2.4.2–3). Although it is steeped in the literary imagination, the conflation of Rhoda and the woman church offers one more indication of the symbolic value of the matron as reflecting the church identity and priorities.

Justin's Roman Matron: Wives of Profligate Husbands

In contrast to the focus on the failures of wives in the texts discussed above, it is the failure of a husband that is highlighted in the apologist Justin Martyr's description of the Roman matron (her name is not given). In this account the matron eventually divorces her pagan husband on account of his refusal to change his licentious ways (Justin, *Second Apology*, 2).[68] Mixed marriage is a favorite theme in the legendary *Apocryphal Acts of the Apostles* and has figured prominently in attempts to understand the role of women in the expansion of early Christianity. As a central aspect of the lives of women in house churches, marriages between Christian women and pagan men (the reverse situation is virtually absent from the literature) will be examined at length in chapter 10, but it is worth mentioning here Justin's Roman matron because she is one of the few wives specifically mentioned in the early Christian literature of the second century and one we can be fairly confident was a real historical person.[69]

It is precisely the superiority of the Roman matron's morals in comparison to that of her profligate husband that serves to enrich Justin's portrait of the tragic circumstances of the first Christians. In telling the tale, Justin contrasts the woman's past (before she became aware of the teachings of Christ), when she shared in her husband's licentiousness, with her new chaste state. Despite her urgings to the contrary, her non-Christian husband continued in his promiscuity. Justin notes the irony of the actions of a husband who should have been taking pleasure in the model behavior of his wife but instead uses it as a basis for accusing her as a Christian: "But this noble husband of hers,—while he ought to have been rejoicing that those actions which formerly she unhesitatingly committed with servants and hirelings, when she delighted in drunkenness and every vice, she had now given up, and desired that he too should give up the same,—when she had gone from him without his desire, brought an accusation against her, affirming that she was a Christian."[70]

Via Justin's description of the actions undertaken by the wife we gain a sense of the differing interpretations concerning the correct course of action for Christians in these situations. How long should one remain in the union and under what circumstances? Contrary to her own inclinations, Justin tells us that the Roman matron was initially persuaded by "her own people" (fellow Christians) to persevere in the hope that her husband might himself be converted, in keeping with 1 Cor. 7:12-16 and 1 Pet. 3:1-6. But the woman's actions, including eventually divorcing her husband (after reports from his exploits in Alexandria proved that he had actually become worse), are closer to Hermas's recommendations that Christians must separate from partners who engage in adultery and sexual immorality (Herm. *Mand.* 4.1.9) than Paul's word on the matter. Justin in fact presents the woman's sentiments in a manner that closely resembles the description of the dangers that Christians face with respect to sexual morality and the pagan world in Hermas: fear of wickedness and impiety by association (graphically reinforced with references to her husband's table and bed!) is what ultimately leads the woman to separate herself from him.

Many features of Justin's account are important to consider in a study of women in house churches. Most obvious, we have an excellent example of how the domestic circumstances of the early Christians were central to the larger conflict between church groups and society. The story of the Roman matron ends with a reference to a petition to the emperor (Antoninus Pius) to grant her permission to first settle her affairs (probably seeking to recover her dowry) and for an opportunity to defend herself, which the emperor apparently granted.[71] Stymied for the time being, her husband then turns his attention to her Christian teacher, who is brought to trial and executed along with two other Christian protesters. The narrative shifts quickly from the domestic realm to the public domains of law and government.[72] But this shifting (and to some extent intermingling) of realms reflects the close association between public and private in Roman family law, concepts of piety, and civic duty. There is in fact a surprisingly public dimension to the Roman matron's circumstances from the outset. Despite its potentially lethal consequences, she is presented as making no effort to conceal her Christian allegiance from her husband; instead she actively tries to evangelize him. Reports of his continuing immoral behavior reach her from Alexandria—perhaps from business associates or the family members of those who lived and worked in the same circles. The suggestion is that the problems between the two are well-known in the church and in the broader society and there are extensive opportunities for exchange of information even across great distances.

The Roman matron described in Justin's *Apology* seems to have been well-to-do. That her past life was characterized by drunkenness and sexual misadventure with "servants and hirelings" implies leisure associated with wealth. The references to her husband's travel to Alexandria (and perhaps a second residence in the city) and her appeal to the emperor to be allowed to set her affairs in order, probably including the negotiation of dowry arrangements, confirm this impression.[73] The Roman matron acted with the kind of independence in domestic matters, including the initiating of divorce, that was associated especially with elite women.[74] The reference to the Christian woman's own people—literally, "the ones belonging to her"—is also worthy of consideration.[75] This appears to be a reference to her own household—most likely an extended household comprised of slaves, former slaves, and dependent workers. The implication of Justin's text is that these people were Christians who initially impressed upon her the importance of remaining married to her husband—perhaps the very head of their household. That no effort was apparently ever made to con-

Fig. 2.2. Collection of silver tableware. Mural inside enclosure of the tomb of Vestorius Priscus, Pompeii. First century CE. Photo by C. Osiek.

ceal her Christian tendencies from her husband leaves open the very real possibility that this woman sponsored church activities in some way that was widely known. It may well have been in her important role as a patron to a church group in Rome that she first came to Justin's attention and why the cruel treatment of Christians associated with her served as such an appropriate example for the elite audience he hoped to convince by means of his apologetic writings.

Perpetua: Wives as Heroines

The account of the life of a third-century Christian wife, "Vibia Perpetua, a newly married woman of good family and upbringing" (*Vibia Perpetua, honeste nata, liberaliter instituta, matronaliter nupta*), makes reference to even more dramatic circumstances and tragic results than Justin's account of the Roman matron. *The Martyrdom of Perpetua and Felicitas* includes a segment purportedly written by Vibia Perpetua herself—a young wife and mother from North Africa.[76] Her diary records her prison experience and is replete with intimate details of her family life, including the struggle she faced in balancing her love for her father, care for her newborn son, and allegiance to Christ. It contains significant material, for example, on the relationship between children and parents in early church circles—a subject to which we will turn in chapters 3 and 4. But in this chapter it is Perpetua's identity as a wife that is of greatest interest.

Perpetua's identity as a wife is shrouded in mystery. There is no mention of her husband.[77] Instead the male-female tension centers on her relationship with her father (as noted earlier, this is perhaps a reflection of the ongoing involvement in marriages of fathers whose daughters generally remained under their *potestas* even after marriage). But even given this strong bond, the complete absence of mention of the husband is striking. Perpetua may have been a widow (but in light of her recent status as mother this seems doubtful), or, more likely, we are meant to understand the absence of a husband as implying that she has been abandoned on account of her Christian allegiance.[78] The family of Vibia Perpetua is not solely Christian. We are told that she has one brother who is a catechumen like herself (2). Almost nothing is said about her mother, but it seems that she is a Christian; Perpetua entrusts her son to her mother and brother early in the narrative (3). Her father, on the other hand, is a not a believer and is clearly opposed to all she is doing.[79] Yet, apparently in contrast to the absent spouse, he is adamant that she reject her Christian allegiance and return to him and to her duties to her family, especially to her infant son (5–6). In one of the most dramatic moments of the tale, Perpetua's father appears at the prisoner's docks with his grandson and proclaims: "Perform the sacrifice—have pity on your baby!" (6). Perpetua finds his appeals deeply moving, and we are left to experience firsthand the interfamilial conflict that could arise as a result of Christian conversion.

The absence of a reference to a husband means that Perpetua's marriage state is certainly less than ideal. But in other respects it is easy to see how virtues associated with ideal wives in the Roman world add to the drama of the narrative. Perpetua displays the qualities of the ideal Roman mother who wishes to care for her child herself, even if it means caring for him in prison. As will be discussed in chapter 3, the refusal to nurse and care for one's own children was a favorite theme of moralists who called for a return to the family values of the past. With a reference to the absence of pain that is so familiar to any nursing mother who has experienced engorgement, Perpetua eventually expresses relief that the child is weaned so easily (6). In the interim between a strong sense of maternal crisis and a type of physical release, there is a period of maternal bliss, when arrangements are made for Perpetua to keep her baby with her in prison, and her prison is subsequently described as a "palace" (3). In the closed world of mother and infant, when life exists on "baby time," all fears and distractions are kept at bay, at least for a little while. The account of the martyrdom of Felicitas (discussed at length in chapter 3), the young slave who delivers her baby while in prison (once again there is no reference to the child's father), also appeals to motherhood ideals. That Felicitas has only very recently experienced childbirth serves to heighten her vulnerable state, with the capacity for her to nurture children graphically portrayed by the image of milk dripping from her breasts (20).

In both of the accounts of Perpetua and of Felicitas, the mothers (and ultimately the readers of the narrative) are reassured that their children will be cared for after their deaths. Perpetua's child is received by her own family (both the child's grandmother and uncle are apparently Christian; 3, 6) and Felicitas's child is adopted by a Christian woman of the community (15). From a literary perspective these adoptions are an important element in resolving the tension between martyrdom and parenthood in the narrative—powerfully conveyed by Perpetua's father's mourning at the loss of his daughter. From a historical perspective these adoptions offer an indication that the children of believers were considered precious and their Christian education vital—all of this at a time when celibacy and virginity were coming to be highly prized.[80] Yet, in the case of Perpetua's child at least, the reader experiences some lingering doubts about the ultimate fate of the child that must reflect real uncertainty about the opportunities for evangelizing the children of "mixed" households. Having refused her final request to turn her child over to the deacon Pomponius, her father remains clearly in control of his legal fate, and his future life as a believer will depend on the possible influence of Christian members of the family (6).

Maureen A. Tilley has pointed out that unlike many of the Christian women who were presented as the ideal in late antique literature, Perpetua and Felicity were not ascetics: "They were wives and mothers whose very embodied activities were part of their identity as holy women."[81] The notion of embodiment is central to an exploration of women in house churches. As wives and mothers, women in early church communities could find themselves having to make difficult choices between loyalty to their own families (Christian or otherwise) and allegiance to Christ. Under the threat of martyrdom, women would have little real choice, and much of the story of Perpetua, including the time spent in prison with her infant, is about maintaining allegiance to both as long as possible.

While the narrative account of Perpetua's life begins with a description of her as "respectably married," in her death the woman whose natural husband seems conspicuously absent is called "beloved of God, wife of Christ" (18). But it is because she has expressed so bravely the ideals of the Roman matron under such difficult circumstances that this final description is so apt. Striking a modern reader as almost to the point of the ridiculous, concern for Perpetua's matronly modesty takes on exaggerated proportions when, in the midst of an ecstatic state under the threat of torture, she fastens up her hair (lest anyone think she might be in mourning) and ensures that her ripped tunic covers as much of her body as possible. Her earthly life has exhibited familial devotion and propriety, but now transcending all the limits of her physical existence, she has reached her goal as wife of Christ. Motherhood is of great symbolic power in such extreme circumstances, as is suggested perhaps most dramatically when Perpetua wakes from one of her visionary dreams to find the taste of sweet curds in her mouth, recalling the experience of the nursing mother whose child has fallen asleep at the breast (4).

Conclusion:
The Importance of Wives

As we come to the end of our survey of marriages, we are confronted with a sad fact: leaving Paul's letters and Acts behind, we have virtually no evidence of specific married couples being presented positively as making contributions to house-church communities. But especially when we keep in mind the physical circumstances of these communities and aspects of family life that have been brought to light by Roman historians, the evidence suggests that these couples were nevertheless vital to the life and infrastructure of the communities. Couples like Prisc(ill)a and Aquila were probably far more numerous than our sources would lead us to believe. The lack of reference to specific partnerships in a positive light may have much to do with the fact that they were simply taken for granted, and it may be in keeping with the limited literary interest of the day in everyday domestic affairs generally and in the lives of wives particularly. It is beyond question, however, that the nature of partnerships that could be embraced by church groups was often a pressing concern, raising a wide range of issues, from whether one could forgive an adulterous partner, to whether remarriage was acceptable, to (though this is less explicit in the texts) sexual propriety in relations among masters, slaves, and former slaves. It is also indisputable that the lives of wives did not always reflect the ideal circumstances described in Eph. 5:22-33. As a result of forces from both within and outside the church, women were sometimes widowed, divorced, abandoned, married to uncooperative, unfaithful, or violent husbands, or even martyred.

Our evidence for the lives of wives in house churches is not easy to evaluate; it simply resists easy categorization and explanation. The cases of sinful couples examined above remind us of how fully women were embedded in male experience, leadership, and reputation. Evaluation of the evidence is also complicated by the obvious merging of influences that occurs in a text like of *The Martyrdom of Perpetua and Felicitas*. Here Roman ideals of motherhood and wifely duty not only confront early Christian priorities and responses, but also shape them in a variety of ways. Moreover, the martyrological construction of Perpetua and Felicitas as "holy women" involves a type of overcoming of sexuality and physical limitation that seems more in keeping with celibacy than the experience of married Christians. But in the combination of symbols of sexual restraint with symbols of motherhood, we have a strong indication of a point we will discuss later in more depth: the lives of married and celibate early Christian women should not be falsely dichotomized.

Even where we have a fair bit of information about a particular early Christian wife like Justin's Roman matron, there is much uncertainty about the parameters of influence and limits of restrictions. Justin's matron was most likely a well-to-do woman who acted as a patron to the church community. The manner in which her efforts to persuade her pagan, profligate husband and ensuing marital difficulties are presented as public knowledge suggests the rather surprising fact that sometimes influential Christian women who were married to influential (and potentially dangerous for the church) pagan men in no way lived their lives in seclusion; they were well-known in the community for their Christian allegiance, possibly sponsored church activities, and may even have held meetings in their houses.[82]

CHAPTER THREE

GIVING BIRTH:
LABOR, NURSING,
AND THE CARE OF INFANTS
IN HOUSE-CHURCH COMMUNITIES

▣▣ ▣▣ ▣▣

A s we have seen, much of the influence of wives in the Roman world was directly related to their active involvement in their children's lives, extending into the lives even of adult children. A full understanding of the significance of motherhood and indeed of the presence of children in early church communities, however, demands that we start at the beginning, with the process of giving birth.

To a much greater extent than is the case for modern western women, ancient women's lives were determined by the realities of procreation. While it is often more implicit than explicit in the texts, the procreating woman's body became a key point of reference for early Christian identity. From the second century, for example, early Christian authors were pointing to differences between Christian and pagan practices and attitudes concerning pregnancy and the rearing of infants. We begin this chapter with an analysis of these apologetic texts. We will then consider descriptions of women in labor and giving birth in early Christian literature in light of what is known of ancient practices, including the role of the midwife. Finally, we will examine the nursing of infants and the challenges involved in caring for them. These were responsibilities that wives shared with other women, including hired wet nurses, nannies, and slaves.

Abortion, Infanticide, and Exposure: Apology and Reality

Although the New Testament is strangely silent on the matter, the avoidance of abortion, infanticide, and exposure is presented in second-century texts as setting Christians apart from others. Here Christians felt that they were choosing the moral high ground in comparison to their contemporaries, but it is evident that there were plenty of protests against such practices also in Greco-Roman literature.

Methods of contraception (with various degrees of success—see dubious methods recommended by Soranus in *Gynecology* 1.61) and abortion were overlapping in the Roman world and seem to have been widely practiced.[1] Pointing to the interpretation of the testimony of Hippocrates, the medical writer Soranus (late first century to second century CE) admits that there is controversy concerning the use of abortives. Soranus himself agrees with those who prescribe abortion in the case of a young woman (when the uterus is small and not able to accommodate the developing fetus) but are against it in the case of adultery or the woman's simply trying to safeguard her figure. Despite his weighing of the arguments, he nevertheless gives detailed instructions for women who intend to have abortions (Soranus, *Gynecology* 1.60, 65). Not unexpectedly, Juvenal, a first-century Roman satirist, associates women seeking abortions with the leisure and laziness of upper-class women, while poorer women suffer the dangers and pains of childbirth and troubles associated with nursing (*Satire* 6.592–601). In the account discussed below concerning the debate over wet-nursing, the philosopher Favorinus similarly associates women who engage wet nurses with those who seek abortions on account of vanity and laziness. Both activities are depicted by him as against nature: depriving a product of one's own blood of "natural" nourishment is tantamount to killing a human being at its very beginnings, while it is being "animated" in the hands of nature, its maker (Gellius 12.1.8–9).[2]

In Jewish writings of this period, abortion (like infanticide and abandonment) is associated with the nations. In his apologetic writing, Josephus, for example, presents the position on abortion among Jews as flowing from their marriage laws: all children are to be raised, and women are neither to cause abortions nor to make away with the fetus—if they do, they will be charged with infanticide (*Against Apion* 2.202–3).[3] Turning to Christian texts from the early second century, in the *Didache* 2.2 commandments against both abortion and infanticide are listed as part of the "Way of Life" in contrast to the "Way of Death," with similar ideas found in the *Epistle of Barnabas* 19.5.[4] Filling out the notion of judgment reflected in these texts with graphic detail, the *Apocalypse of Peter* describes the torments that will befall the woman who has procured an abortion and parents who have practiced infanticide: they are confronted by their children, who stand in a place of delight, and are made to endure great pain. Milk flows from the breasts of the mothers, congealing and smelling foul (*Apoc. Peter* 8).

By the time we get to the apologetic literature of the middle and latter decades of the second century, early Christian attitudes to abortion, infanticide, and exposure have become boundary markers similar to that found in Josephus's work cited above (see Athenagoras, *A Plea for the Christians* 35, referring to abortion and exposure; *Letter to Diognetus* 5.6, referring to exposure; Minucius Felix, *Octavius* 30.1, referring to abortion and infanticide). In his apologetic writing Justin offers rather complex and strange arguments explaining why Christians do not expose their children. Based on the fact that so many exposed children end up in prostitution, not only will Christians be guilty of sending their own children into pollution, but there is the further danger for those who hire prostitutes that they might be engaged in incestuous relationships with their own children (*Apology* 1.27; similar ideas occur in Clement of Alexandria, *Educator* 3.3). Justin is clearly worried about spiraling vices. But we might also sense here some of the anxiety about the correct identity of children that also surfaces in the legal texts concerning procedures for delivery when there are questions about the status of a child. More predictably, Justin goes on to argue that Christians fear exposing their children because of the very real danger that they might not be picked up and therefore Christians would be rendered as murderers (*Apology* 1.28).

Philo of Alexandria claimed that the exposure of children was a common wicked practice among the other nations (*Spec. leg.* 3.110). He offered dramatic descriptions of the calamities that could befall an abandoned child and the horrors of infanticide (3.111–19). In a similar vein, Christian apologists set out to expound their superior morality in relation to pagans. But Roman historians have offered some cautions in interpreting the evidence.[5] Beryl Rawson has argued that although the decision to rear an infant has been viewed as resting in the authority of the *paterfamilias*, both parents would usually have been involved and only the mother in the father's absence; the normal expectation was that a child would be reared.[6] Leaving a badly deformed infant to die or hastening its death was encouraged (Cicero, *On the Laws* 3.8.19; Seneca, *On Anger* 1.15). Yet assumptions concerning the extent to which there was a bias against the disabled and females in practices of infanticide have recently been questioned.[7]

We must not lose sight of the fact that it may have suited the rhetorical purposes of early Christian authors to exaggerate the nature of pagan crimes.[8] Yet, keeping in mind that it is important not to confuse infanticide with exposure,[9] it seems clear that the abandonment of children was a common occurrence, with places for picking up babies such as temples, crossroads, and rubbish heaps being well-known in the community and offering a ready supply of slave bodies.[10] Taken together with the interest in the care of orphans discussed in the next chapter, the texts that speak against abortion, infanticide, and especially exposure point to the rearing of infants as an early ideal of church groups—even though the ongoing occurrence of such practices can certainly not be ruled out. For example, it is important to remember that for women slaves, especially those owned for the sake of prostitution, abortion—and to some extent even infanticide and exposure—could have been used as a type of birth control of last resort. Moreover, although its dating is later than the period mainly under consideration in this book, we know of at least one case of abandonment of a child by early Christians. Cyprian (*On the Lapsed* 3.25) offers evidence for the abandonment of a little girl by Christian parents seeking to escape the Decian persecution in the third century. The little girl, who was subsequently recovered by her mother, was left in the care of her wet nurse, who turned her over to the magistrates.

Labor and Delivery

Children were typically born at home—most commonly the marital home. One possible exception was the case of the widowed or divorced woman where there was a legal dispute concerning the status of the child. In this case sometimes more neutral territory would be sought, such as "the house of a woman of excellent reputation" (D.25.4.1.10, Ulpian). The substitution of another child—perhaps a slave child—for a legal heir seems to have been of significant concern. In setting forth the conditions for disputed births (including appropriate lighting in the delivery room, a single and guarded entry for the room, and the inspection of the newborn infant by the interested parties) legal texts such as the *Praetorian Edict* (D.25.3–4) reinforce the impression one gains from other sources that the birthing process was essentially in the hands of women, both slave and free: "Women of free status, up to the number of five, should be sent, so that in addition to two midwives there are not more than ten free women in the delivery room and no more than six slave women" (D.25.4.1.10, Ulpian).[11] Ancient medical authors like Galen and especially Soranus offer detailed theoretical descriptions of the birthing process and the care and nurturing of infants. We do know, for example, that male doctors could be present and ready to assist in difficult births. But even here there is an awareness of the need to preserve the modesty of the woman in labor, with Galen even suggesting that the male doctor should offer advice from an adjacent room (*On the Natural Faculties* 3.3).[12]

Fig. 3.1: Plaster copy of plaque depicting a midwife at her trade, outside tomb at Isola Sacra, near Ostia. Original in Ostia Museum. Second or third century CE. Photo by Laurie Brink.

Supported by various female assistants, perhaps frequently including the woman's own mother, midwives were in charge of the births. Although many midwives were of servile origin, midwifery was a very important woman's job in the Roman world; it was commemorated on public monuments, and midwives were recognized as having a certain professional standing based on their practice of "a sort of medicine" (D.50.13.1.2, Ulpian).[13] In light of the general apprehension concerning women's involvement with superstition,[14] it is not surprising that we find freedom from superstition listed as a requirement for midwives by Soranus (*Gynecology* 1.4; see D.28.2.4, Ulpian). Despite these stereotypical perceptions, midwives were clearly recognized as a type of moral authority. They were the prime witnesses to the activities in the delivery room and the primary guardians against baby substitution (Paul, *Sententiae* 2.24.8–9).[15] Some of the wealthiest families probably had their own midwives to oversee the births of freeborn dependents and valuable members of the slave *familia*. While their social status and degree of education must have varied significantly, Soranus's list of qualifications for midwives (*Gynecology* 1.3-4) includes the expectation that they be literate. This expectation functions in conjunction with a range of practical (for example, long fingers and short nails) and moral qualifications (for example, respectable and having her wits about her). Soranus envisioned that midwives had substantial formal medical training, and, indeed, his *Gynecology* was probably written with midwives as part of the intended audience, along with doctors and educated laypersons.[16] If midwives were among the members of house churches in the early centuries, they would no doubt have been among the most educated of women.

Since the cultural expectation was that the birth of children was in the hands of women, it is interesting to consider how an ancient audience would have responded to the story of the birth of Jesus in the canonical Gospels. In examining this story, commentators usually focus on such issues as Mary's virginity and Jesus' conception, the theological messages encoded in the evangelists' accounts, the foreshadowing of later Gospel events, and the interaction with the Hebrew Bible. But on one level these are also accounts of a woman's labor and delivery and the early days of an infant's life. For our purposes, it is valuable to reflect upon how such narratives would have been heard in a house-church setting, where infants were being born and nurtured but were also dying—often along with their mothers—at a rate that for us seems unfathomable. Although Soranus's descriptions of obstetrical methods sometimes strike the modern reader as surprisingly sophisticated, the solutions offered for difficult labor within the folk medicine traditions recorded in Pliny the Elder's *Natural History* (involving such aids as hyena's feet, snake sloughs, canine placentas, and vulture feathers) remind us of the high risk of infection for both mother and child associated with many common practices.[17]

Matthew offers scant details about the birth of Jesus itself, stating only that it took place in Bethlehem (Matt. 2:1). Later the Magi visit Jesus in a house (*oikos*) in Bethlehem (2:11), where he is with Mary, his mother. The presence of Joseph in the house is no doubt presumed, though it is not highlighted by Matthew, and no other people in the house are mentioned (compare Luke 2:16). In Matthew's account the gifts from the Magi and the protection of the infant Jesus from Herod's wrath that results from Joseph's premonitory dream are in stark contrast to the fate of the other baby boys from Bethlehem and the surrounding regions. The slaughter of the innocents (Matt. 2:16-18)—as the story in Matthew has traditionally been called—has been passed down through the ages as a prime example of evil of epic proportions. But its impact in a house-church community was no doubt heightened by the commonality of the experience of the death of infants and children. It is probably no exaggeration to say that the majority of women of the community who heard Matthew's Gospel would have readily joined in Rachel's lament (Jer. 31:15; Matt. 2:18), having themselves lost one or more babies under the age of two.

The absence of the usual female support system for the birth of a child that is visible in Matthew's Gospel is even more obvious in the case of Luke. More details are given about the actual birth than in Matthew's Gospel, and an expectation of female support is created earlier in the narrative by Mary's encounter with her pregnant relative, Elizabeth (Luke 1:39-56). An understanding of the rigors and privileges of pregnancy and birth that has always belonged to women is revealed in Elizabeth's famous proclamation: "Blessed are you among women, and blessed is the fruit of your womb" (Luke 1:42 NRSV). Yet, as a mark of the unusual nature of Jesus' birth, neither Mary's own mother (never mentioned in the New Testament), nor Elizabeth, nor any female relative or midwife is with Mary when she delivers. Rather, Mary gives birth in transit, away from her home in Bethlehem on account of the census ordered by Caesar Augustus. Again the presence of Joseph is presumed, but he is given no active role. After the child is born it is Mary herself—not a midwife who would normally have overseen not only the birth but also care for the infant in the early stages—who wraps the babe and places him in the manger. The transient nature of the situation is also stressed by the expression "for there was no place in the lodging area [*katalyma*]" (Luke 2:7). Despite the common belief that the birth is presented as being in a cave or stable, it is more likely that Luke understands it to have taken place in a private house, as in Matthew, but in the part of the house usually set apart for animals and used as guest quarters in an emergency (see Luke 22:11).[18] For an ancient woman hearing this account for the first time, it must all have seemed very strange, perhaps even frightening, no matter how miraculous or befitting of a hero, god, or prophet figure. There is no evidence that husbands typically assisted their wives in labor in the ancient world, and given the lack of explicit reference to Joseph's participation, we are left with the image of a woman in labor alone.

It is perhaps partially in response to the unusual nature of Mary's rather solitary delivery of Jesus in the Gospels that narratives concerning midwives become part of the creative expansion of infancy material in the *Proto-Gospel of James*. Written probably about the middle of the second century in Syria or Egypt, this work tells the story of the births of Mary and Jesus, "weaving stories from the Septuagint into an amazingly free harmonization of the infancy narratives of Matthew and Luke."[19] The ultimate goal of the work is the defense of the virgin birth of Jesus, and the telling of the story of Mary's birth and childhood sets the stage for this defense. But in passing, the author of the *Proto-Gospel of James* offers an important textual representation of the infancy and childhood of a girl—a rarity in early Christian literature (see further discussion in the next chapter).

In the *Proto-Gospel of James,* midwives are involved in some way with the births of both Mary and Jesus. As mothers often do today, Mary's mother, Anna, asks the midwife a question: "What have I had, a boy or a girl?" Upon hearing that the baby is female she rejoices by proclaiming, "My soul is magnified this day" (recalling the words of the Magnificat), lies down, and eventually nurses the baby girl (5:2).[20] Midwives play an even more central role, however, in the account of the birth of Jesus. Concerned to protect Mary's modesty, Joseph leaves her in a cave under the protection of his sons (including presumably the supposed author of the work, James—Jesus' half-brother, usually understood as the "brother of the Lord" known from the New Testament and presented here as Joseph's son by a previous marriage). He then sets out to find a Hebrew midwife. He eventually finds one, but in the end she does little to assist with the miraculous birth. Her presence does, however, bear a certain moral authority, and she acts as a guarantor of legitimate birth in the manner typical of midwives. Along with Joseph, she witnesses the wondrous sign that Joseph's account of his virgin wife giving birth is indeed true—a bright cloud over the cave, followed by a bright light that withdraws only after the baby is born. We are told, as one would expect following a birth, that Jesus immediately took his mother's breast. But to give even more legitimacy to the claim that the birth was miraculous, we are also told of a second midwife named Salome who comes to do a postpartum inspection. Like doubting Thomas, she needs to be convinced on physical grounds. In a truly extraordinary example of Christian storytelling, the account describes her inserting her finger, which is burned and subsequently healed when she touches the child (19–20).

Jane Schaberg is most likely correct in understanding the main intention of the author of the *Proto-Gospel of James* as polemical rather than speaking directly to the circumstances of the ascetic women who lived in a second-century context.[21] The image of Mary in this work opposes the one found in *The True Doctrine*, a work by the pagan intellectual Celsus that was written about 170 CE and is known to us only through a rebuttal composed some seventy years later by Origen. While *The True Doctrine* may well postdate the *Proto-Gospel of James*, there is significant evidence that Celsus drew upon many stereotypical criticisms of early Christianity concerning female initiative and the corruption of households.[22] However one understands the relationship between the two works, the correspondences between the *Proto-Gospel of James* and Celsus's account of the birth of Jesus are remarkable. The presentation of Mary as born of wealthy parents of the noble line of David in the city of Jerusalem, and as the one who had the privilege of spinning the Temple curtain, counters the accusation that Mary was a poor country woman from a Jewish village who made her living of necessity by spinning. Rather than being cast out by a carpenter-husband who convicted her of adultery as recounted in *The True Doctrine*, Mary's purity is protected by her mother, priests of the Temple, her builder-husband—much her senior and more like a guardian than a true mate—and ultimately certified by the midwives. There was no secret birth in Egypt, as Celsus's critique contends, but a true miracle of a virgin birth experienced by many witnesses.[23]

To understand the polemical power of the *Proto-Gospel of James* to respond to critiques like one finds in Celsus's *The True Doctrine*, it is valuable to imagine the recounting of the story in a house-church setting.

Christians of the first two centuries required explanatory narratives to deal with claims (such as virgin birth) and practices (such as the welcoming of subordinate members of the household without the consent of the master of the house) that left them vulnerable to polemical attack. For despite some claims and practices that could easily be interpreted as antifamilial, the majority participated fully in common experiences of family in this era, from the care of children to the management of slaves.

In the creative reworking of infancy material from Matthew and Luke in the *Proto-Gospel of James*, we sense an attempt not only to expand upon the extraordinary events leading to Mary's giving birth to Jesus, but also to communicate these events in a way that would draw upon typical cultural expectations concerning family life in the Roman world. The presence of midwives is one such cultural expectation. But when a reading of this text is informed by an understanding of the Roman family, other elements emerge as well. The portrayal of the older widower Joseph with his grown sons is in keeping with what we know of the frequency of remarriages and the tendency for older men to take younger brides, resulting in the blending of siblings and half-siblings in families, and the wide gaps between the ages of children.[24] Despite the presentation of Mary as a virgin mother, the author makes no attempt to infuse ascetic elements into the other marriages that are presumed, the marriage of Anna and Joakim and Joseph's previous marriage.[25] True ascetics were probably very much in the minority among early church women of the first two centuries. Although they participated in a movement that would come more and more to emphasize the virginal conception and birth of Jesus, the majority of early Christian women were having babies.

Even as we move to the third and fourth centuries, when celibacy and virginity are becoming increasingly prized, the birth of children continues to appear in texts and is clearly being used to communicate early Christian ideals. As discussed in chapter 2, the literary and historical questions raised by the third-century *The Martyrdom of Perpetua and Felicitas* are complex: ideals of motherhood (including birth and nursing images) function in tandem with literary attempts to resolve tensions among physical desires, family responsibilities, ascetic inclinations, and the realities of martyrdom.[26] As many scholars have warned of late, we must be cautious about viewing documents like *The Martyrdom of Perpetua and Felicitas* as direct windows into reality. Nevertheless, when we place them against what we know of childbirth and motherhood in the ancient world, the complexities and tensions revealed by this text often seem to reflect the typical complexities and tensions facing women of procreating age in this era. With careful attention to the literary techniques of the author, we may navigate the complicated relationship between narrative and reality and make plausible suggestions about how the work may have spoken to an ancient audience.

In *The Martyrdom of Perpetua and Felicitas*, the slave Felicitas's labor is dramatized to great literary effect. One of the most poignant moments involves her agonizingly premature labor. Her labor pains are apparently brought on by the prayer of fellow believers who wish for her to share in their martyrdom experience (by law she could not be martyred while pregnant). In reality Felicitas was probably assisted in labor by her companions who were imprisoned with her, but they are not presented as offering assistance in the text. Thus we have one more example of an early Christian birth being presented as an event involving some level of isolation. In fact, the only one who offers commentary during Felicitas's labor offers a criticism of sorts. Felicitas is visibly suffering, and a guard's assistant reminds her that this is nothing compared to what she will face when she is "tossed to the beasts." (Is this the case of a slave chiding a fellow slave?) Her reply gives meaning to her suffering while at the same time highlighting this sense of isolation: "What I am suffering now . . . I suffer by myself. But then another will be inside me who will suffer for me, just as I shall be suffering for him" (15).[27] There is a clear attempt here to give christological meaning to this slave woman's death, and, indeed, there is something striking about a young slave woman in these circumstances being identified with Christ to this degree.

Among the most interesting features of *The Martyrdom of Perpetua and Felicitas* is the manner in which the cultural expectations and ideals of motherhood are both appropriated and to some extent rejected: motherhood is certainly valued in the account, but its ultimate significance is qualified by a new Christian identity. It is interesting to note that at the end of the account, this qualification is expressed through a series of oppositions recalling the rigors of labor and delivery. Here the isolation of Felicitas's giving birth to her daughter fades from view, and references to the presence of a midwife—the normal expectation—serve to highlight the extraordinary nature of her martyrological transformation: "Felicitas, glad that she had safely given birth so that now she could fight the beasts, going from one blood bath to another, from the midwife to the gladiator, ready to wash after childbirth in a second baptism" (18).[28] The reader is drawn into this transformative experience by means of recollections of the common experience of the new lactating mother: "Even the crowd was horrified when they saw that one was a delicate young girl and the other was a woman fresh from childbirth with the milk still dripping from her breasts" (20).

An ancient reader would most probably understand Felicitas's circumstances in relation to her status as a slave; her isolation in giving birth perhaps reflected the circumstances of some slave women who were not fortunate enough to have the usual female support available to better-off freeborn women or to slave women in well-to-do households where significant efforts were made to protect the births within the *familia*. As is also the case with Perpetua, who is presented as a new mother in this text, no father of the baby is mentioned. Perhaps he was a fellow believer martyred along with her.[29] But in a society where the sexual use of slaves was taken for granted, it is possible that the father was her owner or even that she did not know the identity of the biological father. Felicitas's circumstances, however, did not hamper her ability to offer a prime example of faith. Perpetua (the respectable married woman) and Felicitas (the honorless slave) were being presented as complementary role models for their audience.[30] Moreover, the account makes it clear that the higher social status of Perpetua brought no advantages in the arena of martyrdom. In fact, the text hints that whatever social advantages Perpetua may have had in relation to Felicitas may actually have been a disadvantage in securing the Christian upbringing of her child: we are left with doubts as to the ultimate fate of Perpetua's son—he may never have been freed from the bondage of the unbelieving world represented by the powerful intervention of her father. Yet Felicitas's daughter is explicitly said to have been raised by one of the "sisters."

From the fourth century comes another account involving the birth of a baby girl. Gregory of Nyssa's *Life of Macrina* recounts the life of his sister, who became an extremely influential ascetic and founder of women's monasticism. The account of Macrina's birth is remarkable on many levels. For our purposes, it is interesting especially for its depiction of labor and for the way ascetic ideals are intertwined with ideals of motherhood. Macrina's mother is described as having chosen marriage only because, as a beautiful young woman who had lost her parents, she was at risk of being (in our terms) sexually assaulted. Her husband of choice was serious, responsible, and probably older—a suitable protector not unlike Joseph in the *Proto-Gospel of James*. In an unusual turn of events, she fell asleep at the climax of her labor. Immediately before the baby was born, she had a kind of vision in which her child appeared to be outside the womb and a resplendent, more-than-human being named the infant Thecla (the virgin heroine from the second-century *Acts of [Paul and] Thecla* who by the fourth century was an important inspiration to female ascetics). Gregory explains that although known as Macrina in the "outside world" and among her friends, she was known privately as the second Thecla—a sign that she would follow her namesake's way of life.

In contrast to the suffering experienced in labor by Felicitas, the heavenly figure grants Macrina's mother an easy delivery. This seems in keeping with the ease with which Macrina fits into her mother's life and her otherworldly inclinations. Yet despite Macrina's ultimate fate as an ascetic, her preparation for asceticism is rooted in the experience of motherhood and is in keeping with the overlap between the lives of ascetic and married women that is observable in earlier centuries (see chapter 4). Like many an eldest daughter from a large family, Macrina was heavily involved in helping her mother with her younger siblings. As a widow with grown children, Macrina's mother, used to considerable wealth and luxury, was led by her daughter into an ascetic life. This took place by means of a process involving several steps, including the dispersal of property and the recognition of slaves as sisters. By the time Gregory wrote the *Life of Macrina*, the period of house churches was past, but the family continued to play a strong role in defining the identity of ascetic women in practical terms as well as their most attractive virtues.

With the exception of the evidence discussed above and numerous references to the birth of Jesus, actual descriptions of births and infancy are comparatively rare in early Christian literature. Yet the birth experience frequently appears at a metaphorical level. In Paul's letters, for example, such symbolism abounds. There are metaphorical references to a wet nurse (1 Thess. 2:7) and to weaning (1 Cor. 3:1-2; compare Heb. 5:12-14), with childhood generally acting as a state of transition into maturity (Gal. 3:19—4:7; see Eph. 4:14) but also as a symbolic reference point for the relationship between Paul and the community (for example, 1 Cor. 4:14-17; Gal. 4:19 [here Paul depicts his own suffering for the sake of the community as labor pains!]). In some of his most theologically rich passages, Paul speaks of all of creation groaning in labor along with believers in anticipation of redemptive adoption (Rom. 8:22-25). The groaning of labor was probably a sound very familiar to Paul from the houses where he stayed and the churches he founded, as indeed it would have been a common experience of household life in the Roman world. It was, in contrast to screaming, a sound to be welcomed in the laboring woman, who should be advised in proper breathing (Soranus, *Gynecology* 2.6).

With the exception of 1 Thess. 2:7, none of these metaphors of birth and infancy are really feminized in the manner of Philo of Alexandria's metaphorical description of the Creator, who assigns the earth to be both "mother and nurse" and whose bounty of plants offers the same kind of natural sustenance to animals as females who "well up springs of milk" as the time of delivery approaches (Philo, *Concerning Noah's Work as Planter* 14–16),[31] or Tertullian's comparison of the sustenance provided by the church to prisoners in need to that of a mother who offers her "bountiful breasts" (*To the Martyrs* 1; *ANF* 3.693). But if we imagine Paul's metaphors as linked to the family atmosphere of house churches, where, for example, women might well have been nursing during meetings of the *ekklēsia*, the power of the metaphors as encoding feminine experience (useful for teaching on a range of matters from the theological to community relations) becomes strongly apparent. Indeed, it is perhaps the familiarity of this experience within the community that leads the author of 1 Peter to use the insatiable appetite of the newborn for the mother's milk as a metaphor for a spiritual craving for Christ: "Like newborn infants, long for the pure, spiritual milk, so that by it you may grow into salvation—if indeed you have tasted that the Lord is good" (1 Pet. 2:2-3 NRSV).[32]

Nursing and Infant Care

In the Roman world the safe arrival of a newborn baby was often followed by an impromptu party, which would then be followed by a more formal gathering eight or nine days later for the naming day (see Luke 1:57-63; 2:21-22, where the naming of John and Jesus is associated with circumcision and other Jewish traditions). In his apologetic writing Josephus argues that the birth of children among Jews is not viewed as an occasion for parties involving excess drinking but demands sobriety from the beginning (*Against Apion* 2.204). Josephus's comments indicate that sometimes birth parties were raucous events. Among believers the nature of celebrations would have been affected by a variety of factors, including whether parents were from

Jewish or Gentile backgrounds, wealth, and other personal circumstances. But there is no reason to doubt that the earliest Christians would have celebrated births in some way. Roman evidence speaks of these birth celebrations mainly as male affairs with friends congratulating the father, but Beryl Rawson reminds us of what the textual evidence is probably leaving unsaid: "we should remember those women present in the delivery room: they might well have been having their own party, near the new mother, and offering practical advice and making practical arrangements."[33]

Rawson reports the case of a birth in a distinguished senatorial family from the first half of the second century as recounted in the writings of Aulius Gellius (Latin author and grammarian who wrote a twenty-book compendium entitled *Attic Nights*). The case illustrates how the role of women in such celebrations may have flowed naturally from their role as supporters in labor, and how men *and* women might share in postdelivery debates and decision making. Having assisted her daughter through a very difficult delivery, the mother became an advocate for her daughter's well-being amid a group of the father's friends, who were debating the benefits of breast-feeding in relation to wet-nursing (Gellius 12.1.1–5).[34] Because of the philosophical interests of the male party, they were predictably in favor of mothers nursing their babies themselves. Indeed, the protests of Favorinus, the philosopher-teacher of the baby's father, are reported in the text in great detail! The nursing of babies by their own mothers was a practice thought to be virtuous by various intellectuals and social commentators of the day, but dangerously on the decline (Tacitus, *Dialogue* 28.4–5). It was a practice worthy of praise by husbands who were impressed by the determination of wives willing to undergo painful medical procedures to sustain the exercise (Plutarch, *A Consolation to His Wife* 5).[35]

The arguments (Gellius 12.1.5–24) in favor of women nursing babies themselves range from the almost flippant (should one think that women were given nipples for decoration!) to the uncannily modern (nursing greatly assists in bonding between the parents and the baby). The mother's position, however, was closer to that of Soranus, who favored babies being fed with mother's milk in theory but cautioned that that it could lead a woman to age prematurely if the woman spent herself through daily suckling (Soranus, *Gynecology* 2.18). Soranus set out detailed instructions on the selection of a wet nurse (*Gynecology* 2.18–20), listing everything from qualities (such as self-control), to nationality (Greek was best, for in that way the infant would be exposed to the best speech!), to age (neither too old nor too young—ideally having given birth a few times), to excesses in religious matters (superstition and inclinations toward ecstatic states to be avoided—raising the question of how early Christian nurses might have been judged), to her size (milk from large-framed women was more nourishing), to the size of her breasts (medium-size breasts are best, having the right amount of milk). In the case of the debate recounted by Gellius, the mother felt that her daughter was too young and too exhausted by the birth to sustain breast-feeding and argued that the necessary arrangements to hire wet nurses should be made.

Wet-nursing seems to have been a pervasive practice in Roman society at all levels. The debate on the merits of employing a wet nurse (discussed above) might well have also taken place among the earliest Christians. Because the physical setting of these groups was the house church, we should keep in mind that this kind of debate could have occurred in tandem with debate about topics of more obvious ecclesiastical interest, such as who was to preside at the Lord's supper that day or what spiritual gifts were most important. But when we allow ourselves to introduce the world of infants and children within the sacred space of the house church, even what counts as an important spiritual gift might take on new meaning. Wet nurses were often kept on as nannies even after the child was weaned.[36] Their potential as role models and teachers was frequently acknowledged, as in the following excerpt from the writings of (Pseudo-) Plutarch. It occurs amid arguments on the importance of careful selection of wet nurses and foster-mothers, based on their characters and the quality of the lessons they would provide: "For just as it is necessary, immediately after birth, to begin to mould the limbs of children's bodies in order that these may grow straight and without deformity, so, in the same fashion, it is fitting from the beginning to regulate the characters of children" (*Moralia* 3E; *On the Education of Children*).[37] Christian wet nurses, be they slave or free, were certainly in a position to teach their young charges (a spiritual gift highly prized by Paul, 1 Cor. 12:27-31). If Christian wet nurses were owned or hired by nonbelievers, their teaching could easily become an exercise in evangelization.

Beyond nursing an infant, great challenges lay ahead in simply keeping an infant alive. Scholars estimate that about 30 percent of infants died in their first year.[38] A modern parent or childcare provider reading Soranus's detailed directions in caring for a newborn infant will frequently swallow hard, both on account of the tangible vulnerability of infants and the frequent harmful advice—ranging from rubbing a teething baby's gums with chicken fat (*Gynecology* 2.49) to the much more dangerous advice to induce vomiting in a child who swallows his or her own phlegm (*Gynecology* 2.54). Gillian Clark views Soranus's advice on such matters as bathing, massaging, swaddling, and changing babies as optimistic, linking child mortality with "the impossibility of keeping a swaddled baby clean on the fourth floor of a tenement with the water supply at the end of the street."[39] Such would have been one of many concrete challenges facing participants in at least the more humble of house churches.

As discussed above, there are many scenarios, including the potential for multiple pregnancies among slave-prostitutes, where women may have been forced to abandon their babies in an act of desperation. Babies were not always the victims of opportunists, however, and were sometimes the beneficiaries of "the kindness of strangers" in the Roman world (Philo, *Spec. leg.* 3.116). In practical terms, this means that members of house churches not only may have shared a commitment to their own children but may also have been seeking to rescue abandoned infants and to adopt them as part of the community (see Aristides, *Apology* 15, which refers to rescue of orphans by early Christians). Legally, these infants might have been raised as either slave or free. Paul's metaphorical description of adoption as a child-heir of God (no longer a slave) in Gal. 4:7 reflects familiarity with the process of adoption and probably also with the legal options and complexities associated with the process.[40] Within the Gospel material, Luke 18:15-17 offers an especially intriguing indication of a special value attached to infants; people are said to have brought "even infants" (*brephē*; the parallels in Mark 10:13-16 and Matt. 19:13-15 have *paidia*, little children) to Jesus despite the fact that the disciples rebuked them.[41] This reference to infants is in keeping with Luke's theological point about the kingdom belonging to the helpless, the useless, and the outcast[42]—a point sharpened by an awareness that recognition of children's full existence and individuality was a gradual process until about age ten, from which point death invited full mourning (Romans prescribed no formal mourning for children under one year).[43]

Conclusion:
Mothers and Infants in House Churches

Although we are not used to thinking in these terms (perhaps because childbirth most definitely lacks decorum), it is important to remember that house churches were places of women giving birth. They were places of women's labor (including sometimes very difficult labor), delivery, deaths of infants and mothers in childbirth, nursing babies, and the precarious work of keeping a baby alive from the first fragile days into the first few years. One might arrive at a house-church meeting while a woman of the house was in labor or just after a birth. If the household *familia* included many slaves, labor and delivery could have been a frequent occurrence. On the basis of the frequency of births and the presence of children, house-church meetings must have been noisy and bustling places. The sounds of a woman in labor somewhere in the background, the crying of infants, the presence of mothers or wet nurses feeding their children, little toddlers under foot, children's toys on the floor—all could have been part of the atmosphere.

CHAPTER FOUR

GROWING UP
IN HOUSE-CHURCH COMMUNITIES

▣▣ ▣▣ ▣▣

There are signs that the study of Roman childhood is now a burgeoning field. The most important recent work is undoubtedly Beryl Rawson's *Children and Childhood in Roman Italy* (2003),[1] but Rawson is indebted to a wide range of scholarship that has opened up new possibilities for this field: a greater understanding of housing and domestic space, Roman law, epigraphy, iconography, and the conditions of ancient slavery—all of which have laid the groundwork for more systematic childhood studies.[2] Such success in bringing the children of the Roman Empire back to life offers a great opportunity to consider with fresh eyes the limited evidence for the lives of early Christian children.[3] It is useful, however, to begin with a few general methodological observations.

Given the subject of this book, we should carefully consider the nature of the evidence for female children in early Christianity. There are a few Gospel passages that deal specifically with girl children (for example, the raising of Jairus's daughter, Matt. 9:18-26; Mark 5:21-43; Luke 8:40-56; the healing of the daughter of the Syrophoenician woman, Matt. 15:21-28; Mark 7:24-30). The pool of texts expands somewhat if we include women of marriageable years who would really only be adolescents in our own culture, such as the young woman, identified as Herodias's daughter, who dances during the banquet for Herod's birthday (Matt. 14:1-12;

Mark 6:14-29),[4] the ten wise and foolish virgins of the Matthean parable (Matt. 25:1-46), the four unmarried daughters of Philip (Acts 21:9), and the various texts dealing with Mary's betrothal, pregnancy, and giving birth to Jesus.[5] In the last chapter we considered three early Christian works that refer to the birth of infant girls: the description of the birth and childhood of Mary found in the *Proto-Gospel of James*, the reference to the baby girl born to the slave Felicitas in *The Martyrdom of Perpetua and Felicitas*, and the account of the birth and childhood of Macrina in Gregory of Nyssa's *Life of Macrina*. Later patristic literature includes a few other passing references that will be discussed below, but the list of texts above represents the majority of evidence for female infants and girls in early Christian literature.

In seeking to recover the lives of early Christian girls, we encounter an especially strong example of how the constraints facing historians of the family in the Roman world become acute in the case of early Christian communities. Although some texts discuss the situation of children generally, the Roman evidence (including the visual evidence) for the lives of boys significantly outweighs that for girls. In the case of the lives of early Christian girls we have almost no evidence whatsoever—they may in fact be the most underrepresented familial group in all of early Christian literature, if not all ancient Mediterranean literature. In the face of this paucity of evidence, we will by necessity be faced with talking about children in general, rather than specifically female children, when we discuss the process of caring for children in house-church communities. Yet it is here that the comparative perspective becomes especially valuable. Beryl Rawson has argued that much of what was once thought to apply only to boys in the Roman world (for example, esteem for the intellect and education) was also applicable to girls.[6] Therefore, in discussing the few texts that can offer insight into the lives of children who were part of house churches, we will operate under the assumption that girls are to be included unless we know of a clear indication to the contrary or significant comparative evidence that would lead us to think otherwise.

A second methodological issue involves the nature of our focus on women as childcare providers. In a book on women in house churches, it is crucial to examine the lives of children and their relations with women. Yet it is important not to overstate the case concerning the influence of women on the lives of children, as if to imply that children were within their exclusive domain; men clearly played an important role in children's lives not only as legal guardians but also as concerned grandfathers, fathers, stepfathers, teachers, *paidagōgoi*, and so forth. Nevertheless, there can be no denying the special influence of women, especially in the early years of childhood (as in many cultures today), even though influence should by no means be restricted to mothers. In the last chapter we discussed the important role of the wet nurse in the rearing of infants. But the potential for female influences in the lives of children extended even beyond mothers and nurses to include stepmothers, grandmothers, nannies, and slave-attendants of various kinds. Within the context of house churches, we also need to add "sisters" in faith who may well have acted as pseudo-mothers, especially when it came to educating children in the gospel. These women may sometimes have been widows (Herm. *Vis.* 2.4.3) or other unmarried women who included the care of children as part of their ministry.

This chapter, therefore, will include discussion of two interrelated themes: the broad scope of women's involvement in the care of children in house churches and the impact of the presence of children themselves in these communities (with special emphasis on girls). A deliberate focus on the physical setting of the house church will illustrate how thinking about the spaces where children (both slave and free) were born, lived, and died can help us to understand their impact on community life. We will also consider early Christian strategies for caring for children in sickness and health. Finally, we will examine the house church as a space for the education of children. In this last section in particular, our comparative approach will strengthen the case for viewing girls as valued members of early Christian communities.

Household Life

Careful reading of early Christian texts reveals several indications of the presumption of the presence of children in household settings. One of the most charming Gospel stories is the parable of the friend in the middle of the night, in which the householder cries out to a friend who has come to the door looking for food for his unexpected visitor: "Do not bother me; the door has already been locked, and my children [*ta paidia*] are with me in bed" (Luke 11:7 NRSV). The setting suggests a simple house—perhaps only of one or two rooms—and children sharing their parents' bed.

The middle of the night is also the scene for a gathering in a house at Troas, where, according to Acts, Paul and his fellow workers Tychicus and Trophimus gathered with believers in an upper room. A youth (*neanias*; *pais*) named Eutychus (perhaps not coincidentally, his name literally means good fortune! Could this be a slave waiting to go home with his master?) who had been sitting in the window fell asleep "as Paul talked still longer" and fell to his death from the third floor. The boy went on to be miraculously healed by Paul (Acts 20:7-12).

Although it might easily go unnoticed because of the strong focus on the asceticism of women, children are also part of the extensive movement in and out of houses that occurs in the legendary *Acts of [Paul and] Thecla*. In this account Paul's entry into Iconium is facilitated by a certain Onesiphorus, who goes out to meet him with his children, Simmias and Zeno, and his wife, Lectra. They entertain Paul's party at their house, which also serves as a house church, where there is "great joy," "bowing of knees," "breaking of bread," and preaching "of the word of God about abstinence and resurrection" (2–5). Later in the narrative the children of Onesiphorus appear again, but this time in a tomb (on the route between Iconium and Daphne) that has become a temporary home, where they have spent many days fasting. The children eventually protest that they are hungry, and one of them is sent off with Paul's cloak to sell for food. En route, the child encounters Thecla and leads her back to Paul (23).

All of these references to children are found in narrative accounts and do not, therefore, offer direct evidence for the presence and activities of children in house churches. Nevertheless, they reflect the kind of domestic scenes that would have been common experiences for the audiences of these accounts, who listened to them in the house churches where children usually lived: children in bed with their parents; falling asleep at late-night worship; urging their parents to provide food; being sent to run errands; easily falling prey to accidents, and so forth. That children were not merely chance witnesses at early Christian meetings but actually expected to be active listeners to early Christian discourse is made clear by the direct address to them (along with other family groupings) in the New Testament household codes (Col. 3:20; Eph. 6:1).

Imagining the proclamation of household codes with their explicit interest in familial relations within a house-church setting raises the question of whether participants would have drawn any firm distinction between home and church—community worship experience and family experience. A lack of distinction would most obviously be the case when a given house-church membership involved people living in the same house, as may well have been possible if church groups took root in a large *domus* with a large retinue of slaves and clients. But the distinction between home and church could have blurred substantially even for those who physically left their dwellings to attend church gatherings. We might consider the situation of slaves, for example, who seem not to have generally slept in segregated slave quarters but rather simply to have fallen asleep where they worked (in storehouses, kitchens, or stables, or even on the floor of their masters' bedrooms). It is by no means clear that they perceived themselves as being really "at home" (as free members of the house might have) when they were in the houses of their masters.[7] Similarly, we may ask whether the children of the community really ever distinguished between when they were at home and when they were worshipping in the *ekklēsia*. Were they simply visiting the house of friends, where they potentially spent more time than at the houses of their fathers or masters, or was the house church the house where their slave *paidagōgoi* regularly took them as part of a daily routine?

Beryl Rawson has argued that childhood for freeborn persons in the Roman world would often have involved de facto membership in the slave *familia*, with free and enslaved children playing together and even being nursed by the same women slaves. It is against this background of shared space that Rawson reads Celsus's second-century critique of early Christianity, discussed in the previous chapter. According to Celsus, children in house and workshop settings (where slaves often worked) were being encouraged "to leave father and their schoolmasters, and go along with the women and little children who are their playfellows to the wool dresser's shop or to the Cobbler's or the washerwoman's shop, that they may learn perfection" (Origen, *Against Celsus* 3.55).[8] It certainly suits Celsus's purposes to depict early Christianity as a religion of women, children, and slaves, but the physical images in the text are, in Rawson's view, completely believable—reflecting the intermingling of freeborn children, slave children, and slaves.

It is perhaps on account of the shared experiences of freeborn and slave children that they are so often compared in ancient literature, including early Christian literature. Even etymologically, it is not always possible to discern when a text refers to a child or a slave, for one of the principal terms to refer to a child (*pais*) can also mean slave.[9] Ancient texts also make it clear, however, that as freeborn children reached adulthood, the camaraderie of playmates should come to an abrupt end (the extent to which affection among individuals who had been brought up together may have continued despite differences of status should also be kept in mind; see further below). In the following text from (Pseudo-)Plutarch we can see evidence both for what seemed like a natural comparison between the child and the slave and ultimately for the great distance between their positions vis-à-vis the father of the household: "Wherefore Aristippus not inelegantly, in fact very cleverly, rebuked a father who was devoid both of mind and sense. For when a man asked him what fee he should require for teaching his child, Aristippus replied, 'A thousand drachmas'; but when the other exclaimed, 'Great heavens! What an excessive demand! I can buy a slave for a thousand,' Aristippus retorted, 'Then you will have two slaves, your son and the one you buy'" (Plutarch *Moralia* 4F, *On the Education of Children*).[10]

Recent work on slavery both within the Roman world and in early Christian circles has resulted in an increased awareness of the lives of slaves as complex and unpredictable, and has a significant bearing upon our understanding of childhood in early Christianity. For example, as discussed in more detail in the next chapter, the fact that the sexual use of slaves—including slave children—was a common social expectation should guard against assuming that the practice disappeared in early Christian communities. It is impossible to know to what extent symbolism and ethical exhortations, which suggest a certain valuing of slaves, had an impact on the concrete relations between slaves and slave owners in these communities (including some allusions to the benefits of inheritance, which were legally the prerogative of legitimate children [for example, Rom. 8:14-17; Gal. 3:23—4:11; Col. 3:11, 24]). Were Christian slave owners, for example, any less likely to separate slave families that were not recognized in law but certainly existed in reality? Did perceptions concerning the holiness of children affect the treatment of slave children (1 Cor. 7:14)?

Many of the children addressed in the household codes of Colossians and Ephesians were probably slave children (some with no knowledge of or contact with biological parents), and many of the adult slaves who were instructed no doubt had children. We may detect echoes of their past experience in the theological imagery of Col. 2:14-15 (compare Rev. 18:11), which draws upon the public disgrace of honorless slaves and captive families during the triumphal procession of military leaders and applies it to a type of cosmic conquest of Christ over the enslaved powers.[11] It is valuable to compare this textual imagery with evidence for the growing visual use of children for purposes of propaganda in the second century; children were used to great visual effect in the columns of Trajan and Marcus Aurelius, "as symbols of Rome's power and her enemies' humiliation."[12] Children being torn away from foreign mothers by Roman soldiers are among the most pathetic scenes.

Even if we leave aside the question of the impact of early Christian convictions on the lived experience of slaves and slave children, recent work on slavery in the Roman world suggests that straightforward, hierarchical relations between slave owners and slaves should not be presumed always to exist in early church communities. This is the case even when ethical exhortations like the household codes present such relations as ideal. Once again, this has significant bearing on the lives of children in house churches.

Here the work of Dale Martin on inscriptional evidence from Asia Minor (difficult to date, but probably from the second to the third centuries) is especially suggestive.[13] Challenging to a certain degree the impression of rigid demarcation between legitimate children and slaves found in many texts, the inscriptional evidence indicates that some slaves seem to have acted in only a quasi-servile role, as a type of adopted child, perhaps with secondary status. Martin highlights the existence of a Latin inscription from a location near Philippi that pushes the overlap between child and slave even further: Vitalis is described as both a slave and a son of Gaius Lavus Faustus—perhaps the progeny of his master father and a household slave. Thus, Martin asks, "How do we imagine Vitalis experienced his slavery in such a case? How did persons experience their identities when their owners were also their parents?"[14] Martin illustrates that in their slavery and in their "family lives" slaves acted out multiple identities. He concludes that "we must allow our imaginations more room to think about how human beings in antiquity experienced both family and slavery. And that may complicate the way we imagine slavery, family, household, and their relationship to one another in early Christianity."[15]

Sharing Childcare

As noted above, Celsus's critique of early Christianity made reference to the world of children. If one combines his impressions with those of another second-century critic of early Christianity, Lucian of Samosata, one arrives at the following picture: early Christianity welcomes—even encourages—the recruitment of unruly, rebellious, inadequately supervised children. Celsus's discussion of the involvement of children is longer and more graphic, but Lucian's images of "old hags called widows," together with orphans waiting at the gate of an imprisoned Christian at the very break of day, does not fail to get the point across.[16] Both accounts employ images of children to demean early Christian groups, and they reflect plenty of stereotypes. Yet, as discussed above, Celsus's impressions contain many believable elements, and Lucian of Samosata's pairing of widows and orphans is found frequently throughout early Christian literature. In fact, this pairing offers some of the most important evidence for the care of children by early church groups and for the involvement of women—beyond the role of mother—in offering that care.

First, it is important to note that the care of widows and orphans appears frequently in texts as an ethical priority (for example, James 1:27; Herm. *Man.* 8.10; *Barn.* 20.2). Since the grouping was a traditional way of speaking of those in need (for example, Deut. 24:19-22; Jer. 7:6), it might seem to be reading too much into the association to view them as a concrete group in early church communities either living together or associated with one another for some practical purpose. But in addition to Lucian of Samosata's description of the prison scene, other texts indicate that the references to orphans and widows were based in reality. Ignatius (Ignatius, *Smyrn.* 6.2) refers to the neglect of orphans and widows as one of the vices of his docetic opponents in a manner that suggests that he has specific problems in mind (compare Herm. *Sim.* 9.26.1–2).[17] But most important of all is the instruction found in the second-century *Shepherd of Hermas* that Grapte (clearly a literate church leader) should teach the widows and orphans (Herm. *Vis.* 2.4.3).

Grapte may well have been a widow herself, but a relatively well-to-do widow and not one of the many who seemed to require support. Her name is frequently attested for slaves and freedwomen in Rome,[18] but her position suggests that she is more likely to have been a freedwoman of considerable means. She receives one copy of the initial (and evolving) revelation—one of the "little books"—to pass on to her charges. It is safe to conclude that the role envisioned here for Grapte is broader than religious instruction narrowly defined and is rooted in the support she would have offered as patron. (In contrast, note the role of the ministers/deacons [*diakonoi*] who minister badly in Herm. *Sim.* 9.26.1–2—they despoil the living of widows and orphans.)[19] This pattern of a more well-to-do widow caring for other widows is also suggested by the description in 1 Tim. 5:16 of the believing woman who "has relatives who are really widows," the account of the charitable works of Tabitha of Joppa (Acts 9:36-43), and the presentation of the good works of the wealthy widow Tryphaena in the *Acts of [Paul and] Thecla* (3.41). It is important to remember that when the support of widows emerges as an issue of community concern as in 1 Tim. 5:16 (in which personal patronage seems to be preferred where possible instead of centralized relief)[20] or community dispute as in Acts 6:1, the matter almost certainly involves the support of children, although such support is usually a less explicit concern than in Grapte's situation. In the second-century *Acts of Peter* (8), neglect of both orphans and widows is presented as a by-product of the struggle between Peter and his nemesis, Simon Magus (frequently presented in early Christian texts as a "heretic" and father of Gnosticism). The text speaks of a senator who previously followed Christ and opened his house to the poor, offering food to orphans and refuge to widows, now being won over by the magic of Simon Magus and driving away with a stick those who come to his door!

As is suggested especially by Ignatius's greeting in his letter to the "virgins called widows" (Ignatius, *Smyrn.* 13.1), the labels associated with single and celibate women in early Christianity were flexible; in this case the phrase most likely refers to the admission of virgins into the group or "order" of widows that existed in this period in some communities (compare 1 Tim. 5:3-16).[21] If "widows" was a broad category referring to various types of unmarried women (many of whom required support from church groups), we should consider the possibility that "orphans" was similarly broad. When the term "orphans" is paired with "widows," it seems most obviously to refer to the children of the widows themselves, who may sometimes have been quite destitute.[22] But we should remember that, for all practical purposes, the role of motherhood was shared by a variety of people in the Roman world, including nurses, caregivers, and surrogate parents of various kinds, and that slave children and freeborn children often shared the same wet nurse. There must have been many cases in which children (especially of lower status) ended up, for all practical purposes, in the care of others, adopted by default; these orphan children may have been habitually fed, occasionally washed, and put to bed by different people. If we add to this the strong possibility that rescuing abandoned children would have been understood as an act of Christian charity (see preceding chapter), we end up with the likelihood that widows often were caring for children who were not their own.

The second-century depictions of early Christian groups welcoming ragamuffin children with slaves and women in tow, therefore, was probably not too far off the mark—especially if one observed the "orphans and widows" from an outsider's perspective. Beryl Rawson has argued that for poorer families living in crowded urban tenement houses, the street would have been the only playground and the neighborhood an important source of protection and identity.[23] Here it is especially important to consider the testimony of the second-century apologist Aristides, who refers not only to Christians' caring for widows and orphans, but also to Christians' rescuing orphans from those who treat them harshly (*Apology* 15).

The author of 1 Timothy's list of the criteria for enrollment of widows (1 Tim. 5:9) based on past experience (including such home-based activities as hospitality, caring for children, and relief of the afflicted) should probably be taken to mean that these women would continue providing such acts of service after enrollment. This list opens up many possibilities for general service to children in church groups both in sickness and in health. If we include with the list the encouragement for older women to teach younger women to be model wives and mothers in Titus 2:4-5, we discover the important role envisioned for older women in mothering children probably based on three models: indirectly, by acting as a role model for wives who were part of families comprised of a mother, father, and children and by acting as a role model and possibly supporting younger widows who were caring for their own children in their own homes (encouraged by the author of the Pastorals to remarry, 1 Tim. 5:11-14);[24] and directly, by taking in destitute widows and orphans within their own houses (1 Tim. 5:16). That widows' patronage of such groups may have extended to caring for children who had no biological relationship with them and who might otherwise be abandoned is suggested by the fact that the slave Felicitas's newborn daughter was adopted by one of the "sisters." There is no mention of the baby's father and no mention of a husband for the "sister"—we are probably to understand that she is a widow. Although she is a young woman of marriageable age and not really a child (though we would view her as an adolescent today), the virgin Thecla is similarly presented as rescued through the efforts of a wealthy widow in the *Acts of [Paul and] Thecla*. In an important sense, Thecla acts as a replacement for Tryphaena's own daughter Falconilla, who has died (27–31). Vocal about her adoption of Thecla as a second daughter, Tryphaena is struck by the irony of the circumstances as Thecla is led to the arena: "My daughter Falconilla I took away to the tomb, but you, Thecla, I take to fight wild beasts" (31).[25]

Sickness and Death of Children

Members of an ancient audience would easily identify with Tryphaena's poignant cry. Whereas many in our society are spared the agony of watching their children or a brother or sister suffer through serious illness and death, it is no exaggeration to say that almost no one would have escaped this experience in the Roman world. Scholars estimate that roughly 50 percent of all children born died before the age of ten.[26] This perhaps explains the odd (by our standards) fact that Plutarch includes the death of a child as one of the typical misfortunes that might befall a person along with becoming sick, losing money, and failing in public life (*Superstition* 6; see *Rules for Politicians* 32). The great possibility that one would lose a child must have affected the psyche, and scholars of the ancient world have speculated that this reality may have affected the nature of attachment to young children. At the very least, it seems to have affected customs of mourning that progressively became more elaborate in Roman society as the child approached the age of ten.[27] At the same time, it is clear that the death of a child could lead to profound sadness. Among the strongest indications of this is Plutarch's *A Consolation to His Wife*, written to his wife, Timoxena, after the death of their two-year-old daughter, Timoxena the younger.

Scholars debate the extent to which Plutarch's letter reflects the conventions of consolatory letter writing. The letter certainly reflects conventional features with respect to form and content and may, in fact, have been expanded from a shorter, more informal letter to his wife and published later as the version we now have.[28] But there are unmistakable expressions of genuine sentiment in the letter. In remembering her generosity and goodness, Plutarch recalls events that might be described in modern terms as imitative play: "She would ask her nurse to feed not only other babies but the objects and toys that she liked playing with, and would generously invite them, as it were to her table, offering the good things she had and sharing the greatest pleasures with those who delighted her" (*A Consola-*

tion to His Wife 2).[29] The death of the young child might have been espe-cially difficult for her mother, as she was an only daughter born later in life after four sons.[30] Plutarch does offer much consolation to his wife, but his central piece of advice is for her to show restraint in her mourning—counter to cultural expectations in the Hellenistic world, where women were encouraged to vocally demonstrate their grief (see Mark 7:38; Luke 23:27).[31] In praising her for the decorum she has already shown, he may be offering an indirect indication that Timoxena the elder was in reality overwhelmed with grief (and interestingly, for the broader interests of this volume, acknowledging her ability to manage the funerary and household affairs in his absence).[32]

In the world of house churches, the death of two-year-old children like Timoxena the younger would have been commonplace. It is therefore not surprising that the Gospels contain accounts of the healing and raising of children such as Jairus's daughter (Mark 5:21-24, 35-42, and parallels), the daughter of a Syrophoenician woman (Mark 7:25-34 and parallels), and the healing of a demon-possessed boy (Mark 9:14-29 and parallels). In all of these cases it is a parent—either a mother or a father—who intercedes on behalf of her or his child, and in all cases their desperation is palpable.

Beyond the New Testament, the intercession of parents is mentioned in several early Christian healing accounts. In the second-century *Acts of Peter* discussed previously, it is a widow (previously supported by Marcel-lus) who intercedes on behalf of her only son. News of the raising of this poor woman's son eventually reaches the mother of a senator, who in turn experiences the same miracle—even the rich cannot escape this tragedy! The wealthy woman's gratitude leads to her spending all of the money intended to prepare her son's corpse on the support of her slaves now set free, with the remainder, per Peter's instructions, to be divided among the widows (later, she brings two thousand pieces of gold to be divided among the virgins of Christ; 24–29).

Even more elaborate accounts of the healing of children are found in the *Infancy Gospel of Thomas*, which may have been in circulation as early as the beginning of the second century. In this account the character of Jesus as a child is highly developed—to the point at which not only his good but also his mischievous acts are featured (in a fit of childish temper, Jesus in fact strikes a child dead who accidentally runs into him—to the loud pro-test of his parents; 4–5). Many have stressed the entertainment value of the legends contained in the various Apocryphal Gospels, and it is difficult to take a work like the *Infancy Gospel of Thomas* seriously as a piece of religious writing. Yet, in the account of the child who falls off the roof to his death and is healed by Jesus (9), or the account of the child who is healed while bleeding to death after an accident with an ax (10), or the healing of the neighborhood child who died and caused his mother to weep bitterly (17), we sense the attempt to grapple with the serious issues of accident, sickness, and death, and the struggle to believe in Jesus, who is supposed to bring hope to such situations. It may even be the case that the death of a child at the instigation of Jesus is a primitive reflection upon the fact that sometimes a visit from a Christian healer only seems to make a child worse.

Although the presentation of the death of Ponticus, fellow martyr of Blandina, in the *Letter of the Churches of Lyons and Vienne* (Eusebius, *Hist. eccl.* 5.1.2–63; reflecting the persecution in Gaul in 177 CE) is clearly shaped to underscore the drama of the events, one can still sense the fear of an adolescent on the verge of manhood whose "sister in Christ" must urge him on and stiffen him with resistance to meet death. As the last to die, Blandina's bravery and resolve are described with an appeal to bridal and motherhood symbolism; echoing the experience of the mother of the

Fig. 4.1: Amphitheater of Carthage, probably the location of the martyrdom of Perpetua and companions. Photo by C. Osiek.

Maccabees (2 Macc. 7:20-23), she is like "a noble mother encouraging her children." While Blandina offers comfort to fellow martyrs who have become like her children, Perpetua is able to comfort her own brother Dinocrates via her experience of imprisonment and martyrdom. The trauma of watching a brother becoming disfigured and dying "horribly" of facial cancer at seven is recorded in the *Martyrdom of Perpetua and Felicitas*, forming part of one of Perpetua's visions. Perpetua becomes aware of the power of her prayer to secure her brother's happiness, freedom from suffering, and salvation after death; eventually she is granted a vision in which the once hot, thirsty, and dirty little boy is now healed of his disfigurement, drinks to his heart's content, and splashes merrily in the water (7–8). In these martyrological accounts the main point is hope in the resurrection in the face of untimely death, be it as the result of disease as in the case of Dinocrates or in martyrdom as in the case of Ponticus (to what extent the martyrdom of children actually occurred is impossible to determine).

At the end of Gregory of Nyssa's *Life of Macrina*, dating from the fourth century, there is a charming story about parents who brought their young daughter with eye disease to Macrina, who healed it through prayer. Kissing the child and putting her lips to her eyes, Macrina apparently noted her affliction. She offered the family hospitality and promised a special drug, which they later realized was a metaphorical reference to the healing power of prayer. The girl's soldier father recounted the tale to Gregory upon Gregory's return home after Macrina's funeral, but the father's storytelling was frequently interrupted by the sobs and tears of a parent overcome with gratitude.[33]

The stories and legends of the early Christians found both in the canonical Gospels and in the rich body of apocryphal, martyrological, and hagiographic accounts spoke to communities of people commonly experiencing the death of their children. No doubt these stories had to be explained by means of various theological and pastoral expositions. Plutarch offered his own mixture of religious and philosophical advice that would not be that different from sentiments repeated in house churches upon the death of a child of an early church community: she now knows no pain; she cannot be said to be deprived of things she did not know or of which her mind could not conceive; her immortal soul, which has only been here a short time, leaps up naturally toward its natural home (*A Consolation to His Wife* 9–10). In early Christian literature the apologetic writing of Aristides gives a rather chilling explanation of the Christian attitude to the death of children: the birth of a child is a reason for Christians to give thanks to God, but the death of a child offers a reason for even more gratitude, for the child has passed through the world without sins (*Apology* 15).

Education

A frequent theme of ancient literature concerning caring for children is the question of how they should be educated. In the early Christian material, however, the theme includes an interesting twist, for not only are children to be educated, they are also in an important sense educators of the community.

Of all the early Christian material on children, the two Gospel passages in which Jesus points to them as an example of discipleship (Matt. 2:4-5; Mark 9:36-37; Luke 9:47-48) and blesses them (Matt. 19:13; Mark 10:13-16; Luke 18:15-17) are unquestionably the most well-known.[34] What Jesus himself might have meant by his actions with respect to children and how his actions may have been related to his teachings on the kingdom of God are not, however, of central concern in this book.[35] Rather, we are primarily interested in how such teaching may have been heard in the household setting of early church life. The notion that an adult could learn something substantial from a child would have been highly unusual in the Greco-Roman world.[36] Among Jews, children could serve as an example of piety (Ps. 8:2; Matt. 21:16),[37] but this idea is taken to extreme in these Gospel passages, in which children seem to emulate qualities or have knowledge that adults in traditional positions of authority are lacking. In the Gospel of Mark, for example, the use of children as a symbol of the true meaning of discipleship takes place in the context of Mark 9:33-37, in which the disciples argue among themselves about who should be greatest. The true disciple is the one who is last and who engages in service. As an example of the least, the child embodies what it means to be a disciple, but as the one who is welcomed by the disciple, the child becomes a representative of Jesus himself.[38] In this montage of associations, cultural expectations concerning honor and prestige are reversed. Similar ideas occur in Mark 10:13-16 (according to v. 14 the disciples actually rebuke Jesus for his actions), but this time the focus is more directly on children as a central feature of Jesus' ministry. Children are brought to Jesus in order that he may touch (*haptein*) and bless them.

It is probably not coincidental that this episode comes shortly after the three episodes of the healing of children in Mark (Mark 5:21-24, 35-42; 7:25-34; 9:14-29),[39] with reference to "touching" frequently associated with healing and the transfer of divine power (for example, Mark 1:41; 3:10; 5:23, 27-30; 6:56; 8:22).

For the purposes of this study, it is especially important to note that Jesus' teaching on true greatness (using children as an example) takes place in the context of a house setting (Mark 9:33). On the basis of this observation, James Francis has made an intriguing suggestion: "Thus the particular exemplary significance of a child might have had continuing relevance in the (house) church's influence upon the household in interpreting the meaning of subordination."[40] Francis makes another suggestion that is more speculative but nevertheless worthy of consideration. Noting that instructions to subordinates typically precede instructions to superiors in the New Testament household codes, he wonders whether "we might just detect the influence of a wider perspective based upon that logion of Jesus which echoes the metaphorical significance of childhood, 'let the greatest among you become as the youngest' (Luke 22:26)."[41]

The hierarchy inherent in the household codes coupled with practical realities of managing children caution against any romantic notions of the emancipation or leadership of children in house-church communities. The Gospel traditions on children, however, do open up possibilities for the questioning of norms to a certain extent and for valuing otherwise neglected or abandoned children. Celsus accused Christians of leading children to question authority figures like fathers and teachers; a lack of deference to the received tradition emanating from one's elders is implied here, and it is not difficult to find Gospel texts to support it: "At that time Jesus said, 'I thank you, Father, Lord of heaven and earth, because you have hidden these things from the wise and the intelligent and have revealed them to infants [*nēpiois*]'" (Matt. 11:25 NRSV).[42] At the most practical level, the Jesus traditions on children would have provided much justification for house-church communities to teach and evangelize children (both slave and free) that belonged to non-Christian homes (or, more likely, homes in which only the mother was a believer). We cannot be certain that this teaching provided such justification, but as will be discussed in more detail in chapter 10, the spreading of the Gospel by the women of the family to children was, in all likelihood, an important aspect of the early Christian missionary enterprise (see 2 Tim. 1:5).

In keeping with Jewish emphasis on the instruction of children (see Josephus, *Against Apion* 2.173-74, 78, 204; Philo, *Hypothetica* 7.14), many early Christian texts present the education of children in the Gospel as community priority.[43] The teaching on the relationship between parents and children in Eph. 6:1-4 calls on fathers to raise their children "in the discipline and instruction of the Lord." John M. G. Barclay suggests that this refers to an early form of a "specifically Christian way of raising children, and perhaps a specifically Christian body of instruction to be imparted to them."[44] As we move into the period of the Apostolic Fathers, interest in the Christian socialization of children increases (*1 Clem.* 21.6, 8; *Did.* 4.9; Polycarp, *Phil.* 4.2), with such socialization being explicitly presented as the duty of wives in Polycarp's *Letter to the Philippians* (Polycarp, *Phil.* 4.2). From approximately the same period we have the instructions found in 2 Timothy that remind the recipients to continue in what has already been learned: "and how from childhood [*brephous*, literally "infancy"] you have known the sacred writings that are able to instruct you for salvation through faith in Christ Jesus" (2 Tim. 3:15 NRSV).

The association of education with motherhood and with the early stages of childrearing that we find in these texts is in keeping with the detailed attention to education (including the education of the very young) in various Greco-Roman texts. The emphasis placed in the Roman world on the formal rhetorical education of well-to-do boys in their early to mid-teens, who were supposed to be active in public life, is well-known. But in exploring the world of children in a book on women and house churches, it is more important to consider the earlier stages of education at home and school and to consider how education affected the lives of younger children, lower-class children, slaves, and especially girls. Understanding the house church as the educator of children flows naturally from the home as the first locus for the education of children and, in the opinion of some, the best place to educate children.

In the first century CE, Quintillian (*The Orator's Education* 1.1.6–7) presents various examples of parents—both mothers and fathers—being instrumental in the education of their children, and these involve more than the predictable relationship between parents (especially fathers) and sons. Examples of notable individuals who enjoyed superior familial influences include the Gracchi, who benefited from the "highly cultivated style" of their mother, Cornelia (second century BCE); Laelia, whose conversation echoed her famous father's "elegance" in speech (second century BCE);

Hortensia, the daughter of Quintus Hortensius, whose speech delivered before the triumvirs (first century BCE) was still being read in Quintillian's own day.[45] As discussed in the last chapter, nurses too were viewed as having a great impact on the rearing of the child and had to be carefully chosen based on their character, but also to a certain degree on their education. For Quintillian the nurse's standard of speech was especially important, and he applies the same criteria to the slaves who are selected to be brought up with a child (*The Orator's Education* 1.1.4–5, 8). Much of what Quintillian has to say about the education of young children reflects questions that remain the subjects of debate today, such as how early a child should be taught to read (*The Orator's Education* 1.1.15–19). His writings strike one as revealing an almost modern sensibility for child development, with advice to use games in the learning process and to take care not to "turn off" a child who is given difficult work prematurely (*The Orator's Education* 1.1.20; see 1.3.11–12 for a reference to competitions involving all sorts of the "little questions"—perhaps ancient Trivial Pursuit?).

Quintillian also includes a lengthy treatment of the question concerning whether a child should be educated at home or sent out to school. Responding especially to the perception that morals are corrupted in schools and the fact that a schoolteacher cannot offer the individual attention of a private tutor, Quintillian nevertheless comes down on the side of sending a child out to school, while making a case for the importance of what we would term today the "socialization of the child" (*The Orator's Education* 1.2). Education in the home, however, was probably especially beneficial to slaves and girls, who might otherwise not have access to higher levels of education. Beryl Rawson has noted the importance of the visiting intellectual, whose status might actually be that of slave, freed, or freeborn (bringing to mind the visiting apostle or prophet in early Christian circles), in the homes of leading citizens. Even slave entertainers and servers might profit from elevated dinner conversation, and some slave children who experienced life in the intellectual homes as visitors or residents (where they sometimes received literary training—see Nepos, *Atticus* 13)—went on to establish their own literary careers as librarians, tutors, and skilled readers.[46]

Similarly, women who were singled out for their intellectual achievement (though excluded from the higher forms of rhetorical education associated with public life) would probably have received much of their education at home. Rawson offers the following example:

> It is worth noting that Cornelia, daughter of Metellus Scipio, who married Publius Crassus in 55 and Pompey in 52, was said to be a young woman of well-developed intellectual interests. . . . Plutarch (*Pompey* 55) describes her as 'well versed in literature and in playing the lyre and in geometry, and she had been accustomed to listen to philosophical discourses with profit.' She was probably still in her teens, perhaps even early teens, when she first married. This suggests that she had already acquired a good education in her father's home. And that she continued to participate in the intellectual and cultural activities in the houses of her husbands.[47]

Girls would often have had tutors educating them at home. Citing various texts from such authors as Pliny, Martial, Statius, Juvenal (though he is critical), and especially Musonius Rufus (see *Discourses* 3.12–15, in which women are represented as participating actively in philosophical circles), Rawson suggests that the example of educated adult women should be employed to "extrapolate backwards" to support evidence for education of girl children. She argues that such a composite picture greatly strengthens the hypothesis for a climate in which intellectual expectations for girls were not unusual.[48] If Rawson is correct, the rarity of the commemoration of the intellectual qualities of girls (like the epitaph from Rome of the seven-year-old Magnilla, who was "learned beyond her years") among extant monuments should be understood in light of a tendency to articulate female ideals along more limited and traditional lines, rather than as an indication of the lived lives of women and girls.[49]

If a child was sent out to school, he or she would be under the care of a *paidagōgos*, who was usually a slave and apparently usually male, even in the case of a female charge (but see below). The main role of the *paidagōgos* was to accompany a child to school (and protect the child from dangers, including sexual molestation of attractive boys), and he was not technically a teacher.[50] Nevertheless, the *paidagōgos* played an important role in the education process, overseeing a child's lessons and sometimes disciplining the child. Paul reveals an awareness of the responsibility and protection associated with the role of *paidagōgos* when he speaks metaphorically of the law acting as a "tutor" until the dawn of faith in Christ (Gal. 3:24-25). As in the case of parents and nurses, Quintillian believed that the selection of a *paidagōgos* needed to be undertaken with great care, with emphasis being placed on the good education of the candidate (*The Orator's Educa-*

tion 1.8–11). Although some ancient texts register distaste about the matter, there is evidence that slave children sometimes attended schools and
that their education could extend beyond "trades" to the liberal education
usually received by the freeborn.[51]

Some girls went out to school (though more rarely in the case of secondary or "grammatical" education).[52] In recounting the ordeal of the
girl Verginia from the fifth century BCE, who attracted the lustful attention of Appius Claudius, both Livy (3.44) and Dionysius Halicarnassus
(2.28.3) present the attendance of a girl at school as unproblematic (compare Valerius Maximus, *Memorable Deeds and Sayings* 6.1.2). According
to Livy, Appius commissioned his client to claim Verginia as his slave on
her way to school in the Forum. Verginia is presented as being under the
care of female attendants on the way to school; these attendants may have
been female *paidagōgai*, for which we have some limited evidence in the
Roman world.[53] The risks of entrusting a daughter's safety to a *paidagōgos*
is revealed in a tale recounted by Valerius Maximus: the slave-*paidagōgos* of
the daughter of Pontius Aufidianus apparently sold her virginity, with the
end result that the father had both the *paidagōgos* and his daughter put to
death (Valerius Maximus, *Memorable Deeds and Sayings* 6.1.3). In contrast,
the relationship between the (recently deceased) daughter of a friend, a
young girl of thirteen, and the various people responsible for her education
is presented by Pliny the Younger in the most glowing terms: "How warm
her regard for the nurses, conductors to school [*paidagōgoi*], and teachers,
who, in their respective offices, had the care and education of her!" (*Letters*
5.16).[54]

Early Christianity coexisted with and made use of the pagan educational system, and it would be several centuries before Christians would
institute separate schools designed to educate their children.[55] Yet the
world of schools figures in early Christian texts such as a rather comi-
cal account of school-day events found in the *Infancy Gospel of Thomas*
discussed above. This account culminates in a slightly different version
of the familiar story from the Gospel of Luke (19; see also Luke 2:21-
52) in which the twelve-year-old Jesus is located by his worried parents
in the Temple, astounding the teachers with his answers. In the *Infancy
Gospel* this account is preceded by Jesus' encounter with three schoolteachers. After a first teacher fails to teach Jesus (6–7), who himself plays the
role of "teacher," Jesus is again sent to school by Joseph, who is determined
to offer the child proper education. But a rather impetuous remark on the

part of Jesus prompts the second teacher to retaliate by striking him on the head. Jesus in turn curses the teacher, who promptly faints (14). To the great relief of Joseph, a third teacher has greater success and eventually recognizes that Jesus has no need of this kind of schooling and recommends that Joseph take him home (15). As result of this teacher's insight, Jesus agrees to heal the second teacher. The child Jesus never again returns to the world of schools, finding the Jewish Temple a much more appropriate place to impart his wisdom (19).[56]

Ancient readers would recognize the image of the nasty teacher in *The Infancy Gospel of Thomas*, as it was a rather common stereotype, which included a focus on the excessive use of corporal punishment.[57] In fact, a rather curious recommendation in Hippolytus's *Apostolic Tradition* is part of a list of jobs that should be rejected or avoided if possible by catechumens; falling under the latter category is the rather surprising reference to "the teacher of young children." This should probably be taken not as disdain for the role of teacher per se but as a reaction to the idolatrous content of the myths, stories, and pieces of poetry that were part of the "curriculum" expectations for even very young children.[58] While there were a few extreme minority views (see *Didascalia Apostolorum* 12), as Mary Ann Beavis puts it, in general "Christian children at the earliest stages of their education were taught to avoid the 'thorns' of the pagan curriculum while continuing to study it."[59]

The image of the mischievous Jesus in the *Infancy Gospel of Thomas* certainly represents an extreme in early Christian literature, seemingly shaped by both views concerning Jesus' supernatural powers and common perceptions concerning the behavior of children. The negative behavior of children is referred to elsewhere in early Christian texts, however, such as in the *Shepherd of Hermas*, in which the children of Hermas are said to have "renounced God, blasphemed against the Lord, and betrayed their parents by their great wickedness" (Herm. *Vis.* 2.2.2). In chapter 2 we discussed the presentation of the family of Hermas in this work, noting that it is sometimes impossible to distinguish between treatment of the individual family unit and symbolic references to the broader community. The literary structure of Herm. *Vis.* 2.2.2–3, however, counts against the children acting as a mere cipher for the community. It seems likely that the sins of the children were related to the circumstances of some type of persecution (see Herm. *Vis.* 2.3.4), with their material interests perhaps compounding their lack of faith (see Herm. *Vis.*1.3.1–2).[60]

In the early second century, tensions between church groups and society were clearly on the rise, and it should come as no surprise that children (especially adolescents) could be apostates and, as is suggested by the strong language of betrayal used in the *Shepherd of Hermas*, even informants. This negative involvement of children may also be reflected in the reference to boys' and girls' bringing the wood and straw to burn Thecla, evidently anxiously awaiting her execution after the governor's death sentence (*Acts of [Paul and] Thecla* 22). The possibility of children participating in the resistance to early Christianity was the flip side of the possibility of their participation in its growth (to be discussed further in chapter 10).

A more explicit articulation of the complexities of dealing with children is, in fact, found in later patristic literature. As authors increasingly came to treat the main moral and philosophical questions of their day alongside various theological and church issues, it is not surprising that the texts dealing with children have as much to do with the common views on childrearing as they do with any specifically religious education. Writing at the beginning of the third century, Clement of Alexandria (*The Educator* 2) demonstrates concern for every aspect of the Christian's life, including the issue of youths and drinking, which, according to Clement, is especially dangerous because it encourages recklessness in youths already aflame with sexual desire: adding wine to the mix is like "pouring fire upon fire." It is in the writings of John Chrysostom, however, dating from about a century later that we find the kind of detailed treatment of the rearing and education of children that we see in Quintillian's writings. In his *Address on Vainglory and the Right Way for Parents to Bring Up Their Children*, Chrysostom stresses, as many had before him, the example of good speech for the formation of the child, singling out not only the example of the mother, but also that of nurses, tutors, and slaves (31–37). Chrysostom pays detailed attention to how stories should be told to children, focusing especially on the mother's role, but here we see evidence of a program of Christian education with definite ideas on when certain biblical concepts and themes should be introduced: New Testament deeds of grace and deeds of hell are to be saved until the child is older (52).[61]

That such educational choices also involved girls is indicated by the manner in which the education of Macrina is presented in the *Life of Macrina*. In keeping with the reservations concerning the usual content of the curriculum for young children that appear to be reflected in Hippolytus's *Apostolic Tradition*, Gregory of Nyssa tells of how Macrina's mother avoided the usual use of poetry—full of inappropriate references to the passions of womanhood—as a means of training in the early years of childhood. Instead, the girl's studies included especially the Wisdom of Solomon and the Psalms. Not surprisingly, discussion of the formation of Macrina also reflects conventional notions about an appropriate time to marry. At age twelve, when her physical beauty attracted a number of suitors, Macrina was betrothed to an eloquent and steady young man as a result of her father's prudence and good judgment.[62] The young man died, however, before the marriage, and Macrina vowed to remain faithful to his memory and to remain single.

At the beginning of the fifth century, Jerome's dependence on Roman authors for setting forth his ideas on education is unmistakable. He gives advice concerning appropriate methods for encouraging a love of learning in the child and speaks to the importance of example by citing such classical examples as the influence of the speech of the mother of the Gracchi on the development of their eloquence (*Letter* 107, *To Laeta* 4). It is particularly relevant for this book that Jerome's educational recommendations are given within the context of his advice on how to raise girls for an ascetic life. Predictably, he warns against immodest dress, excessive jewelry, makeup, and the piercing of ears: all for the sake of reminding the girl "to whom she is promised" (*Letter* 107, *To Laeta* 5). A mature male teacher is acceptable for an aspiring virgin consecrated to Christ, but boys with wanton thoughts are to be kept away (4; see also Letter 128, *To Gaudentius*).

Lifelong Learning for Women

The story of Macrina's education by her mother is just one example of a long-standing tradition in families whereby women were the principal educators of girls and young women. Daughters of elite families who were to receive a classical education usually had male tutors or were sent out to school, as discussed above. But at every social level, the important tasks of character formation and education in household skills and duties and the girl's future role as wife and mother were performed by mothers and other women in the family, perhaps even by older and experienced female slaves in intergenerational circles. In chapter 7 we will see that young married women even among the elites were expected to know how to spin and weave, so as to exemplify domestic virtue and inspire the slaves of the household to be responsible and industrious. In addition, the young wife coming into a new house was expected to have managerial skills whereby she could immediately assume control and administration of all the activities of the household. These things she could not learn from male tutors!

The Pythagorean Letters contain several letters, probably from Pythagorean circles in the Hellenistic period, in which ostensibly female philosophers give advice about marriage and household management to other women. This advice includes such practical issues as tolerance of the sexual double standard by their profligate husbands and the right way to manage household slaves so that they neither grow slack from too loose a hand nor discouraged and despairing from abusive treatment. These are two questions with which new wives must have frequently struggled. It is much disputed whether the letters in this collection were actually written by women. One wonders especially if women would have been so lenient in condoning marital infidelity, though it was certainly not unexpected, in spite of the criticism of it by some philosophers.[63] Whether or not the Pythagorean Letters were actually written by women, they stand as testimony to the tradition whereby more experienced women were expected to give advice and instruction to girls and younger women.

Christian households of necessity continued this practice of passing down received wisdom and traditions from mother to daughter, from one generation to the next. We catch a glimpse of it in Titus 2:3-5, in the context of general instruction for old and young of both sexes. Older women (*presbytides*) are exhorted to be well-behaved and not given to excessive drinking (the only group for whom this is stated), so that they can be *kalodidaskaloi*, good teachers. This title comes rather strangely into the Pastoral Epistles after the prohibition of women teaching in 1 Tim. 2:12. Here, however, it is a matter not of public teaching nor of teaching men, but of instructing younger women in their duties and behavior: to love their husbands and children, to be virtuously self-controlled, to be submissive to their husbands but good managers of their households, so that no scandal ensues from erratic behavior on the part of young women who might otherwise not follow the domestic role set out for them. The use of the recognized word for teacher (*didaskalos*), however, means that the wisdom imparted by women to the next generation of females was considered to be just as significant as the instruction they and men received from male teachers about other subjects.

The male author writing from the male perspective charges older women to be responsible for the outcome of the next generation, to enforce the rules, so that younger women do not become "idle gossipers going around from house to house telling stories" (1 Tim. 5:13). In the context of the Pastoral author's anxiety about departure from traditional roles that might give scandal to outsiders (1 Tim. 5:14; Titus 2:5), the necessity of virtuous behavior for women is prominent. Older women are responsible to see that everything is done in a socially respectable way.

We may see a more formal aspect of this traditional instruction in the figure of Grapte in Herm. *Vis.* 2.4.3. Her role as teacher of widows and orphans in the early second-century Roman church probably gathered those women and children not embedded in households for their share of instruction. Yet Grapte's commission to exhort widows and orphans with the revelation received by Hermas, while he reads it with the presbyters in the assembly, provides a clue to her further role and that of other women like her. Her responsibility is not only to teach women and girls how to be good wives and mothers. She is also a principal instructor for them in ongoing spiritual formation. She is their catechist and theologian. A few chance comments of Tatian in the late second century confirm that religious education was not restricted by gender, age, or social class. He boasts that the poor and even old women and youths (*presbytides* and *meirakia*) receive instruction. Women and boys, girls and old ladies participate, so that women too pursue "philosophy" (that is, Christian learning and life-style), with the result that the community includes wise women (*Oration to the Greeks* 32–33).

An important part of the wisdom passed down from women to girls and other women in the Christian context would have been instruction for and assistance at the baptism of women. By the third century in the East, this role was institutionalized in the office of female deacons, but the institution of this order only formalized what was already taking place, undoubtedly in the West as well as the East. We know from the third-century *Didaskalia* and fourth-century *Apostolic Constitutions* that female deacons received women who were preparing for baptism, instructed them, assisted in the rite of baptism by immersion, and continued their instruction and help after baptism, becoming patrons and protectors of those baptized.[64]

Our examination of the sources with regard to the education of girls and young women should not be limited to literary and scientific learning. The world of domestic and spiritual formation was also an integral part of their education, communicated not by male authority figures but by the women of the previous generation.

Conclusion: Don't Forget the Girls

In making his case for sending children out to school rather than being tutored at home, and responding to those who view schools as possible sources for the corruption of children, Quintillian (*The Orator's Education* 1.2.8) offered an extremely negative assessment of the influence of home life upon children:

> It was we who taught them, they heard it all from us. They see our mistresses, our boy lovers; every dinner party echoes with obscene songs; things are to be seen which it is shameful to name. Hence comes first habit, then nature. The wretched children learn these things before they know that they are wrong. This is what makes them dissolute and spineless: they do not get these vices from the schools, they import them into them.[65]

Although he is clearly stating the worst-case scenario in order to make a point, Quintillian is offering us insight into a key facet of childhood in the Roman world. Children were present everywhere; nothing—not even sexual activity—escaped their gaze.[66] Here it is interesting to consider the second-century anti-Christian polemic of Marcus Cornelius Fronto, who explicitly included children as participants in the immoral banquets of Christians (*Octavius* 8–9). Singling out the attendance of children would highlight the level of corruption, but their presence at such events would come as no surprise to an ancient audience.

The ubiquitous presence of children is of central importance for understanding house-church communities and the reception they received in the society of their day. The attention given to such "liturgical questions" in later patristic documents as the placement of children during church meetings (for example, *Apostolic Constitutions* 2.57–58; compare 3.13 [on rules for their participation in the Lord's supper]) or the appropriateness of the baptism of infants (for example, Gregory Nazianzen, *Oration on Holy Baptism* 28) reflects a commitment to the inclusion and valuing of children in continuity with the period of the house churches. The incorporation of children now required more thought and planning and did not flow as naturally from daily household life, but it remained a priority.

When read in the context of new research on children in the Roman world, the few textual references we have to the life of children in early

Christianity gain a new dimension. With a greater awareness of the activities of children and the efforts typically made on their behalf, we begin to see that the experience of giving birth and the rearing of infants and children must have been a much more common focus of energy and topic of conversation in early Christian households and house churches than our texts would often lead us to believe. Every new birth would bring new challenges and responsibilities to households and house churches. Women—both slave and free—were at the center of all of this, from assisting at births to nursing and caring for infants (and quite possibly rescuing abandoned infants) and overseeing the rearing and education of children. They were mothers, wet nurses, nannies, older women giving advice to younger women caring for children, and widows caring for orphans. In keeping with conventional expectations, women were educators of children in the home. This education would involve teaching children the Gospel, and, in an atmosphere in which private homes were transformed into house churches, this teaching exercise would no doubt involve groups of children. Although it is only hinted at in the texts, the very nature of the domestic setting of early church meetings suggests that the teaching of children should be recognized as a key aspect of women's ministry in this period.

Among children, we should not forget the girls. Girls are underrepresented in Roman evidence and what is said about them is often highly conventional. Likewise, evidence concerning the lives of early Christian girls is scant. Yet new research on children in the Roman world has revealed that girls were more highly valued and often more highly educated than was previously thought. We should remember their presence among the groups of children receiving religious education at home and in house churches, and we must keep in mind that the detailed advice given by Jerome on how to educate girls in preparation for an ascetic life must have been preceded by much informal exchange—and by no means always to encourage asceticism—on how to raise a daughter in the Lord. This instruction was the beginning of what we would term today a process of lifelong learning. As the discussion of relations between older and younger members of the community in the Pastoral Epistles illustrates especially well, the education of females did not end at adolescence. Moreover, early Christian evidence suggests that the wisdom imparted by women to the next generation of females probably combined elements of domestic and spiritual formation.

CHAPTER FIVE

FEMALE SLAVES: TWICE VULNERABLE

◫◫ ◫◫ ◫◫

From a modern perspective, we would say that the categories "women" and "slaves" are partially overlapping. Some women were slaves, but not all were; some slaves were women, but not all slaves were. But in fact in ancient categories it is the expression "women slaves," which seems to us more inclusive, that is a conceptual contradiction. While women and slaves of the ancient Greco-Roman world shared much in common within the male perspective of the patriarchal household, they did not belong to overlapping categories. Both were, according to Aristotle, fit by nature to be ruled, not to rule. Both shared intimately in the life of the household, including its religion, economy, child-production and nurturing, and burial. Wives and slaves entered the household from outside, with the possible exception of the *verna* or house-born slave. With the Roman marriage custom *sine manu* (without transfer of the wife to her husband's *familia*) largely in place by the first century, the wife remained legally an outsider to her husband's family, yet shared in most of its benefits and liabilities. The slave brought into the family ceased to have any other identity outside the family of ownership, yet remained a marginal member. Both wives and slaves in many ways remained in a state of perpetual liminality. Ancient literature regularly ascribes to one the vices of the other.

Yet there is no evidence that any sense of solidarity was formed between free women and female slaves, based on sex or the common features of their situations. In fact, the opposite seems to have been true. Women owned slaves, both female and male, and women slaveholders, as far as we can tell, were no less brutal or authoritarian than men toward their own slaves. The marital triangle of husband sexually involved with a female slave of the household, jealous wife, and female slave caught in the middle and punished by the wife occurs repeatedly in the comic and satirical literature. If females who were slaves had to be fitted into either the category of women or that of slaves, the ancient thinker, both male and female, would have considered them slaves, not women. As females who were slaves, they were doubly fit by nature to be ruled and dominated.

It has become customary and helpful to distinguish between sex and gender, sex being biological differentiation between the male and the female of a species, while gender is the cultural construction of that biological difference. Gender, what it is to be man or woman, masculine or feminine, as distinct from male or female, differs cross-culturally. In most slave systems, while slaves undeniably have a sex, they do not have gender.[1] Thus a male slave is not a man (*anēr*, *vir*) and therefore cannot have masculine traits ascribed to him, nor socially constructed expectations of masculine behavior placed on him, nor can he claim any of the status inherent in the cultural construct of masculinity.[2] Consequently, a female slave is not a woman (*gynē*, *mulier*) and thus cannot have feminine traits ascribed to her, nor the social expectations of a woman in her culture, nor can she claim any status privileges inherent in the cultural construct of womanhood. Therefore, the safeguards built into the culture to protect women are not to be applied in the case of female slaves, adding a degree of alienation.

In Aristotle's *Politics* 1.1, gender, class, and even race are closely intertwined. Aristotle places free women and women who are slaves in entirely different categories. Female slaves are at the bottom of the dominated heap. They are not to be dominated as members of their sex, as females who are by nature to be ruled by males with constitutional or royal rule as the intellect rules the appetites, but as slaves who are to be ruled despotically as the soul rules the body. All human beings who are as different as body from soul, as animal from person, are by nature slaves (1254b11–13). But the female slave is doubly so, with a body that is to be conquered and dominated, both as female in sex and as slave in class.

In an honor/shame society such as that of the ancient Mediterranean, a woman's honor in the public male world consists of the sexual propriety or chastity appropriate to her state, even though many nuances must be made from culture to culture and from dominant male perspectives to insider female perspectives. But slaves by definition are totally lacking in honor, either ascribed or attributed, in their interactions with free persons. If born as slaves, they are born without honor; if enslaved later, they move into a classification in which honor no longer exists. Nothing they do, no matter how honorably they may conduct themselves, can acquire honor. They are simply outside the honor system of the dominant free society.[3] Thus slaves are not expected to behave honorably; hence the familiar topos, or traditional literary theme, of the lazy, dishonest, unreliable slave, and the equally well-known topos of the exception that proves the rule, the slave who unexpectedly exhibits behavior that would be called honorable in a free person—to the amazement of the slaveholding class. Examples of the latter include Seneca's admission that a slave might rather be beaten with whips and killed than be struck by fist on the face and insulted verbally (*On Constancy* 5.1) and Octavia's slave Pythias, who endured under torture and insulted her torturer rather than slander her mistress (Dio Cassius 62.13.4).

To the female slave therefore, honor, whether of character or of behavior, cannot be ascribed.[4] The female slave can lay no claim to chastity or shame, both of which have no meaning. In the official view, she cannot have sensitivity toward chastity. Her honor cannot be violated because it does not exist, though the property rights of her owner over her can be infringed upon in the case of sexual violation, injury, or death by another who does not hold such property rights. No legal recognition is granted to the sexual privacy of the female slave. In recognition of the anomaly of this situation, the Hellenistic novels and Roman comedies are filled with unfortunate heroines unjustly enslaved, caught between slavery and prostitution, struggling to maintain their honor, vindicated in the end by having their citizen status restored.[5] The contrast between the true slave without honor and the freeborn heroine thrown into the same lot was the stuff of romance.

A familiar story told to explain the origins of a festal day illustrates well the female slave's lack of honor and yet, ironically, her ability to act honorably. Plutarch (*Camillus* 33; *Romulus* 29) relates that after the Gauls sacked Rome in 390 BCE, some of Rome's Latin allies took advantage of the city's temporary weakness to demand its freeborn virgins and widows be taken as wives. While the city fathers were in a quandary, a slave woman, alternately called Tutula or Philottis, suggested dressing female slaves as freeborn women and sending them out to the Latins. This was done, and during the night from the Latin camp, she gave the signal to the Romans, a burning torch from the top of a fig tree, when it was the opportune time to attack. As a consequence, relates Plutarch, July 7 is the *ancillae feriae*, the festival of female slaves, at which time they run out of the city in mock battle calling out Roman men's names, to picnic under a fig tree. The legend only works because of the premise that the female slaves dressed differently from freeborn women (not the case later on) but otherwise looked like them. Most important, underlying it is the assumption that female slaves have no sexual honor to be safeguarded as did the freeborn women.

Orlando Patterson's *Slavery and Social Death* proposes the thesis that slavery is symbolic execution, liminal social death, in some cultures indeed ritualized at the moment of official enslavement. It is human parasitism, in which a relation of domination causes one to grow stronger as the other suffers, yet paradoxically creates a relationship of dependence stronger in the dominator than in the dominated.[6] It is social death because by legal and official recognition, the slave has no family history, identification, or country of origin except that assigned by his or her owner.[7] Slaves' names could be changed at the will of the owner. Even names that would suggest geographical origin might not be meaningful but might have depended on an owner's preference or whim: a German slave with a Greek name, a Phrygian with a Canaanite name, and so on might denote place of *purchase* rather than of origin.[8] Even in situations, which must have been common in the Roman Empire, in which a slave knew well who his or her parents were, familial units could be broken and separated at any time, and blood relatives could be so distanced from each other that they would be unable to maintain contact. In a state of natal alienation, the slave had no past and no future, no ancestry and no possibility of creating a family lineage or bequeathing property to offspring. The slave could not contract a legal marriage, even though slave marriages existed de facto.[9] Slaves' children were not theirs, but their owners'. The slave's total identity was created by the owner and granted for the enhancement of the owner.

Like most studies of slavery and slave systems, Patterson's gives very little consideration to enslaved women except when examining aspects of family and reproduction. Even here, an additional factor must be taken into account with regard to female slaves. Besides natal alienation depriving slaves of a past, an additional reproductive alienation resulted from the fact that they usually had little choice in the matter of whether they would bear children, how much involvement they would have in nursing and raising them, or whether they would ever see their children again. In the slave sale records from Egypt, women in childbearing years commanded high prices and were frequently up for sale, whereas the sale records of women past childbearing years declined noticeably; in the surviving records, there are no sales of women after the age of thirty-five, which may have provided some stability to their lives at that point. Some mothers were sold with small children, but no fathers with them nor couples together. The same records contain numerous instances of children—girls and boys—sold alone, sometimes several times before the age of puberty. Prices of girls seem to have surpassed those of boys in the surviving records of the first two centuries BCE because of their reproductive potential.[10] There was a running legal discussion among the jurists about whether a purchaser could get a reimbursement for a female slave of childbearing age who failed to reproduce.

The Lives of Female Slaves

Attempted discussions of "slave breeding" in the literature on Roman slavery go nowhere. The expression conjures up whole populations of (female) slaves acquired and kept solely or primarily for the purpose of procreation. Nowhere is there any evidence of what would surely have been a very expensive, time-intensive, and not very lucrative practice. Rather, it seems that most slave populations in which males and females lived and worked together were encouraged to reproduce, and the raising of slave children, who in nearly all circumstances followed the servile status of their mother, was often left to others than their own parents. The *lex Papia Poppaea* of 9 CE gave freedom from *tutela* to freeborn women who produced three children and freedwomen who had four. Columella follows suit with his agricultural slaves, giving exemption from work to the slave mother of three and freedom to the one who produced more (*On Agriculture* 1.8.19). Besides giving us the information that large families in any status must have been very unusual and general fertility, or at least survival rate, low, this evidence also tells us that large slave families were a rarity and extra incentive was needed for slaves to reproduce well. Columella would scarcely have offered rewards for what was an average number of children produced by a single female slave, nor was Augustus looking for excuses to waive *tutela*.

Wet nurses and child minders were often hired to nurse and raise children. Whether nurse or nursling was slave or free seems to have made little difference, except that the free nurse could contract for herself. Wet-nursing contracts extended from six months to three years, during which time the wet nurse was under contract not to become pregnant or have sexual intercourse. Though some seemed to think that nursing is a natural contraceptive, apparently most realized that it is not always effective. The further prohibition of sexual intercourse was intended to prevent alienation of affection from the child being nursed. If the wet nurse was a slave, she had no choice in the matter but was subject to the contract arranged by her owner, thereby disrupting any normal familial relations she had.

Apparently it was regular procedure to have slave children nursed by a woman other than their mother, in order to free the mother for work and perhaps for further reproduction. Plautus's reference (*Miles Gloriosus* 697) to "the nurse who suckles the *vernas*" implies a recognized figure for the nursing of slave children in some households.[11] But freeborn children were also often nursed by a slave or freedwoman, known as *mamma* or foster mother;[12] the first meaning of the word *mamma* is "breast." Among the letters of the Pythagorean women philosophers, that of Myia to Phyllis with congratulations and advice to the new mother gives as first point of advice not that she should nurse her own baby, as Plutarch advises (*De liberis educandis* 5), but the necessity of finding a good nurse, one not given to drink or too much sleep, who should not be allowed intimacies with her husband, preferably a Greek rather than a foreigner.[13] Young female slaves were prized for their reproductive potential, yet had little or no control over their reproductive and child-nurturing activity. Evidence for wet-nursing contracts yields twice as many for female foundlings than male, so it must have been considered worthwhile to invest in raising female slaves, even though they were not seen to be as labor-productive as males.

Female slaves as a group have been very little studied. All surviving evidence indicates a larger male slave population in Roman society than female,[14] for a number of reasons. Where child abandonment or other forms of infanticide are practiced in a society that favors males, more female children will be abandoned and die.[15] A heavily agricultural slave society will

depend more on males than females for labor, as also is the case for building, mining, shipping, and other forms of heavy labor. Even in household
staffs, some studies indicate a larger male than female contingent, including the households of aristocratic women. Of Livia's household, 77 percent
were male, as were 66 percent of the slaves and freedpersons of two other
aristocratic households, along with 80 percent of the tomb inscriptions of
deceased slave children of these households, and fifty-nine of sixty-one
slaves in the urban *familia* of an early second-century Roman aristocrat in
Alexandria.[16]

Such a large preponderance of males in the slave population raises serious questions about how this population was maintained. Either the surviving evidence for gender selection of slaves is skewed and there really
were many more female slaves than we think, reproducing at a steady rate
and not largely manumitted during childbearing years, or the slave population was woefully unable to reproduce itself and was dependent on large
numbers entering its ranks through the known nonreproductive means:
child abandonment, self-sale, prisoners of war, and importation from outside the empire.[17]

In every slave society, a larger number of female slaves are manumitted because of sexual relations with masters or other free males and for
marriage, thus reducing further the available female slave population of
childbearing age.[18] Many more female slaves were manumitted to marry
their male owners than vice versa, though Dale Martin presents evidence
of other apparent motivations for freeing female slaves, and the considerations cited above about the ability of the slave population to reproduce
itself must be kept in mind.[19] Marriages between freedmen and freeborn
women were severely discouraged, and even penalized by the *Senatus con-
sultum Claudianum*. Marriages between a male slave and his former female
owner were also strongly discouraged, even when the woman was a freedwoman, yet they continued to occur regularly, as demonstrated both by
continuing legislation and by funerary dedication to *patrona et coniux*.[20] Yet
those to *patronus et coniux*, from freed female slaves to their former owner
husbands, are far more abundant. The early *lex Aelia Sentia* of 4 CE provided that a female slave could be manumitted earlier than the minimum
age of thirty for the purpose of marriage. The overall status of women
with regard to men is a factor here, combined with the dominative nature
of the slave system: for women to "marry up" was considered favorably; to
"marry down" was not, even for freedwomen. That is to say, there was less

Fig. 5.1: Funeral monument of the freedwoman Paccia Helpis, commemorated by both her patron and former master, Gaius Paccius, and her husband, M. Valerius Corvinus. National Museum, Ravenna. Photo by C. Osiek.

compromise of honor involved for men to "marry down" than up. One of the accusations of the Christian theologian Hippolytus against his rival Callistus (a former slave) involved exactly that: Callistus sanctioned marriages of higher-status Christian women with lower-status males, presumably because of a dearth of high-status Christian men (*Refutatio* 9.12). The fact that Hippolytus was Callistus's rival for leadership in the Roman community makes his story suspicious as to all details, but this situation fits known facts.

Female slaves were not spared the harsh treatment often encountered by their male counterparts. Slave whipping, beating, and torture were not confined to males, and references to such treatment, unless specifically applied to males, must be understood to apply to both sexes. Like a travesty of today's service industry, Roman society had professional torturers (*tortores*) who could be hired to discipline slaves deemed to be in need of punishment (see Matt. 18:34) or to extract information in a nonjudicial setting. A chilling testimony is preserved in an inscription from Puteoli that specifies what materials the contractors are to provide for the private punishment of a slave, male or female, by *crux* (crucifixion) or *furca* (impalement on a fork-shaped stake), and how and when the bodies are to be removed.[21] Juvenal refers in passing to sending the female attendants (*ancillae*) of a household to the *tortor* to get information about whether the actor-owner of the house who dresses like a woman is really a woman-chasing male (*Satire* 6.029). Similarly, Pliny the Younger had two slave women (*ancillae*), who held the title of *ministrae* in their church, tortured to investigate Christian practices, though this was official judicial interrogation (*Ep.* 10.96.8). Ulpian specifies, in his legislation about the accountability of slaves under the same roof when their owner is murdered, that the female slave asleep in her mistress's chamber who does not at least cry out when her mistress is attacked is to be put to death (*Digest* 29.5.27). Nor were female slaves less to be feared in the case of rebellion. Diodorus Siculus, for instance, relates that in the Sicilian slave uprising of circa 135 BCE, one couple, Megallis and Damophilus of Enna, were known to have been especially abusive to their slaves, in contrast to their daughter, who tried constantly to undo the damage by kindness. When the slaves revolted, the daughter was given safe passage, while Megallis was handed over to her female slaves, who tortured her and threw her off a cliff (34.10, 13, 39).

Sexual Availability

Inherent in the abusiveness of the slave dominance relationship was the well-known vulnerability of the slave to sexual abuse. Aristotle's definition of a slave is a human being who belongs by nature completely to another, a human being who is also an article of property (*Politics* 1.1254a7). Another way of defining the slave is one who is answerable with his or her body, as to physical punishment, degrading forms of execution, and testimony under torture. Yet another manifestation of this bodily subjection was complete sexual availability to his or her owner and anyone to whom the owner granted rights. All these forms of defenselessness resulted from the lack of honor or *dignitas* of the slave.[22] Seneca remarked of the "passive" or dominated sexual partner: "Unchastity is a crime in the freeborn, a necessity for the slave, a duty for the freedman" (*Impudicitia in ingenuo crimen est, in servo necessitas, in libero officium; Controversies* 4. Praef. 10). This sexual vulnerability was no less for male than for female slaves, but it must have been particularly acute for females, and more complicated because of the possibility of pregnancy. The slave's lack of moral responsibility for sex initiated by a free person was implicit in Roman law, as was that of the initiator.[23] Under the *lex Aquilia, iniuria* (liable damage to property) could be claimed by a slave's owner against someone else who had, against the owner's will, committed "corruption" of a slave, but this is a form of violation of property rights.[24] The crime of *stuprum* seems to have been understood as sexual intercourse in which one person was used to gratify another. *Stuprum* could be committed with a virgin, a widow, or a divorcee (*Digest* 48.5.6.1).[25] It could not be committed with a slave, presumably because the sole purpose of a slave was to be used.[26]

Examples of how this sexual availability was taken for granted abound in the literature. To cite only a few, Horace warns a recipient of his letter not to become enamored of someone else's girl or boy slave, lest the owner not give him the slave (*Ep.* 1.18.72).[27] He also remarks, in a passage lamenting the difficulties of adultery with a matron, that he prefers the more readily available services of an *ancilla* or *verna puer* (boy slave) (*Satires* 2.115–19). Of course, free women could also initiate sexual abuse of slaves. Trimalchio feels no shame in having sexually serviced both his master and mistress for fourteen years, "for it is no shame to do what is commanded" (*Satyricon* 75). It is said of the virtuous Christian woman in Justin's story who divorces her unbelieving husband because of his debauchery that she does not consort with household slaves (*Apology* 2). Clement of Alexandria remarks that modest Christian women who will hardly speak to men who are not their relatives will strip at the baths in front of their slaves (*Educator* 3.6).

The sexual availability of slaves seems to have been completely taken for granted. There is an astonishing lack of specification about slaves even in the literature of marital advice. More ancient authors than might be supposed advocate the marital fidelity of husbands, including Pseudo-Aristotle (*Oeconomicus* 3) and Pythagoras (Iamblichus, *Life of Pythagoras* 47–48), but it is doubtful whether sex with one's own slaves is included. Plutarch, on the other hand, considers it normal for husbands to take their debauchery elsewhere, to go wide of the mark (*exhamartanein*) with a *hetaira* or slave. The wife should be grateful that he does so, reserving a more respectful approach for her (*Advice to the Bride and Groom* 140B). If Plutarch is consistent, then his advice about educating freeborn males not to be overbearing with slaves (*doulou mē perhybrizein*) does not prohibit rape of slaves, even though the word group *hybrizein* with its various prefixes can carry this meaning.[28]

Seemingly the sole dissenting voice, not surprisingly, is Musonius Rufus, who explicitly argues with the husband that if it is not shameful for a master to have sex with his own slave, especially if she is "unmarried" (an interesting reference to slave marriages), nevertheless let him think how he would feel if his wife had sex with a male slave. His seemingly egalitarian ideals, however, have little to do with equality. His motivational appeal to men is not justice to wives or slaves, but justice to men's own power. If they cannot control themselves, they are showing themselves to be weaker than women, thereby reversing the proper order of stronger over weaker as ruler to those ruled. He concludes that it is obvious that for men to take sexual advantage of their female slaves is nothing less than loss of control (*akrasia*, frag. 12). Apparently it was not obvious to everyone.

The effects would be quite different in the two cases of a male or a female slave owner using his or her own slave for sex. The wife's action would be adultery, and the male slave could also be accused of adultery, for male slaves were legally capable of committing adultery with a free married woman. The husband's action would be legally neutral and, for the majority of men, morally neutral. Musonius's example is meant to be strictly moral, not legal. His appeal can only be moral, since the legal implications in each case are considerably different: for the husband legal and (for most free males) moral indifference; for the wife strong social disapproval and a legal charge of adultery, which under Augustan law would require her husband to divorce her if he is aware of it.

Jewish and Christian Slave-Owning

It is sometimes thought that Jews and Christians had different and more humane standards for the treatment of their slaves.[29] Granted, special regulations governed the treatment of Hebrew slaves, and the Torah contains many specifications about the treatment of slaves that severely restrict the power of owners over them. For example, neither male nor female slaves are to be made to work on the Sabbath (Exod. 20:10; 23:12; Deut. 5:14). Domestic slaves are to be integrated as far as possible into family rituals (Exod. 12:44; Deut. 12:12, 18). A Hebrew debt-slave must be set free in the seventh year and sent away with gifts, unless he chooses to remain permanently (Deut. 15:12-17). Though v. 17 suggests the same for a female slave, freeing in the seventh year was not generally interpreted in that

way for women (for example, Exod. 21:7; *b. Qiddusin* 18a). A Hebrew girl
sold into slavery by her father must be married at marriageable age to her
master or his son, or released (Exod. 21:7-11). There is little information
about how these legal stipulations were followed in the Roman period and
later. Most of them did not apply to non-Hebrew slaves, though a female
prisoner of war might be taken as a wife and freed if her captor no longer
wanted her, but not sold (Deut. 21:10-14). Philo justifies Hebrew ownership of non-Hebrew slaves, saying that the law permits it because of the
many situations requiring slaves (*Spec. leg.* 2.123). Male and female slaves
are free from work on the Sabbath, he reports, in anticipation of the full
freedom they may attain if they serve well, because (in disagreement with
Aristotle) no one is a slave by nature, but all are free (*Spec. leg.* 2.67–69).
Slaves have less good fortune but are on the same level with masters, who
should not abuse their authority. Owners should not be excessively cruel to
their slaves, which would reveal their own cruel nature. If a slave dies from
mistreatment, the owner is liable in court, yet if a whipped slave lives two
to three days, the owner is not guilty of murder (*Spec. leg.* 3.137–43; see
Exod. 21:20-21). With incomprehensible logic, Philo concludes that one
who kills his own slave actually injures oneself more by being deprived of
the slave's service and property value (*Spec. leg.* 3.143)!

Ben Sirach says that a slave is to be worked hard, comparably to a
donkey; an idle slave will look for freedom. The disobedient slave should
be tortured, the lazy slave loaded with chains. An owner should not be
ashamed to draw blood on the back (*pleura*, normally side or ribs) of a
wicked *oiketēs*. Yet a single slave, the only one owned by a given person,
should be treated as another self of the owner and not mistreated, lest he or
she run away. And in the midst of these admonitions, quite incongruously,
is one against being overbearing or unjust to anyone, probably an indication of the miscellaneous nature of the collected sayings (Sir. 33:25-30;
42:5).

Most interesting is a text that seems to have been altered from Hebrew
to the Septuagint in the direction of justifying sex with one's own slave.
Exod. 20:17 already prohibited coveting the male or female slave of another.
The passage in Sir. 41:22-23 NRSV (24 LXX; 27 Vg) reads: "Be ashamed of
. . . gazing at another man's wife; of meddling with his servant girl [*apo
periergias paidiskēs autou* LXX]—and do not approach her bed," so that the
meaning prohibits sex with another man's female slave as well as with his
wife. Lucian and Origen read *autēs* for *autou*, so that the prohibition is of

sex with the female slave of another man's wife. But the Hebrew had read *leka* (your), so that the text stated, "of meddling with *your* slave girl."[30] The Hebrew text therefore prohibited a male owner having sex with his own female slave, but the LXX and Lucian altered the reading to avoid that situation and prohibit instead sex with the female slave of another man, something that already carried a penalty in Roman and other legal systems. The Lucianic/Origen reading made the prohibition even more specific, avoiding sex with the female slave of another man's wife, but further removed from the situation of sex with one's own slave.

There are frequent overtones in rabbinic literature of the problems of rabbis with their female slaves. Hillel was known to remark, "The more maidservants, the more lewdness" (*m. Abot* 2.7). Talmudic legislation protects the rights of owners and the honor of wives, but not of female slaves, in spite of the many stories of the chastity and loyalty of the female slave of Rabbi Judah the Patriarch. It was difficult for a freedwoman to marry anyone other than her former owner because of the assumption of her promiscuity (*t. Horayot* 2.11–12; *m. Yebamot* 61). Leviticus 19:20 forbids sexual relations with a female slave, but it is a case of someone else's slave; Lev. 18:8, 15 intends to prohibit a father from having sex with his son's wife or vice versa (compare 1 Cor. 5:1). In this context, see Amos 2:7, in which, in a list of wrongs committed by Israel, father and son have sex with the same female slave (*na' arah* MT; *paidiskē* LXX). But *Sifra Qedoshim* (9.13,92a col. 2 ed. Weiss on Lev. 20:12) excludes female slaves from the prohibition against father and son having sex with the same woman by explicitly referring only to the legitimate wife; thus concubines and female slaves are not included in the prohibition. Another story relates that a prince was thrown out of court for having sex with a slave girl, probably not because of moral impropriety but because he usurped his father's privilege.[31]

Several female slaves appear in early Christian texts, two not among believers: the slave girl in the high priest's household (Matt. 26:69, 71; Mark 14:66, 69; Luke 22:56;[32] John 18:16-17) and the female slave with the spirit of divination at Philippi (Acts 16:16-19), the latter left in a vulnerable position with loss of her ability to earn money for her owners. Among believers, there is Rhoda the doorkeeper in the house of Mary in Jerusalem (Acts 12:12). The self-allusion of Mary mother of Jesus in Luke 1:38, 48 as the *doulē* of God is of course metaphorical, but some of the connotations of female slavery are necessarily attached, especially her lack of honor derived from social status, which only God can bestow on the honorless.

Beyond the New Testament, two *ancillae*, called *ministrae* by their church, are tortured by Pliny the Younger to obtain information about Christian meetings (*Ep.* 10.96): Blandina, the heroic figure of Lyons, and Felicitas of Carthage. Both Blandina and to a lesser extent Felicitas are portrayed as legendary examples of heroism with christological typology. Blandina, whose age is not told, is the rallying point for her fellow martyrs. Her suffering gives them courage to go on, and when she is hanged on a stake and exposed to wild animals, she is explicitly compared to the crucified Christ in the estimation of her companions. She is the last to die and most heroic in her endurance (*Acts of the Martyrs of Lyons and Vienne* [Eusebius, *Hist. eccl.* 5.1.41, 53–55]). Felicitas, of childbearing age, is pregnant at the time of her arrest. Nothing is ever said of the father of her child, any more than the mysterious silence about the husband of Perpetua and father of her newborn. Felicitas gives premature but successful birth in prison after being earnestly prayed over so that her execution would not be delayed beyond that of her companions because of her pregnancy. When she cries out in labor pains, a guard taunts her that she will have to suffer much more in the arena, whereupon she replies that then another will be suffering in her (*Acts of Perpetua and Felicitas* 15). She, like her companions, later goes enthusiastically to death.[33]

Two possible freedwomen are Lydia, the purple merchant of Acts 16, and Rhoda, the former owner of Hermas in Herm. *Vis.* 1.1. Of all of the above, only the story of Felicitas yields any definite sexual information, her pregnancy at the time of her arrest, with no mention of the identity of the father of her child. With Rhoda of the *Shepherd of Hermas*, there is a possible allusion to a sexual encounter with her former slave, Hermas, in the ambiguous opening scene of her bathing in the Tiber under his admiring eye (Herm. *Vis.* 1.1.2).

The *Acts of Andrew* follows the usual pattern of apocryphal acts by featuring a female disciple of the apostle who is won over to chastity, to the dismay of a forlorn fiancé or husband. In this case, the heroine, Maximilla, sends her female slave Eucleia, described as very beautiful but undisciplined, to bed with her husband, Aegeates, who is apparently so drunk every night for eight months that he doesn't notice the difference. To keep her slave's loyalty, Maximilla bribes her with expensive gifts. But Eucleia finally begins boasting anyway to her fellow slaves, who see for themselves what is going on. When the plot is revealed, Aegeates punishes Eucleia (who is not even his own slave) by cutting off her tongue, hands, and feet, leaving her to die of exposure. He crucifies his own three slaves who accepted bribes from Maximilla to keep quiet. The story is typical of the use of slaves, with no Christian difference whatever. Maximilla, in keeping with the theology of the text, is convinced that sexual intercourse even in marriage is sinful, yet does not hesitate to use her slave to fulfill that function to avoid confrontation with her husband. The description of Eucleia as naturally undisciplined repeats slave stereotypes. Aegeates is of course presented as monstrously brutal, but the cruel punishment of the slaves goes without comment, and the story moves on from there.[34]

Porneia and Christian Slavery

How was *porneia* understood in early Christianity? Lexical definitions are very general: fornication, illicit sex. To say that *porneia* means fornication is circular, and the concept of illicit sex only begs the question of what is considered illicit. Long ago Bruce Malina asked whether New Testament *porneia* included all unchastity, or whether the lexica and commentaries were influenced by a culturally conditioned understanding of the New Testament. He noted that in the Hebrew Scriptures *porneia* carries connotations of idolatry or adultery and that the *porneia* forbidden by Torah is not unnatural but unlawful sex. He concluded that, with the exception of the violation of a virgin, which is a different kind of offense, "pre-betrothal, pre-marital, non-commercial sexual intercourse between man and woman" is not a moral crime in Torah.[35] If that were the case in Israelite law, would sex with one's own slave, who is in Roman law legally entirely one's own property and a legal nonperson, be included?

Paul does not address the question we would like answered, whether sex between a slave and his or her owner constitutes *porneia*. Nor do we know whether the same-sex prohibitions of 1 Cor. 6:9 would include it. The case presented in 1 Cor. 5:1, specifically called *porneia*, is usually supposed to be incest and probably is, considering the wording of the sentence, which should best be rendered that the man has taken to himself his father's wife, that is, his stepmother. Presumably the father and the woman are no longer married, or the situation would be called *moicheia* (adultery), not *porneia*. Paul's lack of interest in the woman is taken to mean that she is not a believer. Some, however, have raised the question whether a female slave is the object of the conflict, whether believer or not.[36] This seems unlikely, since the woman somehow belongs to the father (*gynaika tina tou patros*), and a female slave is not likely to have been called simply his *gynē*.

The text of 1 Cor. 6:15-20 is primarily about (Christian) male customers and prostitutes. The sacred temple metaphors recall cultic prostitution, whether or not it was still functioning in Roman Corinth. Here Paul teaches that sexual union with a prostitute (*pornē*, v. 15) violates the identity of the male Christian as a member of the body of Christ and so violates the holiness of the community. *Porneia* is a sin against one's own body, which is a temple of the Holy Spirit, and must therefore be avoided (vv. 18-19). The context refers primarily if not only to prostitution, and that is not our concern here.

In 1 Cor. 7:1-7 Paul begins his comments on sexuality and celibacy by saying—or partially repeating from the Corinthians, "It is well for an *anthrōpos* not to touch a *gynē*, but because of *porneia*, each man should have a wife, and each woman should have a husband." It would be appropriate to conclude from this statement that Paul argues against adultery, and also against prostitution, given the immediately preceding discussion in 1 Corinthians 6. But it is not at all clear that one can conclude from this statement that Paul limits "the legitimate range of sexual expression to marriage" and "implicitly suggests that slaves who oblige their masters sexually are engaged in *porneia*."[37] The use of the word *gynē* in 7:1 personalizes and therefore suggests that the sexual use of female slaves is not envisioned here, just as the use of *pornē* in 6:15-16 depersonalizes the female involved and classifies the particular kind of sexual act that is discussed. Even the reference to lack of self-control (*akrasia*) in v. 5 might therefore be understood to refer to adultery or prostitution. It is possible that the holiness language of 1 Cor. 6:16-20, with its strong assertion of the unitive symbolism of sexual intercourse, precludes the legitimacy of sexual exploitation of one's slave. But even if Paul does include sexual use of one's slave under *akrasia* and *porneia* here, there still remains the question whether his audience would have understood it as such.

Similarly, the enigmatic 1 Thess. 4:3-5 exhorts abstention from *porneia*, adding that each Christian should keep one's own *skeuos* in holiness and honor, so as not to offend against a "brother" in this matter. Whereas 1 Pet. 3:7 uses the expression for "wife," its more familiar meaning in this kind of context is the human body or vulnerability (2 Cor. 4:7), or even the genitals (cf. LSJ and BDAG s.v.; 1 Sam. 21:5). Again, there is no doubt that Christian moral teaching prohibits *porneia*. The question, still not clarified, is whether sex with one's own slave was included in what constituted *porneia*.[38]

Obedient Slaves in Early Christianity

In the early years, Philemon; 1 Cor. 7:21-23; Eph. 6:5-8; Col. 3:22-25; 1 Tim. 6:1-2; Titus 2:9-10; 1 Pet. 2:18-25; and Ignatius, *Letter to Polycarp* 4.3 all speak to some degree of the submission and obedience expected of slaves. Philemon, of course, deals only with one specific male slave, Onesimus, and this case is not relevant in a study of female slaves. None of the other texts distinguishes male from female slaves, so we must read both sexes into the passages unless there is compelling reason to do otherwise. The texts 1 Cor. 7:21-23 and Ignatius, *Polycarp* 4.3 both speak of expectations of manumission, and both discourage setting it as a priority. First Corinthians makes it a matter of indifference, and Ignatius speaks against an expectation that the church will be the agent of manumission, which must therefore have been a custom beginning to develop in some places. Ignatius's paternalistic advice continues to set the tone of the church's general attitude to slavery and slaves for years to come: let slaves not think to be manumitted at church expense, lest they become slaves of desire (*epithymia*).

More to the point are the various household codes and advice to slaves. Ephesians 6:5-8 enjoins slaves to obey earthly owners with fear and trembling and simplicity of heart as they would Christ, not in appearance but as true slaves of Christ, as if serving the Lord, knowing that the reward from God will be the same for both slave and free. Likewise, Col. 3:22-25 in very similar terms exhorts slaves to obey their owners in everything as if serving the Lord. Their inheritance is sure because they are really serving the Lord Christ. Colossians adds that the wrongdoer will also be repaid in kind. What does it mean to obey *in everything*? The stress of the authors of these two letters on the fact that obeying an earthly master is really obeying Christ would at first glance lead us to think that the authors did not intend to include sexual availability as one of the factors in obedience. Yet in the previous and somewhat parallel exhortation to wives, the admonition "Wives, submit to your husbands as to the Lord . . . in everything" (Eph. 5:22, 24) certainly does include sexual availability. Much of the rest of the passage about husbands and wives, Christ and the church, is clearly sexual in connotation (vv. 26-31). Given societal expectations, it cannot therefore be ruled out that the exhortation for slaves to obey in everything might include sexual service.

On the other side, it can be countered that some sayings in the same literature seem to exclude an atmosphere in which sexual exploitation of slaves could be countenanced. For instance, Eph. 6:9 tells slave owners not to be overbearing or threatening because they too have an impartial heavenly Lord. Colossians 4:1 goes further with the same point to say that owners should relate to slaves with justice and fairness or equality (*to dikaion kai tēn isotēta*, but this refers not to equality between slave and owner, but to showing partiality to one slave over another—a situation that could easily arise in which one slave in a household is concubine of the owner).

The passage in 1 Tim. 6:1-2 is less explicit about the theological underpinnings of servitude. Owners are to be regarded with full honor so that outsiders do not see disobedient slaves and judge the teachings poorly. Slaves with believing owners are not to be less respectful for that reason, but to serve all the better. Titus 2:9-10 bids slaves to be submissive and pleasing in every way to their owners, not obstinate but completely faithful. The most difficult passage, 1 Pet. 2:18-25, tells slaves to be submissive not only to kind and gentle owners but also to abusive ones, after the example of Christ who suffered abuse. Clearly, the ideology of complete slave submission was little altered in Christian discourse.

In the immediate noncanonical literature, both the *Didache* and the *Letter of Barnabas*, in nearly parallel texts, pick up both the expectation of slave obedience and the tempering factor of admonition to slave owners against abuse (*Did.* 4.10–11; *Barn.* 19.7). Slaves must obey their owners as representatives (*typos*) of God, in reverence and fear (*aischynē* and *phobos*). Owners must not command in bitterness their male or female slaves, who believe in the same God. Christian slaves seem to be supposed here. The motive for forbearance is a piece of good psychology: being abused may lead them to abandon fear of the God who is over both slave and owner. The appeal to owners to restrain their behavior toward their slaves is both theological and practical. The same God rules over all without respect for persons. At the same time, that very fear of or respect for God is part of the motivation that keeps slaves in their place of subservience.

Three questions must be asked: First, what did a particular author intend to include under the category of obedience? Second, what did slave owners hear and do with these teachings? Third, how did slaves hear and under-stand what was given them as official teaching? Generations of women have been told to endure abusive husbands because it is God's will as set out in the Bible. What of slaves suffering not only physical but also sexual abuse from their owners? The text does not differentiate between male and female slaves, good and bad believing owners, or good and bad unbelieving owners, and there is no caveat or exception given to the total obedience that is expected, even to unjust and abusive owners. The incentive to full obedience continues further in the tradition. A later text, the Ethiopic *Apocalypse of Peter* 11, delights in describing special torments devised for special crimes. One group of men and women "who ceaselessly chew their tongues and are tormented with eternal fire . . . are the slaves who were not obedient to their masters. This then is their judgment forever."[39] The way in which the text specifies here and in several other instances in the same context "both men and women" suggests that the differences in males' and females' situations are taken fully into account and that the author explic-itly wants to include both.

Even if the Christian authors of texts such as the above do not intend to include sexual use as part of slaves' obedience (and that is never clear), the question still remains how new Christians, used to the sexually abusive patterns of slavery as normal and morally neutral, would have heard these directives in the absence of anything more specific. It is intriguing that, in the texts that have been preserved, no such exception to the demands of obedience is specified. We would like to know whether it was so specified in oral instruction, but there is no way to know. It is also clear that not every instance of sexual exploitation in slavery would have been experienced by the victim as abusive. Many female slaves both Christian and not would have found a certain degree of status, security, and perhaps even power in the relationship, as long as they were not mistreated and not threatened by jealous wives. Some may have attained a great deal of power, like Marcia, the probably Christian concubine first of Quadratus, nephew of Marcus Aurelius, then of Commodus (Hippolytus, *Ref.* 9.12; Dio Cassius 73.4.6–7; 22.4; 74.16.5), from which position she was able to do good for Christians whom she favored.[40] From a modern perspective and perhaps an ancient one as well, even if the victim feels fortunate, it is still abuse.

Tertullian does compare the exploitation of female slaves to the fre-quenting of brothels, which he argues against, not out of concern for prostitutes and slaves, but out of the bizarre purity concern that, because abandoned girls were often raised as slaves and prostitutes, someone might unknowingly commit incest.[41] The *Apostolic Tradition* of Hippolytus gives a list of occupations and conditions of persons that might pose problems for admission to the church as catechumens. Among them, a male catechumen not living with a wife should be taught not to fornicate, but to take a lawful wife or remain as he is. Whether this precludes sexual exploitation of his own slave depends on whether the understanding of fornication included this form of exploitation at that point. Again, a male living with a concubine should cease and take a lawful wife. While this situation may refer to a woman of free but inferior social status, it also covers the situation of a man using his female slave as common-law wife. Like most of the examples usually cited about sexual liaisons with slaves in the Greco-Roman texts, it implies a long-term relationship and says nothing about occasional sexual exploitation.[42] A slave concubine—and this is the only time in the reconstructed text of the *Apostolic Tradition* that "slave" is specified—who has reared her children and remained faithful to one man is not to be held blamable, but may be admitted (*Ap. Trad.* 15–16). Here the situation of slave concubinage is recognized and opposed, but it is still not certain that occasional sexual abuse of one's own slave is included in the prohibition. A separate sexual standard is held for free men, who are in control of their sexual activity, and female slaves, who are not.[43]

Thus what Jennifer Glancy calls a "moral conundrum" is recognized. Either the Christian community had to exclude some slaves whose sexual behavior, through no fault of their own, could not follow the general moral standard, or the community tolerated some whose sexual behavior did not conform to those norms. This situation adds a new dimension to the implications of 1 Cor. 7:21: given the opportunity for manumission, should the sexually exploited female slave take it, even though otherwise slavery or freedom is held by Paul to be morally and soteriologically neutral?[44]

Glancy rightly frames the dilemma faced by early Christians in this way: either it is not true, as was maintained even by Paul and ever since, that servile status was no impediment to membership in the church, or there were some forms of extramarital sex that were overlooked. By the fourth century, concepts of *moicheia* and *porneia* no longer follow the older Roman legal distinctions.[45] The old Roman *stuprum* becomes the Byzantine *phthora* (corrupting influence).

There was even some critique of slavery itself. Thus for Gregory of Nyssa, slave owning is an aspect of the sin of pride (*Hom. 4 on Eccl. 2.7*).[46] There is no doubt, however, that slavery by Christians continued, as attested, for example, by the fourth- or fifth-century slave collar on the neck of a slave of archdeacon Felix, inscribed with the owner's name,[47] or another of a slave belonging to Victor, an acolyte of the church of Clement in Rome.[48] A fifth-century epitaph with Christian symbols commemorates Theodora, slave of Dorotheus.[49] Many other examples could be added.

Expectations of slave obedience also continued. Severity of legislation shows no change. *Canon* 5 of the Council of Elvira decrees that a woman who in rage flogs her *ancilla* so severely that the slave dies within three days must do seven years of penance if she did it deliberately, five years if there was no intent to kill (how intention was to be discovered is not specified). If, however, the penitent should fall ill during the time of her penance, she can receive communion. The abuse is clearly considered wrong but is in no way likened to murder or attempted murder. In Constantinian legislation, the death sentence was prescribed for a free woman who had sex with her own slave and for the slave as well,[50] and it was ruled that if a slave died as the result of whipping, the owner was not to be charged with murder, since the use of a whip was evidence of intent not to kill.[51] Richard Saller argues that later Christian thinking actually expanded the use of whipping to children, since all are created equal in the sight of God![52] Augustine opines that misbehaving slaves should be whipped for their own benefit, since it is no kindness to let someone fall into greater evil by not acting (*City of God* 19.16). He also reports as nothing extraordinary—in a story about his mother's virtue—that when the female slaves in his household of origin created tensions between Monica and her mother-in-law by slandering the daughter-in-law, Monica continued deferential to the older woman and thus regained her confidence. When the mother-in-law realized what was happening, she asked her son, Augustine's father, to have the slaves beaten. After that, there were no more problems (*Confessions* 9.9.20).

Written evidence of some awareness of the problems does exist. Basil of Cappadocia writes that a female slave who cohabits with a man against the will of her owner commits *porneia*, because contracts made by those under authority are invalid, but that if the relationship continues after she is freed, it becomes *gamos*, marriage. This simply follows Roman law in part. But further in the same letter, he states that a woman raped by force is innocent, even a slave raped by her master (*Ep.* 199.40, 49). The passage is part of a series of opinions about the sexual guilt of women in various situations. The text still raises no suggestion of culpability on the part of the master. Basil acknowledges that the double standard is not right but is the custom (*Ep.* 188, 199). The *Apostolic Constitutions* of the late fourth century forbid at least clerics from having a *hetaira* or an *oiketis*, a household slave as concubine (6.17.2), perhaps considered legitimate by some when marriage for clerics was discouraged. The issue, however, is not slave ownership but the sexual propriety of the cleric.

Other Christian writers by this time were speaking out against the sexual double standard, including the sexual availability of female slaves to their owners, but nearly always from the point of view of what is required of the virtuous Christian male, not the rights of the slave. Thus Jerome assumes that where there are female slaves, lust reigns, but he also insists that rules about chastity that apply to women must apply equally to men (*Ep.* 77.3). Eusebius of Emesa, in the context of securing the vow of a consecrated virgin, lashes out at Christian males who blame a "fallen virgin," while they are unfaithful to their good and chaste wives by wronging their *ancilla* (*On Virgins* 11.B1, 182–83).[53] While authors expressed their moral views, they also acknowledged that neither the government nor men themselves did much to change the custom.[54] Later in Byzantine law, *porneia* explicitly includes intercourse with a female slave.[55] Though one's own slave is not specified, it can probably be presumed by this time. The crime is not *stuprum* but *porneia*, which has now become a legal category.

Did earlier Christian writers not speak of sexual exploitation of one's slave because a prohibition was self-evident (unlikely), because it was not done by Christians (also unlikely given the prevailing acceptance in the culture), because it was too much of a problem to tackle (ignore it and maybe it will go away), or because they did not consider it a problem? Probably in the earliest years this was a part of the culture that they had not yet sorted out as something to reject explicitly, though there may have been some awareness of the problem. Gradually an awareness of the wrongness of sexual exploitation of slavery was built into the legal code, but slavery itself was still too much of a cultural convenience to be questioned for many centuries.

Conclusion:
An Ambiguous Legacy

The entrance of Christian faith into families seems to have made little difference to the institution of slavery. The best that can be said is that writers picked up the most humane thinking of their day with regard to how unwise it was to abuse slaves, both from the philosophical perspective of God's indifference to the status of persons and their mutual responsibility to facilitate the growth of faith, and from the practical perspective that happy slaves work better. We can only assume that the views preserved in the writings more or less matched the behavior of the majority. The lingering question with regard to sexual abuse is whether or not, contrary to accepted custom, Christian teachers would have thought from the earliest years that making use of the sexual availability of one's own slaves was abusive and wrong. Discipline was expected to be kept as strictly as ever. Obedient slaves were part of the demonstration that Christians kept law-abiding and respectable households. Even if Christian opinion was against sexual abuse of slaves, the strong admonitions to slave obedience could have caused severe conflicts in the well-intentioned Christian slave who happened to be in an abusive household. Perhaps the equally strong family ideology of Christian teaching would have encouraged slave owners to respect the integrity of slave families and keep them together, though they had no legal pressure to do so.

Any discussions of slavery in this literature must be assumed to include female as well as male slaves unless the context obviously indicates the opposite. Female slaves bore the same liabilities as male slaves to exploitation, torture, and abuse. The eventual entrance into the equation of an encouragement to celibacy might have been confusing, since the celibacy of slaves would be an economic liability. On the contrary, in later years, beginning in the fourth century, there are narratives of aristocratic women who begin monasteries that incorporate their former female servants. In such a case, one wonders if these servant women had any choice in the matter.

The evidence for the conversion of household slaves to Christianity along with their owners is mixed. Blandina's mistress was arrested with her. We cannot be sure that was the case with Felicitas. The *Apostolic Tradition* envisions both cases in which a slave in a believing household will later seek baptism on his or her own and cases in which the slave in an unbelieving household takes the initiative to do so. It seems that one of the things that characterized early Christianity, as was also true of Judaism and a number of private cults, was that slaves were expected to make their own choices of religious adherence. The silence of most sources about the lives of female slaves in early Christian communities is a magnification of the common phenomenon of the silence of women's voices in general.

CHAPTER SIX

EPHESIANS 5
AND THE POLITICS OF MARRIAGE

◻◻ ◻◻ ◻◻

Thus far we have concentrated on the daily lives of women and girls in house churches, with a special focus on their roles and relations within the family as wives, daughters, and slaves. But at the same time as female participants in house churches were contributing substantially to the movement, their lives were increasingly becoming the subject of ideological discourse. Given the great interest in women and asceticism among scholars of Christian origins, it is somewhat ironic that in the early period at least, it is the wife that is of greatest ideological interest. In this chapter we give detailed consideration to arguably the most important textual representation of female identity in the literature of the latter decades of the first century and the first half of the second century CE: Eph. 5:22-33. We will discuss how the idealized Christian wife in this text plays a key role not only as an ethical role model but also as a symbol of community identity and interaction between church and society.

Our analysis is indebted to recent scholarship on Ephesians using Roman imperial ideology as an interpretive grid. This approach helps us to identify important points of contact among political elements, family values, and features of Christian identity reflected in this text. While our study focuses especially on the textual idealization of wives, we also make cautious suggestions about how an understanding of the socio-political impact of Eph. 5:22-33 can enhance our picture of the *significance* of the life of the Christian wife—the married woman who brought up children in the faith and continued to guide adult children into maturity, who combined household management with organizational efforts for church meetings. This picture helps prepare the way for our discussion of women leaders of households and Christian assemblies in chapter 7.

Ephesians and Empire

Scholars in general have recognized the importance of reading the teaching on marriage in Ephesians, as seen within the broader framework of the household code of Eph. 5:21—6:9, against a background of Greco-Roman ethical ideals. It is generally accepted that the New Testament household codes draw their origins from the traditional expositions of the topos "concerning household management" (involving the three pairs: husband-wife, parent-child, master-slave) found in the teaching of various philosophers, moralists, and political thinkers from Aristotle (*Politics* 1.1253b.1–14) onward.[1] Because of the detailed treatment of marriage in Eph. 5:22-33, which seems so deliberately to build upon the brief treatment of marriage in the Colossian household code, many scholars have attached great significance to this segment of the letter; some even see the text as the key to unlocking the purpose of the work as a whole.[2] But commentators are far from agreeing on the place of the passage within Ephesians, and many questions remain about the significance of the points of contact between Ephesians and Jewish and Greco-Roman texts from this period that display interest in household management.[3]

The content and the place of the household code within Ephesians reflect and condense what the document as a whole recommends as a stance in relation to the wider world. Here it is especially valuable to keep in mind that commentators are beginning to view imperial ideology as an important interpretive grid for Ephesians. The familial ideals of the Ephesian household code are intertwined with other texts in Ephesians that offer insight into the *ekklēsia*'s political response to the *Pax Romana* (imperial propaganda for Roman rule).[4] Moreover, in recent years there has been growing awareness of the socio-political impact of marriage ideals among ancient historians working on the Roman family, and such work strengthens the case for viewing the marriage teaching of Ephesians as an important socio-political statement.

Although there is much historical uncertainty concerning the identity of its addressees (the words "in Ephesus" are missing from several important witnesses), Ephesians is frequently dated at about 90 CE and most often set within the context of Asia Minor. By the time of the composition of Ephesians, Roman imperial marriage values had spread to Eastern centers,[5] and depictions of harmonious unions between couples were seemingly everywhere. We might consider, for example, the artwork of ancient Pompeii that includes a portrait of Paquius Proculus and his wife. The two are strikingly similar in appearance, achieving harmony even in the nature of their gaze. The image is a particularly lovely example of a trend that can be seen in the art (especially funerary art), inscriptions, and literature of Rome from the late Republic onward: the tendency to demonstrate the ideal of the Roman family, including the concord of the married couple.[6] Such ideals no doubt are rooted in real social expectations and aspirations about marriage (no matter how different the reality), but their presence in the speeches of emperors and various political rhetoricians and moralists reveals the broad appeal of such ideals for purposes of social comment and political propaganda.[7] The tendency for civic harmony to be linked with marital concord has led historian Peter Brown to describe Ephesians in turn as presenting "an image of unbreakable order that the pagan world could understand."[8] The symbolic use of marriage to explain the relationship between Christ and the church meant that in the church, as in the larger society, the married couple was idealized as a microcosm of the society as a whole.

Nowhere else in the New Testament do we find such a deliberate attempt to articulate the ideal of the married couple as in Eph. 5:22-33. The description of hierarchical relations between husband and wife is unmistakable, but the text is also infused with notions of affection and unity that have points in common with the most sentimental ideals of the Roman family. At one level, Eph. 5:22-33 is a highly conventional text. But the author of Ephesians also makes use of major themes from the work as a whole to infuse the code's traditional marriage teaching with meaning, creating new patterns of identity. In other words, with a focus on the pure bride who has one true husband, the author of Ephesians encodes central values and theological messages of the community; the author articulates the boundaries of the *ekklēsia* in a manner intended to set it apart from so much other discourse and social expression of this time. Thus, in what follows we will be confronted with one of the major interpretive puzzles of Ephesians: the heavy stress upon conventional marriage in a document that in many respects presents believers as having already escaped the boundaries of conventional existence (for example, Eph. 2:6). This ironic disjuncture serves to alert us to a methodological caution key to the present discussion and recalls the questions about the role of Nympha of Laodicea at the beginning of this book: when it comes to the lives of wives, much more may be going on than appears on the surface of texts.

Before we focus specifically on the household code and its instructions to wives, we need to consider how the text as a whole reflects engagement with the *Pax Romana* as a whole. An obvious place to begin is with Eph. 6:10-20, a text that Andrew Lincoln has argued constitutes Ephesians' *peroratio* (the typical concluding section of persuasive communication designed to make the audience ill-disposed to any enemy and arousing the emotions of hearers). He notes that this *peroratio* takes the form of a "call to battle" and is similar to the speeches of generals before battle, reminding soldiers of their superior strength, bracing them for a successful outcome.[9] The final section of Ephesians encourages the community's disdain for the enemy: the Gentile nonbelieving world that is in the grip of evil spiritual powers—hostile spiritual beings (compare Eph. 2:2; 6:12) that can still make inroads into the community (compare Eph. 4:17-24).[10] Lincoln has, in fact, argued that Eph. 6:10-20 serves as the conclusion not only for the ethical exhortation section that begins in Eph. 4:1 but also for the entire epistle. This suggests that the passage is of central significance for understanding the tenor of the work as a whole.

For all of its points of contact with imperial ideology and the militarization of society, however, it is immediately clear that Eph. 6:10-20 is intended to distance the way of life of believers from the usual standards and priorities of society. With what may well be an ironic jab at the imperial propaganda for Roman rule, the *Pax Romana*, the armor of God is presented as including the equipment of the "gospel [*euangelion*] of peace" (Eph. 6:15)—reversing the usual meaning of the term "gospel" to refer to the message of peace and security of Augustus and his successors (compare Eph. 2:14-18).[11] An awareness of the political overtones of the language of doing battle with evil in Eph. 6:10-20 leads to a greater appreciation of the text as a valuable indicator of the epistle's response to the nonbelieving world. Although the limits of space prevent a full illustration of the matter here, Ephesians displays an extremely strong sentiment of separation from the Gentile world.[12] The household code is in fact sandwiched between two key texts dealing with the relationship between the church and outside forces of various kinds: a long articulation of the vices of nonbelieving society and virtues of believers (Eph. 4:17—5:20) and the metaphorical description of doing battle with evil (Eph. 6:10-20). Both of these texts serve essentially the same function: they instill a repulsion for the lives of unbelievers and encourage cohesion through the adoption of a common ethical stance. In the latter "warrior" text, this call to adopt a common ethical stance is explicitly presented as a strategy of defense. What this might mean for our understanding of the household code and its presentation of marriage will be explored below.

When we read Eph. 5:21 as closely related to Eph. 5:20, it becomes evident that "being subject to one another" is characteristic of a way of life that sets believers apart from the nonbelieving world. Some interpreters suggest that the whole of the household code needs to be understood in this light.[13] The household code of Eph. 5:21—6:9 clearly has points in common with other household codes in the New Testament and displays significant links with the traditional topos "concerning household management" found throughout Hellenistic literature. But two aspects of the text need to be taken particularly seriously: the author's deliberate effort to create transition between the code and the previous ethical exhortations (in contrast, for example, to the seemingly abrupt insertion of the code within Colossians [Col. 3:18—4:1]) and the significant points of contact between the teaching on marriage and the remainder of the epistle. In fact, the transitional nature of Eph. 5:21 offers an important textual indicator of a dual separating and accommodating orientation of the Ephesian household code. Although frequently viewed as one of the strongest signs of accommodation to the world, and obviously deeply embedded in Greco-Roman ethics, the household code is presented as that which ultimately sets believers apart.[14] Ethical teaching directing church members on how to live in a manner distinct from the Gentiles begins at Eph. 4:17 and is resumed again at Eph. 6:10. At several junctures in the code, ethical teachings are infused with reflection on the meaning of baptism, love, and unity and with a presentation of believers as the "holy ones" set apart from all impurity—themes also found throughout Ephesians.

The household code of Ephesians represents a defensive strategy in the sense that it promulgates a vision of marriage that is integral to an emerging identity in opposition to those on the outside. What is ironic about the social impact of the exhortations, however, is that they do not in fact create a visibly distinct identity in the social realm. Understood as shaped by "reverence for Christ" (Eph. 5:21), but nevertheless providing concrete patterns for daily life that are conventional, the household code provides a type of balance between flight from society and confrontation with society. The code ties the community defensively to a social structure that has the power to render members fairly invisible among their neighbors. But lest anyone misunderstand the overarching program, the author of Ephesians moves immediately from the code imbued with the socio-political agenda of traditional household management to a call to do battle with evil (Eph. 6:10-20). This strategy for survival often manifests itself outwardly in highly conventional terms, but it is rooted in the conviction that there is no compromise to be made with a profoundly evil world.

Conventional and Countercultural Elements

Within the Text of Ephesians 5:22-33

Some echoes of a strong sentiment of world-rejection are even embedded within the hierarchical marriage teaching itself, especially in Eph. 5:25-27. The command for husbands to love their wives in Eph. 5:25a leads immediately to an exposition of the identity of the church and its relationship to Christ. Human marriage does not become an immediate concern again until Eph. 5:28, serving primarily in 5:25b-27 as an analogical tool for discussing the human-divine relationship.[15] In Eph. 5:25-27 three *hina* clauses ("that," "in order that") spell out the purpose of Christ's love for the church, of his giving up of himself on her behalf: in order that he might sanctify her; in order that he might present the church to himself in splendor; in order that she might be holy and without blemish. Particularly noteworthy is the language of sanctification recalling biblical notions of sanctification tied to God's appropriation of Israel and reflecting a theme that is very useful in articulating the call for dissociation from nonbelievers: the *hieros gamos* or "sacred marriage."[16] The use of this recurring motif from ancient Near Eastern literature allows the author to draw the attention of the audience to sexual union and especially to the sexual purity that serves as such an apt metaphor for dissociation from a corrupt society.[17] Though tempered by the propriety associated with scriptural allusions and citations (Eph. 5:26 [Ezek. 16:9]; Eph. 5:28 [Lev. 19:18]; Eph. 5:31 [Gen. 2:24]), hearers are nevertheless confronted in Eph. 5:22-33 by the image of a bride's prenuptial bath and the suggestion of a purity inspection conducted by the bridegroom-Christ, who eventually takes her as his own.[18] The role of the husband in relation to his wife is presented as being analogous to the role of Christ, who sanctifies (*hagiazein*, "makes holy") the church (Eph. 5:26). English translations mask what is ultimately a statement concerning the identity of believers. Members of the church are very frequently called saints or holy ones (*hagioi*) in Ephesians (for example, Eph. 1:1, 4; 2:19; 5:3). That the notion of being a "holy one" is linked to the household and house-church life of believers is suggested especially by Eph. 2:19, in which recipients of the epistle are described as "fellow-citizens with the *saints* and members of the household of God."

The idea of believers being set apart is further reinforced by the manner in which bride and bridegroom imagery is juxtaposed with allusions to baptism in Eph. 5:26. The bride/church is cleansed with a washing of water "by the word." The preparation of the woman for marriage by washing (Ezek. 16:9; see Ezek. 16:8-14) becomes a metaphor for the baptized community faithful to the gospel message. The strongest statement of the identity of the *ekklēsia* with its concomitant rejection of the wicked world outside comes in Eph. 5:27. Like the beautiful bride of Ezek. 16:10-14, the church represents human perfection and purity. Preceded by the detailed description of the tainted and corrupt society outside the church in Eph. 4:17—5:20, the presentation of the church as being without spot (*spilos*) or wrinkle (*rutis*), as holy and without blemish (*amōmos*), becomes a central metaphor for believers' engagement with the world and withdrawal from the world (Eph. 5:27). That such negotiation of boundaries underlies this text is supported by the fact that the terms "spot" and "blemish" are brought together in 2 Pet. 2:13 to refer to false teachers (the "unrighteous," 2 Pet. 2:9)—the only other place in the New Testament where these terms occur together.[19]

Links between communal identity and marriage are created in two main ways in the undisputed letters of Paul: through the symbolic depiction of the community as the bride of Christ (2 Cor. 11:2-3) and through instructions to marry with an attitude and attention to purity that separates the community from the immoral Gentile world (1 Thess. 4:4-5; 1 Cor. 7; compare 2 Cor. 6:14—7:1).[20] In Ephesians, these two tendencies are brought together. The holiness, purity, and submission of the church as the bride who is loved by Christ (Eph. 5:23b, 25b-27, 29b) serves to justify and explain why wives should submit to the authority of their husbands and why husbands should love and cherish their wives (Eph. 5:22-23a, 24-25a, 28-29a, 33). Moreover, marriage between believers is sanctified in the context of exhortations more broadly concerned with distinguishing Christians from nonbelievers (see Eph. 4:17—5:20; 6:10-20). It would not be appropriate to state that the marriage teaching of Ephesians constitutes endogamy rules, because marriage between believers and nonbelievers is not ruled out explicitly and undoubtedly continued in this period (see 1 Cor. 7:12-16; 1 Pet. 3:1-6). In addition, it may well be the case that the audience to which Ephesians was addressed included wives whose husbands were nonbelievers (mixed marriages involving believing men and nonbelieving women are possible, but virtually unheard of in the literature)[21] and who may have interpreted the instructions as a call to remain married no matter what the circumstances. But a move to idealize marriage between believers by means of christological language is unmistakable in the text, no matter how different the realities lived by many church members.

When Ignatius of Antioch offered instructions at the beginning of the second century concerning marriage and described the ideal union as a reflection of the love of the Lord for the church, he went one step further than the author of Ephesians—essentially calling for endogamy measures with the appeal that marriages should take place with the permission of the bishop (Ignatius, *Pol.* 5:1-2).[22] It is important to note, however, that a move toward endogamy does not mean that marriage becomes a matter of internal concern only, devoid of significance for relations with outsiders. This can be seen clearly in Josephus's apologetic work *Against Apion* (probably dating from about the same period as Ephesians), in which marriage between Jews under the Law comes to be explained as a central aspect of identity following an explanation of the Jewish conception of God and the Temple (*Against Apion* 2.190–203).[23] Josephus sets out to present a harmonious and unified Jewish people, pointing to the example and witness of women and subordinate members of the household as a particularly revealing sign of identity: "Even our women-folk and dependants [*tōn oiketōn*] would tell you that piety must be the motive of all of our occupations in life."[24]

The text in which Josephus sets out to explain the marriage teaching of the Jews (*Against Apion* 2.199–201) has frequently been compared to the

New Testament household codes in general and has certainly been seen as reflecting a typical interest in household management that is found in the literature of this period. Yet it might be objected that the usefulness of a specific comparison between Eph. 5:22-33 and Josephus's *Against Apion* is called into question by the strongly internal focus of the Ephesian household code (compare 1 Pet. 3:1-6) and its lack of explicit apologetic interests.[25] Recent work on the Roman family, however, has highlighted the importance of marriage for assertions of identity in society generally and suggests that marriage practices among the early Christians would be one of the most important vehicles for communicating the essence of the church and for negotiating life with neighbors. The passionate concern with the identity of the church in Ephesians, coupled with the fact that marriage could never really be merely an internal affair for a group immersed in an ancient city, leads us to see the public presentation of the church as bride of Christ as the flip side of the concern with internal cohesion.[26] Domestic behavior is a valuable tool for communicating messages to the world—even if these messages are largely nonverbal and designed primarily to deflect social tension rather than really to encourage new membership. Directed to the members of the community in the first instance, but of crucial importance for community deportment and image, Eph. 5:22-33 is the New Testament's most complete answer to Josephus's question, "What are our marriage Laws?" (*Against Apion* 2.199).

Recognizing the complex and multifaceted messages encoded within Eph. 5:22-33, drawing upon both common familial ideals and the core beliefs of the *ekklēsia*, is vital to understanding the implications of the text for the lives of women in house churches. As we have seen, the Ephesian household code essentially encourages conventional behavior and repeats associations that would have been familiar to its audience. But such a mirroring of cultural values extends only so far. The author also creatively interweaves such elements with the major themes and concepts of the epistle such as unity, holiness, mystery, and the body of Christ. At least one intriguing aspect of the textual interplay within Ephesians for understanding the lives of women has received little attention from commentators: traditional language that appears to assimilate the church into society nevertheless works in conjunction with the major themes of the epistle to forge identity and to reinforce an ethos of separation from the nonbelieving world.

Intertextuality and Ephesians 5:22-33

To offer examples of how themes from earlier in the work reenter the passage and give shape to this ethos, we might briefly consider the head/body language that begins at Eph. 5:23 and surfaces more or less explicitly throughout the text. The notion of Christ as "head" (*kephalē*) of the church, his body, has already been introduced in the epistle (see Eph. 1:22-23; 4:15-16) and is a concept that Ephesians shares with Colossians (see Col. 1:18, 24; 2:10, 17, 19). In Ephesians, however, the focus on Christ's universal reign (implicit within the concept of headship) becomes a central means of articulating the majestic parameters of his body, the *ekklēsia* (Eph. 1:22-23; compare Col. 1:15-20). In addition, the first appearance of the notion of Christ's headship (Eph. 1:22-23) in the context of the thanksgiving and prayer of Eph. 1:15-23 is closely connected to the concept of Christ's enthronement at God's right hand in the heavenly places (Eph. 1:20-21; see 2:6; 3:10; 6:12). In essence, Ephesians presents believers as belonging to a heavenly *ekklēsia* under Christ's headship. Such associations are also central to the vision of the harmonious community found in Eph. 4:1-16. Believers are presented as growing up into the head, Christ (Eph. 4:15-16; see 2:21), the one who engages in a heavenly journey (Eph. 4:8-10).[27]

Thus, by the time we come to the author's analogy in Eph. 5:23 (that the husband is the head of the wife as Christ is the head of the church), the audience has been prepared to think in majestic and heavenly terms not only about Christ's reign but also about the boundaries of the community. Moreover, the author's use of such headship language in the context of marriage teaching is facilitated by Paul's previous statement (which may have been familiar to the audience) that Christ is the head of man as man is the head of woman (1 Cor. 11:3; see 11:2-16). In Ephesians these motifs are combined in a new way.[28] The husband is head of his wife as Christ is head of the majestic and heavenly church. Human "wifely" behavior within the church becomes an indicator of the community's dislocation as an apparently conventional but nevertheless heavenly body.

A similar sentiment of dislocation emerges when one compares Eph. 5:21-33 to Eph. 2:11-22 and sets out to understand how the theme of unity, associated earlier in the document with such broad realities as nations and citizenship, is reworked within a passage with a specifically domestic focus. Once again Josephus's *Against Apion* (where unity serves as an apologetic motif) is useful in alerting us to intertextual dynamics within Ephesians:

> To this cause above all we owe our admirable harmony. Unity and identity of religious belief, perfect uniformity in habits and customs, produce a very beautiful concord in human character. Among us alone will be heard no contradictory statements about God, such as are common among other nations. . . . Among us alone will be seen no difference in the conduct of our lives. With us all act alike, all profess the same doctrine, one which is in harmony with our Law and affirms that all things are under His eye.[29]

The emphasis on God-ordained harmony among Jews calls to mind the lofty proclamations of unity in Eph. 2:11-22, but the focus on ethics points to the presentation of unity in the Spirit in Eph. 4:1-16, which marks the beginning of the ethical exhortation segment of the letter in which the household code (Eph. 5:21—6:9) occupies a central place. Like the author of Ephesians, Josephus turns his attention easily from the wider political and religious sphere to the domestic sphere when he presents women and other members of the household as communicators of the piety (*eusebia*) of all their occupations in life (*Against Apion* 2.181).

Both Eph. 2:11-22 and Eph. 5:22-33 rely heavily on metaphors to explore the identity of the church, with Eph. 2:11-22 representing the macro vision of heavenly citizenship and Eph 5:22-33 representing the micro vision of household holiness and loyalty.[30] In fact, the relationship between these two texts calls to mind the understanding of the household as the microcosm of the state in Aristotle's *Politics* and in subsequent Hellenistic discussions of household management (as is also reflected in Josephus's comments cited above). In addition, the relationship between "macro" and "micro" runs through each of the texts of Eph. 2:11-22 and Eph. 5:22-33, even though one side of the equation is emphasized more than the other. In depicting the submission of wife to husband as a reflection of the relationship of the church to Christ, the household code itself embraces the concept of household relations reflecting the wider realities of the relationship between the human and the divine. In Eph. 2:11-22 these wider realities are cast in civic terms, but links with the micro setting of household holiness and loyalty are revealed when believers are described in Eph. 2:19 as "fellow-citizens with the saints and members of the household of God"—a text that sets the stage for the triumphal proclamation in Eph. 3:15 of God as the great *patēr* ("father") from whom every home (*patria*) in heaven and on earth is named.

Beyond the general terms of the macro/micro relationship described above, the political perspective of Eph. 2:11-22 extends its reach to embrace the household code by anticipating the household code teaching in specific ways.[31] Preparing the way for the marriage teaching that also incorporates elements of unification, both Eph. 2:14 and 2:15 (with slight differences in terminology) refer to Christ's actions "making two [Gentiles and Jews] into one," reflecting traditional baptismal notions (see Col. 3:10-11; Gal. 3:27-28) that celebrate the new creation in terms of unification (or reunification) of opposites. The male-female pair figures prominently in these traditional formulations (Gal. 3:27-28).[32] In addition, Eph. 2:14-16 refers to Christ's actions leading to the incorporation of believers into his body. This corporeal symbolism calls to mind the celestial union (presented in vividly physical terms) of Christ and church and the use of body concepts and imagery in Eph. 5:22-33. Throughout the text the church is presented as Christ's partner, but it is especially interesting to consider how the metaphor of church as "bride" and church as "body of Christ" merge to a significant degree. This can be seen especially in Eph. 5:23, in which Christ is presented as "the savior of the body" and in Eph. 5:28-30, which describes Christ's love for the church as a love for "his own flesh" and offers the justification for the instruction by explaining that "we are members of his body" (Eph. 5:30).

In the context of the house-church setting of early Christianity, it is especially striking that the household code is anticipated most directly by the reference to the identity of the community as the "household of God" in Eph. 2:19 (see also Eph. 3:15). This verse offers one of many examples in the New Testament of metaphors linking the experience of salvation to the physical gathering place of church groups (see also Gal. 6:10; 1 Pet. 2:5; 4:17; 1 Tim. 3:15). The household metaphor of Ephesians is especially intriguing for the study of women, however, because of the presentation of the church as symbolically female in Eph. 5:22-33. Read in relation to the image of the bride-*ekklēsia* of Eph. 5:22-33, the household of God takes on a feminine persona. While it is important not to press symbolic language too hard for logical equivalence and literal meaning, it is nevertheless suggestive for the present discussion to conceive of the *ekklēsia* as a household of women. Conceived as such, what are we to make of hierarchical household code teaching that clearly reinforces the authority of the *paterfamilias*?

With respect to the metaphorical language of Eph. 2:11-22 at least, it is clear that the author does not intend for us to focus too long on the conventional shape of dwellings and other structures.[33] The author leads the reader away from neighborhood ground through a series of architectural metaphors, shifting attention away from the concrete and physical to conceive of the community as in the process of being built up as a heavenly and spiritual temple, a dwelling place for God (Eph. 2:20-21). The transition operates via a shift from house to temple—a shift from the domestic realm to the realm of city and state. This is suggested not only because of the significance of the Jerusalem Temple (see Eph. 2:14), but also because of the importance of the construction of temples for prestige and the securing of imperial favor in the Roman world.[34] The transition, however, continues upward and outward to transcend even the most important monuments of city and state. Although they draw upon the ideological underpinnings of the empire, ultimately these architectural images constitute a critique of conventional notions of sacred space, including temples and various politically approved arrangements for meeting; in household cells believers live in a sacred community whose boundaries transcend the horizontal and earthly realm. If one considers that a similar relationship between the conventional and the countercultural might be at work in the metaphorical description of marriage in Eph. 5:22-33, could the reference to the woman-church, the *ekklēsia* conceived as a female body/space, encode its own critique of the politically approved arrangements for meeting?

To ask such a question is not to deny the restrictive and patriarchal impact of the household code. Because the desire to reinforce the boundaries of the community in Eph. 5:22-33 is expressed mainly in terms of preserving the bride's purity, it is firmly tied to controlling and defining the identity of women. They are the passive and chaste vessels who are to be taken, unblemished, the exclusive possessions of divine or human partners.[35] This is in keeping with a social system that placed much less weight on sentiment in the arrangement of marriages than is the case in modern society, and in which women, especially in more elite circles, sometimes found themselves to be pawns in political arrangements. With respect to acceptance of traditional values for the life of women in the early church, it is clear that the household code teaching stands in contrast to other strands of the tradition that challenge ideals of the human bride in favor of asceticism (for example, 1 Corinthians 7) and that women's behavior is being "scripted" in highly conventional terms. Women are presented as

carrying a heavy burden for the community—they are the human convey-
ers of purity par excellence. But it is actually very difficult to know if the
women who heard these instructions would have interpreted them as a call
to change their behavior in any way (for example, perhaps relinquishing
earlier ascetic inclinations) or whether the specific ethical recommendations would sound so familiar as to seem banal, perhaps even to be quietly
ignored.

Household Management and Informal Conventions

Discussion of a final aspect of the tension between traditional and countercultural elements reflected in Eph. 5:22-33 involves consideration of
conflicting forces associated with marriage in the Roman world generally.
Research on the Roman family has revealed that marriage combined elements of hierarchy with those of mutual responsibility, companionship,
and coordinating spheres of authority (even if, in the case of wives, this was
most frequently informal). The most "romantic" of these sentiments are
perhaps best represented by Plutarch, who preserved a hierarchical understanding of marriage but nevertheless described marriage as a type of symbiotic relationship: "The marriage of the couple in love with each other
is an intimate union; that of those who marry for dowry or children is of
persons joined together; and that of those who merely sleep in the same
bed is of separate persons who may be regarded as cohabiting [*synoikein*],
but not really living together [*symbioun*]."[36]

It is easy to observe points of contact between Plutarch's thought on
the married couple and texts like Eph. 5:22-33. What is much less obvious, however, but extremely important for our understanding of the rule-
like statements found in the household codes is that even apparently very
restrictive legal pronouncements function in conjunction with a multitude
of conventions lacking formal authority. Recipients of the household codes
may have assumed that wives and mothers were being granted powers in
managing the affairs of the household that were associated by convention
with the traditional model of family life. This may not seem very remarkable in and of itself, but when we consider that the venue for meetings
was the house church, an implicit recognition of the role of the mother
in the household codes may have fairly significant consequences for the
running of the community. As will be explored in more detail in the next
chapter, among the virtues prized in wives in the Roman world was that

they should be good managers of the household. This included frugality in the first instance but also a number of domestic duties, such as overseeing the proper running of the household and care of guests.[37] As we discussed in chapter 2, the autonomy of Roman wives tested the boundaries of the legal prerogatives of the *paterfamilias*, with women being involved in such activities as the negotiating of good matches for their children or, in widowhood, essentially managing the affairs of their young children.

When one thinks about all that could be involved in wives' management of households, their potential involvement in the house church comes to the fore. Such understanding should perhaps even cause us to rethink our view of some of the most patriarchal-sounding texts in early Christian literature. While they no doubt restricted choices offered to women, the instructions that young widows should marry, bear children, and manage their household also created opportunities for women to exercise influence in a house-based movement (1 Tim. 5:14). Assuming that most recipients of early Christian texts were far removed from the classes in which the ideal of the Roman matron was articulated in sophisticated ways, Dixon's comments about lower-class women are also worth pondering: "Within the slave and freed-slave families of Rome, the mother must sometimes have been an anchor in a very uncertain world. She probably occupied an important place within the family structure but it is difficult to determine whether it was one of great authority and, if so, what that authority might have rested upon."[38] The authors of the New Testament household codes have little doubt as to where the authority of mothers rests. The authority of mothers, like that of fathers in relation to their children, rests "in the Lord" (Eph. 6:1-3; Col. 3:20). Despite the clear reinforcement of the authority of the *paterfamilias* in the household, the authority of the mother in the Lord may often have been a far more present reality for many people.

Household and House-Church Images and Ideologies of Masculinity

To focus on the informal authority of wives in our discussion of hierarchical marriage arrangements is admittedly to concentrate on only one side of the equation. The reinforcement of the formal authority of husbands and fathers in the household code clearly has important consequences for the women of the community. Yet the reinforcement of the authority of *paterfamilias* was at least as much about "image" as about the reality of social structures. For a movement organized in terms of household groupings, the symbolic significance of marriage was bolstered by the closely related symbolic significance of the physical house. The first-century writings of Valerius Maximus offer an especially fine example of the close association between marital concord and the harmony of the house in traditional Roman values. He tells of ancient Roman times when, on account of a disagreement, a couple left their own house and went to the Temple of Viriplaca, known literally as "the Placater of Men." Both relating their side of the story, they were able to work out their problems before the goddess and return to the "*domum in concordiam.*" According to Valerius, the natural inferiority of the wife to the husband meant that this procedure for solving disagreements was especially appropriate. But, as Geoffrey Nathan has noted, of far more significance is the implication that disagreements should not occur in the physical house, offering a clear indication of its symbolic significance.[39] The lofty presentations of the unity of the *ekklēsia* that are so characteristic of Ephesians (and of which the married couple is a prime symbol) are meant to reinforce an image of order and decorum in which division, disagreement, and impropriety have no place.

The issue of masculine authority is especially important when seeking to understand the importance of image in the formulation of the household codes. The resemblance between Plutarch's observation ("a man therefore ought to have his household well harmonized who is going to harmonize state, forum, and friends") and the directive for bishops in the Pastoral Epistles ("If a man does not know how to rule his own house, how can he take care of God's church?") is striking.[40] Both remarks are highly conventional, and their similarity offers an especially strong indication of the close link between household norms and expectations and the articulation of male leadership structures both inside and outside of the *ekklēsia*. (But in the case of the Pastoral Epistles, there is a certain irony in the remarks. It is not the city or state that the bishop will oversee, but the *oikos* of God that meets in his own home!)

The detailed study on the ideologies of masculinity in the Roman world by Craig A. Williams can shed further light upon the social impact of household code teaching, which reinforces male control of paternity and, as illustrated especially well by the vivid sexual imagery of Ephesians 5, male control of women's sexual experience. Williams's conclusions are worth citing at some length:

> I have suggested that control and dominion constituted the prime directive of masculinity. A man must exercise dominion over his own body and his own desires as well as the bodies and desires of those under his jurisdiction—his wife, children, and slaves—just as the Roman citizenry as a whole ideally dominates most of the rest of the world. A man might lose his grip on masculine control, and thus be labeled effeminate, in various ways: by indulging in an excessive focus on his appearance or making himself look like a woman, by seeking to be dominated or even penetrated by his sexual partners, by subjugating himself to others for the sake of pleasuring or entertaining them, or by yielding to his own passions, desires, and fears. Masculinity was not fundamentally a matter of sexual practice; it was a matter of control.[41]

If control and dominion were indeed the prime directive of masculinity, then the household codes and household regulations that spill over into directions for ruling the church need to be recognized as prime assertions of masculinity.

One aspect of Williams's work is particularly suggestive for understanding the impact of household code teaching within a house-church setting: the tenuous nature of masculinity. Masculinity needed to be achieved; it did not flow naturally from anatomical sex. The display of even one effeminate trait was enough to compromise the entire performance of masculinity. Boldness and courage in the arena of public life would not be enough to protect the man accused of excessive grooming or a luxurious, self-indulgent life.[42]

The accusation of violation of gender boundaries was a central feature of second-century pagan critique of early Christianity. According to Celsus, early Christianity drew its membership from the inconsequential members of society, including the dishonorable, the stupid, women, and little children. His harsh polemic may include an indirect acknowledgment that (formerly) honorable men are among the group's membership, but he is insistent that adherents display none of the ideals of masculinity: "Moreover, we see that those who display their secret lore in the market-places and go about begging would never enter a gathering of intelligent men, nor would they dare reveal their noble beliefs in their presence; but whenever they see adolescent boys and a crowd of slaves and a company of fools, they push themselves in and show off."[43] With his focus on the meeting places of church groups as "private houses,"[44] Celsus declared early Christianity to be a religion of women's spaces in a manner that is in keeping with the studies of anthropologists of Mediterranean cultures, who have noted that men who are "too much of the house" can be subject to public "shaming" and ridicule.[45] Instead of becoming "men" and following religious practices that properly belong to the honorable public domain of men, the easily duped adolescent boys are lured into a group in which religion has been privatized and feminized and by leaders who "show off." Self-indulgence emerges among Roman writers as a major indicator of effeminacy.[46]

Williams has also explored the importance of the notion of masculine dominion over foreigners and women in Roman ideologies of masculinity. His work raises interesting questions about the gender-stereotyping implications of Roman writers' descriptions of early Christianity as a foreign superstition.[47] Among the most revealing examples cited by Williams concerning the loss of control over women among foreigners is one from Valerius Maximus: "But even more effeminate was the male population of Cyprus, who patiently allowed their queens to climb into their chariots on top of their women's bodies, which were arranged as steps so that they might tread more softly. It would have been better for those men—if they were in fact men—to die than to submit to such a delicate dominion."[48] Williams points to a "conceptual anomaly" in the expression "delicate dominion" (*delicato imperio*). Masculine *imperium* is usually the very opposite of *delicatum*, and therefore, according to Williams, "a *delicatum imperium* is a self-contradictory impossibility, and these men are depicted as gender deviants."[49]

Although it is not usually described in these terms, the notion that early church members were gender deviants may be encoded in the Roman judgment that early Christianity was a "depraved and excessive superstition" (*superstitio prava, immodica*).[50] This was Pliny the Younger's assessment of the group at the beginning of the second century, and he offers it immediately after a reference to the interrogation and torture of two slave women (*ancilla*) whom he called deacons (*ministra*)—the only two individuals singled out for mention in his letter to Emperor Trajan.[51] In drawing attention to some kind of female leadership in the group—to the exclusion of references to male leaders—Pliny was implying that the ideals of masculinity were being compromised. Women were in control. Torture and interrogation were intended to lead them to cede control—a marker of their feminine nature.[52] But Pliny's dismissive remarks suggest that this did not happen. Pliny's silence with respect to the specific content of the women's confessions suggests that they revealed nothing at all. Although it would certainly not suit Pliny's purposes to reveal it, perhaps they displayed the "manly" valor that women were said exceptionally to attain.[53]

While the gendered critique of early Christianity comes from the second century and most likely after the composition of most of the New Testament household codes, there is good reason to believe that such accusations occurred before they became embodied in the texts that come down to us as the first Greco-Roman impressions of the rise of Christianity. This is clearly evident, for example, in 1 Peter, which reveals that the community is being burdened by slanderous rumors (1 Pet. 2:12; 3:15-16) and whose marriage teaching includes the difficult circumstances of marriages between believing women and nonbelieving men (1 Pet. 3:1-6). However, even in the case of a text like Ephesians, in which we do not find explicit evidence of a need to respond to external accusations, it is important to recognize the defensive qualities of the language. The need for a defense of masculinity was such a common social expectation that it would have arisen even if there had been no specific charges brought against the community. As the previous detailed analysis of Eph. 5:22-33 illustrates, both on a symbolic level and in terms of the practical realities of household management in a house-based movement, in many respects this was an *ekklēsia* of women. The wives who acted as perfect reflections of the church and facilitated church functioning in the household, within a society in which masculinity needed to be achieved on an ongoing basis, indeed were required to exercise a delicate dominion (to borrow the expression of Valerius Maximus)—at times exercising their authority in a manner that could never be officially recognized.

The Politics of Marriage at the End of the Second Century

In leaving the behind the world of Ephesians, we need to wait until about the end of the second century CE before we begin to see the same or even more detailed reflection on the meaning of marriage and the significance of the life of wives in early church literature. In chapter 2 we saw clear attempts in the early decades of the second century to distinguish believers from outsiders with respect to marriage and sexual morality. Moreover, the occasional Christian wife is mentioned, but this is usually for behavior that is less than ideal by Christian standards or, as in the case of Justin's Roman matron, admired by Christians but unappreciated by pagans. There is virtually no information about the daily contribution of wives to the church and little theological reflection on the significance of marriage. But by the end of the second century, this begins to change. Although the literature from this era lies just outside the period of house churches, it contains important indirect acknowledgments of the contribution of wives to church groups and the significance of their lives for the formation of Christian identity, shedding light upon earlier material.

We find a fairly positive evaluation of marriage in the writings of Clement of Alexandria, who was inspired partly by a desire to contain ascetic extremism.[54] Clement associates the necessity of marriage with the production of children, and his teaching on the benefits of marriage has much in common with that of the Greek philosophers, whom he cites in tandem with various texts from the Hebrew Bible and the New Testament. Marriage, like celibacy, is a place where one must exhibit self-control. Clement gives very precise instructions on how to do this within matrimony, even to the point of giving advice on when intercourse should be avoided (for example, early in the morning, after coming home from church or from the marketplace).[55] But even under cover of darkness one should not lose sight of the value of restraint. The display of honorable behavior that should characterize relations with one's neighbors should also characterize relations with one's wife: "For if we must practice self-control, as certainly we must, we ought to manifest it even more with our own wives by avoiding indecent embraces, and we should show at home the same trustworthy proof of chastity that we display toward our neighbors."[56]

Marriage is urged upon Christians by Clement as biblically sanctioned, for wives are necessary help (Gen. 2:18). In keeping with the tendency to draw connections between marital harmony and stability of the empire, which is found in much imperial ideology and propaganda, Clement proclaims boldly, "By all means, then, we must marry, both for the sake of our country and for the succession of children and for the completion of the world, in so far as it pertains to us. . . . For if people do not marry and produce children, they contribute to the scarcity of human beings and destroy both the cities and the world that is composed of them."[57] It is the combination of the view of marriage as an opportunity to exercise self-control and an appreciation of the broader significance of marriage for the church and society that leads Clement to the remarkable validation of marriage as a ministry on a par with celibacy:

> Just like celibacy, marriage has its own distinctive services and minis-tries for the Lord; I refer to the care of one's children and wife. The special characteristic of the marital union, it seems, is that it gives the person who is committed to perfect marriage the opportunity to show concern for everything that pertains to the household he shares with his wife. That is why the apostle says that bishops must be appointed who have learned how to supervise the whole church by supervising their households (cf. 1 Tim. 3:4-5). So, then, let each one complete his ministry by the work to which he was called (cf. 1 Cor. 7:24), so that he may be free in Christ and may receive the proper reward for his ministry (cf. 1 Cor. 7:22).[58]

Clement recognizes service to the family as a model for service to the church. His insight is no doubt based, if not on firsthand experience of house churches, then surely on firsthand experience of households as places of Christian formation, where able householders became bishops of communities and whose wives and children (as part of these model house-holds) were embedded in their leadership.

The wife in Clement's thought is a construct of tradition and conven-tion. Drawing upon the scriptural notion of the wife as a necessary help (Gen. 2:18), he illustrates the necessity of marriage by noting the value of a wife in times of physical illness, whose loving care, faithfulness, and sympathy surpass the commitment of even the closest friend.[59] But this partnership is qualified by the most conservative, seemingly outdated sen-timents calling for the seclusion and modesty of wives and linking them exclusively with household life: "If a wife does not adorn and decorate herself beyond what is proper, she will not be subject to slanderous accusa-tions. She should devote herself to constant prayer and avoid leaving the house too often; she should shut herself away as much as possible from the gaze of all but her relatives; she should consider the care of the household as much more profitable than worthless chatter."[60] The reference to worth-less chatter here calls to mind the description of Hermas's wife's sin and, as discussed above, its association with violation of family integrity and purity. From much later, Gregory Nazianzen's fourth-century funeral ora-tion for his sister Gorgonia (*Oration* 8) also offers an interesting point of comparison: Gorgonia is presented as exemplar to her whole household, "acting as a silent exhortation to her house" (*Oration* 8.8; see 1 Pet. 3:1-6). Particularly in the case of Clement of Alexandria, however, in which such teaching occurs in the context of general exhortations concerning the importance of pure and undefiled marriage, one would be tempted to conclude that this conventional language was simply more grist for the patriarchal mill. However, the fact that the inappropriate household behavior of women was clearly the subject of slanderous accusations against Christians in the second century should lead us to suspect that more is going on at the historical level than Clement reveals explicitly. Comparison with Tertullian's writings confirms this impression.

An initial hope that one might find valuable material on the lives of wives in Tertullian's treatise *To His Wife* (*Ad Uxorem*) quickly leads to disappointment. Tertullian, who wrote in North Africa at the end of the second century and in the opening decades of the third, was primarily interested in this work (written between 200 and 206) in ensuring that his wife knew how to act upon his death. While remarriage was not presented as a sin in the treatise, he strongly advised his wife against it.[61] Tertullian's instruction on remarriage certainly is bound up with a sense of what separates Christians from outsiders, no matter how much it may have in common with cultural ideals that placed high regard on women's sexual purity. His thought reflects more than the Roman ideal of the *univira*, in which wives married only once were held in esteem. The woman married more than once—commonplace in the Roman world generally—came progressively to be seen in Tertullian's thought as a representative of all that should be excluded from the Christian fellowship.

In general Tertullian, following Paul's lead, viewed marriage as a means of containing sexual immorality. But his acceptance of marriage was more reserved even than Paul's position on the matter. Citing Paul's famous proclamation in 1 Cor. 7:9, he went one step further in encouraging celibacy: "What sort of good is it, I ask, that is commended only by comparison with an evil, so that the reason why marriage is better is because burning is worse? How much better is it neither to marry nor to burn!"[62] But what Tertullian finds particularly reprehensible is women who, "given the chance to practice continence" on account of divorce or death of a spouse, instead choose not only to remarry but even to remarry pagans—contrary to Paul's teaching in 1 Cor. 7:39, which he understands as allowing remarriage between Christians only.[63]

Whereas Clement associates the ideal Christian wife married to a Christian husband with the house dutifully managed and modestly preserved, Tertullian depicts just the opposite scenario when a Christian woman marries a pagan. Marriage to pagans means wives will be enticed by worldly ornamentation and tainted sexual acts associated with the pagan world. Above all, as a servant of the devil, a pagan husband will do all to thwart the duties of a believing wife. Attempts to attend prayer services will be squelched by plans that the couple should attend the baths that day. Fast days will be met with plans for a banquet. Attempts to go out on church business will be stopped on account of pressing household business. In the following remarkable text, Tertullian presents the duties of a Christian wife in such a manner that should lead us to question Clement's image of the static indoor wife. Believing wives of this era—most likely whether they were married to pagans or not—probably rarely exhibited such conservative virtues. Here Tertullian adopts the perspective of the pagan husband in relation to his Christian wife:

> Who would allow his wife to run around the streets to the houses of strangers and even the poorest hovels in order to visit the faithful? Who would willingly let his wife be taken from his side for nightly meetings, if it be necessary? Who, then, would tolerate without some anxiety her spending the entire night at the paschal solemnities? Who would have no suspicions about letting her attend the Lord's supper, when it has such a bad reputation? Who would endure her creeping into prison to kiss the chains of the martyrs? Or even to greet any of the brothers with a kiss? Or to wash the feet of the saints? To desire this? Even to think about it? If a Christian traveling on a journey should arrive, what hospitality will he find in the house of a stranger? If anyone needs assistance, the granary and pantry are closed.[64]

In this text Tertullian reveals the dangerous duties of the Christian wife. It is a precious source among an abundance of early Christian texts that tell us very little about how Christian wives served the church. We should by no means think that these duties only pertain to wives married to pagans; Tertullian's main point is that the lives of Christian women married to pagans will be especially difficult precisely because these duties and tasks are expected of Christian wives in general. The emphasis on Christian women's visiting various houses—among the rich and the poor—is striking, as is the emphasis on wives' exercising hospitality. Clearly, Christian wives did more than tend the hearth; both in their own homes and in the houses of others they offered service to fellow believers. Specifically with respect to mixed marriage, debate among scholars continues about the extent of marriages between pagan men and Christian women and their influence on the growth of early Christianity.[65] Tertullian clearly is interested in limiting the phenomenon with his harsh warnings against Christian widows and divorcees entering into unions with pagans. But with this text it becomes evident that at the very least Tertullian has thought carefully through the ramifications of the scenario, and it is difficult to avoid the conclusion that he was very familiar with a phenomenon that was quite widespread.

Conclusion:
Both Conventional and Countercultural

In many respects an ancient audience of Jews and Gentiles would have been prepared for the content of Eph. 5:22-33 in the way that a modern audience is prepared for a romantic film. One is familiar with the genre, and one can anticipate much of the script. The literary and visual evidence for viewing the married couple as an expression of social and political ideals is so extensive that we can be confident that people from a variety of social strata were articulators and recipients of the message. Within a house-church setting an audience listening to Eph. 5:22-33 would probably have heard aspects of the familiar combined with aspects of the novel, important messages concerning Christian identity communicated via well-established cultural codes. As has been illustrated above, when one sets out to understand the marriage teaching within the context of the text as a whole, one encounters strong indications that the traditional teaching may mask elements of strong countercultural responses to the world.

All of this, along with the fact that hierarchical conceptions of marriage in the Roman world functioned in conjunction with informal conventions concerning the influence of wives, makes it very difficult to be certain how wives would have been affected by Eph. 5:22-33. The household code was probably addressed to many women who would have been anything but the model *matrona* of elite Greco-Roman literature, whose idealized life underlies these traditional ethical exhortations: slave women, divorced and abandoned women, women disobeying their pagan husbands on account of Christian allegiance. One might argue that the author of Ephesians was setting forth an ideal that very few women in the community could reach and thus creating a hierarchy of women within the church itself. But when one considers the variety of possible circumstances of women in the community, the female personification of the *ekklēsia* as a pure bride remains quite striking. We cannot know whether the "bride of Christ" imagery would have bestowed dignity on women who had very little control over their own bodies and destinies. But the conventional hierarchical marriage teaching should not blind us to this possibility. It is perhaps no accident that when it comes to the concepts of purity, fidelity, and unity, the links with Jewish scripture become especially visible in Eph. 5:22-33, and the connections with the Greco-Roman household topos "concerning household management" become less obvious. It is precisely when the author of Ephesians seeks to set up the *ekklēsia* as opposed to the standards of the world that biblical concepts and points of contact with Jewish literature become most apparent.

To view Eph. 5:22-33 as part of a political strategy of resistance to the dominant social order is not to exonerate the author, however, nor to downplay the significance of the problematic nature of the text in shaping the lives of celibate and married women throughout the ages.[66] But it is nevertheless important to realize that the unnamed wives who are celebrated in this text, and who led perhaps the most conventional lives of all women, may have had a greater significance for the life and identity of church groups than is often realized. By the time Tertullian wrote his treatises, church authors were demonstrating a clear preference for women as ideological constructs of purity and identity rather than for recounting any specific details of their lives. It is somewhat ironic, therefore, that it is Tertullian who provides perhaps the most important evidence for the vital, but largely conventional, work of wives in sustaining early church communities.

The conflicting forces associated with Roman marriage would continue in early church groups, sometimes revealing themselves in new Christian manifestations of familiar gender-based tensions. The fourth-century funeral oration for his sister Gorgonia by Gregory Nazianzen offers a particularly vivid illustration of these conflicting forces in their new Christian form. Gregory portrays both his mother, Nonna, and his sister Gorgonia as emulating the ideal of the silent wife, while he recounts their valiant deeds that undercut the ideal. Gregory's interpretation of Gorgonia's relationship to her husband is particularly striking in this regard, echoing Pauline teaching in 1 Cor. 11:2-16 and Eph. 5:22-33: Gorgonia's respect for her husband as her head did not prevent her from recognizing her first Head. Once her husband was won over, he became her fellow servant rather than an unreasonable master. Even more remarkable is Gregory's lengthy description of his sister's ability to combine the best of both the unmarried and married states, seemingly carrying double and potentially conflicting responsibility for sexual purity (*Oration* 8.8).

CHAPTER SEVEN

WOMEN LEADERS OF HOUSEHOLDS AND CHRISTIAN ASSEMBLIES

In chapter 2 we saw how the idealization of what today we would call the "intact" family influenced not only Greco-Roman thinking about the family but the New Testament texts and further early Christian thinking as well. Here we will attempt to ascertain what actually happened when women were in charge of households and the implications for Christian house churches led by women. The household codes of the New Testament convey to modern readers a rather passive submission of wife to husband, with no suggestion that a wife was expected to take any initiative. Contemporary readers of the household codes, however, would have read them in light of what was expected of a wife in the management of a household. In other words, they would have had a context in both other literature and real life that is lost to the modern reader.

Authority of Women Household Managers

The married woman, the Roman *matrona*, had a surprising amount of authority and autonomy in her own household, and this social reality predates the Christian era. Women managers of their households were expected to be independently responsible and efficient, even though much of the literature wants to suggest that they are under the benevolent supervision and guidance of their husbands. We catch glimpses of this independent functioning of wives in several literary references.

From late Persian or Hellenistic Palestine, "earlier rather than later,"[1] comes the discourse on the wife manager in Prov. 31:10-31. The dating of Proverbs is disputed. The later it is dated, the more likely is the presence of Greek and Hellenistic influence.[2] The text describes in detail the responsibilities of a "Woman of Substance,"[3] the wife manager of a large household. Her efficiency in accomplishing all the expected tasks with ease is obviously idealized, "an unattainable male fantasy of the perfect spouse, who does her husband proud and brings up a clutch of perfectly adorable children while engaged in a daunting range of managerial tasks."[4] Yet the list of her activities reflects real expectations of an elite wife householder. She sees to provisions and the care of everyone in the household. She purchases necessary materials, secures wool and flax, spins and weaves clothing, provides food, supervises the work of the slaves, buys fields, plants vineyards, sells the produce of the household, including linen garments, and sees to distribution of goods to the poor and needy. For all this her children and her husband call her blessed.

The earlier and more traditional interpretation of the passage has been to see the woman as an incarnation of Wisdom. Only in modern times has the text been approached as a datum of social history. Either way, the description of her activities, while idealized, is based on the reality of elite women's responsibilities in household management. Here is the image of a household manager who acts totally independently of her husband in the management of the household, while he busies himself with civic affairs outside the house, at the city gate. This idealized description reveals both the gendered division of labor and the independent management expected of a wife householder. She is not confined to the house, as will be the case in later Greek idealization, for she directs agricultural activity of the family and carries on its business; yet her domain is domestic in the broadest sense, for she is not engaged in political activities, which belong to the world of men. The traditional public-private division at the core of Mediterranean life is interpreted in different ways in different situations. Here it is interpreted very loosely, yet remains part of the male idealization. The passage from Proverbs, though different in genre from what follows, is not dissimilar in content.

Late classical and Hellenistic discussions of household management also sometimes include a surprising amount of detail about a wife's expected duties, for example, Xenophon's *Oeconomicus* from late classical Greece, which we know was read in the Roman period by such figures as Cicero, Philodemus, and Galen. In the text Socrates, in conversation with Xenophon, sees husband and wife acting as partners (*koinōnoi*) in the household. Property comes in largely through the husband's activity and is dispersed through the wife's activity, so that she contributes an equally important (*antirropon*) service toward its success. Both are fully responsible for the prosperity of the estate. Socrates defers to Aspasia, legendary mistress of Pericles, and offers to introduce Xenophon to her, because, knowing it all from a woman's point of view, she will be able to explain it all better than he can (3.14–16).[5]

Later in the *Oeconomicus*, Socrates engages in conversation with Isomachus about the proper training of his fifteen-year-old wife for her duties. The usual age disparity between husbands and wives at first marriage is reflected here and probably did not differ greatly from what is known from epigraphical evidence of the Roman period: girls being twelve to eighteen at first marriage, boys twenty-five to thirty, and older men frequently in second or third marriages to younger girls.[6] The more elite the family, the younger the bride is likely to be, since among elites, a girl's value lies more in the politically advantageous marriage for which she is the instrument than in her labor. Using the conventional argument that the creator destined men for the outdoor life, women for the indoor, Xenophon compares the wife's duties to those of the queen bee in a hive but then goes on to specify what her responsibilities are: supervision of all comings and goings in the house, protection and distribution of supplies, supervision of weaving and food production, care of sick slaves, instruction of slaves in household skills, rewarding and punishing slaves, in short, independent management of an entire household (7.36–43). She is to be the guardian of its laws, like a military commander, a city councilor, or a queen, rewarding the good with praise and honor, meting out punishment where deserved (9.15).

The shy young girl of course protests that she feels overwhelmed by it all, and the husband patronizingly encourages her. The young age of the girl is not unrealistic, and it is not difficult to imagine the trauma of such a girl, well trained though she might be by her mother at home, suddenly leaving that home as the wife of a man she may hardly have met, with whom she has had her first sexual relationship but as yet no adequate personal relationship. She must step immediately into the role of authoritative manager of a considerable household economy, supposedly in charge of experienced household slaves much older than she. It must have made for some very difficult personal dynamics.

The gist of the whole discussion in the *Oeconomicus* reflects the patriarchal assumptions of author and reader that the wife will only be as good as the husband teaches her to be. Here the literary convention and the premise of a young wife's needing instruction preserve for us what wives and other women who managed households really did and were expected to do on their own initiative. Of course, many women entered second and third marriages not so young and inexperienced, and quite used to independent management of their households.

Pseudo-Aristotle's *Oeconomica* Book One, the work of an unknown Greek author probably of the late classical or early Hellenistic period, likewise assumes a patronizing, all-knowledgeable husband who must educate his young wife. The work is briefer and far less detailed than Xenophon's treatise. It begins with the traditional comparison of household management to political administration. Whereas the state is ruled by various components, the rule of the household is one. The household is composed of persons and material objects (1.1–2). Among persons, the wife has pride of place as the one with whom the householder will live and raise up legitimate children. Nature dictates that the man is destined for action outside the house, the woman for quiet indoor tasks that guard the household (1.3). The first responsibility of the husband toward his wife is to do her no wrong, which includes marital fidelity (1.4). Husband and wife together keep watch over the whole household in partnership (*koinōnia, societas*), especially the slaves, together setting good example by their own leadership.

Book Three[7] is entirely about the relationship of husband and wife and the duties of the managerial wife in the household. The good wife rules her home (*dominari*), controlling everything that happens within it, all within the limits and approval set by her husband, of course, but she is primarily responsible, for it is inappropriate (*indecens*) that he should know everything that happens in the house (3.1). Again, a husband's fidelity to and just treatment of his wife will be the inspiring motivation for her loyalty and fidelity (3.2). Together they will give appropriate honor to each other's parents and appropriate attention to the raising of their children (3.3). The public-private difference is again reinforced. While the husband is general supervisor, he entrusts the running of the household entirely to

his wife. He is occupied with public life and should not even know everything about the management of the household, for this would compromise
his public image and role.

The Pythagorean collection contains fragments and whole letters supposedly written by five philosopher women, some treatises on philosophy
and mathematics, and others letters of advice to other women. The texts
are of uncertain date, anywhere from the fourth century BCE to the second
century CE. They are ascribed to illustrious known-earlier Pythagorean
women: Theano, wife of Pythagoras; Myia, his daughter; and even Perictione, Plato's mother. Whether these treatises and letters were actually
written by women is much debated and in fact doubtful in the case of
most. Yet it is known that later Pythagoreans took names of earlier revered
figures, so it is not out of the question that later women bearing these
names may have had a part in the authorship.[8]

In general, the conservative male perspective is represented in the letters, but there is an interesting reversal from what we have seen. A string
of Hellenistic and Roman treatises on household management written by
men and directed to the husband specify that the best way to secure his
wife's loyalty and fidelity is for him also to be faithful to her.[9] This position
is echoed later by Christian writers, even if the double standard continues
and is acknowledged as such.[10] Yet in the Pythagorean letters purportedly
written by women to other women, the double standard is expressly tolerated. Marital infidelity is allowed to men, but not to women. The treatise of Perictione, *On Feminine Harmony* 3, supposedly extracted from a
book on the subject, warns the female reader to avoid illegitimate passions
that would alienate her not only from husband but also from children and
household personnel. Such conduct will destroy everything that husband
and wife hold in common, because she will invent subterfuges to conceal
her actions. After inveighing against too much care for personal appearance, the author reminds the reader that after the gods, parents are to be
given the greatest respect and honor (an interesting aside somewhat out
of context, but revealing of the networks of familial relationships in the
Greco-Roman family). The wife must remain steadfast with her husband,
even in reversal of fortune and even if, through weakness or drunkenness,
he consorts with other women. "Such a failing is pardonable to men, but
not to women," so she should accommodate this custom.[11]

The Letter of Theano to Nicostrate echoes the same themes. It begins,
"I have heard of your husband's indiscretion, that he has taken up with a

courtesan, and you suffer from jealousy." The wife's role is not to spy on her husband, but to be his indulgent companion and put up with his indiscretion. It means that the courtesan is ruling him, not the other way around. What he does with a courtesan, he does from passion; what he does with his wife, he does for mutual advantage (*pros to sympheron*). She will do well to continue in docile fidelity, governing her house and treating her children well.[12]

This explicit tolerance of the double standard, not sanctioned in many male discussions of household management, may be one of the best indications that the letters are really written by men, who resorted to pseudepigraphy to preserve it. However, the whole idea of letters written by women for the instruction of other women,[13] whether the letters are authentically so or not, reveals that such activity of educated women was not surprising, especially on the part of Pythagoreans, who attempted the closest thing to sexual equality that we know from Mediterranean antiquity.

Beyond this discrepancy, the Pythagorean Letters continue to address the role of the wife as mistress of the house. The treatise of Phyntis, *On the Modesty [sōphrosynē] of Women*, asserts that, while the chief virtue of a woman is modesty and her main occupation to manage her house, stay home, and please her husband, nevertheless wife and husband share certain qualities: courage, justice, and temperance (*andreia, dikaiosynē,* and *phronēsis*). The man is called on to manifest courage more, the woman more often temperance, yet they must both possess these qualities.[14] Theano's Letter to Eubula discusses details of child raising with no mention of paternal intervention. Her Letter to Callisto seems to echo Xenophon's picture of the young wife, as it asserts that by virtue of marriage lawful authority is given to young women to rule (*archein*) their households and, in first place, the domestic servants. In this task she must in every case maintain her own dignity and authority. Some women in this position are skinflints who try to exact ever more from their slaves and give them ever less of what they need. This profits nothing in the long run. At the same time, it is necessary to maintain discipline, to punish justly when necessary, but not with excessive cruelty, which exhausts slaves and inspires them to seek release either by running away or by suicide. But if excessive resistance persists, such a slave must be sold. Both the mistress of the house and the discipline maintained within it should be like the stringed instrument that is out of tune when too loose and breaks when too tight.[15]

Similar pieces of advice can be found in many Greco-Roman authors, male to male. Many philosophers and householders were sufficiently astute to know that pushing too far the people upon whose labor your comfort and even survival depends will pay decreasing dividends (see even, for example, Col. 4:1; Eph. 6:9). But the fact that here this advice is represented, whether authentically or not, as coming from women and addressed to women is another demonstration that the woman manager of the household had full authority over the material and human resources of the household, the *oikos* or *familia*, and was expected to administer those resources wisely.

The Roman Stoic Musonius Rufus (first century CE) asks whether women should study philosophy, after having clarified that men and women have the same virtue and both need to acquire virtue. He answers that the woman who studies philosophy will be better equipped to be a good manager (*oikonomikē*) and accountant (*eklogistikē*) of the household and ruler (*archikē*) of its slaves (frag. 3).[16] The conventions surrounding

Fig. 7.1: Women reclining and sitting at a banquet, surrounded by female assistants. Mosaic from the Tomb of Mnemosyne; portrayal of the woman buried there or a mythological scene. Antioch. Fourth century CE. Worcester Art Museum.

weddings suggest the same, for marriage poetry portrayed the woman's role as guardian of the house.[17]

Philo, following the tradition of Hellenistic discussions of household management, says that there are two kinds of *polis*, or social entity: the greater one is the city, managed by men (*politeia*), the lesser one the household, managed by women (*oikonomia*) (*Spec. leg.* 3.170). In both cases, the managers exercise *prostasia* or position of authority. Such statements echo the philosophical commonplace that the household is the micro version of the state, but not all acknowledge women's control of one of them.

In Plutarch's treatise on marriage, the husband is of course leader and initiator, in keeping with patriarchal ideals, but the wife is several times called mistress of the household (*oikodespoinē*) in contexts that are not about her household management and thus do not require the title. This would seem to indicate that it was a recognized way of referring to a wife (*Advice to the Bride and Groom* 140C, 141D, 141F, 142B).

Plutarch also asks why a man returning from abroad sends a message ahead to let his wife know he is coming (*Roman Questions* 9). He gives several answers. First, it is a question of confidence: if he arrived unannounced, he would give the impression that he doesn't trust her. He also wants to hear news from home and wants to hear that his wife is longing for him. But also, in his absence, says Plutarch, the wife has had more household hassles to deal with, and the advance warning gives her time to settle everything so that his arrival will be pleasant. In this husband-centered discussion, we can read between the lines that a wife often got quite used to running the household without interference from her husband and no doubt carried on essentially the same, with or without him. He, of course, wants to know that she is longing for his return. But we do not know that she really is.

From earliest discussions of the wife's role in household management, she was expected to take part in the labor of the house, not just supervise. The woman manager in Proverbs 31 spins wool and flax with her own hands and rises before dawn to organize preparation of food and the work of the slaves (v. 13, 15). Athenaeus of Attalia (mid-first century) writes that wives should imitate the action and simplicity of the servants for better health; in other words, they should get some exercise by working.[18] The idealized Roman *matrona* was one who not only maintained her virtue but also spun and wove the cloth for clothing the household. Musonius Rufus says that the woman who studies philosophy will be energetic and strong, nurse her own children, and be willing to do what is thought of as slaves' work (frag. 3).[19] Because all of this literature is written from the perspective of male idealization, it is surprising how much responsibility is expected of wives: total management of household resources, personnel, and production—quite a different picture from the passive image of the wife in the New Testament household codes. This literature gives us insight into how wives and hence widows were perfectly used to being independent household managers and how men expected them to be just that.

This expectation that women are the managers of their household is picked up in passing in Christian literature, first in 1 Tim. 5:14, in which younger widows are to remarry and rule their households (*oikodespotein*), then in Titus 2:4-5, in which older women are to teach younger women domestic virtue: to love their husbands and children, to be submissive to their husbands, but also to be good household managers (*oikourgous agathas*). Later Christian writers picked up the same themes. John Chrysostom, for example, echoes the "men in the forum, women in the house" commonplace, then admits that women know more than men about household affairs and have their own opinions about them. Wives manage all of these things so husbands do not have to. A wife, Chrysostom says, "takes care of all the other tasks that a man could not undertake appropriately or easily, even if he were determined to try ten thousand times."[20] This constant theme tells us that, in spite of a veneer of male supervision in the household, it was really a system run by women. The household was women's space.

Mistress and Slaves

We cannot read this literature without asking questions about the relationship of this female household manager to the household slaves. We have seen that enlightened philosophical perspectives recognized that motivating slaves to obey out of loyalty was far better than forcing them through cruelty and fear. The ideal *matrona* led by example as much as by word. Yet her authority had to be clearly acknowledged and followed, even by slaves older and more experienced than she.

We can only speculate about the mistress-slave relationship in a Christian household, or one in which at least the mistress was Christian.[21] The question is part of a larger one about how if at all Christian faith made a difference in these relationships. Because women, some of them freedwomen who had once been slaves themselves, also owned slaves, New Testament admonitions to "masters" about the treatment of their slaves must also be understood to apply to women slave owners. Likewise, exhortations to slaves, whether female or male, to obey their "masters" must also be understood as instruction to obey their mistresses. The frequent warning that slaves should not think of themselves as on equal footing with their owners because of their baptismal status could not have arisen from sheer speculation that perhaps some slaves might get the idea (1 Tim. 6:2-3; Titus 2:9-10; Ignatius, *Pol.* 4.3). Indeed, some slaves must have been taking seriously what they were told about the dignity conferred upon them in baptism. Already the stage was set for social change that would in fact not happen for centuries.

It is difficult for us to imagine how women slaveholders could live on intimate terms with their female slaves, who bathed them, set their hair, adorned them with their jewels, cooked their food, washed their clothes, suckled their newborns, and raised their children, and not feel some solidarity with them against the male world of politics and authority. But the sources are silent on this point. It does not seem that any union of common experience or purpose was formed on the basis of sex that traversed the lines of legal and social status. If indeed it was so, the stories are lost to us in the oral world of antiquity.

Did Christianity make any difference here? Would belonging to the same house church have created a new bond? Again, the sources are silent. The two early Christian narratives in which female slaves feature are the story of Blandina in the account of the martyrs of Lyons and Vienne and of Felicitas in that of Perpetua and Felicitas. In the former, Blandina the slave has a Christian mistress who is arrested with her; her only recorded concern is whether Blandina will be strong enough to endure (Eusebius, *Hist. eccl.* 5.1.17). In spite of the persistent popular idea that the slave Felicitas was the slave of Perpetua, there is no suggestion of this connection in the *Acts*, and the two have little to do with one another in the story, with one touching exception.

Toward the end of the account, both young women are put together in the arena in nets, to be tossed by a wild heifer. When Perpetua sees that Felicitas is down, she raises her up, and, in an intriguing statement, *ambae pariter steterunt* ("They both stood together," chap. 20). One wonders whether the author intended to convey more with these words than a simple statement of their bodily positions. Perpetua, who has been the central character throughout the narrative, acts here consistently with her status, taking the initiative as she has throughout the story. But perhaps the author knew more than we suspect and was telling of a solidarity that had grown between the two women of unequal social status who stood together as equals to face death. Perhaps, too, that is why, in spite of the discrepancy in the importance of the two women in the narrative, their *Acts* came to be known by their two names rather than that of Perpetua alone.

Women Managing Households for Themselves

Not every household had an ultimate male source of authority, in spite of the presumption in this regard in the literature. The material presented above demonstrates not only that married women were quite capable of running entire households by themselves, but also that they were accustomed to doing so. In the case of an experienced woman household manager, the presence or lack of a man in the house probably changed very little the way the household was conducted.

Students of Roman social history are familiar with the term *paterfamilias*, often used and often misused in modern discussions. Richard Saller has shown that the term was used in ancient sources in reference to the head of household as property owner, but not in regard to his relationships to other free persons. A *paterfamilias* was a male citizen *sui iuris*, that is, not in the *potestas* of another male. The term is used in legal texts only as property owner, with no necessary connotations of familial relationships. He is a *paterfamilias* who has *potestas* over children (and wife in *manus*), slaves, and family property. But he does not have to have wife or children to be a *paterfamilias*; he only has to have property.

The similar term *materfamilias* is not parallel to *paterfamilias*. The jurists did not agree on its meaning, some thinking it had to do with maternity, others with chastity and personal female honor,[22] in other words, with virtue and personal qualities. Its meaning seems close to the social connotations of "matron." Only Ulpian among the jurists tried to understand the word as referring to "a woman independent of the *potestas* of her father and with a capacity to own property" (*Digest* 1.6.4), in an attempt to have a parallel female word to the male word *paterfamilias* designating one capable of independent property ownership. But even Ulpian, when attempting a formal definition, fell back on honor, concluding that what really makes a *materfamilias* is not birth or marital status but "good character."²³ The term is therefore more a social than a legal one and does not carry the same connotations as *paterfamilias*. In spite of Ulpian's best efforts, there was no clear common way in language or in law to designate female property owners.

A woman *sui iuris*, that is, not in the *potestas* of father or husband, also owned property and slaves. Saller notes that "it is essential to remember (as some social historians have not) that female property owners are subsumed in many categorical legal discussions cast in terms of the *paterfamilias*."²⁴ In other words, just as a slave "master" must sometimes be understood to be a woman, so, too, sometimes a *paterfamilias* is a woman.

The evidence for women property owners and slave owners is clear in both literature and inscriptions. But this is not the same thing as a woman managing her household on her own, for it was quite common for women property owners to bring their property into a marriage and continue to administer it independently or, in the case of domestic slaves and household objects, jointly. Slaves in a combined marital household could belong to either husband or wife, yet the wife was expected to manage the unified household as if all were common property. One can easily see how this arrangement was a setup for the ability of clever household personnel to play off the authority of the mistress of the house against what was in theory the superior authority of her husband. Many a slave belonging to the husband, especially if he was of higher social status, may not have taken well to being commanded by the *domina* of the household, especially if she was very young or not from a very prominent family. This situation would compound the challenges to a new wife.

Beyond this double arrangement in households in which husbands were alive, however, the evidence for women, usually widows managing their own households in the absence of husbands, is indirect but persistent. Cornelia, mother of the Gracchi, was known to have remained a widow and refused a second marriage in order to raise her twelve children, of whom only three survived. Plutarch attributes to her an education of her children more influential than nature (*Life of Tiberius Gracchus* 1.4).

Valerius Maximus (2.6.8) tells a story of "assisted suicide," about a noble woman in the town of Iulis, on the island of Kea. A woman over ninety years of age formally gathered her family, which consisted of two daughters and seven grandchildren. She invited Sextus Pompeius, son of Pompey the Great, who was on his way to Asia, and made a great fanfare of his presence at her demise. He arrived, gave a speech urging her not to die, but then attended her death. After a libation to Mercury, she drank poison, surrounded by her family, and described the increasing numbness of her limbs in a manner reminiscent of the death of Socrates. One of her daughters closed her eyes. There is no mention of any male relative even present, and even Sextus Pompeius did not consider himself authorized to prevent her.

Ummidia Quadratilla presided over a household in which the grandson of Pliny the Younger was living for a while. Pliny (*Ep.* 7.24) described her lifestyle as "pleasure-loving" and did not approve of her choices of in-house entertainment by mimes, but neither he nor anyone else seemed able to control her. Pliny contented himself with the assurance that the boy was shielded from it by being forbidden to attend the dinner parties in which the objectionable entertainment took place.[25] Matidia, great-aunt of Marcus Aurelius, had a household outside Rome in which the emperor's daughters were staying in the year 161, according to Cornelius Fronto (1.301). Catullus (27) refers to attendance at a dissolute banquet presided over by one Postumia, whom he calls *magistra*. She seems to be "calling the shots," as we would say. Philostratus twice alludes to a mother taking over the household upon the death of her husband (*De gymnastica* 2. 23; 272.30–31).[26] A woman named Hiereis invites guests to a banquet in the Serapeum of Alexandria; it is unlikely that she would do this were she not the extender of hospitality.[27]

There are a number of surviving papyri in which a woman registers on the tax list her own house and family as her property.[28] Especially interesting is P.Wisc. 72, from a soldier named Caecilius Gemellus to a woman named Didymarion, whom he addresses as sister and lady (*kyria*). It would not be unusual for a husband to refer formally to his wife as sister and lady, but what he writes in the final lines (23–29) is unlikely to be to his own wife: "Greet all of your people and all those in your household [*oikos*]."[29] He would never refer to his own household as hers. Didymarion could be his sibling or other relative. What is clear is that she is head of her own household; compare especially Ignatius, *Smyrn.* 13:2 ("I greet the house [*oikos*] of Tavia"). A possible exception is Ignatius, *Pol.* 8.2 ("I greet everyone by name, and [she who belongs to] Epitropos, with her whole household [*oikos*] and her children"). If Epitropos is a proper name and a living husband (not ex-husband or father, both of which are possible), it must mean that she is Christian and functioning rather freely, while her husband is not. Probably most if not all of these women are to be understood as widows. Besides the examples listed above, there are many probable others, for example, tax records from Egypt in which women pay property taxes for themselves.[30]

Christian Women Who Host House Churches

These portraits of women's activities in the management of their houses give us some glimpses and perspectives with which to approach the activities of women in house churches in early Christianity. The examples furnish the backdrop for what we read in the New Testament and early Christian literature, texts that also supply some of the best references to women managing their own households in the ancient Greco-Roman world.

The mother of John Mark in Jerusalem has a household in which a good number (*hikanoi*) of the believing community are gathered in nocturnal prayer, expecting to hear in the morning that the imprisoned Peter had been executed. Instead, as the story goes, Peter is miraculously freed from prison and in the middle of the night goes straight to Mary's house, where the slave Rhoda leaves him standing at the door in her confusion (Acts 12:12-17). The narrative indicates that Mary's house is the recognized center of activity for the community and the natural place where they would assemble in time of crisis. Moreover, Peter knows exactly where to go to find members of the community awake and assembled, or, in another scenario, he doesn't know they are there, but out on the street in the middle of the night, where will he go? Mary's house is the obvious answer. It is even possible that Luke wishes to infer that since Peter is not from the city, she is providing hospitality to him and many others from Galilee. In this case, Peter, released from prison, is heading to his home away from home.

Lydia the purple merchant of Philippi has her own household (*ho oikos autēs*), all of whose members receive baptism with her together.[31] This kind of communal solidarity in conversion occurs rarely in the Pauline letters (for example, the household of Stephanas baptized by Paul, 1 Cor. 1:16), but is narrated elsewhere in Acts (10:44-48, of the household of Cornelius in Caesarea; 16:33, of the anonymous jailer's household in Philippi). The complete loyalty of the household to its head, even to the extent of accepting a new religious allegiance, is perhaps Luke's ideal, and it conforms to the classic ideology of the subordinate household fully obedient to its head. Implicitly, therefore, the authority of the head of household over slaves extends even to their religious practices, something that otherwise does not seem generally to have been the case. Slaves belonged to various private cults and *collegia* seemingly with no intervention on the part of their owners. Other Christian texts suggest that conversion of subordinate members of households did not happen all at once, but was more individualized (for example, 1 Cor. 7:12-16, 21-24; 1 Pet. 3:1).[32] Paul and Silas accept hospitality at Lydia's insistence for an indefinite period, so that her house becomes the center of evangelization and instruction as well as ritual celebration. Later, when the difficulty that led to their imprisonment makes it expedient for them to leave, they do not do so without first meeting in Lydia's house with "the brothers and sisters," that is, all who had become part of the house-church assembly that met there regularly (Acts 16:14-15, 40).

Nympha in Colossae hosts an *ekklēsia* in her house (Col. 4:15). The authorship and therefore the authenticity of references in Colossians are disputed, but it is difficult to understand why a later author would fabricate this reference, since it goes so against the very household order he had earlier advocated (Col. 3:18-19).[33] Tavia in Smyrna has an *oikos* to whom Ignatius sends greetings (Ignatius, *Smyrn.* 13.2). Tryphaena in the *Acts of [Paul and] Thecla* heads her own household. All of these passages are definite allusions to women who have at least no *believing* husband or other male with authority in the house, and it is difficult to imagine a woman hosting regular meetings of a house church with an unbelieving husband in residence. Tertullian reminds us of the difficulties faced by a believing wife of an unbeliever (*To His Wife* 2.4–6). By Tertullian's day the church was probably no longer meeting in private houses, so he does not even entertain the idea of a Christian wife hosting a house church if her husband is not a believer, but the difficulties he describes were not less, and probably more, relevant in earlier years.

Other possibilities for women running their own households include the independently traveling Phoebe (Rom. 16:1-2), who is also *diakonos*, some kind of recognized local ministry, and *prostatis*, a term of authority at least in the patronage system.[34] It is not out of the question that she also had a husband at home, though this does not seem likely. Another possibility is Grapte in Herm. *Vis.* 2.4.3, who seems to conduct a center of instruction for widows and orphans. If Euodia and Syntyche are significant leaders of the church in Philippi, as seems likely, they may also each be leaders and hostesses of a house church (Phil. 4:2-3).[35] The widows of 1 Tim. 5:9-10, who must show certain qualifications to be enrolled, and the widows of other texts in which they are encouraged not to remarry could have remained in the house of a son or other male relative. If not, they surely managed their own houses, which is more likely if they were expected to take the initiative to show hospitality to visiting Christians and perform works of charity (1 Tim. 5:10).

Presiding at Meals

The commonly held scholarly opinion is that the earliest traditions would allow women to be present at meals with men only in intimate family circles and even then, if men reclined, women sat next to their couch. More formal occasions would necessitate either the complete absence of women or their accommodation in separate dining rooms. The more official and public an event, the more likely that traditional customs would hold sway. Thus Valerius Maximus early in the first century CE tells us that the traditional Roman way of dining is for women to be seated next to their husbands' couches but that Roman women were now reclining at banquets alongside their husbands (2.1.2). Several generations earlier, Cornelius Nepos included among his reasons for the superiority of Romans over Greeks that among the Greeks, women are segregated, not taken to dinner parties, and kept in the inner recesses of the house, whereas Roman women participate in dinner parties with their husbands and appear in public, with no shame attached to this behavior (*Preface* 6–7).[36] At approximately the same time, however, Livia, who is reported to have reclined next to Augustus at their wedding in the new way, still gave separate banquets for women when Augustus gave his banquets to celebrate important occasions and military victories (Dio Cassius, *Roman History* 48.44.3; 55.2.4, 8.2; 57.12.5).

Most of the evidence suggests that by the imperial period, married women were attending meals alongside men, in one way or another. There does seem to have been more of a tendency to separate women from male company in Eastern meal customs as opposed to Western, but perhaps we are reading the evidence too strongly through the biased view of Cornelius Nepos. By the early first century, regional variances may have made little difference, at least in more elite circles, because of the pervasiveness of Roman customs and desires to imitate them.

Despite the assumption that by the first century Romans in Italy would have fully accepted the presumably newer customs of integrated couches, some house layouts in Pompeii feature two rooms side by side, both of which would seem, by everything we know, to be intended as dining rooms. These are sometimes interpreted as sexually segregated dining facilities, but the physical remains do not indicate one way or another, and interpreters are thrown back on the literary evidence.[37]

The received wisdom, based on Valerius Maximus and Cornelius Nepos, has been that the full participation of respectable wives with their husbands in public activities and dinner parties, and specifically reclining with them at dinner, was a newly introduced custom in Roman gatherings around the turn of the era. This view has recently been questioned by Matthew Roller, who argues that from considerably earlier days, women reclined with their husbands in practice, signifying a licit sexual connection. But the artistic convention of the virtuous woman who does not recline remained in public consciousness, especially among subelites, so that women who wanted to symbolize sexual propriety were often portrayed sitting.[38] This would explain the depiction of women sitting alongside their reclining men, as represented in many late funerary monuments, and even in some of the late third- and early fourth-century catacomb meal scenes like those at the Catacomb of Pietro and Marcellino discussed in chapter 8. In these later periods we can be fairly certain that the seating custom pictured there, of women sitting alongside reclining men, was no longer the norm.

The depiction, then, of the seated female figures alongside men on couches probably says more about social symbols than about actual practice. If this is true, then at least by the time of the New Testament, if not certainly earlier, in actual practice married women would have reclined at formal banquets alongside their husbands. Would the same be true of widows like the elite Ummidia Quadratilla or Matidia when they hosted dinners for guests in their own house, complete with the entertainment of which Pliny disapproved? What about subelites? If reclining was the position of free status and leisure, it is difficult to imagine that a seated woman alongside a couch of reclining men could exercise the position of hosting and leadership.

We do not know for sure if participants in the common weekly meal in house churches reclined or sat. Reclining was the formal and festive position. Depictions of seated banqueters probably reflect one of three contexts: old-fashioned simplicity, less formality, or a lower-class context such as a *caupona* or tavern.[39] The second two reasons are unlikely in the case of the Christian assembly, while the first is possible. If women who hosted house churches did so on their own authority, and if reclining was the position of participants in the *ekklēsia*, then women must have reclined with men, including the woman leader in the case in which the assembly met in a woman's house. If the position of all was sitting, then a woman leader would also sit. The host of the meal would have been the ordinary leader of any toasts that took place and, in Christian groups, of the special blessing and sharing of bread and cup with ritual words toward the end of the eating portion of the meal.

Paul's concern in the well-known passage in 1 Cor. 11:17-34 is for the quality of the social and ecclesial dimensions of the meal and says nothing about qualifications for leadership. To be sure, there are recognized leaders in every community (1 Cor. 12:28; Phil. 1:1; 1 Thess. 5:12-13). Their sex is not specified in the generic masculine plurals used in these texts. Only with Ignatius in the early years of the second century—for the first time—is there any concern expressed about when and where a true Eucharist is celebrated. Ignatius's model of church leadership requires the knowledge and consent—though not necessarily the presence—of the *episkopos* (Ignatius, *Smyrn.* 8.1). By this point the *episkopos* is unlikely to be a woman, though among the earlier *episkopoi* in Philippi (Phil. 1:1), there could well have been women leaders of house churches, especially Euodia and Syntyche (Phil. 4:2).

The order of the meal must have followed that of the familiar banquet or symposium, with eating first, followed by either entertainment or philosophical discussion. The reading of Scripture and of apostles' letters, followed by preaching or discussion or both, must have replaced this part of the ordinary banquet. This order is of course the reverse of the celebration of Eucharist today, where the service of word precedes that of the table. The change of order probably happened sometime in the second century, when the ritual became detached from a real meal in a private house, in favor of a more formal assembly in a hall.[40]

It is clear from the earliest years that there is no particular anxiety about the qualifications of leaders of the ritual meals. The same cannot be said for the qualifications of teachers. Leadership of the assembly in the role of host is not necessarily the same as the role of teacher. The banquet tradition of turning to others (for example, philosophers) to speak after the meal lent itself quite naturally to having someone other than the host lead the second part of the assembly order, the reading and reflection on written texts. Here a trained person with the skills of a reader was required, someone who would read the texts aloud with interpretation (performance cues to the reader sometimes appear in the texts, for example, Matt. 24:15; Mark 13:14; Rev. 1:3). Then the teacher would have taken over, reflecting aloud on the meaning of what was just read, with exhortation and spiritual guidance about living a way of life to which they had committed themselves. Great care was given to the selection of persons for this leadership of teaching.

Women had always been, and continued to be, the most important teachers of other women.[41] But some women were recognized as teachers of mixed groups. Prisca along with her husband, Aquila, instructed Apollos, though presumably in private (Acts 18:26). The author of Revelation acknowledges the effectiveness of the teaching of a woman prophet at Thyatira, whose name is unknown to us because her attacker speaks of her only with the dubbed name "Jezebel," whom he threatens with violent language (Rev. 2:20-23). Irenaeus preserves the name of the "heretical" teacher Marcellina, whom he grudgingly admits to be very powerful ("She destroyed many" [*Against Heresies* 1.25.6]). The Montanist women prophet-teachers of the late second century, Maximilla, Prisc(ill)a, and later Quintilla, are well-known. There seems to have been a pattern of preserving the names of teachers, both female and male, with whom a certain writer disagreed, but less care is taken to record the names of teachers with whom one is in agreement. A few later Christian women of the fourth century and beyond were given the title of teacher.[42] We do not know the full extent of the ministry of women of the Pauline churches such as Euodia and Syntyche (Phil. 4:2), Phoebe, Maria, and Junia (Rom. 16:1, 6, 7), or Nympha (Col. 4:15). Undoubtedly, there were many more whose names have not been preserved. Resistance to women in this magisterial position of authority in a mixed assembly soon arose (most notably and explicitly, 1 Tim. 2:11-15, but also possibly 1 Cor. 14:34-36), due to traditional norms that sought to silence women in public functions. Women with the gift of teaching must certainly have been active in the earliest communities, yet they may have met with obstacles to the exercise of their gifts from the beginning. This in no way detracts from their recognized leadership of meals hosted in their house. The two functions of presiding and teaching were seen as distinct, probably until some time in the second century, when the model of the teaching presbyter bishop developed.

Conclusion:
What We Know about Women Leaders

Women were expected to independently manage their households, with or without a husband. Therefore, to step into a Christian house church was to step into women's world. This was true even when the leader of the assembly was male. Further, it can be established that women, probably for the most part widows who had autonomous administration of their own households, hosted house churches of the early Christian movement. This fact in itself does not necessarily mean that they had leadership in teaching or other spiritual responsibilities. That conclusion, however, might be inferred from several cultural patterns. First, it was normal procedure for the person in whose house a group met to dine, to preside, to select the menu and the entertainment that followed the meal, and to facilitate conversation, philosophical or otherwise. The entertainment could take a number of forms, and here an invited expert could be brought in, a philosopher or wisdom figure for the edification of attendees.

In Christian assemblies the reading of Scripture and teaching no doubt took place at this point. In the case of both women and men hosts, it would not be out of the ordinary for a recognized teacher who was not the presider at the meal to speak. Second, as we have seen, women were expected to be in complete management of their households without male interference. Third, contrary to some older scholarship, the civic leadership of women in positions of political appointment by the early Roman period was not uncommon.[43] Fourth, women both retained administration of their property and were actively engaged in businesses on their own and thus had funds at their disposal. Based on all these factors, it is safe to say that those texts that seem to indicate women hosting Christian house churches mean just that.[44]

CHAPTER EIGHT

WOMEN LEADERS
IN FAMILY FUNERARY BANQUETS

JANET H. TULLOCH

▣▣ ▣▣ ▣▣

During the last twenty years scholars working in the area of women and
early Christianity have increasingly turned their attention to visual
and material culture to augment their understanding of the New Testament and Late Antique worlds. In the search for evidence of women's
roles in the early church, artifactual data (primarily frescoes, mosaics, and
tableware) can provide supplemental or even alternative representations of
the past to those offered by ancient texts.

What has captured the historian's interest is a set of frescoes (wall paintings) located in the underground funerary district outside the old city of
Rome in a catacomb known as SS. Marcellino e Pietro, hereafter referred
to as Marcellino and Pietro. These frescoes depict eight banquet scenes
with painted inscriptions created some time around the late third or early
fourth century for the burial chambers of wealthy Roman Christians. The
banquet scenes have always been important to early Christian art historians and archaeologists because, for paintings that are approximately seventeen hundred years old, they are well preserved and demonstrate a kind of
Roman Christian hybrid in the history of early Christian art.

Recent attention to these scenes, which depict female figures raising cups, has been piqued not so much by the aesthetic gaze of the art theorist but by the historian's question: What, if anything, can these pictures tell us about women's roles in the early church? The visual content appears to show aspects of the life of the rich and famous: dress, hairstyles, jewelry, meal etiquette, tableware, cooking utensils, and diet associated with the Roman household. What has especially captured the historian of religion's interest is a pattern of repeated cup-raising gestures by female figures in a number of different banquet scenes. Specifically, these frescoes show a female figure who dominates the action by raising a cup at the beginning of a meal shared by four to seven participants, including children.

For approximately two hundred years a debate has raged among scholars over the specific meaning of the prominent female figures in the banquet scenes. Indeed, the constellation of eight banquet scenes raises more questions than scholars have asked to date, namely: What does the cup-raising action signify? Is there religious or ritual significance (other than the Eucharist) to the action? Do male figures raise a cup too? What is the difference, if any, between this action performed by a male and the same action performed by a female figure? In those scenes in which both a male and a female figure raise a cup, what is the order of the action? Is there significance to this order? Is there a ritual significance to the inscriptions *Agape* and *Irene*, repeated on a number of the banquet scenes? How do we account for the bilingual nature (Greek and Latin) of the inscriptions? In other words, what degree of actuality, with regard to early Christian funerary meals and, in particular, female roles at those meals, can be deduced from these wall paintings?

At the end of the twentieth century the challenge to explain the figures' actions resulted in a stalemate between contending schools of early Christian art and archaeology. Two main arguments dominated the debate. The first, supported by scholars from the German school, argued that the female figures with cups are representations of real people, most likely servants of wealthy Roman Christian households. The counterargument, held by the Roman school, posited that the female figures are personifications of the Christian virtues Love-Affection (*Agape*) and Peace (*Irene*). Within both schools, depending on the specific fresco being discussed, nuanced interpretations of the dominant arguments were also offered.[1] At the beginning of the twenty-first century a third type of interpretation has been advanced by a German scholar who interprets the female figures with cups as painters' types or *Assistenzfiguren* offered to the banquet scene to visually balance the picture at the request of the patron.[2] While each of the above views has contributed to our knowledge of early Christian art and archaeology, none of these explanations adequately accounts for all the artifactual data, including the inscriptions painted on the frescoes. Rather, the figures in the banquet scenes represent real people or a typology of real people who once lived and were in some way connected to those buried in the underground household chambers in Marcellino and Pietro and its early Christian community. The main difference between this interpretation and that of the German school is that the female figures that raise a cup are not servants but are meant to represent female family members who were heads of influential households in the Marcellino and Pietro community. In contrast to the Roman school, the words *Agape* and *Irene* inscribed on the paintings do not refer to the names of any female figures represented in the banquet scenes, real or personified, but rather form part of a funerary toast said with wine and shared among the participants at the banquet.[3] And while Norbert Zimmerman rightly argues that a case-by-case interpretation for each meal scene must be undertaken, the identification of the prominent female figures as "painters' types" would have more strength if the female figures were less individualized. Even Zimmerman acknowledges that the male-female pair with "cups" depicted in the banquet scene on wall three of chamber 78 (see figure 8.5, p. 179), which are also depicted in the prayer posture on wall two of the same chamber (see details, fig. 8.4, p. 187), are probably portraits of the Roman Christians originally buried in the privileged sites of the chamber.[4]

After a brief orientation to the use of art and artifactual data as a historical tool, we will examine what took place at a Roman funerary banquet, with the consideration that some of the best evidence for understanding the patterns of behavior at the banquet is from art and archaeology. Then we focus on four of the primary banquet scenes in Marcellino and Pietro, with specific attention paid to the female figures and inscriptions. Finally, we will discuss what evidence can be drawn from frescoes of early Christian funerary banquets for female leadership in the early church. Although this visual data is later than most of the literary evidence for house churches, a continuity of practice in family funerary meals can be assumed, given the long-established history of funerary banquets in the Mediterranean world and women's involvement and leadership in them.

Art and Artifactual Data

There is currently a growing appreciation in the academy for interdisciplinary research, especially the methodological question of integrating archaeological and textual evidence to achieve a broader understanding of historical periods. Two-dimensional pictures and three-dimensional objects provide different challenges for scholars when considered as historical evidence. When we interpret a work of art for its relevance to social context, the question naturally arises: How much actuality or historical reality can be extracted from a work of the imagination? The short answer is quite a lot, if we proceed with caution, are patient, and set up clear parameters for our investigation. As researchers, we must be skeptical toward viewpoints that see the image qua image as enough reason to discount the historical elements that may be part of it. Jas Elsner, an art historian of Late Antiquity, warns that "because art forms the setting where the fantasies and ideals of a society may be represented, imagined, negotiated, it is, for that reason, a dangerous guide to actuality."[5]

Many early Christian textual scholars would agree that Elsner's caution toward images could be voiced with equal justification toward literary texts. However, various methods of textual analysis have enabled scholars to work with the elements of historicity embedded in literary documents. Similarly, for visual materials, one must be knowledgeable of representational strategies that provide structure for visual content. The introduction of fantasies and ideals into pictures and texts is not a reason, however, to discard any possibility of historical investigation. While acknowledging that architectural remains and artifacts are "in no way intended to act as mirrors of reality," classicist Katherine Dunbabin states, "From such sources, much information can be derived that illuminates the patterns of behavior at the banquet and the social intercourse of the diners, more clearly than any surviving written material."[6]

The Roman Funerary Banquet

In the Roman world of Late Antiquity, care of one's ancestors was an important part of familial and moral duty (*pietas*). Unless the deceased was a renowned military hero or a member of the patrician class, funerals were considered to be private affairs, the province of one's family.[7]

Private funerary societies or *collegia* existed, usually with the aid of a wealthy patron, for assisting members with the expenses of the funerary banquet, among other responsibilities. Roman funerary practice required that on the day of the deceased's funeral, and on the ninth day after that, the family hold a banquet (*refrigerium*)[8] at the site of the tomb for family members and close friends.[9] Elaborate meals for the dead, which included wine, were consumed on the masonry couches built for this purpose inside or outside family tombs or in a space collectively owned by the society near the cemetery. Private commemorations of the family's ancestors may also have taken place inside the home at the shrine to the *Lares*, the spirits who protected the household.[10] As well as private ceremonies, elaborate public festivals for the dead called *Parentalia* were held once a year from February 13 to 22. At this festival an entire community's ancestors were honored; banquets took place first privately in the home and then publicly on the *Feralia* or last day of the festival.[11] A more private celebration in memory of the household ancestors called the *Lemuria* was celebrated on May 9, 11, and 13.[12] These ritual activities, taken together, ensured well-being and honor for the dead, purification for the living, and order, continuity, and prosperity for the empire. Such a private cult of the dead involved the entire household, including slaves, freedmen, and freedwomen; it was the responsibility of household members and their descendants to ensure that their forebears would not be forgotten or dishonored through the regular practice of commemorative banquets and rites.[13]

As part of the expression of familial duty, an entire industry grew up dedicated to the permanent praise of the deceased through the creation of the banquet funerary monument. The scene of the deceased reclining on a *klinē* couch (one- or two-person bed), surrounded by loved ones and attendants who carried food and drink, became the signature piece of a Roman's earthly farewell for those who could afford it. Roman *klinē* scenes from the Republican period to the third century show male and female figures reclining on a couch individually or with each other, the male figures typically reclining at the back or upper section of the couch.[14] In this posture the male figure frequently holds a cup or *patera* (shallow dish), while the female figure holds an object associated with funerary rites such as an incense box, garland, flower, or fruit. A small three-legged table rests in front of the *klinē*, on top of which is a platter of food, a roast or fish. Amphorae, jugs, or flasks of wine in baskets are frequently found beside the table.

In Roman funerary visual motifs the iconographical convention of the *klinē* monument or relief focuses on the faces of the central figures as the place where features of the deceased were recorded. The remainder of the figures, however, could be subject to heroization through semi-nudity (for males and for elite females shown reclining alone) or through representation as a deity (often combined with semi-nudity). The setting was also idealized through reference to the countryside and a bountiful array of goods. Along with side attendants, these features represented the ideal of the good life—a sign to those who visited the graves that the interred led a prosperous and productive life.[15]

A second type of banquet scene known as the "sigma-meal" was first introduced in art around the reign of Augustus (27 BCE–14 CE). A painting from the columbarium of the Villa Doria Pamphili shows a group of six figures sitting on the ground in a semicircle.[16] Some of the figures are holding cups, and a platter of food rests on the ground in front of them. The sigma-couch or *stibadium*, as it was also called, was originally a large semicircular cushion or set of cushions used for outdoor banquets. Dunbabin contends that the *stibadium* banquet fashion "derived at first from the numerous religious festivals in the Roman, and earlier in the Greek world, which called for outdoor feasting."[17] Archaeological evidence for this eating configuration indoors in the form of rooms marked out through a C-shaped floor pattern is found only in the late second or early third century. What began as an informal meal on a cushion with friends became an elaborate indoor feast by the Severan period (193–211 CE), as evidenced by extant curved floor mosaics such as the examples from houses in Antioch, Argos, and Dargoleja.[18] It is this sigma-meal formation that we find in the banquet scenes in Roman catacombs.

Women and Roman Funerary Banquets

In Roman households the task of caring for the dead fell to the survivors. Sons were ultimately responsible for the cult of their parents, but the actual management of the funerary meals consumed at the tomb fell to the primary caregivers of the living—the women of the family. As the managers of household goods, women not only directed the banquet feasts for their own kin but may have also hosted them for well-liked slaves. Petronius (d. 66 CE) writes satirically about a matron by the name of Scissa who "was holding the ninth-day feast for her poor little slave that she'd freed on his

deathbed" (*Satyricon 65*). House tombs from the second and third centuries
CE at Isola Sacra, near Rome, had space for multiple cremation urns, and
some of the larger ones also included ovens for cooking funeral meals on-
site.[19] As well as hosting banquets, Roman women were known for having
been patrons (*patrona, mater, matrona*) of Roman *collegia* or professional
organizations, including those whose purpose included the underwriting
of funerals for their members.[20] In Jean-Pierre Waltzing's four-volume
study of Roman professional corporations, an inscription from the year
153 CE tells us about a female patron who made a very generous gift of
some of her property (just outside of Rome) with a roofed terrace and vine
trellis to the College of Aesculapius and Hygeia, a burial club, in order to
accommodate its members' need for cult and dining space:

> Decree of the collegium of Aesculapius and Hygeia Salvia Marcellina,
> daughter of Caius, in memory of Fl. Apollonius imperial procurator,
> who was in charge of the picture galleries, and Capito freedman of
> Augustus, his assistant, her most devoted husband, gave as gift to the
> collegium of Aesculapius and Hygeia a place for a shrine with a trel-
> lis and a marble statue of Aesculapius and an adjoining covered sun
> deck in which the members of the collegium enrolled above may dine,
> which is on the Via Appia near the temple of Mars, between the first
> and second milestones for those going out of the city, on the left side
> between the boundaries of the property of Vibius Calocaerus and the
> public domain.[21]

The patronage of wealthy women, whether given individually or as co-
patrons along with their husbands,[22] other male family members,[23] and
other women,[24] supported the empire's less fortunate population while
accruing honor and status to Rome's upwardly mobile females.

The question of women's posture, that is, reclining, sitting, or standing, in
funerary banquet scenes is an extremely important one as it relates closely to
the perception of female status and morality in Roman society.[25] In Roman
funerary banquet iconography from the early Imperial period, the visual
convention dictates that servants stand and wives either sit on an upright
chair or recline at the foot of a couch occupied by their husbands.[26] Evidence
of women's posture at banquets from classical texts and funerary monuments, however, does not always agree. The literary evidence relates that
respectable Roman matrons fully reclined and participated in banquets with
their husbands.[27] When depicted as part of a reclining couple on a funerary

monument, however, the woman is rarely portrayed holding a drinking cup, a sign of full banquet participation. Such a representation would introduce ambiguity into the woman's legal status and moral behavior based on sexual activity. Matthew Roller suggests that among subelites (that is, Roman freedmen and freedwomen), the representation of a woman's restrained convivial behavior developed in order to signal the woman's legal status as wife (not mistress) and the couple's "juridical status as free citizens."[28] Dunbabin relates that among elite Romans it was the strength of a long-standing social taboo that sustained a sense of "inappropriate[ness] for a woman to be represented on her grave monument as a reclining banqueter holding a wine cup."[29] Women with drinking vessels who reclined beside males in domestic banquet scenes, such as those from Pompeii and Herculaneum, were generally perceived to be sexual companions of the men and not respectable Roman matrons.[30] Thus, on the funerary monument the typical banquet posture of actual Roman women was a visual convention that communicated the ideals of sobriety, sexual loyalty, and social legitimacy in relation to one's spouse. It did not reflect what a woman's actual banquet behavior might have been. Finally, unmarried women, or young women who may have died before their spouses, were sometimes depicted as reclining alone. Even in these cases, the respectable female who reclines alone is unlikely to be represented holding a drinking cup in Roman funerary banquet art.[31]

The Role of Wine

As well as pouring wine over the mortal bones of the deceased, another important function of the gods' ambrosia in Roman funerary rites is related to the deification and immortalization of the dead. Using archaeological and inscriptional evidence from the early empire, we can detect a cultural pattern that reflects the notion that if the dead were to attain immortality, a very uncertain and inconsistently held view in Roman thought, it would be through the process of becoming divine. It is probable that the deification process for the Roman emperor and empress introduced the idea of the deification of the dead into Roman culture on a popular scale.[32] From his study of themes in Greek and Latin epitaphs, Richmond Lattimore demonstrates that the idea of the dead as divine was prevalent among ordinary citizens of the empire from the first to third centuries.[33] The offering of wine to the deceased at the funeral banquet or religious festival would act to strengthen the family member's (new) status as a divine-like being.[34] Material evidence also confirms the idea of the divinity of the deceased. Funerary urns in the shape of altars from this time period are found in museums of Rome and elsewhere. Some of these urns have holes in the lid for the pouring of wine libations. Funerary reliefs showing men and women represented in the guise of specific gods or goddesses are also common among elite families.[35] Statuary representing the deceased as a specific deity can also be found from this time period, but is less abundant due to greater cost and fragility. Together this evidence suggests that one function of the Roman cult of the dead was to elevate and maintain the status of the deceased as a divine-like being. Wine, given as an offering to the deceased, functioned as a symbol and possible catalyst of this deification process.

With regard to wine at memorials for the dead, Christians are told that they are certainly allowed to drink, "otherwise it would be to the reproach of what God has made for cheerfulness," but that they are not to drink to excess, which only brings "sorrow," "uneasiness," and "babbling" (*Apostolic Constitutions* 8.44). Archaeological data found in Marcellino and Pietro, such as holes in the covering plates of subterranean *loculi* and later in the plates covering graves inside the mausoleums built on the surface of the cemetery, shows that early Christians continued the pagan practice of sharing wine with the deceased well into the fourth century.[36]

Roman Christian Funerary Banquets

Like their Roman pagan counterparts, Roman Christian funerals were considered to be private affairs.[37] The management of private family death rituals by the church hierarchy was only assumed over a very gradual period of time.[38] Since there were no institutionalized rites for death that would have required the presence of a priest, the path was clear for women to act as leaders in private funerary ceremonies and the commemoration rites after burial. Women participated in funerals as professional mourners, as those who washed and anointed the body of the deceased, and as those who prepared or managed the preparation of the funeral feast. We know that care for the sick, from which the sacrament of extreme unction eventually developed, was also delegated to deaconesses in the church (*Didascalia Apostolorum* 3.12). Since women were allowed to minister to the sick, it would have seemed a "natural" extension to have women also minister to the dead. It is probable that those who washed and prepared the body for inhumation also administered communion to corpses, a practice first condemned at an ecclesiastical council in North Africa in 393 CE.[39] In the Eastern church Christians were to add two additional days to the Roman pattern of commemoration, which included psalms, lessons, and prayers on the third day in imitation of the resurrection and on the fortieth day "according to the ancient pattern" (*Apostolic Constitutions* 8.42). This was to be done in imitation of the lamentation for Moses. In the West an additional two days were added on the third and thirtieth days after death.[40]

Other textual evidence for early Christian behavior at funeral banquets is slim and, generally speaking, negative. Tertullian speaks about Christians returning from the graves "staggering under the effects of wine" (*On the Testimony of the Soul* 4.4). And Augustine's reforms of the cult of martyrs toward the end of the fourth century were directed at removing the "rioting and drunkenness" that ensued among Christians during these celebrations (*Epistle* 22.3). With regard to banquets that celebrated the anniversaries of martyrs in Rome, we have strong evidence from the calendar of the martyrs (354 CE) that anniversary celebrations took place at each of the cemeteries for which there are banquet scenes. Anniversary banquets for martyrs buried in Marcellino and Pietro took place on the ninth of September and November every year.[41] There was also an anniversary celebration in the cemetery of Priscilla on July 10 for the martyrs Felix and Filippus.[42] As one of the oldest cemeteries, Callixtus is mentioned as the site of anniversary celebrations five times during the calendar year. Excess drinking by Christians over their dead at the tomb (along with the worship of pictures) continued in Rome into the late fourth century, as evidenced by Augustine in his polemic against the Manicheans (*The Way of Life of the Catholic Church* 1.34.75).

Archaeological remains in Marcellino and Pietro show the presence of thirty-three small tables or *mensae* constructed out of stone, tufa, or brick and mostly found in funerary chambers, including chamber 45, where one of the banquet scenes discussed below (fig. 8.2, p. 178) is found.[43] Jean Guyon, head of an archaeological team that studied Marcellino and Pietro, believes that these *mensae* were used for the funerary meal as evidenced by in situ fragments of glass and ceramic plates attached to the top surface of the tables. On other *mensae* large plate impressions are inset within the actual stone. These same types of tables are found beside the remains of shrines to the martyrs, including saints Marcellino and Pietro, and were probably used in their cult, one of the primary functions of the cemetery after 325 CE.[44]

Selected Banquet Scenes from Marcellino and Pietro[45]

The total number of banquet scenes in Marcellino and Pietro is around fifteen.[46] Of these, eight have female figures of interest to the topic of women's roles in the early church because female figures that raise or hold a cup are dominant in most of the scenes. The cup-raising action occurs at the start of the main course of a funerary meal. While the images form a group due to their many shared visual elements, each image must be treated as a unique document with important iconographical and archaeological differences. The images also share inscriptions in common. The words *Agape* and *Irene* are repeated five and six times, respectively, on seven of the banquet scenes. Scholars generally agree that these inscriptions represent speech. Because of space limitations we will examine only four of these scenes here.

Fig. 8.1: Fresco from chamber 45, wall 3, SS. Marcellino and Pietro, early fourth century CE. Seated male figure gestures toward a platter of food resting on a stone mensa. An actual stone mensa is found in this chamber directly across from the fresco near the entrance. Photo © Pontificia Commissione di Archeologia Sacra. Used by permission.

Household Chambers (*Cubicula*) Underground[47]

Most of the banquet frescoes are found in what is generally thought to be household or family-unit underground chambers (*cubicula*), where multiple burials of related individuals could be accommodated. A range of different grave types occurs in these chambers, from *arcosolia* dug out of the tufa (volcanic rock) walls, in which a large sarcophagus could be placed and the surface contours decorated, to body-length shelves (*loculi*) also dug out of the tufa in drawer-type formation. This latter type of burial space was reserved for lesser members of the household, such as slaves and their families. Elaborate *arcosolia* also occur in the underground galleries or narrow passageways of the catacomb alongside numerous rows of the shelf-type graves. The *loculi* were the cheapest and most common type of burial place. Of the four banquet scenes discussed in this chapter, one is found in an independent *cubiculum* (fig. 8.2 [Lau 45]), one is found in an *arcosolium* in an underground passageway (fig. 8.3 [Lau 47]), and two are found within the same funerary chamber (fig 8.4 and fig. 8.5 [Lau 78]).[48] While an *arcosolium* in a passageway was a step up in status from the common *loculus*, a private chamber off a passageway would have been the most expensive type of funerary site to purchase and decorate. The total number of funerary chambers excavated by 1987 numbered around 187, of which seventy-five are estimated to have been built before 320 CE and 112 after that date. The oldest of these underground chambers appears to have been dug out sometime toward the end of the third century, between 290 and 300 CE.[49]

Dating of Frescoes

The most recent study on the dating of the frescoes in Marcellino and Pietro is by early Christian art historian and archaeologist Norbert Zimmerman, who uses a method of analyzing the paintings according to workshop styles and even individual artists.[50] His method attempts to harmonize the dating results by Jean Guyon in his topographical analysis of the catacomb and stylistic analyses made by archaeologist Johann Deckers and earlier art historians. Zimmerman claims a continuous development for the two regions of banquet paintings located in the north and south sections of the western end of the cemetery, where the banquet scenes are found. According to Zimmerman, these paintings were made during "the enormous expansion of the huge community cemetery starting with the reign of Constantine the Great" (306–37 CE).[51] His study places the dating of the banquet scenes at the beginning of the fourth century at the earliest. In some instances, for example, in the case of figures 8.4 and 8.5 (chamber 78), Zimmerman suggests a date as late as 320–40 CE for the frescoes.[52]

Theoretical Framework

In order to understand the representational strategies that provide structure for the visual content of the Marcellino and Pietro scenes examined here, a visual-studies approach is used. This framework bridges a traditional iconographic and comparative approach to art and artifactual data with the significant insights that have emerged from recent art and cultural theory relating to visual culture. These insights include but are not limited to the relationship between representation and actuality;[53] intertextuality or the interplay between text and image or between image and image; the visual communication among figures within a scene such as gesture, gaze, and posture; the influence of the physical context on the meaning of the image; and viewer practices of looking.[54] Visual-rhetoric theory, which understands still images as performative works of communication to an imagined audience, is used to analyze the individual images.[55] This theory is especially useful in analyzing ancient art that depicts figures making oratorical gestures. A visual-studies approach acknowledges that even if none of the human-looking figures in an image can be shown to represent actual people, the image can still expose anthropological or sociological relationships that are typical for the culture and time period studied. Also, changes in iconography, especially within a visual tradition lasting as long as the banquet scene (more than a thousand years), are attributed less to the whims of individual artists than to external changes in cultural conditions. In the case of changes in the visual conventions of Roman funerary monuments, in which the delicate question of a family's reputation was at stake, a visual-studies approach argues that these changes reflect larger cultural shifts in the perception of important status indicators such as honor, moral reputation, and wealth (including size of client base and household). Applied to the banquet scenes in Marcellino and Pietro, visual-rhetoric theory can help elucidate speech communicated through the looks and gestures among the various figures depicted in a scene, and the relationship of the inscriptions to the visualized action. In conjunction with an iconographical analysis that identifies changes in visual conventions within Roman art and between Roman Christian and Roman pagan funerary banquet scenes, a visual-studies approach argues that such variations were due to changing convivial practices of real men and women in the external environment. The argument is made that these changes in real life eventually exerted enough pressure on the standard custom of their representation to evoke a change in the visual convention. In the case of the Marcellino and Pietro scenes, it is likely that the represented action had been an accepted practice for some time in the early Christian community with the representation of the behavior lagging behind the actual practice. Thus, a visual-studies approach proposes a relationship between the "real" and its representation, which is not one of direct imitation, but rather a negotiated tension between the two.

The Banquet Scenes

With the understanding that changes in visual conventions of banqueting practices can point to possible changes in convivial practices of real men and women, we begin our discussion of the four Roman Christian banquet scenes by focusing on the female figures with cups, comparing some of the main differences of these figures with a few examples from Roman funerary art (see figs. 8.2, 8.3, 8.4, and 8.5, pp. 178–79).

Of the four female figures, one sits (or possibly reclines) to the viewer's left very near to the sigma-couch (fig. 8.2), while two stand near the couch on the viewer's right (figs. 8.4 and 8.5). The fourth figure stands in front of the couch slightly to the right of center (fig. 8.3). All are richly dressed, wearing wide-sleeved ankle- or near-ankle-length dalmatics (robe or overgarment) with stripes (*clavi*) and ornaments in their expensive coiffures. One figure wears jewelry around her neck (fig. 8.5). Of the standing figures, one wears a diadem (fig. 8.3), and another figure displays a diaphanous veil (fig. 8.5). The actual cups that each figure holds are quite different in size and shape. The seated figure (fig. 8.2) holds a large conical-shaped cup, while the standing figure in fig. 8.3 raises a large stemless goblet. In fig. 8.4, the standing figure holds a delicate clear glass cup, as do the reclining male figures. And in fig. 8.5, the standing figure holds a small shallow dish (*patera*), probably made of clay.

Of the representations of Roman pagan funerary banquets with female figures in the *stibadium* or sigma-shape configuration, one of the best-known frescoes is from the Hypogaeum of Vibia in Rome (fig. 8.6, p. 180). This fresco shows six banqueters, one of whom is Vibia, who reclines near

Fig. 8.2: Banquet scene fresco from chamber 45, wall 2, SS. Marcellino and Pietro, late third or early fourth century CE. Painted on lunette of arcosolium. Dark oblong shape is an empty loculus. Photo © Pontificia Commissione di Archeologia Sacra. Used by permission.

Fig. 8.3: Banquet scene fresco found on the lunette of an arcosolium dug out along a gallery, no. 47, SS. Marcellino and Pietro, late third or early fourth century CE. A large terra-cotta platter (not shown here) is affixed to the arch with mortar just left of the center point of the arch. Photo © Pontificia Commissione di Archeologia Sacra. Used by permission.

Fig. 8.4: Banquet scene fresco from chamber 78, wall 2, SS. Marcellino and Pietro, early fourth century CE. Painted on lunette of arcosolium. One of two banquet scenes in this chamber (see below). Photo: Estelle Brettman, The International Catacomb Society.

Fig. 8.5: Banquet scene fresco from chamber 78, wall 3, SS. Marcellino and Pietro, early fourth century CE. Painted on lunette of arcosolium. One of two banquet scenes in this chamber (see above). Photo: Estelle Brettman, The International Catacomb Society.

the center of the couch in what is the place of the honored guest. (She is identified by the inscription above her head.) Her head is uncovered, and she wears a small mantle (*palliola*) around her shoulders.[56] She does not hold up a cup, but there is an amphora on a stand to the viewer's far right. Male servants, as identified by their short tunics and developed calf muscles, clean the ground in front of the banqueters: one tips a vase toward the ground, and one brings in a platter of food. Vibia holds up her right hand with the palm facing the viewer.[57] There is nothing in it.

A second banquet scene dated from the late fourth century shows an all-female banquet in the form of a floor mosaic in "Mnemosyne's tomb" in Antioch (see chapter 7, p. 150 [fig. 7.1]). The heads of three of the female figures have unfortunately been destroyed. The female figure seated beside the cushion on the viewer's left holds an open scroll in her hands. The standing figure on the viewer's right extends a large shallow dish in her right hand and holds the handle of a jug in her left. There are two reclining figures on the small couch. With her right hand, one of the reclining women touches the head of the seated woman. The right arm of the other figure has

Fig. 8.6: Induction and banquet scene of Vibia, hypogaeum of Vibia, Rome, mid fourth century CE. Painted on lunette of arcosolium. Photo by Estelle Brettman, The International Catacomb Society.

deteriorated so that we cannot tell if it held a cup. All are sumptuously dressed with elaborate coiffures and earrings. A wine amphora is shown behind the standing figure on the viewer's right. In this representation, drinking from a shared cup (the shallow dish) is implied but not shown.

In Marcellino and Pietro early Christian representations of women banqueting include three banquet images[58] not discussed here; fragments of banquet scenes also extant in the catacomb;[59] and the marriage at Cana shown as a sigma-meal scene.[60] Another early Christian banquet scene with female figures includes the famous fresco in the catacomb of Priscilla. In almost all of these scenes a cup is found in the hands of a female figure in the process of being brought to another female figure or is placed in front of female banqueters, as in the case of the banquet scene in Priscilla. In the marriage at Cana scene the lack of wine is the central visual motif: the middle banqueter holds his cup down, while Jesus, who stands to the viewer's right, places his wand over the jugs of water. Holding one's cup down in front of the sigma cushion may be an oratorical gesture indicating the cup is empty.

The representations of banqueting males from Roman Christian funerary monuments frequently show the end figure (to the viewer's left) on the sigma-couch with a cup or about to receive one from an attendant.[61] Typically, a second cup is being drained by the middle male figure (similar to the action in fig. 8.2). With regard to host-guest relationships at the banquet, scholars disagree as to which place in the sigma formation is reserved for the guest of honor and which is reserved for the host. Generally, the visual evidence of male banquet scenes on sarcophagi and tomb paintings demarcates the middle figure on the sigma-couch in some way, while the end figure (to the viewer's left) holds a cup and gives direction to servants when they are present in the scene. This visual convention has been interpreted by some scholars to signify that the middle figure is regarded as the honored guest (the deceased at funerary banquets),[62] while the host occupies the right end position on the sigma-couch.[63]

The depiction of two figures each holding a cup in funerary banquet scenes suggests that drinking rituals, such as toasts, occurred in pairs. Surviving examples of Roman cups designed as pairs from Pompeii and Hockwold, Norfolk, reinforce this idea.[64] Late third- and early fourth-century sets of ceramic drinking vessels and vases with Latin inscriptions found in excavations of grave sites from North Africa to northern Europe suggest toasts were also made to the deceased as a regular practice.[65]

Of course, there are other images of women banqueters in the sigma-shape formation in Roman art, such as the image of Dido's feast from the *Codex Vergilius Romanus*, in which only the honored guest, Aeneas, raises a cup. But these images are not from a funerary context and might suggest other types of drinking rituals carried out at the Roman banquet. As discussed above, the lack of female figures holding cups in Roman pagan funerary banquet scenes is a visual convention meant to signal to the viewer the high moral standing of the depicted woman. This observation would seem to be further borne out by the visual evidence of elaborately decorated sarcophagi from the third century, some owned by individuals from Rome's upper classes.[66] These monuments feature a sculpture of a husband and wife reclining together as part of the lid design. The typical motif depicts the male figure holding a cup while the female figure does not. As our early Christian frescoes in Marcellino and Pietro show, female figures dominate the cup action at the funerary banquet. If Roller is correct about the representation of drinking wine on Roman funerary monuments as a cultural index of female morality, then some explanation for the difference in banquet iconography between pagan and early Christian funerary monuments is warranted. One possible explanation of the variation is that early Christian funerary practices by women in real life over time changed the cultural perception that only disrespectable women drank wine at banquets. If this is the case, this change in practice would only have been inserted gradually into the iconography of early Christian art, given the Roman moral sanction in representational practice against showing respectable women drinking wine and the early Christians' desire to blend in with pre-Constantinian Roman society.

Early Christian women's use of wine at funerary banquets probably occurred much earlier than the end of the third century. The banquet scene in the catacomb of Priscilla, which dates from the early to mid-third century, shows a single cup in front of one of the female banqueters, but none of the female figures appears to actually hold a cup in her hand.[67] As this is an older fresco, it may be that the Roman taboo of representing respectable women reclining with a cup on their funerary monuments precluded the depiction of an early Christian female figure actually holding a cup of wine. The only surviving text we have of a respectable Christian woman sharing a cup of mixed wine in a funerary context relates to the late fourth-century story of Augustine's mother, who

> never poured more than a small cupful of wine, watered to suit her
> sober palate, and she drank only as much of it as was needed to do

honor to the dead. If there were many shrines to be honored in this way, she carried the same cup around with her to each one and shared its contents, by now well watered and quite lukewarm, with any of her friends who were present, allowing each to take only the smallest sip. For her purpose was to perform an act of piety, not to seek pleasure for herself. (Augustine, *Confessions*, Book 6, Chapter 2)[68]

Monica quit this practice not out of concern for her own moral reputation in relation to wine, but out of concern for the reputation of the church, as instituted by Ambrose, and to disassociate herself from the pagan cult of the dead. By the middle of the sixth century, women's association with the drinking cup in the Eastern church had become a highly respectable visual convention, as evidenced by Empress Theodora's depiction offering the chalice to a member of the clergy inside the Basilica of San Vitale, Ravenna, Italy. In the banquet frescoes of Marcellino and Pietro, it is probably the more relaxed and later, accepted status of Christians under Constantine that allows the emergence of the visual convention of female figures raising a cup, a practice that was already familiar to Christians in real life, to be expressed openly in representations of funerary banquets.

So far we have discussed the female figures in the Marcellino and Pietro scenes as though they were merely enjoying a cup of wine at an intimate dinner party. An analysis of the looks and gestures among the banqueters, however, shows this to be far from the case.

Looks and Gestures

In three of the four frescoes discussed here, there are two figures in each banquet scene (one male and one female) shown with drinking cups. As discussed above, it is likely these cups and those who hold them form a pair for the purpose of toasting (see details of figures, pp. 184–85).

From the looks of banqueters without cups that are directed at those holding a cup (or the cup itself), it is clear that this action is a significant one and happens at an important moment in the banquet. The figures look intensely at the object they hold, which suggests the importance of this particular drinking rite (see especially fig. 8.5 details, p. 185). The visual evidence suggests that the pairs of figures with cups make the first toast at the beginning of the funerary banquet. Of those male figures with cups, it is interesting to note the oratorical gesture of their free right hands. In fig. 8.3, the end figure's right arm is raised in exhortation, while the end male

Detail of Fig. 8.2:
Female figure
shown giving
(opening?) toast
of *Agape* [Love-
Affection]" at the
banquet. Photo
© Pontificia
Commissione
di Archeologia
Sacra. Used by
permission.

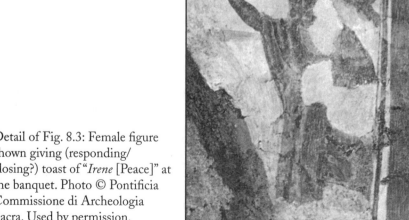

Detail of Fig. 8.3: Female figure
shown giving (responding/
closing?) toast of *Irene* [Peace]" at
the banquet. Photo © Pontificia
Commissione di Archeologia
Sacra. Used by permission.

Details of Fig. 8.5: Details show host pair (male and female figures with *patera*) giving a joint (or reciprocal) toast of "*Agape*." Photo © Pontificia Commissione di Archeologia Sacra. Used by permission.

figure in fig. 8.5 points at the platter with his outstretched right arm (as do his fellow banqueters without cups). Like inscribed words that can stand for speech, stylized gestures in ancient figures enhance or stand in for oral communication. The right arm raised in exhortation by the end male figure in fig. 8.3, combined with the cup in his left hand, strongly suggest that he is one of the speakers of the banquet toast. The inscribed speech above his head is most likely meant to be identified with him, while the other inscription in fig. 8.3 is meant to be identified with the female figure as speaker. In the raising of her right arm, her gesture of exhortation is combined with that of a toast.

In the case of fig. 8.4, of those reclining figures whose hands are visible, we see they are holding delicate clear glass cups, though it is impossible to tell from the image if they are a match to the glass cup held by the standing female figure. The female figure and those reclining at the sigma-couch are shown in a state of suspended animation, while the servant hurriedly brings in the platter of food. In this scene their toast is simple, "*Irene*" (Peace). As no one figure's arm is raised in exhortation, there is no clear speaker of the toast. Perhaps the inscription close to the female figure is meant to identify her as the speaker.

Analysis of the hand and arm gestures in the banquet frescoes shows that fig. 8.5 is very different from all the other scenes. While it is related to the banquet scene shown in fig. 8.4 (it is on the adjacent wall in the same funerary chamber), the action is stiff and formal. There are no gestures suggesting informal speech among the figures, as there are in figs. 8.2 and 8.3. Compared to the other banquet frescoes in Marcellino and Pietro, it is a highly stylized scene, with the male figures represented similarly except for the middle figure's dress. He wears a tunic with embroidered patches on his shoulders, while the other male figures wear striped dalmatics.[69] Both of the middle figure's hands point at the platter in front of the sigma-couch. The special significance of this figure and the standing female figure is underlined by their secondary appearance in individual frescoes above the banquet scene in fig. 8.4 in the same funerary chamber (see details, fig. 8.4, p. 187).

In these individual frescoes, probably meant to be portraits, both figures are shown in the praying posture. As the female figure is wearing a veil in both representations, it is possible that this garment signals her special status in the community, with the banquet picture showing a celebration that she co-hosts. While the banquet scene in fig. 8.4 depicts the moment before the anticipated toast, fig. 8.5 depicts the pinnacle moment of the funerary banquet—the toast itself. As the banquet host, it is the female host's job to utter the toast, "*Agape*" (Love-Affection).[70] The Latin word *misce* (mix) in the inscription forms part of the truncated speech that appears as host-client dialogue on common Roman drinking vessels from the third and fourth centuries. This brings us to the discussion of the function of the inscriptions painted on the banquet scenes. We will now see how the inscriptions reinforce the female figures' roles as hosts or co-hosts of the banquet.

The Relationship of Inscriptions to the Banquet Scene

I have suggested that pairs of figures with cups are meant to represent the act of making a toast. A comparison of the banquet inscriptions with Roman drinking salutations found on glassware, cups, and vases (see pages 188–89) buried with the dead shows that the banquet inscriptions in Marcellino and Pietro are part of a Roman wine-toasting tradition. In an examination of a number of Roman terra-cotta cups with Latin inscriptions from the late third and early fourth centuries,[71] it is possible to dis-

Details of Fig. 8.4: The above figures also appear in the banquet scene on wall 3 (fig. 8.5). It's probable that these figures are meant to represent the owners of the funerary chamber. Photo © Pontificia Commissione di Archeologia Sacra. Used by permission.

cern correlations between the message of the inscription and the size of the tableware for some of the artifacts. For example, the word *misce* (mix) appears on small individual cups more frequently than on any other type of drinking container.[72] Cups with the word *nobis*[73] (for us) painted on their sides are three times the size of the *misce* cups, suggesting the contents of the *nobis* cups are to be shared among banquet participants (see fig. 8.7).

The words *Da caldam* (give hot water and wine mixed together) (see fig. 8.9) and *Misce mi* (mix for me) appear more typically on vases or jugs for pouring.[74] Latin words for manager or host, such as *copo* (male host or manager of a tavern or inn), are also found on jugs for pouring wine (see fig. 8.8) and in some cases on amphorae.[75] The inscription *hospita* or female host has been found in fragment and beaker form.[76] This remarkable parallel with the Marcellino and Pietro inscriptions suggests that the Latin part of the texts painted on the banquet scenes should be read in the context of the host-guest relationship; the female figure raising a cup or holding a jug could be equally interpreted as the host or as the co-host of the banquet.

In the banquet frescoes discussed here, the words *Agape* and *Irene* are repeated three times each in the inscriptions:

Fig. 8.7: Examples of single- and multiple-user beakers. Cup on right—made in Trier, circa late third or early fourth century CE—has faded "*Nobis*" (for us) inscription. (Cups were photographed in close proximity on same shelf.) Photo by Janet H. Tulloch.

Fig. 8.8: A dark-colored ceramic vase made in Trier, circa late third or early fourth century CE. Inscription reads: upper register—R•E•P•L•E•M•E lower register—C•O•P•O•M•E•R•I (Refill me, worthy host.) Photo by Janet H. Tulloch.

Fig. 8.9: Terra-cotta cup and vase with painted inscription done in "en barbotine" style. Photo © Rheinisches Landesmuseum Trier. Used by permission.

Fig. 8.9: Inscription on small cup is: "*Dami*" (give me); on vase it is: "*Da Caldum*" (give hot water and wine mixed together). These Rhenish wares were made in Trier circa late third or early fourth century CE. Photo © Rheinisches Landesmuseum Trier. Used by permission.

Fig. 8.2	AGAPE . MISCE	IRENE
	NOBIS	[P]ORGE[E]
		C[A]LDA

| Fig. 8.3 | AGAPE | IREN[E] |
| | [PO]RGE CALDA | MISCE |

| Fig. 8.4 | IRE | |
| | NE | |

Fig. 8.5	AGAPE.	
	MISC	
	E	

The above inscriptions have always been interpreted as a continuous sentence even though the words *Agape* and *Irene* appear alone or on a single line in five of the six inscriptions reproduced above. The interpretation offered here is that the separation of the words both spatially and linguistically (Greek from Latin) suggests the inscriptions are meant to represent two parts of a conversation, a command and a response, that is, a dialogue rather than a single command. This interpretation is supported by other examples of similar inscriptions using *Misce* on the Roman drinking cups and vases discussed above. For example, *Misce vivas*, painted on the same line of a wine jug, has been interpreted by Matthias Bös in his study of Roman drinking cups with inscriptions as representing part of a dialogue between a host and a guest: *Misce*, or "Give mixed wine," says the guest; *vivas* or "To Life" or "Cheers," says the host.[77] Applied to the Marcellino and Pietro banquet inscriptions, this interpretive model suggests that *Misce mi* or *Misce* is the command given by the guest, and *Agape* or *Irene* is the response or toast spoken by the host or co-host. In the banquet scene from chamber 76 (not shown here), this is the actual order of the speech painted on the scene if one reads left to right, top to bottom.[78] Two other Greek words, *Pie/Zeses* (Drink/Live), associated with Roman drinking salutations and frequently inscribed as a pair written in Latin letters, are commonly found on Roman pagan ceramic tableware and gold-glass as well as Roman Christian gold-glass.[79]

Thus, when the inscriptions are analyzed independently from the banquet scenes, in the context of familiar Roman drinking salutations found on cups and vases from the same time period, we find that the speech model of "command and response" fits well with the interpretation of "the toast" from the visual data presented in the gestures of the figures with cups. The Greek words in the Latin inscriptions serve to emphasize the dieretic nature of the speech as well as signify the high status of the tombs' occupants, who may have spoken some Greek, the language of culture. Like the image action of the banquet scenes, the inscriptions should be read in the context of Roman host-guest relationships.

With this analysis it is now possible to suggest that, in the case of figs. 8.2 and 8.3, the following dialogue exists between the banquet guests, who request that the hosts offer mixed wine to them, and the hosts, who respond:

Fig. 8.2	Guest 1:	*Misce nobis*	(Mix wine for us…)
	Host 1:	*Agape*	(Love and Affection!)
	Guest 2:	*[P]org[e] c[a]lda*	(Offer warm water…)
	Host 2:	*Irene*	(Peace!)
Fig. 8.3	Guest 1:	*[Po]rge calda*	(Offer warm water…)
	Host 1:	*Agape*	(Love and Affection!)
	Guest 2:	*Misce*	(Mix [wine] …)
	Host 2:	*Iren[e]*	(Peace!)

In the case of fig. 8.4 there is no inscribed request, only the utterance of the toast, "*Irene.*" In fig. 8.5 there is one inscribed request, "*Misce*," and one response, "*Agape.*"

The order in which these early Christian funerary toasts were spoken may have been significant. However, the answer to this and related questions about the nature of early Christian banquet toasts requires further research.

Conclusion:
Evidence for Women as Banquet Hosts

The Marcellino and Pietro banquet scenes represented in the various underground household chambers document the cultural memory of the hospitality provided by female heads of households in a funerary context. The inscriptions on the banquet scenes point to a funerary toast given with wine that occurred before the start of the banquet and uttered by the co-hosts of the meal. The words *Agape* and *Irene* do not refer to the names of any of the female figures represented in the banquet scenes, but rather are the hosts' response, as part of the host-guest dialogue, to the guests' requests for wine. These toasts were no doubt uttered in honor of the newly departed but were also directed to everyone in the household, living and deceased.

We now return to the question with which we began: What degree of actuality, with regard to early Christian funerary meals and, in particular, female roles at those meals, can be deduced from the banquet scenes examined in Marcellino and Pietro?

In comparing the female figures in Roman pagan funerary scenes and those in Roman Christian funerary scenes, we were able to account for the iconographical differences in the latter images by reading the Marcellino and Pietro banquet scenes as visual evidence for the changed cultural perception of female respectability. Just as representations of Roman female figures in private funerary banquet monuments were an index of women's status and morality in Roman society, the representation of Roman Christian women in early Christian banquet scenes can be seen as an index of women's status and morality in the formation of the early church. While the funerary representations of respectable Roman pagan women were tied to perceptions of their banquet drinking behavior as an index of their status to the *paterfamilias*, representations of early Roman Christian women in the funerary scenes discussed here suggest that a new visual index of women's status and morality was developed for Christian female believers. By the end of the third and early fourth centuries this new index for female status and morality begins to show up in the early Christian banquet scenes of Marcellino and Pietro. No longer is the cultural perception of female respectability tied to a legal relationship with the *paterfamilias*; instead, it is visually indexed by the woman's role in relation to her household, as someone who has reared children and provided hospitality for family, close relatives, and friends.

By the late third and early fourth century, the Christians of Rome were no longer assembling for worship in private homes, but some households, and therefore some family celebrations, continued to be led by women, and certainly women continued to participate in important roles in those family celebrations whether led by women, men, or both. Since visual representation tended to lag behind actual practice, the material presented here can be assumed to reflect continuity with the earlier Christian roles of matrons, widows, and women leaders of households that can be seen in the textual evidence discussed in other chapters.

CHAPTER NINE

WOMEN PATRONS
IN THE LIFE OF HOUSE CHURCHES

◻◻◻ ◻◻◻ ◻◻◻

The role of women patrons in the life of the early church is a subject that has received little attention, yet it is central to the understanding of women in house churches in the earliest years. To see it in context, we must back up and look first of all at the wider phenomenon of patronage in the ancient Greco-Roman world, a subject about which a considerable amount has been written, and how it functioned with regard to women, about which not nearly so much has been written.

The phenomenon of patronage in ancient Roman society has been well studied. There are major cross-cultural studies of the social construction of patronage (Gellner and Waterbury, Eisenstadt and Roniger, Elliott)[1] and of its specific exercise in ancient Rome (Saller, Wallace-Hadrill, Krause).[2] Patronage in early Christianity now occupies the attention of biblical scholars and historians; significant examples are Frederick Danker's influential *Benefactor* in 1982[3] and the ever-insightful E. A. Judge's work in the 1960s, 70s, and 80s.[4] In all of the above cases, however, the androcentric norm prevails, and women are hardly mentioned, in spite of the fact that they participated heavily in the patronage system on both sides, as patrons and as clients.

This chapter will consider first a quick survey of patronage and how it functioned; second, women's exercise of patronage in the Roman world;

third, the role of patronage in early Christian life; and finally, the role of Christian women in this social system.

Patronage in the World of the Early Roman Empire

In their cross-cultural study of patronage, Eisenstadt and Roniger[5] list nine characteristics of patron-client relations. They are usually "particularistic and diffuse." They are characterized by simultaneous exchange of different kinds of resources, economic and political on one side, and "promises of reciprocity, solidarity, and loyalty on the other." The exchange of resources usually comes as some kind of package deal, in which none can be exchanged separately but only in full combination. They contain an ideal of "unconditionality and of long-range credit." They bring with them a strong sense of interpersonal obligation that is intricately connected with concepts of honor and shame. Patron-client relationships are not fully legal but rather more informal and at times go directly against or furnish a means to circumvent laws. These relationships are entered into and can be abandoned more or less voluntarily, though social constraints can certainly set up a situation in which a client has little choice. They are formed in vertical personal relationships and tend to undermine any sense of horizontal solidarity. Finally, they are "based on a very strong element of inequality and of differences of power between patrons and clients."

John Elliott notes that patronage "involves issues of unequal power relations, pyramids of power, power brokers, protection, privilege, prestige, payoffs and tradeoffs, influence, 'juice,' 'clout,' 'connections,' *Beziehungen*, *raccomendazioni*, 'networks,' reciprocal grants and obligations, values associated with friendship, loyalty, and generosity, and the various strands that link this institution to the social system at large."[6] Richard Saller, in his study of Roman personal patronage, synthesizes it all into three pivotal characteristics: there is reciprocal exchange of goods and services, the relationship is personal and of some duration, and the relationship is asymmetrical.[7] A fourth characteristic is often added to the consensus: that it is voluntary and not legally enforceable.[8]

One of the contributions of the patronage system to the social order is to give the weak a means of influencing the powerful.[9] The client could expect to receive economic and political benefits, such as gifts of food; invitations to dinner (for the importance of this dinner invitation as a symbol of patronage, see Juvenal, *Sat.* 5.12–15); gifts of land, house, or sometimes cash; low- or no-interest loans; lodging in the town house or villa of the patron; favorable recommendations and appointments; help with matchmaking; and bequests and inheritance.[10] The patron in return could expect loyalty, public support, economic assistance if needed and possible, votes, and, most important, public praise and presence, especially at significant times for the political advancement of the patron. Clients found themselves in a double bind: it was expected that they would publicize the generosity of their patron's *beneficia*, but the admission of having received them marked one's own lower social status.[11] A client who did not give proper praise was considered *ingratus* (ungrateful) and unworthy of more.

It is recognized by ancient social historians that patronage systems definitely existed to some extent in the cities of classical Greece even though there seems to have been no terminology to refer to it exactly.[12] For example, the word *prostatēs*, so important to us for understanding Rom. 16:1, was in classical Athens the term for the required citizen patron of a *metoikos*, a resident alien. The term thus carried connotations of social superiority versus inferiority, so no citizen would acknowledge having one. Yet, in the Roman period, Plutarch understands *prostatēs* as the equivalent of *patronus* (*Romulus* 13).[13] However, the institution of patronage never developed in earlier Greece in the extensive way that it did in Roman society. Moreover, the end of the Republic and beginning of the empire signaled a new resurgence in patronal relationships, as the old structures of government and power gave way to the uncertainty of newly developing ways of exercising power. The new figure of the *imperator* took advantage of the vacuum of power to seize control of major power networks, governing by an intricate balance of relationships with the elite families. Augustus was able to consolidate power and set up a system in which "the inaccessibility of the center except through personal links" deepened and nourished the patronal structure of society, and to cast himself as *pater patriae*, chief benevolent father figure of the entire Mediterranean world.[14]

While the Latin language of patronage contained such direct words as *patronatus, patronus/a, clientela,* and *cliens,* by the time of the early empire this language was generally considered too abrasive to the delicate honor system, and a new set of terms was adapted into the structures of patronage: that of friendship. Thus the semantic field of *amicitia* becomes the preferred language.[15] Because the patronage relationship was by definition asymmetrical but the language of friendship could also be used in the topos of true friendship, one could speak of *amici minores* (Pliny, *Ep.* 2.6.2), *amici pauperes* (Pliny, *Ep.* 9.30), *amici inferiores* (Seneca, *Ep. Ad Lucilium* 94.14), or the like, all of which were meant to be less condescending than the bald word *cliens*.[16] Seneca (*On Benefactions* 6.34.2) credits Gaius Gracchus and Livius Drusus as the first to classify their "friends" into three categories, and suggests that the classification is reasonable and to be continued: *amici primi* who are received in private, *amici secundi* received with others, and *numquam veri* (never trustworthy) to be received all together in one group. Some preferred the term *cultor* for one who was attempting to ingratiate himself or herself with a patron and, more commonly, the verb *colere*, which also applied to honor and reverence due to the gods, a meaning that carried over into Christian usage. One of the major ways of exercising patronage was with regard to artists, poets, and writers; here words like *patronus* and *patrocinium* are never used.[17]

The range of terms employed for this informal but essential social custom varies greatly: *amare/amor, sodalis, diligere/dilectus, contubernium* (also used for a nonlegal marriage), *caritas/carus, familiaritas/familiaris*, even *meus* and *noster*.[18] The exchange of goods and services was connoted by such terms as *meritum* and *gratia*, but primarily under the name of *officium* and *beneficium*, originally a gesture of duty and loyalty from the inferior versus a gesture of largesse and generosity on the part of the superior. Gradually, however, the terms became almost interchangeable and are thus used even by Cicero in his treatise *De officiis*.[19] The language of friendship could be used in an upward as well as a downward direction, that is, toward one's patron as well as toward one's client. The patronal relationship was often between two persons of distinctively different social classes, but it need not be. It could exist between near equals, for example, between a senior and a junior senator. Even senators could be referred to as imperial *clientes*. While one would think that the loyalty inherent in the patron-client relationship should have implied that a client could have only one patron, there is some evidence that it was possible to have more than one, perhaps in a way that would make it possible for the client to subtly play them off against each other.[20] In the fourth century the famous orator Libanius delivered at Antioch his oration against patronage (*De patrociniis vicorum*) in the context of social and political upheavals that were driving peasants to align themselves in clientage with powerful military patrons, undermining the authority of aristocratic landowners over their peasants. In this context he argues strongly that there must be only one patron: the landowner. Here, in the interest of wealthy landowners (Libanius's own class), we see both the ideal and the reality.

Two further aspects of the patronage system deserve further comment. The first is the particular relationship between patron and freed slave. Most of the characteristics of patronage still apply here, the main difference being that the *officia* and loyalty owed to the patron, under the title of *operae* and *obsequium*, was specifically designated, not at all voluntary, and enforceable by law. Here the terminology of patron and *libertus/a* was used, even in funerary inscriptions. The relationship was certainly not voluntary on the part of the freedperson, who often continued doing pretty much what he or she had done as a slave. Jennifer Glancy[21] cautions that the patron-client model was not an appropriate one in this more coercive case. Nevertheless, the terminology was used, and some of the same mutually advantageous benefits were applied.

The second further aspect of patronage is the phenomenon of public patronage, or euergetism,[22] and of an intermediate form that is important for early Christianity, patronage of a private group. While the essence of the patronage system was a relationship between two individual persons who were not social equals, in fact the relationship of one dominant person to groups of social inferiors had always been part of the system as an extension of the personal relationship into one with a collectivity, whether a professional guild, a club, a group of the poor, the devotees of a private religion, or a city. Building public facilities like fountains or baths, providing free meals to the needy or to children of the city, or holding banquets at civic celebrations are all examples of public patronage. Building meetinghouses and temples for groups or providing economic assistance or banquets to devotees were examples of the exercise of private patronage to groups. In return, the patron was named in thankful inscriptions or had a statue erected in his or her honor, was seated in a place of honor at official gatherings of the group, was appointed to an official position (which may be honorary), and was generally hailed as a VIP. Of course, the role of the emperor constituted the highest form of public patronage. The giving of public banquets by the emperor or by wealthy private citizens on the occasion of a feast or celebration was a familiar form of patronage, and those forms that we would call charity or social aid were exercised not primarily out of compassion, but for the motive for which all patronage was exercised: honor, (*philotimia, philodoxia*).[23]

Women's Patronage in the Roman World

Both private and public patronage were activities in which women were deeply involved. Women could attend the morning *salutatio*, the obligatory greeting of clients to patron, in which the client could ask for favors and might receive a gift or even an invitation to dinner, but might also be asked for required service (Juvenal, *Sat.* 1.120–16). There is ample evidence of women's participation in business. Women who had the legal status *sui iuris*, that is, they were not under the *potestas* of a man, could conduct their own transactions, though the law imposed some limitations. The earlier institution of *tutela*, male guardianship requiring permission to alienate property, was mostly inactive by the Augustan age, though former owners could still exercise considerable control over the property of a *liberta* (freedwoman). Other legislation was enacted that prevented women from taking on liability for the debts of others. Roman legal scholars think that this restriction was primarily aimed to protect women from unscrupulous husbands.[24] As is often the case with Roman law, what was on the books was not necessarily what was done, and there were perhaps more exceptions than strict applications of the law.

The social and political patronage of elite women can be well documented. First, of course, women often served as patrons for other women. Cratia, the wife of M. Cornelius Fronto, tutor of Marcus Aurelius, was called in one of his letters to the emperor a *clienta* of Domitia Lucilla, the emperor's mother. As such, she visited the imperial family, staying with them in Naples without her husband to celebrate her patron's birthday.[25] An otherwise unknown woman named Valatta on the British frontier wrote to the commanding officer of the Vindolanda outpost, Flavius Cerialis, about a favor mediated by his wife, Sulpicia Lepidina.[26] The epitaph of Epiphania, a second- or third-century benefactor, the well-traveled daughter and wife of shipowners, reports that she was generous with her wealth, motivated by *eusebeia* (devotion), especially to abandoned friends *hōs gynē gyneksi*, woman to woman.[27]

Women's patronage was not limited to women, however. Though women could not vote or hold elective office, elite women were heavily involved in the exertion of political pressure and the informal negotiations that were always included. Indeed, it seems likely that all elite women were involved in politics at some level by reason of their family connections. The influence of powerful women in the palace and the law court through their exercise of patronage, *amicitiae muliebres*, was ever present.[28] Moreover, Valerius Maximus cites situations in which women argued their own cases in court (8.3). Though he thought this self-defense unusual, he does not at all imply that it was unusual for women to be involved in legal suits, as either defendant or plaintiff.[29]

Roscius of Ameria, later defended by Cicero in a parricide case that involved political machinations against Sulla, fled for protection in Rome to the aristocrat Caecilia Metella, not to any of her abundant male relatives or her husband, because of her *amicitia* with his deceased father. Whatever the political intricacies in the story, it was recognized that she, not one of the male members of her family, was his patron.[30]

Augustus's wife, Livia, was exalted in public imagery as the paragon of wifely virtue, *patrona ordinis matronarum*, and upholder, with her husband, of "family values," in spite of their utter failure as parents to instill the advantages of the virtuous life in their daughter, Julia (Livia's stepdaughter). Livia had her own entourage and client loyalties, even receiving the Senate in her house during her widowhood. Josephus recounts her benefactions to the Herodian family, including marriage advice to Salome (*Ant.* 17.10).[31] Upon her death the grateful Senate voted the erection of an arch in her honor, which had not been done before for a woman, but Tiberius never allowed it to be built. The senators' gratitude arose because she had saved the lives of some Senate members, provided for their orphaned children, and helped many by paying their daughters' dowries. She was so popular that she was called informally, in parallel to Augustus's title, *mater patriae*, a title that was denied to her officially, however, even after her death (Dio Cassius 58.2.3).[32]

Nero's aunt Domitia had clients, and the schemer Agrippina, Nero's mother, was known to be patron for numbers of men eager for political advancement. It was she who succeeded in getting Seneca's exile rescinded (Tacitus, *Annals* 12.8). On the death of her father, Germanicus, his *clientela* passed to her as well. At one point, Nero had her residence moved from the palace to the house that had belonged to Antonia in order to prevent the crowds that arrived for the morning *salutatio* to their patron (Tacitus, *Annals* 13.18.5). Her political enemy, Junia Silana, got two of her own male clients to charge Agrippina with inciting revolt from imperial authority in the person of Rubellius Plautus.[33] Antonia Caenis, freedwoman of Claudius's mother, Antonia, became mistress of Vespasian until her death. Dio Cassius (65.14.1–5) vividly describes her patronal power and wealth: she gave in exchange for money various kinds of public offices and priesthoods, and she obtained imperial decisions and secured imperial pardons in favor of her clients.

Many more individuals could be mentioned. The names of Poppaea Sabina with Nero, Plotina with Trajan, Marcia with Commodus, and Julia Domna with Caracalla are among them. These stories of political involvement of elite women, or women who gain access to elite status through consorting with an elite male, are well-known.

Less attention has been paid to lesser women and their exercise of patronage. Cornelius Nepos's comment about the presence on the dining couches of Roman women—as contrasted to Greek women—at dinner parties indicates greater social freedom of movement for first-century Roman and Romanized women, but it also means greater access to the corridors of informal power and greater ability to influence them (Preface, *Illustrious Lives*). Juvenal complains of women who not only attend mixed dinner parties but also host them and discourse on politics and literature (*Sat.* 6.434–56).[34] He also hints that the best way to social advancement is through the patronage of some aging wealthy woman (*Sat.* 1.39).

The exercise of women's patronage was not limited to the elite, however. The evidence from Pompeii reveals women active in a variety of businesses and trades. They rented out and leased buildings and sold various commodities. The 154 wax tablets in the business files of the auctioneer L. Caecilius Iucundus, for example, contain references to fourteen women who transacted business with him, including Umbricia Ianuaria, who received 11,039 sesterces from the proceeds of a sale he had conducted for her (*CIL* 4.3440).[35] Other women lent money and, though they could not vote, supported local candidates for public office on wall graffiti like this one: "Statia and Petronia ask you to vote for Marcus Casellius and Lucius Alfucius for *aediles*. May our colony always have such citizens!" (*CIL* 4.3678).[36] Many women earned income from use of their property,[37] like the enterprising Julia Felix, probably a freedwoman, who owned a vast urban property in the southeast corner of Pompeii that contained a parking lot for horses and carriages, private dining rooms (one with its own fountain), baths, swimming pool, wine shop, and more modest areas for dining—and probably for takeout as well. She had more than what meets the eye today, for her notice on the outside wall advertised for lease "the Venus baths, fitted up for the best people, taverns, shops and second story rooms."[38] The property is situated just across the street from the city *palestra* (gymnasium) and amphitheater. One suspects that this was *the* place to stop off before and after the local games or an afternoon exercising at the *palestra*.

This kind of evidence is important for seeing the wide range of possibilities for women's personal patronage. All of these nonelite women who had accumulated even a modest amount of wealth and connections could be active in patronage relationships. A freedwoman named Manlia T. l. Gnome, for example, boasts on her epitaph that she had many clients (*clientes habui multos*; *CIL* 6.21975). Women were also patrons of their own freedmen and freedwomen, with the differences that this legal relationship carried. A *patronissa* whose name has been lost from the inscription is honored on a second- or third-century Roman Greek epitaph by the freedman Gaius Fulvius Eutyches.[39] The freedwoman Naevoleia Tyche at Pompeii erected a monumental tomb for herself, her freedman husband, Gaius Munatius Faustus, and their slaves and freedmen and freedwomen at the Herculaneum Gate cemetery. The inscription tells us that Munatius

Fig. 9.1: House of Julia Felix. Large recreational complex with dining rooms, swimming pool, and gardens for rent. Property owned by Julia Felix. Pompeii, first century CE. Photo by C. Osiek.

was an *augustalis* (member of an important college of freedmen) and *paganus*, official in charge of a district of the city or suburbs. Yet the ashes of Naevoleia and her husband were actually buried in another simpler monument at the Nucerian Gate, erected by the husband.[40] Whichever came first, Naevoleia decided to make the best of her wealth and to tell the world (in two places!) how important she and her husband were.

The same laws and customs applied to female as to male patrons. They set up their *libertus* or *liberta* with loans or gifts of money to start a new business, with a certain amount of legal control and the expectation of generous bequests in their former slave's will.[41] They provided in their funerary monument that their freedmen and freedwomen should also be buried there: *libertis libertabusque posterisque eorum*. Marriages between a *patrona* and her *libertus*, though heavily discouraged by social disapproval and even forbidden by law at some points, are not unknown (see, for example, *CIL* 6.14014; 14462; 15106; 15548; 16445; 21657; 23915; 25504; 28815; 35973). Some of these were likely cases in which the *patrona* herself came from originally servile status, but at least one is not: T. Claudius Hermes in Rome commemorates his freeborn wife, Claudia, as *patrona optima* (best patroness) and *coniux fidelissima* (most faithful wife) (no. 15106). Alimentary and funerary foundations provided sustenance in life and burials and commemorations at death, whether in the patron's lifetime or by bequest, for members of the *familia*, that is, predominantly slaves and former slaves.[42]

Patronage of Groups

Women's patronage of unofficial groups is an activity that bears directly on our understanding of their patronage in early Christianity. Euxenia, priestess of Aphrodite in Megalopolis in the Peloponnesus in the second century BCE, donated a guesthouse and a wall around the temple (*IG* 5.2.461).[43] Tation, daughter of Straton son of Empedon, from Kyme either built or remodeled at her own expense the building and the surrounding precinct of a synagogue, for which the Jews honored her with two traditional ways of rewarding a patron: a gold crown and a place of honor (*proedria*). The wording of the inscription ("the Jews honor her") and the family names suggest that she was not Jewish, but an outside benefactor (*CIJ* 2.738).[44] Similarly, Julia Severa of Acmonia in Phrygia, who held a number of distinguished priesthoods and city offices and was of a family sufficiently prominent that her son entered the Senate, donated property to the local synagogue, perhaps because two of its archons were freedmen or clients (*CIJ* 2.766; *MAMA* 6.264).[45]

Eumachia, a public priestess of Pompeii, patroness of the fullers' guild, in her own name and that of her son, Numistrius Fronto, erected at her own expense a gallery, cryptoporticus, and portico for the fullers' building in a prominent place in the forum, dedicating them herself to *concordia* and *pietas augusti*, important concepts of social harmony propagated during the reign of Augustus. In gratitude, the guild erected a dedicatory statue of her

Fig. 9.2: A copy of a statue of Eumachia, patron in Pompeii, behind the meeting place of the fullers' guild. Original in Archaeological Museum, Naples. Pompeii, first century CE. Photo by C. Osiek.

with inscription, a copy of which still stands behind their building at the forum in Pompeii. She also built a tomb for herself and her *familia* outside one of the city gates (*CIL* 10.810, 811, 813).[46]

Alimentary programs for poor children were popular ways for both men and women to exercise civic patronage. Besides imperial subsidy of these charitable projects, such as those in memory of the two imperial Faustinas, other wealthy women found this a suitable outlet for their money and a suitable way to be immortalized. Crispia Restituta of Beneventum set up one such project on income from her farm in 101 CE (*ILS* 6675). Caelia Macrina set up a fund to distribute a monthly meal to one hundred boys and one hundred girls in Tarracina (*ILS* 6278 = *CIL* 10.6328). Fabia Agrippina of Ostia contributed the sizable sum of one million sesterces to such a program for one hundred girls, in memory of her mother (*CIL* 14.4450). Since officially sponsored alimentary programs favored boys, these deliberate acts of attention to the needs of girls may have been a conscious effort on the part of women benefactors to create a balance.[47] Menodora in first-century Sillyon in Pisidia gave wheat and money to her city, including three hundred thousand denarii for the support of its children. She also erected a statue of her deceased son, all the donations being in his memory.[48]

Other forms of public patronage by women are also common, including in Asia Minor those connected with the holding of public office. The same Menodora held quite a number of public offices, including priestess of Demeter and of the imperial cult, *hierophantis* (a priest involved in initiations), *dekaprōtos* (a committee of ten who supervised public revenue and collected taxes), *ktistria* (founder), *dēmiourgis* (magistrate), and *gymnasiarchos* (superintendent or supplier of the *palestra*). She was honored with many statues and inscriptions, as was the early second-century benefactor of Perga, Plankia Magna, who held the titles of *dēmiourgos* and *gymnasiarchos*.[49] Vedia Marcia of late third-century Ephesus had held the title of *prytanis*, representative of the official cult of Artemis and also one of the principal magistrates of the city.[50] Tata of second-century Aphrodisias bore the title of *stephanēphoros* (crown bearer), as did her husband, Attalus. She, however, supplied oil for athletes, was a priestess of the imperial cult, and many times held banquets for the citizens, supplying dining couches and the best entertainment.[51]

Junia Theodora of first-century Corinth, originally from Lycia, provided an anchorhold for Lycians passing through this commercially strategic city.

Fig. 9.3: Plankia Magna, patron of Perga. Second century CE. Attalya Archeological Museum. Photo by Barbara Bowe.

In return for her benefactions, the Lycians set up in or near Corinth (the stone was discovered nearby in secondary use), five inscriptions on a single stone dedicated to her honor from the Lycian cities she had served. The combination of Latin and Greek names for Junia Theodora may indicate her Roman citizenship. The monument was set up during her lifetime, for the inscription from the federal assembly of the Lycians says that the assembly sends her a gold crown "for the time when she will come into the presence of the gods." A second decree of the assembly offers her not only a gold crown but also "a portrait for her deification after her death," painted on a gilt background. Among the services she performed for trav-

Fig. 9.4: Dedicatory inscription on a statue base, from Plankia Magna to Artemis/ Diana, in Greek and Latin. Perga, second century CE. Photo by C. Osiek.

eling Lycians were hospitality in her own house, cultivating the friendship of the Roman authorities in their favor, and designating her heir, Sextus Iulius, who gave every sign of carrying on what she began. Her patronage was not only directly to the Lycians but also on their behalf with the political powers. The decree of the Lycian city of Telmessos speaks of her *prostasia* (patronal leadership) in the context of hospitality and mediation.[52] Because of her location in first-century Corinth and because of the use of the word *prostasia* for her activity, Junia Theodora is an important comparative figure for the work of Phoebe *prostatis* in Rom 16:1-2.

Another important civic patron from the time of Nero is Claudia Metrodora of Chios, again probably a Greek woman with Roman citizenship besides that of her native Chios. She was an illegitimate daughter of Claudius Calobrotus, adopted by another man named Skytheinos, a rare instance of the adoption of a girl to supply an heir in a wealthy family. Like other civic patrons, she held some of the highest offices, gymnasiarch four times, *agōnothetēs*, and *stephanēphoros*, likely in exchange for public benefactions. Among them was an entire public bath complex. She also held the office of lifetime priestess of Empress Livia under the title Aphrodite Livia. She was elected "queen" of the federation of thirteen Ionian cities, a title that is probably completely honorary whenever it or "king" occurs in this context (something like "homecoming queen" or "rodeo queen" or "Miss Ionia"?). At some point she married a man whose name is lost and lived in Ephesus, where together they carried on their civic benefactions by erecting a portico.[53]

Sergia Paulina hosted a burial society in her house in Rome (*CIL* 6.9148), and Pompeia Agrippinilla, wife of a consul, was patron of a second-century Dionysiac association near Rome that boasted more than three hundred members, who gratefully erected a statue to their patron and priestess (*AE* 1933.4).[54] Memmia Victoria, freeborn woman of third-century Italy, whose son was a decurion, or cavalry officer, was named "mother" of an artisan group (*CIL* 11.5748), while Claudia, wife of a freedman from Faleri Piceni, Italy, was hailed as "mother" of a fullers' brotherhood (*CIL* 11.5450). Six Jewish women in Italy are known to have been given the title "mother of the synagogue."[55] Salvia Marcellina, daughter of Gaius, was patron of a *collegium* between the first and second milestones on the Via Appia (*CIL* 6.10234 = *ILS* 7213). The freedwoman Nymphidia Monime, widow of their patron Q. Cominius Abascantus, was adlected (appointed rather than elected, a common action for patrons) into the Augustales (a *collegium* of imperial freedmen) at Misenum in 149 CE, the first known example of a woman in the Augustales, apparently elected without approval of the local magistrates.[56] Women exercised leadership widely in other types of *collegia*, however, holding such titles as *quinquennalis, sacerdos, curator, honorata, quaestor,* and *decurio,* all titles of office.[57]

Others were town benefactors for public works. The unflappable Ummidia Quadratilla, grandmother of a friend of Pliny the Younger, caused mayhem during her life by indulging her taste for gambling and pantomime entertainment, both carried on in her own home, to the dismay of many of her friends. Visitors had to accommodate. Pliny breathed a sigh of relief when she turned over her grandson to him to train: no longer would he be subject to this negative influence. However, her hometown of Casinum remembered the lady differently when she died at the age of seventy-nine. There she was commemorated for her benefactions of amphitheater, temple, and theater, a glory of the city and not an embarrassment (Pliny *Ep.* 7.24.5; *CIL* 10.5813 = *ILS* 5628; *AE* 1946.174).[58]

Other specific women were hailed as patrons of their cities. In North Africa, Aradia Roscia Calpurnia Purgilla was acclaimed in the third century as patron of Bulla Regia (*CIL* 8.14470) and Caecilia Sexti f. Petroni-

ana Aemiliana patron of Thuburbo Minus (*AE* 1931.42). Egnatia Certiana
was hailed as a patron of Beneventum in the second or third century (*CIL*
9.1578) and Publilia Caeciliana and Publilia Numisiana at Verecunda in
the third century. Laberia Hostilia Crispina is proclaimed patron of the
women of Trebulae, though it is not clear why (*AE* 1964.106).[59]

In Herculaneum, where the hardened mud that covered the city made
immediate retrieval of precious items much more difficult than at Pompeii, more statuary was preserved than at Pompeii. At Herculaneum, 40
percent of the dedicatory statues are of women, mostly large and in bronze
and metal. They were set up alongside those of men in the theater and the
forum area, without any perceptible gender pattern.[60]

This selection of evidence makes clear that both personal and public
patronage were widely practiced by women in much the same way that it
was practiced by men. The older interpretation that public offices and titles
when held by men were actual, but when held by women were honorary, is
no longer tenable. The burden of proof is on those who would so contend.
Indeed, many of these titles and offices in cities, temples, and synagogues
were in fact honorary, but equally so for both men and women.[61]

The major difference for women was that they were excluded from voting and elected office, though at least in Asia women did hold some of
the highest public municipal appointments. The prohibition of women
from the elective process, however, by no means kept them out of politics or the patronage system. We are accustomed to thinking systemically
about women in this society in terms of gender dichotomies in a gender-based hierarchical structure. But in face of the evidence, we can only
conclude that women *of sufficient social status* in the Roman world exercised a great deal of freedom and power with regard to business and social
activities. What made this possible? Riet Van Bremen in his perceptive
essay "Women and Wealth" notes that traditional ideas and laws about the
subjection and confinement of women seem to have changed little. What
did change is the concentration of wealth in the hands of some women
and the lessening of the social controls over them through weakening of
the distinction between the public and private dimensions of social life.
Another factor, however, is that in the Roman social system, as distinct
from the older Greek ways, status took precedence over gender as a marker
of prestige and power. A person of higher social status and access to power
could function as mediator and dispenser of favor regardless of sex, with
the same expectations of reciprocity in terms of honor, praise, and loyalty
on the part of clients.

Christians and the World of Patronage

Scholars now see that the model of social networks based on informal and asymmetrical relationships for the exchange of goods and resources is the social reality underlying the relationships that created the early Christian communities. They are "a series of overlapping but not systematically related circles," in the words of E. A. Judge.[62] Patronage underlies exchanges of hospitality, the hosting of Christian gatherings, and most relationships of persons to other persons and to groups. Let us recall the kinds of things clients could expect of patrons, realizing that the same relationships were present in Christian communities: material and cash gifts, food and dinner invitations, lodging, favorable recommendations and appointments, help in matchmaking, and bequests and inheritances.

Civic benefaction specifically as Christians would not be open to them for several centuries. However, just as there must be some surviving burials of Christians from before the late third century, though they did not leave any signs that mark them as Christian burials, even so, there may be civic benefactions done by Christians with no sign of their Christian identity. But in this case, as with burials, there is no way to know. Private and unofficial group benefaction were the areas in which their patronage primarily functioned, as far as we know.

Roman historians tend to assume that the social patterns documented among the elite were replicated insofar as was possible by the rest of society, a sort of "trickle-down" effect. It is regrettable that there is so little non-Christian or non-Jewish evidence preserved for the social exchanges of nonelites in the same period. Some funerary commemorations provide a few glimpses. Even there, however, those who could not afford inscriptions are excluded. In one sense, early Christian literature is one of the best bodies of evidence for the life of nonelites in the first centuries of the empire. But there are, of course, key differences.

A number of questions must be asked about the function of patronage in the early church, especially with regard to hierarchy and authority. First, the Roman world loved honor, prestige, status symbols, and signs of precedence. It is now generally understood that any exchange between two males outside the familiar setting was an implicit contest for honor. In the literature of the period the love of honor and praise (*philotimia*) is the primary motive for benefactions. Would the portrait of the humble, crucified Jesus and Paul's proclamation of the cross and strength in weakness have any effect on the instinctive scramble for honor? Paul puts a great deal of effort into changing the mind-set in his language of the cross in 1 Corinthians 1 and Galatians. The schismatic tendencies in the Corinthian community suggest that the lesson was not well learned in Paul's day, and the behavior of many bishops in the better-preserved Christian records of the fourth and fifth centuries suggests that it never was. In other words, we are talking here not about ideals but about realities. It is important to remember that the other side of the proclamation of the cross was that Christ was raised in power and subjected his enemies under his feet, a triumph in which the Christian believer was promised an eventual share (1 Cor. 15:24-25; compare Ps. 110:1).

Second, patronage nearly always presupposes an unequal relationship, because the whole point of it is access to power that the client would not otherwise have. Where do figures like Jesus and Paul fit here? Does their charismatic authority take precedence over the usually established criterion of status? And does not Paul have some relationships in which he is alternately patron and client? Third, network theory tells us that it is not ideas but personal contacts that create the environment for joining, for continued allegiance, and therefore for conversions. How did those social networks operate among the nonelites of the Roman cities who were brought into contact with Christian evangelizers?[63]

This is not the place to examine the traditions about Jesus in depth, but it is worth looking briefly at the figure of Jesus as it functions in patronal and brokerage roles. The proclamation of the reign of God is the announcement of efficient patronage: all who approach it will receive what they ask (Matt. 7:7; compare Heb. 4:16). The relationship is certainly asymmetrical, and it is reciprocal: loyalty and praise are expected of clients in return for favors granted. Jesus is God's authorized agent on earth, dispensing such favors as healing, exorcising, and, above all, forgiveness of sin, the release of debt. The disciples are empowered at various levels to carry on the same work of dispensing God's patronage. In view of the emperor's claim to be chief father figure and Pontifex Maximus, that is, major mediator between gods and inhabitants of the empire, these were dangerous views.

Through Paul's letters we know more about him than about any other apostolic figure. There is a remarkable paucity in his letters of the terminology of friendship (only the closing greeting in 1 Cor. 16:22, which may be a quoted formula), despite efforts to portray his relationship to the communities as one along the traditional lines of the literary topos of friendship.[64] There is, however, an abundance of talk about *charis*, understood theologically as grace, but in the world in which Paul developed this new meaning, the semantic field of *charis* is that of favor, graciousness, benefaction, and therefore of the asymmetrical relationship of patronage. It is God's *charis* that Paul emphasizes, and in doing that, Paul is indeed, as many have claimed, creating a new dimension to the patronage pattern that will be followed by Luke and others: to God be the glory, praise, and honor, and therefore the patronage.[65]

Paul's skittishness about dependence on the Corinthians, when he gratefully received gifts from other churches, has always been an interpretive problem. While we do not have enough information about how this patronage was organized in other communities, it does seem that, for example, at Philippi a communal collection was delivered to Paul rather than gifts from individuals (Phil. 4:16-19; God will reciprocate). Jerome Murphy-O'Connor suggests this as the reason for Paul's resistance at Corinth: there, it was to be personal patronage, into whose entangling alliances Paul did not wish to venture.[66]

He seems not to have been able completely to avoid such entanglements at Corinth, however. Why did he baptize Crispus, Gaius, and the household of Stephanas if he did not see baptizing as part of his mission (1 Cor. 1:14-17)? The best answer is that these were the ones Paul perceived as most prominent, those who would sponsor his gospel to their dependents, and the ones under whose patronage he could carry out his mission and the church could thrive.[67] Paul has set up his own patronage system, in which their gratitude to him will cultivate loyalty. Stephanas particularly can be singled out for his social prominence, for he hosts Paul and the whole church, the members of which are expected, as good clients, to be submissive to him (1 Cor. 16:15-16). He has also taken part in the Corinthian delegation to Paul at Ephesus, all of which leads Murphy-O'Connor to remark that his role "implies a degree of leisure difficult to associate with those who had to sweat for every morsel of food."[68] At a later time, Gaius hosts the whole Corinthian church (Rom. 16:23).

From the submission language about Stephanas and the language of respect and esteem for those who "labor among you, who preside over you and admonish you" in 1 Thess. 5:12-13, it would seem that the expected way to deal with leadership figures very early was with respect and submission. That should not be surprising. In return, loyal church members could expect to receive the benefits of clientage. What *is* surprising to note is that, apart from one passage in *1 Clement* (1.3) and in the long recension of Ignatius, *Philadelphians* 4, the language of submission (*hypotassein*) appears in early postcanonical Christian literature only in the context of the deference owed to church leaders (also in *1 Clem.* 1.3). In the household codes of the New Testament, by contrast, such language is closely associated with marriage relationships and slavery, even though it occurs in many other contexts there, including civic authority (Rom 13:1). Hence the language of submission has migrated from household to patronally organized church.

The policies of church leadership toward personal patronage of individuals and especially of groups within the church fluctuated in the following centuries. Diotrephes, the burr under the saddle of the Elder in 3 John 9, is characterized as *philōproteuōn*, which means more than liking to put himself first, as the NRSV renders it: he is overbearing about his patronal claims and does not wish to acknowledge those of the Elder. Hermas criticizes the wealthy for shirking patronal duties: they get so tied up in their business interests that they avoid lesser persons because they do not wish to be asked for favors (Herm. *Sim.* 9.20.2–4). This would have been considered not only bad but stupid behavior for the wealthy anywhere. Such people would incur the disdain not only of Hermas but of the Christian poor as well, to say nothing of their peers. Their repentance will consist of "doing some good," namely, generosity with their riches and the establishment of patronage relationships. The traditional titular churches and catacombs of Rome witness to the benefactions of early patrons. In nearly every instance, what later becomes church-owned and -administered space for burials and funeral meals begins with a wealthy benefactor who allows communal use of privately owned property.[69]

Other later writers under a growing church centralization are not so encouraging. The *Apostolic Tradition* of Hippolytus discourages individuals from holding charity meals for the needy without clerical supervision.[70] Cyprian, probably like most bishops of his time, wanted to consolidate patronal power in his own office by weakening the power of wealthy members of the church, encouraging centralized charity, and rejecting the charismatic claims that martyrs forgave sins. The consolidation of charity, already evidenced by Justin and Tertullian, gradually becomes the normal way for Christians to exercise their generosity. By then, the patronage system has been vastly overhauled, and there is only one major patron left: the bishop.[71]

The Patronage of Christian Women

Having now described the general functions of patronage and the participation of women in the system, and having taken a brief look at how patronage functioned in early Christianity, we turn at last to Christian women. Both personal and group patronage are evident. Women extend benefaction to individual leaders like Paul and Ignatius, and they open their houses for Christian gatherings. The evidence of women's hosting house churches is clearly present in the New Testament: Mary mother of John Mark in Jerusalem (Acts 12:12), Nympha (Col. 4:15), Lydia (Acts 16:14-15, 40),[72] and Prisca with Aquila. The examination of how those households and church gatherings were conducted is the subject of another chapter. The assumption can be made that they were conducted in the same way as any other patronage situation, with deference, respect, and submission owed to the patronal figure who expected to be the center of attention and of honor, except at those times when founding apostles were present.

Several more general remarks in Acts leave the gaps to be filled in. In Acts 17:4 and 12, Paul's preaching in Thessalonica and Beroea, respectively, results in the conversion of some important men and distinguished women.[73] In both cases, the same should be assumed as with Paul's dealings with important people in Corinth: that he welcomed these prominent connections as opportunities to establish patronage networks whereby the less distinguished, especially their dependents, would be favorably impressed and even perhaps pressured toward conversion. The reverse is true at Acts 13:50 in Pisidian Antioch, where the leading Jews incite the leading men and distinguished women *against* the missionary preachers. Here the power connections are already too well established, and they are not in Paul's favor. Given what we know about women's patronage, we need not assume in any of the above three cases that by the mention of both men and women, married couples are meant.

Ignatius's letters mention several more prominent women who must have provided patronage for him and probably hosted a house church: Tavia with her household (*Smyrn.* 13.2) and perhaps the highly placed Alke, "a name that is dear to me," probably the same Jewish woman whose brother Niketas was later inimical to Polycarp (*Smyrn.* 13.2; *Pol.* 8.3; *Mart. Pol.* 17.2). One suspects a story there of a woman who sacrificed some family ties for her continued support of Ignatius. There is another woman referred to in *Pol.* 8.2, an unnamed wife of an unnamed steward (*epitropos*) or of a man called Epitropos, with her whole household and children. This must be the case of a Christian *materfamilias* with an unbelieving husband. We are accustomed to thinking of widows as women in a position to be benefactors of Christian groups, but this passage cautions that married women too might have performed patronage roles to Christian groups independently of their husbands, just as their non-Christian counterparts did to synagogues and temples. The inclusion of the household and children in this case suggests hospitality of some kind, with the husband not objecting.[74] The absence of the woman's name is surprising. It may be a way of protecting her or her husband from public shame by being associated with a convicted criminal—or perhaps Ignatius has just had a "senior moment" and has forgotten her name!

And so we come to the Paul-Phoebe connection in Rom. 16:1-2, where Phoebe is called both *diakonos* and *prostatis*. We will not take up here the question of what a *diakonos* would do in the middle of the first century in Cenchrae, except to agree with those who suggest that the context in Rom. 16:1-2 hints that representation of one church to another has something to do with it, since representation or agency is one of the principal connotations of the *diakonia* word group.[75] A parallel may perhaps be found in two passage of Ignatius. In *Letter to the Philadelphians* 10.1 he encourages the church to appoint (*cheirotonēsai*, the term that will later be the most common for clerical ordination) a *diakonos* as representative (*eis to presbeusai*) to the Syrian church.[76] In *Smyrn.* 10.1 two men named Philo and Rheus Agathopous, who accompany Ignatius (*Letter to the Philadelphians* 11.1), were received by the Smyrnaeans as representatives of God (*hōs diakonous theou*) when they came to Philadelphia. Margaret Mitchell has shown that the officially designated envoy, in the context of epistolary conventions, was to be received in the same way as the sender would be received and is the authoritative representative of the one who sends.[77] Phoebe functions this way with regard to Paul, as do Timothy and Titus in other situations.

The ascription *prostatis* is the one of most concern here. Taking account of everything we have already seen, it becomes clear that the connotations are not so much "presider" as in a liturgical assembly, though that is not ruled out by reason of the privileged place of the patron in an assembly, but the patronal benefaction and therefore the prestige and authority that come from the position.[78] While it is true that neither the masculine *prostates* nor the feminine *prostatis* necessarily includes hospitality, this role cannot be ruled out either, by reason of the *prostasia* of Junia Theodora, Phoebe's Lycian contemporary in Corinth, whose role description does clearly include hospitality to Lycians passing through Corinth.[79]

Some have suggested specific strategy on Paul's part by entrusting his letter to Phoebe. Robert Jewett sees Phoebe as Paul's front-runner and ace in the hole for his Spanish mission. Since he knows no one in Rome and there is not a sizable Jewish community to which he could attach himself, he relies on the wealthy and influential Phoebe to pave the way in Rome and stimulate there the desire to finance his Spanish mission once he arrives. The greeting list of Romans 16 is then "a roster of potential campaign supporters . . . the first stage in the recruitment process."[80]

On the other hand, Caroline F. Whelan sees Romans 16 as intended for Ephesus, where Paul relies on Phoebe to secure his interests there while he heads west. Paul relies on Phoebe's network of clients and at the same time introduces her to his network as a way to reciprocate her patronage to him. She sees their relationship as "an agreement of 'equals,' albeit with vastly different spheres of interest," this equality on some levels creating a different kind of patron-client relationship, in which there is some kind of mutuality.[81] This may be so. We saw early on that patronage between two near equals, for example, senior and junior senator, was possible. But from what we know of relationships in general, seldom was the concept of equality part of the equation, and almost never between men and women until the later days of the Christian ascetics several centuries later. Otherwise, however, in Rom. 16:2 we have the odd case of a client, Paul, commending his patron, Phoebe. But this may be justified in the case that the patron is moving into new territory that the client already knows to some extent, as is probably the case here.

Whether one considers Romans 16 as addressed to Rome or to Ephesus will necessarily influence one's interpretation of Phoebe's role. But whichever it is, it is likely that Paul is not just commending Phoebe to a new group but is participating in some greater plan, which may have been initiated not by Paul but by Phoebe.

An unusual Christian inscription from fourth-century Jerusalem commemorates a "slave and bride of Christ" named Sophia, a deacon (*diakonos*), "the second Phoebe" (*hē deutera Phoibē*). It is doubtful that she is hailed as second Phoebe because she is a deacon, a title held by many Christian women of the period. G. H. R. Horsley proposes several parallels in which men are hailed in inscriptions as "new Homer," "new Themistocles," "new Theophanes," and "new Dionysos," the last also applied to two emperors, Commodus and Gallienus.[82] In every case, the person so titled seems to have been a major benefactor of his own or his adoptive city. The title probably began with popular acclamation and stuck to the man's public identity. The same is likely true of Sophia because of her benefactions to the church of Jerusalem.

A few more glimpses of Christian women patrons must be mentioned. The reference to "Chloe's people" in 1 Cor. 1:11 means that Chloe is the central person in some kind of household staff. Her "people" are either members of her immediate household or of her extended network of clients. If they have written from Corinth to Paul in Ephesus, Chloe herself is probably not a Christian, since her dependents would not be referred to in this manner. Rather, the reference would be to "Chloe and her people." On the other hand, if some members of her household are now in Ephesus for some reason, or passing through en route to another destination, and are reporting orally to Paul, it is possible that Chloe herself is a believer, at home in Corinth. A certain number of Christians in her *familia* are functioning either independently with regard to religion, which would not be unusual, or under the patronage of this woman who may or may not have been a member of the community, much as a synagogue received the patronage of Tation at Kyme or Julia Severa at Akmonia, two women patrons who were probably not Jewish.[83] Marcia, concubine of Commodus, is known to have interceded in imperial machinery for the release of a group of Christians condemned to the mines in the early third century, among them Callistus, according to his rival Hippolytus. One of the things that Hippolytus found objectionable about Callistus's policies once he became bishop of Rome is that Callistus allowed women of higher status to marry men of lesser status, a practice always frowned upon by society at large (*Ref.* 9.12). Though not specified further, this is likely to have meant a freeborn woman, an *ingenua*, marrying a freedman, a *libertinus*. The old objection about women patrons marrying their own freedmen may have risen once again, this time in a Christian context.[84]

The evolution of the office of widow also gives glimpses into what was happening with Christian women patrons. While the text of Acts does not say that Tabitha is actually a widow (Acts 9:36-42), she is a benefactor especially to widows, and there is no mention of her husband in the narrative of her restoration to life. First Timothy 5:16 encourages women patrons to care for needy widows so that the church does not have to carry the burden. This is an acknowledgment of the power of wealthy and influential women and an appeal to a particular way in which women could be of service, by befriending other women in need.[85] While widows are presented in many texts from 1 Timothy 5 onward as predominantly recipients of charity, the "enrollment" to which they are subject also implies a certain status of honor. In Tertullian's Carthage the order of widows is seated with the clergy to receive petitions for a second marriage and for the ritual prostration of public penitents (*Monogamy* 11.1; *Modesty* 13.7). Beginning in 1 Tim. 5:13, the traditional fear of the power of widows is raised: since they no longer link two families and are no longer under the direct authority of a man, they have too much freedom, and their integrity is suspect.

The long recension of Ignatius's *Philadelphians* 4 includes at the end of an extensive discussion of submission relationships an exhortation to widows not to wander about and be lacking in austerity, but to be serious like Judith and Anna. The same motif recurs in the third-century *Didascalia Apostolorum* 15 (*Apostolic Constitutions* 3.5–11).[86] Here widows, asked about the faith, must only respond about the basics, leaving catechesis to the qualified, for if outsiders were to hear about the incarnation and passion of Christ from a woman, their response would be derision. The whole idea of women's teaching or baptizing is disapproved of, but the obsession, returned to several times in the text, echoing 1 Tim. 5:13, is with widows' moving around from house to house. They may not instruct, visit the sick, or lay hands on anyone without the bishop's permission. From earlier tradition, widows are compared to the altar of God. Just as the altar stays in one place, so should they![87] Thus there is a deliberate attempt to thwart the mutual aid system that usually functions in women's subgroups and to make the widows entirely dependent on the bishop and his representatives, the deacons. The widows are expressly told that they should not know, and may not reveal if they do know, the identity of their benefactors. The expected desire of clients to be personally connected to their patrons is suppressed in favor of centralized coordination. By this time, we can see a conscious attempt on the part of church authority to control women's patronage as well as men's and to break the network of personal patronage that had been the backbone of social relationships.

The patronal activity of women did not entirely disappear in this new centralized system. Their role in providing burial for the Christian poor continued into the fourth century.[88] Wealthy women continued to be major donors to the church and as such to command at least a great deal of respect, if not social power. They also participated as deacons throughout the empire, especially but not exclusively in the East, where often the preferred title for such women was *diakonos* rather than *diakonissa* through the sixth century. Male deacons were responsible for carrying out the patronage program of the bishop. Female deacons participated in that work, especially in a ministry to other women. Female deacons also contributed to churches and cities and exercised their own charitable works. The deacon/ness Matrona of fourth-century Stobi, for example, paved an exedra (temple room) in fulfillment of a vow, as did the *diakonos* Agrippiane a mosaic floor in Patrae, while Mary the deacon in sixth-century Archelais, Cappadocia, in keeping with the description in 1 Tim. 5:10, "raised children, exercised hospitality, washed the feet of the saints, and distributed her bread to the needy."[89]

Conclusion:
The Evolution of Patronage

The extent and importance of women's patronage in the Greco-Roman world and especially in early Christianity have been neglected and are still in need of exploration. But to appreciate the nature of women's patronage, to catch the nuances, we need to be sensitive to the social signals, networks, and hierarchical relationships inherent in ancient Mediterranean society. Whereas we would think that one who supplies material assistance to another is in a subordinate position, there it was the opposite: the one who received had to recognize subordination. With honor came the expectation of authority. There is no evidence that in ordinary patronage relationships this was any different for women than for men.

While real legal and ideological differences remained, it is doubtful whether in the everyday practice of patronal relationships much difference could have been perceived between the practice of patronage among men and women, except for voting and holding elective office, and even there, other aspects of the political process are very similar. Likewise, in early Christianity there was little difference between the patronage of men and women, but the patronage function was an essential ingredient in the life of house churches. Ultimately, the patronal power began to be absorbed into the hands of the bishop. But in that case, both women and nonclerical men found that it was a different world.

CHAPTER TEN

WOMEN AS AGENTS
OF EXPANSION

ⓞⓞ ⓞⓞ ⓞⓞ

In concentrating throughout the last three chapters on women leading house-church communities, presiding at banquets, and acting as
patrons, we have been shifting our focus away from the more domestic
roles of women to their more public roles. It should be stated at the outset, however, that any firm distinction between the domestic (or private)
realm and the public realm in the Roman world can quickly lead to a false
dichotomy. The existence of early Christian house churches illustrates
this especially clearly. In houses—the domain traditionally associated
with women—male and female believers were hosting a movement with
an unmistakably public thrust. While we must always be ready to qual-
ify our distinctions, in this chapter we will examine the involvement of
women in the most obvious dimension of this public thrust: early Christian expansion.

Women and the Christianization of the Roman Empire:
Ancient and Modern Impressions of Prominence

We begin with ancient impressions of the prominence of women in early
church groups. We have already discussed Celsus's second-century pagan

critique of early Christianity on a few occasions in this book. For example, in chapter 4 we discussed Celsus's impressions of the involvement of children in early Christian communities, and in chapter 6 we considered how his critique reflects stereotypical notions of the violation of gender boundaries associated with foreign religious groups. Here we will concentrate specifically on Celsus's impressions of women leading to the expansion of early Christian groups.

For Celsus the Christian family is at the very heart of the growth of a troublesome new movement. The subordinate members of households are especially prominent among the gullible crowds. As recorded by Origen, Celsus describes the early Christian missionary tactics as follows: "Their injunctions are like this. 'Let no one educated, no one wise, no one sensible draw near. For these abilities are thought by us to be evils. But as for anyone ignorant, anyone stupid, anyone uneducated, anyone who is a child, let him come boldly.' By the fact that they themselves admit that these people are worthy of their God, they show that they want and are able to convince only the foolish, dishonorable and stupid, and only slaves, women and little children."[1] According to Celsus, Christians lead adherents to turn against the heads of households and those in legitimate positions of authority—they encourage insubordination within the family group:

> In private houses we see wool-workers, cobblers, laundry workers, and the most illiterate and bucolic yokels, who would not dare to say anything at all in front of their elders and more intelligent masters. But whenever they get hold of children in private and some stupid women with them, they let out some astounding statements as, for example, that they must not pay any attention to their father and school teachers, but must obey them; they say that these talk nonsense and have no understanding, and that in reality they neither know nor are able to do anything good, but are taken up with mere empty chatter. But they alone they say, know the right way to live, and if the children would believe them, they would become happy and make their home happy as well. And if just as they are speaking they see one of the school teachers coming, or some intelligent person, or even the father himself, the more cautious of them flee in all directions; but the more reckless urge the children on to rebel. They whisper to them that in the presence of their father and their schoolmasters they do not feel able to explain anything to the children. But, if they like, they should leave father and their schoolmasters, and go along with the women

and little children who are playfellows to the wooldresser's shop, or the cobbler's or the washerwoman's shop, that they may learn perfection. And by saying this they persuade them.[2]

In Celsus's account women and children are clearly depicted as targets for Christian missionaries, but they are also presented as active in the missionary enterprise themselves. Teachers are said to instruct the prospective members to go along with women and children to the various shops in order to attain perfection, seemingly to receive further instruction and initiation. While we should probably not press the text for logical consistency, there is an interesting movement from house to house or house to shop (which could presumably mean one section of the house to another) in this text. The initial contact is made in houses where gullible, illiterate, and subordinate members of the household are present, but the possibility of someone in authority overhearing is very real indeed. Bolder recruits (children mostly) are presented as being accompanied by women and children to the wool dresser's shop—or to the cobbler's or to the washerwoman's shop—apparently a place where there will be greater opportunities for instruction. All of this suggests an intriguing relationship among secrecy, concealment, and the involvement of women and children that will be explored further below.

In analyzing Celsus's depiction of women's involvement in the evangelizing tactics of the early Christians, we are confronted immediately by one of the most difficult methodological issues facing historians who investigate the involvement of women in the expansion of the movement: the problem of drawing historical conclusions based on texts in which women are represented in such a way as to further the agendas of male authors. From the target audience for missionary efforts, to the nature of the shops propounded as the locus of activities, to the secretive and insubordinate behavior of adherents, to the stress on the initiative of women and children, the attempt to denigrate early Christianity by appealing to the gender and status of its main proponents is unmistakable. In fact, women figured prominently in Celsus's polemical critique of early Christianity as he set out to attack the religion on the basis of its origins, major tenets, and social manifestations.[3] Celsus's approach was to be expected. New and illegitimate religious groups in antiquity were typically attacked by highlighting their attraction for women and their corrupting influence upon women.[4] Predictably, we see these themes repeated in the pagan criticism of Christianity, which predates or is contemporary with Celsus. Celsus's treatise has much in common with the reactions of such authors as Marcus Cornelius Fronto or Lucius Apuleius, but it also differs from these others in a significant way.[5] His account surpasses mere rumor, general impression, or stereotype. He clearly had a detailed knowledge of Christianity and had read such important texts as the Gospel of Matthew and probably various Gnostic sources.[6] Moreover, the picture Celsus painted of the importance of the house to the expansion of Christianity finds support in early Christian texts, which speak of groups meeting in houses (for example, Rom. 16:5; 1 Cor. 16:19; Philemon 2) and of entire households joining the church (for example, Acts 16:11-15; 1 Cor. 1:16).

In this book we have examined significant evidence for the participation of women in early Christian house churches, and, though it is not free of ambiguity, it has points in common with Celsus's presentation. When evaluated critically, pagan opinion about early Christianity can offer an alternate window into the lives of early Christian women to complement what can be deduced on the basis of Christian sources.[7] To stress the involvement of women and children in the expansion of Christianity clearly suited Celsus's rhetorical purposes, and his treatment certainly cannot be taken at face value, but there is enough corroborating Christian evidence that we may reasonably ask the question: Was Celsus right?

The impression of prominence, even of predominance, of women in early Christian circles that one finds in pagan critique of early Christianity has found a counterpart in modern scholarship on the Christianization of the empire. In his magisterial study *Pagans and Christians*, Robin Lane Fox has written that "Christian women [were] prominent in the churches' membership and recognized to be so by Christians and pagans," and he recalls the claims of Adolf von Harnack about women playing "a leading role in the spread of this religion."[8] More recently, the involvement of women has been central to Rodney Stark's thesis about the involvement of women in the rise of Christianity (published in his 1996 work *The Rise of Christianity*). In his chapter on women Stark makes claims about women outnumbering men in early Christian circles, about their enjoying higher status in church circles than in the Greco-Roman environment generally, and about their ability to affect church growth on account of marriages to pagans. It is this last aspect of Stark's work that is of most interest for this chapter. Stark is clearly drawing on a particular sociological notion of conversion that focuses on the use of available social "networks" in contributing to the expansion of the group.[9] The network in question in this case is the extended household of antiquity.

Yet some interpreters (sometimes adopting a feminist perspective) have been reluctant to ascribe a major role to women in the Christianization of the empire and have warned against an uncritical reading of the evidence. They have argued that when dealing with ancient literature, including both early Christian texts and pagan critique of early Christianity, the depiction of women's influence may have much more to do with the intention of male authors than with the activities of real Christian women. Focusing particularly on the Christian literature of the later empire, Kate Cooper has spoken of a "topos of womanly influence" in Christian literature as an element of "cultural continuity with the earlier Empire."[10] Concentrating on evidence from Jerome, Chrysostom, and Augustine, Cooper argues that texts that describe the influence of women on their male partners, and that have been understood to mean that married men were converted by their wives, should not be taken at face value. Her thesis is that such discourse was part of a rhetorical strategy in power competitions between men, such as that between married, householder clergy and celibates over Christian leadership.[11] In a similar vein Judith Lieu has raised critical questions about earlier evidence concerning the involvement of women. Noting some parallels with Josephus, she has argued that a novelistic tendency may well shape the account of the conversion of Lydia (Acts 16:11-15) and of the noble women of Thessalonica in Acts (17:4, 12; compare 17:33-34) and, for similar reasons, that the story of Thecla "tells us little about 'real' women's conversion to Christianity in the second century."[12] She concludes: "The gendering of conversion is a matter of rhetorical and not of statistical analysis. The move from rhetoric to social experience must remain hazardous."[13]

The disjunction between the bold claims of Stark and some ancient historians and the sobering cautions of other interpreters (to the point where one might become hesitant to make any claims about real women at all) calls for a reexamination of the evidence. In investigations of the role of women in the expansion of Christianity, scholars have dealt with two types of evidence. They have made claims about the number of women attracted to early Christianity and about the greater attraction of women to early Christianity. It follows that women may have contributed to the expansion of early Christianity by the sheer force of their presence.[14] Second, they have focused on the specific activities of early Christian women (such as their role in evangelizing pagan partners) in contributing to the expansion of Christianity. This study is of the latter type. In this chapter we will concentrate on literary texts that suggest that women—many of them unnamed in the texts and probably quite ordinary according to the standards of their day—were actively doing things that contributed to the expansion of church groups.[15] Much of the discussion of the role of women in the Christianization of the empire has concentrated on the Roman aristocracy of the fourth century because of the significant body of evidence from this period. But here we will focus on the earlier periods, about which much less is known but which are clearly critical for the expansion of early Christianity—the first and second centuries CE, the period of house churches.

Women in the Pauline Mission

If one is to study the role of women in the expansion of Christianity, an obvious place to begin is with the women who participated in Paul's mission. Clearly, women such as Prisca and Phoebe had leadership roles in the Pauline circle, but can we say for sure that they contributed in direct ways to the group's expansion? Of course, the difficulty of answering this question is compounded by the fact that the manner of Christianization of the empire remains a subject of debate; even Paul's own modus operandi is far from certain,[16] especially given the problem of harmonizing Paul's letters with the depiction of Paul as a missioner in Acts. Despite these difficulties, however, many recent interpreters have confidently asserted the involvement of women in the missionary efforts of the Pauline circle. The fascinating references to women leaders in the Pauline churches have been analyzed by Elisabeth Schüssler Fiorenza and others, and it is impractical to repeat the results of their analysis here.[17] However, it is important to note that interpreters have usually not distinguished precisely between women's involvement in the expansion of early church groups and the other types of leadership they undertook among believers. This is no doubt due to the fact that the New Testament evidence does not at all suggest a rigid demarcation among types of leadership. A woman leader of a house church such as Prisc(ill)a (Rom. 16:3-5; 1 Cor. 16:19) is also depicted as engaging in evangelizing efforts (Acts 18:24-26). But for the purposes of this chapter, it is essential to try to distinguish as much as possible between local leadership and leadership efforts with an outward orientation—indications of activities that clearly win new members.

Among the strongest evidence we have that some of the women mentioned in Paul's letters understood themselves and were understood by others as fostering the spread of the gospel is the fact that they are named as partners—missionary partners—continuing the practices of the Jesus movement (see Mark 6:7; Luke 10:1—though here not presented as male-female pairs).[18] Because they are described as prominent among the apostles—clearly a designation of paramount significance for Paul's identity and in earliest Christianity—Andronicus and Junia are especially intriguing missionary partners (Rom. 16:7).[19] It must be admitted that the term "apostle" (*apostolos*) carries a broad range of meanings in Paul's letters and can refer simply to a messenger or emissary of the church (for example, 2 Cor. 8:23). But Paul frequently uses the term to refer to itinerant preachers of the gospel (2 Cor. 11:4-6, 13; 12:11-12). If we place the description of this pair of "apostles" within its context of Romans 16, which often alludes to precarious activities undertaken for the sake of the gospel, there seems little reason to doubt that Paul referred to Andronicus and Junia (described as Paul's fellow prisoners) as apostles who partook in the missionary enterprise.

Of the male-female pairs, however, we possess the most information about Prisc(ill)a and Aquila, discussed at length in chapter 2. They are both called Paul's coworkers (Rom. 16:3: *synergos*), a term that Paul can use to single out males in leadership roles (for example, Rom. 16:9; Phil. 2:25), including such important fellow workers in the spreading of the gospel as Timothy (Rom. 16:21; 1 Thess. 3:2) and Titus (2 Cor. 8:23). Euodia and Syntyche also belong to this group (Phil. 4:3). Paul even describes himself, along with Apollos, as God's fellow workers who plant what in the end only God can grow—the community (1 Cor. 3:9). Like Paul himself, the "fellow workers" seem to do things that are understood as expanding the church while at the same time nurturing existing communities. One of the most remarkable texts in all of the New Testament concerning the evangelizing role of a woman is Acts 18:24-26, in which both Prisc(ill)a and Aquila are said to have taught Apollos in Ephesus, a learned Jew who had great knowledge of the scriptures. Although Apollos already had some knowledge of the Christian message, Prisc(ill)a and Aquila are said to have taken Apollos aside and "explained the way of God more accurately" (Acts 18:24-26).[20] The author of Acts probably meant for us to understand that

Prisc(ill)a and Aquila took Apollos into their home, which also served as a house church, the basic cell of Christian organization (Rom. 16:5; 1 Cor. 16:19). But, as we discussed in chapter 2, we should not underestimate the influence of the "settled" life of house churches on winning new members and the success that Prisc(ill)a—usually named first when the pair is mentioned—had as an agent of expansion.

While Prisc(ill)a and Aquila's teaching of Apollos might offer evidence for the involvement of women in a type of evangelization, it cannot be used to provide evidence of women making initial contact with nonbelievers—Apollos was already familiar with the Christian message to a certain extent. Yet the evidence from Acts is suggestive, especially when one considers Celsus's description of Christians' leading the recruits back to their shops for further instruction. Moreover, Paul describes the efforts of Prisc(ill)a and Aquila with language that recalls the perils of mission. He states that they have risked their necks on his behalf and on behalf of others; we may surmise that he is talking about the dangers of travel and perhaps also the risks of initial contacts with people whose family members objected to this association (see 1 Cor. 7:12-16). Such an association between danger and the life of missionary partners is also evident in the description of Andronicus and Junia (Rom. 16:7), and especially in the description of Euodia and Syntyche's contribution to Pauline Christianity (Phil. 4:2-3). While we cannot be absolutely certain of this, Paul's language implies that these women were involved in the evangelization of nonbelievers. They were apparently successful despite having experienced opposition from nonbelievers (though opposition from internal opponents cannot be ruled out entirely). Using a verb that recalls the struggles of war or the violent contests of the games (*synathleō*), the text describes them as coworkers who fought at Paul's side in the gospel. The only other use of the term in the New Testament appears earlier in Philippians to refer to the struggle of the community against some external threat that Paul himself experienced (Phil. 1:27-30; see also Acts 16:19-40; 1 Thess. 2:2).[21]

With Euodia and Syntyche's leadership (Phil. 4:2-3; compare Rom. 16:12) we have evidence of women clearly conducting their work for the sake of the gospel in the first instance without male counterparts. This type of independence is even more striking with respect to Phoebe (Rom. 16:1-2; Mary [16:6] and Persis [16:12] may also be women working for the sake of the gospel without specific partners), the woman who traveled to Rome perhaps bearing Paul's letter or for business purposes or both.

Among the most tangential theories about her identity, but among the most suggestive for our purposes, is that Paul viewed Phoebe as a central player in his plans for a Spanish mission (Rom. 15:23-24).[22] In calling Phoebe a "benefactor" (*prostatis*) of many community members and of Paul himself, Paul implies that he has been dependent upon her sphere of influence to expand his mission in Cenchrae or elsewhere (the commendation Paul offers Phoebe, however, is also an indication of her dependence upon him). Perhaps Phoebe offered her house for meetings or acted as a host to traveling Christians; she may well have been of service to Paul by introducing Paul to others who became community benefactors.[23] The titles used to describe Phoebe offer evidence that the extension of her influence included the winning of new members. Like Apphia, the prominent member of the house church greeted in Paul's letter to Philemon, Phoebe is called a "sister" (*adelphē*)—a term that could be used to refer to the female member of a missionary partnership (compare 1 Cor. 9:5) and whose male equivalent was a frequent designation for Paul's collaborator Timothy (2 Cor. 1:1; 1 Thess. 3:2; Philemon 1). The significance of the use of the term "deacon" (*diakonos*) to describe Phoebe's role is not completely clear.[24] But it is indisputably a term (often translated as "minister," "servant," or "helper") that Paul uses to describe his own identity and the identity of coworkers who are involved in spreading the gospel (for example, 1 Cor. 3:5; 2 Cor. 3:6; 11:23; compare Rom. 11:13; 1 Cor. 16:15; 2 Cor. 5:18; 6:3; Col. 4:7).[25]

There is strong evidence suggesting that the women named as leaders in Paul's letters engaged in activities that contributed directly to the expansion of the movement. Such terms as "sister," "deacon," "coworker," or "apostle," which are used to describe these women, are not unambiguous. But when taken together and compared to their usage (or the use of masculine equivalents) to describe men, including Paul himself, we are left with a very strong impression of missionary activity. Describing the precise nature of this activity is much more difficult. The references to travel and crafts, especially with respect to Prisc(ill)a and Aquila (see chapter 2), indicate opportunities to circulate the gospel on the road, in shops, and in the midst of trade. Allusions to the institution of patronage, the leadership of house churches, and sequestered teaching opportunities point to women using their households in various ways to foster the growth of the movement. Among the most fascinating information emerging from this survey is the ever-present suggestion of danger. These women were clearly taking risks for the sake of the gospel.

Rhetorical attempts to control the lives of women and to use female identity as a means of articulating community norms and boundaries are present in Paul's letters (for example, 1 Cor. 11:2-11; 14:33b-36) and become even more pronounced in later periods. As we move beyond Paul's day, incidental references to "real" women become rarer and women's identities increasingly become constructs operating through such literary genres as apology, martyrology, and novelistic accounts. It is difficult to judge the impact of such texts on women's lives or to what extent they reflect the reality of the existence of women. Thus, we are fortunate indeed that Paul revealed so much incidentally in the exchange of greetings and recommendations about real women. As if by accident we are informed that the roles of women coworkers were like those of men. With respect to missionary couples, for example, there is no indication of the female partner's having a different or diminished role in relation to the male partner. Later patristic exegetes offered the women partners a much more restricted script. Clement of Alexandria interpreted 1 Cor. 9:5 as a reference to spiritual marriage, in which the woman missionary partner acted as a helpmate who ministered in her own right only to other women. He stressed the fact that only women could enter the women's quarters in houses without scandal being aroused.[26] Clement's reading is shaped by the intention to present an appropriate male and female division of labor at the end of the second century CE, but his presentation does raise interesting questions about the role of women in making initial contact with other women. Clement is writing at about the same time as Celsus, when suspicions about the illicit activities of Christians are clearly high. The secret penetration of the house emerges in the comments of both pagan and Christian as a Christian missionary strategy. Similarly, in the fourth century, the ministry to women in pagan households was described as a special duty of the deaconess because it would have been too dangerous to send a male official.[27] All of this should not be read uncritically back into Paul's day, when tension between the church and the world was much less pronounced and Christianity would most likely not have appeared to an outsider as a clearly distinct entity. The named women leaders we encounter in Paul's letters were probably continuing in the leadership roles they had as pagan and Jewish women in other groups and associations.[28] Yet even in the earliest period there is evidence that women's joining church groups was causing household tensions (1 Cor. 7:12-16; see also 1 Pet. 3:1-6) and, as discussed above, that women were taking some types of risks for the sake of the gospel.

Widows, Teachers, and Prophets

The evidence concerning widows in early Christian literature indicates that networks of women contributed to the expansion of Christianity among women and children. Both Paul's letters and Acts bear testimony to the importance of the presence and influence of widows among the first generations of believers (for example, Acts 6:1-2; 9:36-43; 1 Corinthians 7). In keeping with the tendency to stress the involvement of well-to-do women in the rise of Christianity, the author of Acts presents Tabitha of Joppa as a community patron who bestowed goods on widows who were less fortunate. Tabitha may have been a widow herself, though one of independent means.[29] Perhaps as a reflection of the importance of widows to the expansion of church groups, the author presents the miraculous raising of Tabitha from the dead as the catalyst for a missionary thrust with news circulating by means of the witness of the saints and the widows (Acts 9:41-42).[30] That well-to-do women in early Christianity opened their homes to other women is also suggested by 1 Tim. 5:16. The practical support that early church groups could offer women and children in otherwise destitute circumstances was in all likelihood an important factor in winning new female members. If this was not the case, it is difficult to make sense of texts such as 1 Tim. 5:16, in which their sustenance is clearly an issue of community concern, if not at the center of a community dispute (see also Acts 6:1).[31]

In the literature coming from about the beginning of the second century, we find conclusive evidence of organized groups of women, some even exercising the "office of widow." In chapter 4 we discussed the association of these women with orphans, their ministry in house churches, and their roles as childcare providers and educators of young women and girls. Here our focus is on widows as agents of expansion. A key text for us to consider is 1 Tim. 5:3-16. In this passage the author of the Pastoral Epistles sets out to limit the burden of widows on the church, to define and to limit the "office of widows," and generally to control the behavior of widows. But unwittingly, the author may have offered us a window into the network of women that contributed to the expansion of Christianity. In critiquing the lives of widows, the author appeals to stereotypical opinions about the excessive and inappropriate religious inclinations of women. Among other things, they are said to be idlers, gossips, busybodies, and gadabouts, going from house to house, saying things that should not be said (1 Tim.

5:13; see also 2 Tim. 3:6). They are in all likelihood perpetuating an ascetic teaching that the author of the Pastorals cannot abide (compare 1 Tim. 4:3). Yet, if we consider the great interest in the reputation of the community in these texts and the author's admission that some widows have already contributed to the defamation of the community, it seems likely that the author is aiming to limit activities that were designed to draw new recruits into their ranks.[32]

The vision of roving women in the Pastorals has much in common with Celsus's depiction of the church as contributing to insubordinate behavior among women and children. Both bear the strong imprint of conventional views concerning the effect of illegitimate religion upon women. But the polemic does not mask the historical activities of women completely. In terms of widows in particular, the evidence is solid enough to suggest that by the end of the first century the activities of groups of women would have been visible to outsiders and, as the story of Tabitha and the treatment of widows in 1 Tim. 5:3-16 suggest, a contributing factor in the expansion of Christianity. Widows as a group were visible enough in the wider world to be singled out by at least one pagan author. When Lucian of Samosata told the tale of the conversion to Christianity of the philosopher Peregrinus, he spoke of aged widows and orphan children waiting near the prison, at the very break of day, presumably to pray or to offer some type of service to those who were in prison.[33] But the strongest evidence for widows engaging in "evangelizing" activities comes from just outside the period we are mainly discussing, the early third century.

The *Didascalia Apostolorum* displays many conventional views on the virtues and vices of women. The relationship between the teaching concerning widows and the specific activities of women is by no means always clear. But the instructions concerning how widows should relate to non-believers are precise and nuanced enough that we may be fairly confident that they are based on actual encounters between pagan and Christian. In the opinion of the author of the *Didascalia Apostolorum*, these encounters can often lead to problems. But interestingly, the author does not ban them altogether. Rather, the writer allows the widows to answer preliminary questions "in refutation of idols and concerning the unity of God." More complicated questions concerning Christology and eschatology, however, need to be referred to male church leaders: "For when the Gentiles who are being instructed hear the word of God not fittingly spoken, as it ought to be, unto edification of eternal life—and all the more in that it is spoken to them by a woman—how that our Lord clothed Himself in a body, and concerning the passion of Christ: they will mock and scoff, instead of applauding the word of doctrine; and she shall incur a heavy judgement for sin."[34] The attempt to restrict the activities of widows severely once again is unmistakable. But the small amount of latitude given to widows to answer rudimentary questions might well represent an indirect acknowledgment of the power of widows to make initial contact with potential converts and to generate interest in Christianity (even if, in the author's view, such interest subsequently needs to be perfected by the appropriate male authorities).

The treatment of widows in the *Didascalia Apostolorum* is in keeping with a common attitude displayed in early Christian texts toward women teachers, prophets, and visionaries, many of whom were celibate. The texts bristle with often indirect acknowledgments of their power and strong measures to control them (for example, 1 Cor. 11:2-16; Rev. 2:19-23). This ambivalence is no doubt related to the ambivalent reaction these women received as ambassadors of the new faith. In Lucian of Samosata's account mentioned above, the presence of old women and children in early Christian circles clearly serves to strengthen an already negative picture. But, in contrast, drawing special attention to the presence of women among church groups, Galen of Pergamum praised their "restraint in cohabitation" and defined their nature as a philosophical school.[35] In highlighting the involvement of both men *and* women, Galen's comments recall Philo's favorable description of a Jewish ascetic community, the Therapeutic society, and also have much in common with Justin's description of celibate men and women who proudly display their example before the whole of humanity.[36]

Judith Lieu has argued that Galen's description of Christian women and the involvement of women in Gnosticism and Montanism offer evidence that some women may have found Christianity intellectually attractive and may have been drawn to church groups for that reason.[37] At the end of the second century, Celsus's investigation of early Christianity turned up a number of women teacher-leaders, apparently as founders of groups. Although it suited his agenda to stress this female initiative, these women do figure prominently in Gnostic and apocryphal sources: Helena, Marcellina, Salome, Mariamme, and Martha.[38] Celsus also speaks of the early Christian belief in a "power flowing from a certain virgin Prunicus" and calls some Christians "Sybillists"—the Sybil was a prophetess of obscure origin known from Jewish and pagan sources and also mentioned in *The Shepherd of Hermas*.[39] It seems likely that Celsus had encountered early Christian groups—including Gnostic groups—in which women were prophets, visionaries, or teachers.

At about the same time as Celsus composed his critique of early Christianity, two women, Priscilla and Maximilla, were greatly honored leaders in a revivalist movement known as the New Prophecy (or Montanism), and their oracles were written down and accorded high status.[40] Further evidence for the prophetic activities of women is found in *The Martyrdom of Perpetua and Felicitas*. This document presents Perpetua as a powerful visionary, and, though it is by no means certain, has been understood as reflecting Montanist elements rooted in an early third-century, North African context.[41] Because a portion of this work claims to have been written by Perpetua herself, it has frequently been judged to be highly significant for the history of early Christian women. Although some scholars have recently raised reservations about the historicity of the document and claims of female authorship,[42] the document nevertheless raises many interesting questions about the relationship among conversion, martyrdom, and the religious displays of women more generally. Although it enhances the martyrdom discourse to speak of the conversion of jailers[43] and the power of a prison love feast to lead witnesses to faith,[44] the prison and martyrdom arena was clearly a place where early Christian women might have made a public impression.

The Household and Conversion

While asceticism and marriages between pagans and Christians (see below) continued to challenge the boundaries of conventional family existence, it is fair to say that by the latter decades of the first century Christianity became grafted onto conventional patterns of family life in some church circles.[45] At times, the household base of early Christianity was actually sanctified, with familial images merging with metaphorical descriptions of the relationship between the human and the divine (see Eph. 5:22-33; 1 Tim. 3:15). Ephesians even names God as the father from whom every home (*patria*) is named (3:14-15), suggesting "the sanctification of lineage as a divinely-ordained gift."[46] This reinforcement of conventional life is revealed most explicitly, however, in the household codes found repeatedly in the literature of the late New Testament and early patristic era (see Eph. 5:21—6:9; Col. 3:18—4:1; 1 Tim. 2:8-15; 5:1-2; 6:1-2; 1 Pet. 2:18—3:7; Titus 2:1-10; 3:1; *Did.* 4:9-11; *Barn.* 19:5-7; *1 Clem.* 21:6-9; Ignatius, *Pol.* 4:1—5:2; Polycarp, *Phil.* 4:2-3). Modern research on the origin and functions of the codes has revealed that the degree of explicit apologetic interest varies from one document to the next, but we should clearly look to the need for apology if we wish to understand why this type of hierarchical ethical exhortation emerged in church groups at this time.[47] Generally speaking, the tendency to include household code teaching surfaces when Christianity emerges as a clearly identifiable group in ancient society and struggles to survive in an increasingly hostile environment. Moreover, the emergence of household codes occurs largely simultaneously with what Ramsay MacMullen has identified as a decline in references to explicit missionary activity starting at the turn of the second century. He argues that Christians of this period were essentially cautious when it came to large-scale public appearances and identifies the fairly sequestered settings of home and work as the circumstances in which most conversions took place.[48]

What MacMullen describes as a move in the literature toward greater seclusion corresponds to what interpreters have identified as a shift with the household codes away from the fairly open possibilities for women's leadership in Paul's day toward increasing restriction within the household. We noted in chapter 6, however, that hierarchical conceptions of marriage in the Roman world functioned in conjunction with informal conventions concerning the influence of wives and that the unnamed wives of Eph. 5:22-33 may have had a greater significance for the life and identity of church groups than is often realized. Moreover, it is important to remember that the restriction of women's leadership opportunities does not mean that women necessarily played less of a role in the growth of the movement in all cases. With all of the limiting of women's authority inherent in the household codes, the codes nevertheless include at least one tacit acknowledgment of women's influence. As the instructions concerning the relationship between believing wives and nonbelieving husbands in 1 Pet. 3:1-6 illustrate, sometimes hierarchical teaching masked tacit acknowledgment of the ability of women to influence the household by perpetuating the growth of the movement. The ideal Christian wife could serve as a symbol of group identity (see Eph. 5:22-33) and the perfect, modest, and discreet mediator between the church and the nonbelieving world (1 Pet. 3:1-6).[49]

Although it is communicated through literary artistry rather than ethical exhortation, an apologetic agenda also underlies the Acts of the Apostles. In an effort to link the rise of Christianity with family institutions and modes of operation, the author of Acts highlights a pattern of early Christian expansion for which Paul's letters (for example, 1 Cor. 1:16) provide important corroborating evidence: the conversion of the head of the household followed by the remainder of the household.[50] Acts includes four stories of household conversions, beginning with the programmatic story of Cornelius (Acts 10:1—11:18; compare Acts 16:11-15; 16:25-34; 18:1-11). All of these speak of conversions using the same *oikos* formula, "and/with [all] his/her household," apparently recalling for the reader the mission of evangelizing households given to the Seventy-Two in Luke (Luke 10:5-7).[51] With a specific focus on Acts 16, which includes the story of the conversion of Lydia and her household, Michael White has demonstrated the problems with establishing direct historical correlation between the narrative and the situation in first-century Philippi, noting the tendency for the narrative instead to revolve around the conventional. He argues that the author of Luke-Acts is interested in making a point about the shape of the Christian movement using an established model from the environment: "That model asserts the position of the extended household (including the *pater-* or *mater-familias*, children, slaves, friends, freedmen, and other clients) is the locus of the movement."[52]

In the story of the conversion of Lydia and her household (Acts 16:11-15), the interest of the author of Acts in highlighting the conversion of households intersects with the desire to highlight the attraction of well-to-do women to Christianity.[53] As a dealer in purple dyed garments with a house large enough to host several guests, Lydia obviously meets the grade. The setting for Lydia's conversion is Philippi, but in other cities Paul finds converts among leading women, including Thessalonica (Acts 17:1-9), Beroea (Acts 17:10-15), and Athens (Acts 17:16-34). An interesting corollary to this success among leading women is the failure at Pisidian Antioch, where "prominent" and "devout" women team up with leading men to oppose Paul (Acts 13:50).[54] The sympathy of powerful women seems to be one of the themes developed by the author of Acts in an effort to communicate the respectability and independence of early Christianity.[55] In addition to its apologetic crafting, Judith Lieu has argued that Acts shares the novelistic tendency of second-century Greek and Jewish novels that appear to exaggerate the social influence of women.[56]

It is probably best not to look for direct correlation between the story of Lydia and the real circumstances of Paul's day. Rather, for the author of Acts Lydia represents the ideal woman convert, a facilitator of Christian growth to the ends of the earth (Acts 1:8) whose own house serves as a base for the movement (16:15, 40). Lydia herself may never have existed, but women like her almost certainly contributed to the rise of Christianity from Paul's day onward. Lydia has been compared to such "real" women as Phoebe (Rom. 16:1-2), discussed above, and Nympha (Col. 4:15), who is described as a woman leader of a house church in the context of the document that introduces the household code into Pauline Christianity. The inclusion of traditional household ethics in works of the latter decades of the first century and early decades of the second century did not mean that influential women completely disappeared from early Christian texts. The works of Ignatius of Antioch, for example, contain both household code teaching (Ignatius, *Pol.* 4:1—5:2) and references to prominent women such as Tavia (who is apparently at the head of a household or may lead a house church), the wife of Epitropus (who is greeted along with her house and children), and Alke (Ignatius, *Smyrn.* 13.2; *Pol.* 8:2-3). As male authors began to propound more restricted and conventional roles for women, they nevertheless continued to offer considerable latitude to well-to-do women. This may be in part because women such as Nympha or Tavia were very important to the success of the mission, but it was also no doubt due to the fact that their exertions of influence as heads of households and patrons were within the boundaries of societal expectations for the prominent women of their day.[57]

Christian women who were married to pagans, however, posed a definite challenge to societal expectations concerning the prerogatives of the *paterfamilias.*[58] Rodney Stark argues that such marriages were nevertheless ultimately of great importance for the growth of early Christianity, noting that they were a mechanism by which "Christians managed to remain an *open network*, able to keep building bonds with outsiders, rather than becoming a closed community of believers."[59] Central to his thesis is the ruling by Callistus in the early third century that women could live in "just concubinage" with their mates.[60] This ruling apparently responded to the problem of upper-class women seeking to preserve their wealth, for legal marriages with Christians of lower rank would have meant the loss of inheritance. Thus, Stark asks, "If highborn Christian women found it so difficult to find grooms that the bishop of Rome permitted 'just concubinage,' how was he to condemn middle- and lower-class Christian women who wed pagans, especially if they did so within the church guidelines concerning the religious training of children?"[61] As Stark himself acknowledges, many voices, including that of Tertullian, strongly condemned the practice of Christian women entering into new marriages with pagan men, but he sees this as a further indication that such marriages were actually occurring in significant numbers.[62]

All of this evidence needs to be evaluated carefully. There is no question that marriages between pagans and Christians existed in the church from Paul's day and that they virtually always involved a Christian woman (though 1 Cor. 7:12-16 speaks of such marriages both ways). Despite the encouragement to let these marriages continue under some circumstances (for Paul it is the nonbelieving partner's willingness to remain in the union that is the determining factor [1 Cor. 7:12-16]), these marriages are clearly problematic. Most obviously, there is the problem of pollution (see 1 Cor. 6:15-20; 2 Cor. 6:14; 1 Thess. 4:4-5). In chapter 2 we discussed Justin Martyr's description of the circumstances of the woman from Rome who eventually divorces her profligate husband. Although his argument is clearly shaped by his apologetic genre, Justin nevertheless describes the situation in a manner that may offer insight into typical reactions of Christians to mixed marriages: he speaks of her revulsion at having to share his table and his bed.[63] Tertullian states categorically that believers contracting marriages with Gentiles are "guilty of fornication" and should be excommunicated, citing 1 Cor. 5:11: "with persons of that kind there is to be no taking of food even."[64] Drawing upon the examples from pagan life in which wealthy householders forbade their slaves to marry outside of the household, Tertullian describes Christian women who seek marriage to pagan men as "conjoining to themselves the devil's slaves." In Tertullian's view it is the wealthiest Christian women who are subject to such temptations, those with a proclivity for the more capacious house (in our terms, the bigger house in the suburbs!).[65] Such forceful language may indicate that some women wish to enter into marriage with pagans, but it is equally possible that Tertullian is using such aspirations as a particularly good example of the moral weakness of women without there being necessarily many instances of women seeking out such arrangements at all.

In addition to the problem of pollution, the theory that exogamous marriage (particularly the contracting of new marriages between Christian women and pagan men) was central to the growth of early Christianity must be measured against evidence of mounting tension in the households of those engaged in mixed marriage (see 1 Cor. 7:15) that culminates in violence against Christians. Instructions concerning marriage between believing women and nonbelieving men in 1 Pet. 3:1-6 include the call for silence and reserve, coupled with a clear attempt to bolster the confidence of these women with the instruction that they are to let nothing terrify them (1 Pet. 3:6).[66] Clement of Rome connects the suffering of believing women who were divorced by pagan husbands with the indignities suffered by women during martyrdom (*1 Clem.* 6:1-4; compare Tertullian, *Apology* 3). While often more fantastic than historical, the *Apocryphal Acts of the Apostles* nevertheless include many accounts of women's attraction to Christian asceticism culminating in refusals to marry or to go on living with pagan men, the result being blind rage and violence directed especially at apostles.[67] There are enough points of contact with other early Christian texts to suggest that, at least to some degree, these texts reflect the circumstances that real women faced.

Given all of this tension, violence, and concern about the polluting influences of the pagan partner, we are left with the question of why these marriages were tolerated at all. Part of the reason may have been pragmatic. In order to survive, Christian women may sometimes have needed to keep their allegiances secret and Christian exhortation may have justified a way of life from which there may well have been no safe escape. But the motives announced by the texts themselves fit to some degree with Stark's theory. For Paul and the author of 1 Peter the motivation to preserve the union is clear: such marriages bear the inherent potential of spreading the gospel. In 1 Pet. 3:1-6, the woman is cast in the role of quiet evangelist in her own home. Justin presents the Roman woman as trying to persuade her unchaste husband initially, apparently heeding Paul's advice (2 *Apology* 2). If church texts present these marriages as potentially winning converts, we should perhaps be hesitant to discount them. But the problem is that there is very little evidence of success in the convincing of husbands in this period. In fact, there is evidence in the distinctly opposite direction. In Justin's account, the woman ends up divorcing her husband despite numerous attempts to reform him. The *Apocryphal Acts* time and time again describe the husband's opposition to the wife's attraction to ascetic Christianity and rarely include the conversion of husbands.[68] But if women were not very often successful in converting their husbands, perhaps they contributed to the preservation of an "open network" (to use

Stark's phrase) in other ways: by influencing children (1 Cor. 7:12-16; 2 Tim. 1:5) and perhaps also slaves (1 Tim. 6:1). Perhaps the preservation of the marriage was often not based on any real hope of the Christianization of the marriage per se, but on the hope of winning some members of the household and those with whom the wife might come into contact as she went about her daily affairs.

In chapter 4, our chapter on growing up in house-church communities, we discussed the education of children at length. But in the present chapter it is valuable to reflect briefly upon the overlap of evangelizing and educating children. While Eph. 6:1-4 already hints at the existence of a specifically Christian body of instruction to be imparted to children,[69] the Christian socialization of children is repeatedly listed as a priority in the teaching of the Apostolic Fathers (*1 Clem.* 21:6, 8; *Did.* 4:9; Polycarp, *Phil.* 4:2). In Polycarp's letter to the Philippians such socialization is presented as the special duty of wives. The Pastoral Epistles offer specific evidence of women being involved in the Christian socialization of children. Timothy's faith is said to have been kindled by the influence of his grandmother Lois and of his mother, Eunice (2 Tim. 1:5).[70] Given modern expectations of mother-child relations, one might naturally suppose that this type of socialization took place primarily between mothers and young children. But Suzanne Dixon has brought evidence to light indicating that Roman mothers continued to exert considerable influence on their adolescent sons, even in such areas as education and career patterns.[71] That the grandmother Lois and mother Eunice are presented as sharing this agenda is also not particularly surprising, as a good deal of evidence points to a strong bond between married daughters and their mothers.[72]

We should also consider the circumstances of children who were part of families in which only one parent was a member of the church. Paul mentions them for the first time in the midst of his argument concerning the preservation of mixed marriages in 1 Cor. 7:12-16.[73] The manner is which Timothy is presented as the child of two generations of believing women suggests that he is being presented by the author of the Pastorals as the "fruit" of a family circumstance in which faith was propounded by the women of the house. It is likely that many children simply accompanied their believing parent into the church without making a deliberate choice to join a new movement. But, at the parent's side, faith would have been absorbed. As we have seen, young children were left in the care of, or came into contact with, a variety of people in the ancient household, including slaves, nurses, and surrogate parents of various kinds.[74] In chapter 3 we considered the possibility of Christian wet nurses taking advantage of opportunities to evangelize very young children. If Celsus's views even somewhat accurately reflect church efforts to recruit children, there is also good reason to suspect that children themselves would have contributed to the expansion of Christianity. Although it comes from a much later period, there is at least one delightful text that envisions the specific missionary activity of a child. In his correspondence with Laeta, Jerome casts Laeta's daughter in the role of unrelenting child-evangelist in relation to her pagan grandfather: "When she sees her grandfather, she must leap upon his breast, put her arms around his neck, and, whether he likes it or not, sing Alleluia in his ears."[75]

Thecla the Missionary

We turn finally to the most dramatic image of a woman winning household members (though not members of her own household). In the *Acts of [Paul and] Thecla*, Thecla is portrayed as a missionary teacher who dies only "after enlightening many with the word of God" (3.43).[76] But the evidence from this work is by no means easy to evaluate. Earlier theories about the prominent role assigned to a woman offering a window into the ascetic world of women have given way to great hesitation to view this account and other stories contained in the *Apocryphal Acts of the Apostles* as historical in any way.[77] Because these works have so much in common with ancient novels, their value for describing the lives of real women is difficult to judge. In comparing the *Acts of [Paul and] Thecla* to ancient romances, Kate Cooper has argued that even the centrality of asceticism in the work should be evaluated critically and from a literary perspective:

> The Acts of Paul makes clear the usefulness of the heroine's continence as a narrative device to propel the conflict between the apostle and a symbolic representative of the ruling class of the cities he visits. ...The challenge by the apostle to the householder is the urgent message of these narratives, and it is essentially a conflict *between men*. The challenge posed here by Christianity is not really about women, or even about sexual continence, but about authority and the social order. In this way, tales of continence use the narrative momentum of romance, and the enticement of the romantic heroine, to mask a

contest for authority, encoded in the contest between two pretenders to the heroine's allegiance.[78]

Cooper's important work calls into question naïve historical readings of the *Acts of [Paul and] Thecla* and theories about women's storytelling or authorship underlying the text. But while it is clear that authority and the social order are central to the true meaning of this work, to say that the challenge posed by Christianity "is not really about women" is probably to overstate the case.[79] It is important not to lose sight of the significant points of contact between the *Acts of [Paul and] Thecla* and other less novelistic texts. We know that ascetic communities of women existed, such as seem to be in view in this work, especially in the depiction of the household of the widow Tryphaena. We also know that the prerogatives of the pagan *paterfamilias* were threatened by women who were attracted to early Christianity, ascetic or otherwise. We know that marriages between pagan men and early Christian women existed, even if it is difficult to determine their frequency. Perhaps most important, the literature speaks of church groups dealing with awkward situations on account of the involvement of Christian women in such arrangements. When women were converted to Christianity under such circumstances, we can only assume that they took the initiative. This is not to suggest that Thecla ever existed or that the influence of a woman has not been exaggerated greatly, surpassing the bounds of history. But in the case of this early Christian text, women's influence appears to be exaggerated because women's influence was real and perceived as dangerous. Christianity's conflict with the social order and civic responsibility involved both the real and imagined activities of women. Cooper may be correct in identifying the two main conversation partners in the *Acts of [Paul and] Thecla* as men, but this conversation makes sense in this early Christian text only because of a combination of women's initiative, social expectations concerning women's proper roles, and the special significance attached to the honorable behavior of women in defining group identity.[80]

At its most basic level, the battle about authority and social order in the *Acts of [Paul and] Thecla* is expressed in terms of a battle for houses in the city, with a special concern for the activity of women in these houses. The work has significant points in common with the other texts we have been considering. As it is presented in the *Acts of [Paul and] Thecla*, the church meets in houses (for example, 3.2-7; see also 3.41) and conversion is a household affair (for example, 3.7, 23). Onesiphorous, for example, is described as having left the things of this world to follow Paul with all of his house (3.23). Recalling the widows of 1 Tim. 5:13-15 who perpetuate a network of false teaching from house to house, the text describes Thecla's frequent movement from house to house. But this time such movement is celebrated. The wealthy widow Tryphaena, whose own daughter has died (see 3.27-29), offers shelter to Thecla. Thecla is presented as resting in the house of Tryphaena for eight days, instructing her in the word of the Lord. The maidservants are said also to believe, and there is great joy in the house (3.39). A new family has been created whose bonds are not of flesh and blood, but of Christian commitment.[81] Even after Thecla sets out on the road again, Tryphaena continues to support her work, sending her gifts of clothing and gold for the poor (3.41). The households of women envisioned in 1 Tim. 5:16, Ignatius's *Smyrn.* 13.1, and Herm. *Vis.* 2.4.3 come to mind, as do the hints in various texts that women spread the gospel to other women, children, and slaves, and supported those in need.

In the *Acts of [Paul and] Thecla*, Thecla takes on masculine characteristics (for example, 3.25) and adopts a public and visible evangelical role of the type for which there is very little evidence either for Christian men or for Christian women in this period.[82] But, if we understand the text as a symbolic depiction of what was at stake especially for women who joined the church and worked to secure its survival and expansion in various ways (and for men who were seen to be associated with such women), we are much closer to history. The suspicions of shamelessness and sexual immorality that follow Thecla through the account are echoed throughout pagan critique of early Christianity. The fantastic depictions of the violence endured by Thecla find a corollary in the usually much more subtle depictions of household strife and violence found in other texts. Yet what is perhaps most interesting about the *Acts of [Paul and] Thecla* and most useful as a means of clarifying the historical indications we find in other texts is the importance attributed to household settings in the expansion and struggle for success of early Christianity.

Conclusion:
The Household and the Spread of Christianity

In this chapter we have drawn attention to the existence of divergent scholarly opinion concerning the involvement of women in the expansion of Christianity. With respect to the first two centuries CE, the evidence justifies neither the bold claims of some scholars concerning the influence of women in the Christianization of the Roman Empire nor the extreme skepticism of others. For the earliest period in particular we find incidental references to women who contributed to the expansion of the movement. But the evidence also includes many texts in which women are represented in order to further the agenda of male authors in various ways; the relationship between these texts and the lives of real women is much more difficult to determine. Yet the results of literary and rhetorical analysis of such texts can be incorporated within the process of historical reconstruction. Comparison of the relevant early Christian texts, consideration of the Greco-Roman setting, and careful attention to literary genre can work together to produce a reliable picture of the involvement of women in the expansion of early Christianity. This picture, however, is not uniform (that is, mainly stemming from marriages between Christian women and pagan men), but multifaceted, involving women in such diverse roles as patrons, heads of households, mothers, teachers, and various kinds of ambassadors of the new faith. Nevertheless, the picture has a unifying element: household life. The attempt to identify the specific activities of women that contributed to the expansion of the gospel leads time and time again to the household: women meeting together in a house, seeking to build believing homes, or struggling to preserve Christian allegiance in the home of a pagan householder.

To return, then, to the question with which we began: Was Celsus right? If we look beyond the polemic (though the polemic is part of the story!), largely, yes. Women did move in and out of houses and shops, taking risks and leading people—including children—to join the movement without permission from the proper authorities. They did so, it seems, while conducting their daily business. No doubt they sometimes remained largely invisible, but in other cases they met with real resistance both inside and outside of church groups. This combination of boldness, affront, and concealment is one of the most interesting and little understood features of the rise of early Christianity.

CHAPTER ELEVEN

CONCLUSION:
DISCOVERING A WOMAN'S PLACE

▣▣ ▣▣ ▣▣

I n this book we have combined the study of house churches with analysis
of the lives of early Christian women. We now offer a few concluding
reflections on how this exploration has contributed to our understanding
of early church women in particular and of the atmosphere of early church
communities in general.

Research on early Christian women has been an extremely important
branch of the study of Christian origins for over two decades now. It must
be admitted, however, that early enthusiasm for recovering women's lives
by means of historical methods has been giving way in recent years to a
clearly discernible trend in the direction of greater pessimism.[1] This pessimism has resulted especially from more sophistication in literary and
rhetorical analysis of early Christian texts and a growing awareness of how
women were represented in order to further the agendas of male authors.
In its most extreme form, this greater pessimism leads to a hesitation to
draw any conclusions about real women at all.

We hope our study of women within the context of house churches
might in fact restore some confidence in the possibility of the historical
reconstruction of the lives of early Christian women. Nevertheless, we
have aimed to listen carefully to our colleagues engaged in rhetorical and
literary analysis, who urge us to pay careful attention to how the represen-

tation of women is affected by genre, metaphor, novelistic tendencies, and ancient topoi (literary themes). As Judith Lieu has written so succinctly, "The move from rhetoric to social experience must remain hazardous."[2] It has been useful for us throughout our study to navigate the complicated relationship between rhetoric and reality. With Janet Tulloch's contribution, we have even broached the hazardous subject of the relationship between artistic representation and social experience. We believe that in so doing, we have discovered more than the dutiful wife inscribed in the Ephesian household code (Eph. 5:22-33).

In our investigation we have discovered more than a static image of obedience and compliance. We have found traces of women's multifaceted influences in households and house-church communities—women acting as patrons, teachers, and dinner hosts. It is important to emphasize, however, that some of these traces of influence have been precisely of women acting as dutiful wives. Conservative rhetoric such as that found in Eph. 5:22-33 or in Tertullian's arguments against women marrying pagans, in which he inadvertently reveals many of the services provided to the church by Christian wives (Tertullian, *To His Wife* 2.4), has called us to consider the significance of traditional women's work for the life of the community. We have reflected upon how aspects of such rhetoric may function in conjunction with, and to a certain extent even facilitate, elements of resistance to the dominant imperial order in early Christian discourse. We have also considered how informal conventions tied to traditional family arrangements actually gave wives and mothers considerable latitude in house-church communities and were widely accepted in society at large.

If we have succeeded in furthering understanding of the history of early Christian women, this is in large part due to our reliance on the significant work on the Roman family that has occurred in recent years. Like scholars of early Christianity, historians of the Roman family have been acutely aware of the shaping of female identity to suit wider rhetorical, moral, and political purposes in discourses and narratives of various kinds. But in their attempts to reconstruct life from the past, they have been able to balance textual witnesses against evidence that is simply not available for early church groups in the period of house churches: material evidence of various kinds, including archaeological remains of houses, inscriptions, and art. In engaging scholarship on the Roman family as a conversation partner, as well as being informed by the growing body of literature on the Jewish family, we have been able to draw upon examinations of this wider range of evidence to shed light upon the world of women in early church circles. We have been able to expand our understanding of the familial constituency of house churches and the physical conditions of communities. In turn, we hope that this book will be of help to historians of Roman and Jewish families and of women in the Roman world, from whom we have learned so much. For example, when it comes to the lives of women, textual scholars often bemoan the dominance of an elite perspective in the sources. Early Christian evidence from the first two centuries offers arguably very important evidence for family realities and the lives of women in less-than-elite contexts.

Understandably, there has been a tendency to focus on exceptional women in the study of early Christianity: women like Prisc(ill)a, Phoebe, Perpetua, and the legendary Thecla, who, admittedly, also have a prominent place in this study. But in drawing upon work on the Roman family, which invites reflection about relations between wives and other members of the household such as children and slaves, we have been urged to think carefully about daily responsibilities and actions—to concentrate somewhat less on the exceptional and somewhat more on the ordinary. This has resulted in two main features of our work. First, while acknowledging the importance of asceticism for the lives of some women in house churches, we have highlighted the contributions of married women to church groups, many of whom are unnamed or named only with reference to their husbands, such as the wife of Valens (Polycarp, *Phil.* 11.4), the wife of Hermas (Herm. *Vis.* 2.2.3), or the wife of Epitropus (Ignatius, *Pol.* 8.2). We have also discussed patterns of continuity between the lives of unmarried women, especially widows, and their married sisters. In the period of house churches the lives of married and unmarried women overlapped, to the point where widows may have combined ministries involving prayer and various good works for the community with caring for children and the domestic training of younger women (for example, 1 Tim. 5:5, 9; Titus 2:3-5). Second, our focus on the ordinary features of familial life has allowed us to gain a greater sense of what women were doing most of the time and to savor the atmosphere of the communities.

In our chapters on giving birth and growing up in house churches, we endeavored to capture something of the domestic flavor that would have permeated early church meetings. In allowing the world of babies, children, and female caregivers to enter our imagination when it comes to house-church meetings, we ended up with a picture of church life that challenges preconceived notions of solemnity in favor of the boisterous and somewhat chaotic exchanges of household life. House-church meetings took place in a setting where midwives were hired, babies were born, nursed, and nurtured, and children grew up. References to infants and children occur largely in passing in early Christian texts, and sometimes their presence must be gleaned through the lens of metaphorical expressions of domestic experience in the Gospels or from such narrative accounts as the *Proto-Gospel of James* or the *Martyrdom of Perpetua and Felicitas*. But the more complete picture of childhood in the Roman world that has been emerging from the work of ancient historians, including the greater appreciation for the lives and education of girls, can help us to gain new insight into the meaning of these fragmentary impressions.

As part of the process of re-creating the domestic atmosphere of house churches, we have also set out to capture some of the emotions and difficult choices that would accompany life with children. We have examined presentations of healings of children in early church texts in light of the frequency of the death of infants and children in the Roman world. Contrary to some earlier theories, there seems little doubt that the death of a young child was experienced profoundly in this era. The sickness and death of children require further attention on the part of scholars as typical (but largely undocumented) features of early church life. We have also stressed the ongoing involvement of early church women in such decisions as whether to rear an infant, to rescue an abandoned infant or child, or to nurse an infant oneself.

In the case of the latter, we have examined ancient sources suggesting that this was a topic of considerable social debate, not only about the merits of nursing or hiring a wet nurse but also about the importance of the choice of a wet nurse as an early educational influence in the life of the child. Leading women of the community probably had a strong voice here as advocates for their own daughters and other young women of the *ekklēsia*, and just as in society at large, church members may have chosen wet nurses because of their potential as teachers of their young children. This raises the possibility that believers sought other believers as wet nurses and that Christian wet nurses, either as slaves or as hired workers, may have played a role in evangelizing nonbelievers. At the very least, within the setting of early church groups, it is safe to assume that conversations about nursing and rearing children were part of daily life and were intermingled with conversations about what we would normally consider as more typical church concerns, such as who would preside at the Lord's supper or who should be sent out with news for a neighboring community.

The roles of older women as advocates for and teachers of younger women and girls have been one of the many dimensions of women's exercising leadership roles in the community that we have explored. Another is women's role in the leadership of the assembly. By exploring the expected role of the wife as competent manager of her household, with or without a husband, we have found a new approach to the question of leadership in those assemblies that met in a woman's house. While husbands or other males represented authority, *potestas*, in both home and public forum, it was their wives who knew intimately the house and its inhabitants, who could truly welcome visitors into a place that they knew well. When women were widowed or divorced and remained in charge of their own house, it was not unnatural for them to be initiators and central figures of hospitality. In a Christian context, accordingly, it was no less natural for them to be hostesses and thus presiders at the common meal.

The role of hospitality did not end in the house. Janet Tulloch's new interpretations of some catacomb meal scenes reveal depictions of women in roles of leadership in the family funerary banquets portrayed on the walls. While the paintings themselves are several centuries later than most of the material we have been discussing, and while artistic portrayals must be approached with caution when assuming that they reveal anything of real life, nevertheless we know from literary texts that such funeral meals were being held earlier and even well before the Christian era. The same ancient practices were then adapted by believers to express both their continuity with the past and their new faith.

The social structure of the Roman world was heavily based on the informal unequal relationships known as patronage. The participation of women in the public and private patronage system has been little studied, but they were present and active in it. We have provided context by bringing forth some of the extensive evidence for women's patronage in the wider Roman world, in order to investigate how the same social structures may have functioned in nonelite and especially Jewish and Christian circles. Important women in house churches, whether independent heads of households or wives, exercised leadership by using patronage to respond to social needs and to wield influence and power for the sake of the nurture and expansion of church life and missionary efforts.

In our discussion of the leadership of women, however, it is valuable to reiterate the position stated in the introduction: early Christian women did not exercise unique or more advanced leadership roles in early church groups in comparison to other women of their times. Rather, their roles sometimes reflected the greater social freedom and public visibility that was happening already in Roman society. Justin's Roman matron (Justin, *Second Apology* 2) offers an especially good example of the independence of some well-to-do women. This is evident not only in the manner with which she handles divorce arrangements but also in her apparently quite public allegiance to early Christianity, despite the dire consequences for some Christian supporters. An understanding of broad societal patterns can be helpful on many levels with respect to the lives of women, however, even beyond demonstrations of independence and leadership patterns. For example, new research on educational possibilities for girls in the empire can help bring this severely underrepresented constituency of early church groups back to life and also strengthen the case for viewing females as intellectual contributors in their own right to early Christianity.

It is also important to point out, however, that in exploring the lives of women in house-church settings, we have found evidence both for women's leadership, solidarity, and participation in communal life at all levels and at times for women's powerlessness and suffering. Early Christian women would not have escaped many of the terrible choices and situations that faced women of this era. Our attention has turned especially to the plight of the most powerless women in the system, whether Jew, Christian, or other: slaves. The society was founded on slavery and could not exist without it. Most households, however modest, were partially based on slave labor. The sexual availability of slaves to their owners and anyone allowed by their owners was a given. Christian female slaves of childbearing years must have often found themselves in nearly impossible situations, being instructed to live according to a strict moral code and finding it impossible to do so. We cannot rule out, for example, the possibility that, for some, chastity and fidelity to their own children and the father of their children were impossible and that, for some desperate slave women who were members of church groups, perhaps especially if they were owned by non-Christians, the act of abandoning an infant would seem like a necessity of survival. We would hope that in a believing household life would be different, but there is no hard evidence that this is so, and there is abundant evidence that whole households often did not convert to the new faith together. There were probably many Christian slaves in predominantly non-Christian households, whose life of faith was hard indeed.

We have also argued that the lives of wives (many of whom would not be legally married by Roman standards) in church groups by no means always matched the ideal circumstances described in Eph. 5:22-33. On account of circumstances both within and outside of the church, women were sometimes widowed, divorced, abandoned, married to uncooperative, unfaithful, or violent husbands, even martyred. In terms of marital problems, it is not difficult to find evidence of tensions surfacing in the texts. Where Christian wives are associated with failure, it is easy to see that they have been implicated in male leadership and reputation, even when the extent of their personal wrongdoing seems far from clear. But it is in the texts dealing with mixed marriage that one often senses a potentially explosive situation, despite the promise recognized by early church authors of women acting as agents of early Christian expansion in such circumstances.

In combining the study of house churches with analysis of the lives of early Christian women, we have gained a greater awareness of the complexity of the situation of women in house-church communities. We have by no means discovered either utopian communal relations or even distinct roles for women in comparison to the broader society. Nevertheless, we come to the end of this study with greater conviction concerning the influence of women in the creation of early Christian infrastructure, their roles as hosts, teachers, and leaders, and their significant contribution to the expansion of early Christianity in the empire.

ABBREVIATIONS

▫▫ ▫▫ ▫▫

1 Clem.	*First Epistle of Clement*
2 Clem.	*Second Epistle of Clement*
AB	Anchor Bible
AE	*Année epigraphique*
ANF	*The Ante-Nicene Fathers*
ANRW	*Aufstieg und Niedergang der römischen Welt.* Edited by H. Temporini and W. Haase. Berlin: de Gruyter, 1972–.
Ant.	Josephus, *Jewish Antiquities*
ANTC	Abingdon New Testament Commentaries
Apoc. Peter	*Apocalypse of Peter*
Apol.	*Apology*
Ap. Trad.	*Apostolic Tradition*
b.	Babylonian Talmud
Barn.	*Letter of Barnabas*
BDAG	Walter Bauer, Frederick W. Danker, F. W. Arndt, F. W. Gingrich, *A Greek-English Lexicon of the New Testament and Other Early Christian Literature.* 3rd ed. Chicago, 2000.
B.J.	Josephus, *Bellum Judaicum (Jewish War)*
BR	*Biblical Research*
BTB	*Biblical Theology Bulletin*
CH	*Church History*

CIJ	*Corpus inscriptionum judaicarum*
CIL	*Corpus inscriptionum latinarum*
Cod. justin.	Justinian Code
Cod. theod.	Theodosian Code
CP	*Classical Philology*
CSEL	Corpus Scriptorum Ecclesiasticorum Latinorum
Did.	*Didache*
Ep.	*Epistle*
FRLANT	Forschungen zur Religion und Literatur des Alten und Neuen Testaments
Herm. *Mand.*	Shepherd of Hermas, *Mandate*
Herm. *Sim.*	Shepherd of Hermas, *Similitude*
Herm. *Vis.*	Shepherd of Hermas, *Vision*
Hist. eccl.	Eusebius, *Church History*
Hom.	*Homily*
HTR	*Harvard Theological Review*
HTS	Harvard Theological Studies
ICC	International Critical Commentary
IG	*Inscriptiones graecae.* Editio minor. Berlin, 1924–.
ILS	*Inscriptiones Latinae Selectae*
JAAR	*Journal of American Academy of Religion*
JAC	*Jahrbuch für Antike und Christentum*
JBL	*Journal of Biblical Literature*
JECS	*Journal of Early Christian Studies*
JFSR	*Journal of Feminist Studies in Religion*
JR	*Journal of Religion*
JRS	*Journal of Roman Studies*
JSNT	*Journal for the Study of the New Testament*
JSNTSup	Journal for the Study of the New Testament, Supplement Series
JTS	*Journal of Theological Studies*
LCL	Loeb Classical Library
LSJ	Liddell, H. G., R. Scott, H. S. Jones, *A Greek-English Lexicon*. 9th ed. with revised supplement. Oxford, 1996.
LXX	Septuagint
m.	*Mishnah*
MAMA	*Monumenta Asiae Minoris Antiqua*. Manchester and London, 1928–93.

Mart. Pol.	*Martyrdom of Polycarp*
MT	Masoretic Text
NewDocs	*New Documents Illustrating Early Christianity,* edited by G. H. R. Horsley and S. R. Llewelyn. 9 vols. Macquarie University: Ancient History Documentary Research Centre, 1981–2002.
NIGTC	New International Greek Testament Commentary
NovT	*Novum Testamentum*
NovTSup	Novum Testamentum Supplements
NRSV	New Revised Standard Version
NTA	*New Testament Abstracts*
NTOA	Novum Testamentum et Orbis Antiquus
NTS	*New Testament Studies*
PBSR	*Papers of the British School at Rome*
Phil.	Polycarp, *To the Philippians*
Pol.	Ignatius, *Letter to Polycarp*
P.Wisc.	The Wisconsin Papyri
QL	Qumran Literature
Ref.	Hippolytus, *Refutation of All Heresies*
RivB	*Rivista biblia italiana*
Sat.	Juvenal, *Satirae* (*Satires*)
SBLDS	Society of Biblical Literature Dissertation Series
SBLMS	Society of Biblical Literature Monograph Series
SecCent	*Second Century*
Smyrn.	Ignatius, *Letter to the Smyrnaeans*
SNTSMS	Studiorum Novi Testamenti Societas Monograph Series
SP	Sacra Pagina
Spec. leg.	Philo, *On the Special Laws*
SR	*Studies in Religion/Sciences religieuses*
t.	*Tosefta*
TAPA	*Transactions of the American Philological Association*
Vg	Vulgate
WBC	Word Biblical Commentary
WUNT	Wissenschaftliche Untersuchungen zum Neuen Testament

NOTES

◻◻ ◻◻ ◻◻

1. Introduction

1. Frequently called in modern discussion a *paterfamilias*. But Richard Saller has shown that this term was used in antiquity to refer to a property owner, not necessarily a patriarchal head of family; Richard P. Saller, "*Pater Familias, Mater Familias,* and the Gendered Semantics of the Roman Household," *CP* 94 (1999): 182–97.

2. Especially David D. Gilmore, ed., *Honor and Shame and the Unity of the Mediterranean* (American Anthropological Association Special Publication 22; Washington, D.C.: American Anthropological Association, 1987); John G. Peristiany, ed., *Mediterranean Family Structures* (Cambridge: Cambridge University Press, 1976); John G. Peristiany and Julian Pitt-Rivers, eds., *Honor and Grace in Anthropology* (Cambridge: Cambridge University Press, 1992); Halvor Moxnes, "Honor and Shame," in *The Social Sciences and New Testament Interpretation*, ed. Richard L. Rohrbaugh (Peabody, Mass.: Hendrickson, 1996), 19–40; Bruce J. Malina, *The New Testament World: Insights from Cultural Anthropology*, 3rd ed. (Louisville: Westminster John Knox, 2001).

3. Especially Kathleen E. Corley, "Feminist Myths of Christian Origins," in *Reimagining Christian Origins: A Colloquium Honoring Burton L. Mack*, ed. Elizabeth A. Castelli and Hal Taussig (Valley Forge, Pa.: Trinity Press International, 1996), 51–67; and idem, *Women and the Historical Jesus: Feminist Myths of Christian Origins* (Santa Rosa, Calif.: Polebridge, 2002).

4. Bernadette J. Brooten, "Jewish Women's History in the Roman Period: A Task for Christian Theology," *HTR* 79 (1986): 22–30; and Judith Plaskow, "Christian Feminism and Anti-Judaism," *Cross Currents* 28 (1978): 306–9.

5. For references, see Carolyn Osiek and David Balch, *Families in the New Testament World: Households and House Churches* (Louisville: Westminster John Knox, 1997), 57–60.

6. For example, Susan Treggiari, "Jobs for Women," *American Journal of Ancient History* 1/2 (1976): 76–104; and Deborah Hobson, "The Role of Women in the Economic Life of Roman Egypt," *Echos du monde classique/Classical Views* 28 n.s. 3 (1984): 373–90.

7. The now familiar Latin term is often misused by modern writers. It was used in Roman antiquity not for the father of a family of persons, but for a property owner—who could sometimes be a woman! See note 1 above as well as chapter 7 for further discussion.

8. Discussion in Osiek and Balch, *Families*, 6–10. It has been argued by others that in fact the architectural evidence of Greek houses from the classical period does not support this gendered division of space in the Greek house: Michael H. Jameson, "Domestic Space in the Greek City State," in *Domestic Architecture and the Use of Space: An Interdisciplinary Cross-Cultural Study*, ed. Susan Kent (Cambridge: Cambridge University Press, 1990). So, even here, we may be dealing with a conceptual or cultural stereotype.

9. Stephen C. Barton, "Paul's Sense of Place: An Anthropological Approach to Community Formation in Corinth," *NTS* 32 (1986): 225–46.

10. Sharon Lee Mattila, "Where Women Sat in Ancient Synagogues: The Archaeological Evidence in Context," in *Voluntary Associations in the Greco-Roman World*, ed. John S. Kloppenborg and Stephen G. Wilson (London: Routledge, 1996), 269.

11. Kerstin Aspegren, *The Male Woman: A Feminine Ideal in the Early Church*, ed. René Kieffer (Uppsala Women's Studies, Women in Religion 4; Uppsala: Almqvist & Wiksell, 1990).

12. Bonnie Bowman Thurston, *The Widows: A Women's Ministry in the Early Church* (Minneapolis: Fortress, 1989), 64–65.

13. Stevan L. Davies, *Revolt of the Widows: The Social World of the Apocryphal Acts* (Carbondale: Southern Illinois University Press, 1980); Carolyn Osiek, "The Widow as Altar: The Rise and Fall of a Symbol," *SecCent* 3 (1983): 159–69; and Thurston, *Widows*.

14. Slave marriages were, however, tacitly recognized even in funerary inscriptions; see Dale B. Martin, "Slave Families and Slaves in Families," in *Early Christian Families in Context: An Interdisciplinary Dialogue*, ed. David L. Balch and Carolyn Osiek (Religion, Marriage, and Family; Grand Rapids: Eerdmans, 2003), 207–30.

15. A good introduction to the topic is Moxnes, "Honor and Shame." To the bibliography given there should be added Sally Cole, *Women of the Praia: Work and Lives in a Portuguese Coastal Community* (Princeton: Princeton University Press, 1991); Jill Dubisch, ed., *Gender and Power in Rural Greece* (Princeton: Princeton

University Press, 1986); and Frank Henderson Stewart, *Honor* (Chicago: University of Chicago Press, 1994).

16. Stewart, *Honor.*

17. Lila Abu-Lughod, *Veiled Sentiments: Honor and Poetry in a Bedouin Society* (Berkeley: University of California Press, 1986); Dubisch, *Gender and Power*, and Uni Wikan, "Shame and Honor: A Contestable Pair," *Man* 19 (1984): 635–52.

18. Cole, *Women of the Praia*, 77–107.

19. Ramsay MacMullen, "Women in Public in the Roman Empire," *Historia* 29 (1980): 208–18; cf. Plutarch, *Moralia* 267A, on veiling of women as the usual custom in the Roman East.

20. Partial lists in Osiek and Balch, *Families*, 52; L. Michael White, *The Social Origins of Christian Architecture*, 2 vols. (HTS 42; Valley Forge, Pa.: Trinity Press International, 1996–97), 1:81–82. See also chapter 9 below.

21. It has long been argued by some that Romans 16 was really directed to Ephesus. The argument has not won general acceptance, however. For a discussion of the issues, see Karl P. Donfried, "A Short Note on Romans 16," in *The Romans Debate*, ed. Karl P. Donfried, rev. ed. (Peabody, Mass.: Hendrickson, 1991), 44–52; Joseph A. Fitzmyer, *Romans: A New Translation with Introduction and Commentary* (AB 33; New York: Doubleday, 1993), 57–59.

22. For further discussion of the sexual double standard, see chapters 2 and 5.

23. Ulpian, *Digest* 47.10.5.5. See further discussion in chapter 7 below.

24. "Tenement Churches and Communal Meals in the Early Church: The Implications of a Form-Critical Analysis of 2 Thessalonians 3:10," *BR* 38 (1993): 23–43.

25. For example, the large, luxurious House of the Vettii at Pompeii was probably owned by two freedman brothers, the ample house of Caecilius Jucundus was owned by the son of a freedman, and Julia Felix, owner of a large rental property in the southeast section of the city, was surely a freedwoman. For different domestic constructions, see, for example, the following: Alexander G. McKay, *Houses, Villas, and Palaces in the Roman World* (Baltimore: Johns Hopkins University Press, 1998); Andrew Wallace-Hadrill, *Houses and Society in Pompeii and Herculaneum* (Princeton: Princeton University Press, 1994); Paul Zanker, *Pompeii: Public and Private Life* (Cambridge: Harvard University Press, 1998). Of course, housing patterns were not everywhere like Pompeii, but they were not totally different, either.

26. Katherine M. D. Dunbabin, "Triclinium and Stibadium," in *Dining in Classical Context*, ed. William J. Slater (Ann Arbor: University of Michigan Press, 1991), 121–48. All the meal scenes depicted in the Roman catacombs (third and fourth centuries) are *stibadia*. For further discussion, see chapter 8.

27. Generally, Kathleen E. Corley, *Private Women, Public Meals: Social Conflict in the Synoptic Tradition* (Peabody, Mass.: Hendrickson, 1993), 24–34, 66–75; see also Sir 9:9.

28. *Didascalia* 20 (*Apostolic Constitutions* 2.57–58) of the early third century depicts men in front and women behind, undoubtedly now in a rectangular hall.

29. John H. Elliott, "Patronage and Clientage," in Rohrbaugh, *Social Sciences*, 144–56. Women patrons are the subject of chapter 9 below.

30. Richard A. Bauman, *Women and Politics in Ancient Rome* (London: Rout-ledge, 1992); Suzanne Dixon, *The Roman Mother* (London: Croom Helm, 1988).

31. L. William Countryman, *The Rich Christian in the Church of the Early Empire: Contradictions and Accommodations* (Texts and Studies in Religion; New York: Mellen, 1980); Charles A. Bobertz, "The Role of Patron in the *Cena Domi-nica* of Hippolytus' *Apostolic Tradition*," *JTS* 44 (1993): 170–84; and idem, "Alms-giving as Patronage: The Role of Patroness in Early Christianity," unpublished paper, American Academy of Religion annual meeting, 1992.

32. Full references in Osiek and Balch, *Families*, 167–73.

33. Dennis R. MacDonald, *The Legend and the Apostle: The Battle for Paul in Story and Canon* (Philadelphia: Westminster, 1983); Davies, *Revolt of the Widows*.

34. MacDonald, *Early Christian Women*, 240–43, 247.

2. Dutiful and Less Than Dutiful Wives

1. For more detailed discussion of Nympha see Margaret Y. MacDonald, "Can Nympha Rule This House? The Rhetoric of Domesticity in Colossians," in *Rhet-orics and Realities in Early Christianities*, ed. Willi Braun (Studies in Christianity and Judaism; Waterloo, Ont.: Wilfrid Laurier, forthcoming). On women lead-ers of house churches see chapter 7 of this volume. The leadership of a house church by a woman created such a scandal for subsequent readers and copyists of Colossians that attempts were made to masculinize the text, with some manu-scripts presenting Nympha as a man. For textual variants and discussion of issues of translation see Margaret Y. MacDonald, *Colossians and Ephesians*, ed. Daniel J. Harrington, S.J. (SP 17; Collegeville, Minn.: Liturgical, 2000), 182–83.

2. See, for example, James D. G. Dunn, *The Epistles to the Colossians and to Philemon: A Commentary on the Greek Text* (NIGTC; Grand Rapids: Eerdmans, 1996), 246.

3. See Col. 3:18—4:1; Eph. 5:21—6:9; 1 Pet. 2:18—3:7; 1 Tim. 2:8-15; 6:1-2; Titus 2:1-10; compare 1 *Clem.* 21:6-9; Ignatius, *Pol.* 4:1—5:2; Polycarp, *Phil.* 4:2-3; *Did.* 4:9-11; *Barn.* 19:5-7.

4. In this latter case, the greeting to believers in Laodicea would be reiterated to single out Nympha. In other words, "and to Nympha" would mean "and spe-cifically to Nympha" (see Rom 16:23). See Markus Barth and Helmut Blanke, *Colossians: A New Translation and Commentary* (AB 34B; New York: Doubleday, 1994), 486. Note, however, that despite the likelihood that Nympha's house was in Laodicea, a location in either Hierapolis (see Col. 4:13) or even Colossae itself cannot be ruled out entirely.

5. See Suzanne Dixon, *The Roman Mother* (London: Croom Helm, 1988), 31. See also Keith Hopkins, "The Age of Roman Girls at Marriage," *Population Studies* 18 (1965): 309–27; Keith Hopkins, "Men's Age at Marriage and Its Consequences in the Roman Family," *Classical Philology* 82.1 (1987): 21–34. In the surviving Christian inscriptions of the fourth and following centuries, median age at marriage for both boys and girls appears to be slightly older than in the previous population: Carlo Carletti, "Aspetti biometrici del matrimonio nelle iscrizioni chritiane di Roma," *Augustianum* 17 (1977): 39–51.

6. Keith R. Bradley, *Discovering the Roman Family* (New York: Oxford University Press, 1991), 171.

7. *Laudatio Turiae* LS 8393, col. i, 11.30-3. Cited in Geoffrey S. Nathan, *The Family in Late Antiquity: The Rise of Christianity and the Endurance of Tradition* (London: Routledge, 2000), 196.

8. Compare, for example, Gregory of Nazianzen's fourth-century funeral oration for his sister Gorgonia, who is portrayed as an ideal married woman. See *Oration* 8.

9. Craig A. Williams, *Roman Homosexuality: Ideologies of Masculinity in Classical Antiquity* (Oxford: Oxford University Press, 1999), 30–31.

10. On the details of the Augustan legislation of 18 BCE and 9 CE (*lex Julia et Papia*) in general, see Jane F. Gardner, *Women in Roman Law and Society* (London: Croom Helm, 1986), 77–78; on adultery see 127–31. See also Judith Evans Grubbs, *Law and Family in Late Antiquity: The Emperor Constantine's Marriage Legislation* (Oxford: Clarendon, 1995), 94–98; Antti Arjava, *Women and Law in Late Antiquity* (Oxford: Clarendon, 1996), 77–78. It should be noted that the Augustan legislation was directed primarily at elite senatorial classes for the purposes of guaranteeing sufficient legitimate progeny for the health of the Principate and included measures that would have been especially meaningful to the elite such as restrictions on inheritance. However tangentially related to the specific lives of many early church members, they nevertheless offer insight into the values and socio-political ideals of society that resonate also in early Christian literature.

11. See also interesting evidence for a sexual double standard among Pythagorean traditions, in which the advice to "look the other way" is purportedly given by women to other women. See discussion of these texts in chapter 7.

12. The lone dissenting voice appears to be Musonius Rufus (frag. 12), who encourages husbands to think of sex between masters and their slaves as shameful. See detailed discussion of the sexual use of slaves in chapter 5 of this volume. See also Williams, *Roman Homosexuality*, 30–31, 51–52.

13. Jennifer Glancy, *Slaves in Early Christianity* (Oxford: Oxford University Press, 2002). See also chapter 5 of this volume.

14. See full discussion in Margaret MacDonald, *Early Christian Women and Pagan Opinion: The Power of the Hysterical Woman* (Cambridge: Cambridge University Press, 1996), 220–25. On slave marriages and family relations among slaves

see Dale Martin, "Slave Families and Slaves in Families," in *Early Christian Families in Context: An Interdisciplinary Dialogue*, ed. David L. Balch and Carolyn Osiek (Religion, Marriage, and Family; Grand Rapids: Eerdmans, 2003), 207–30.

15. Gardner, *Women in Roman Law and Society*, 31–32. See also discussion of inscription evidence in Dale B. Martin, *Slavery as Salvation: The Metaphor of Slavery in Pauline Christianity* (New Haven: Yale University Press), 2–7; Martin, "Slave Families and Slaves in Families."

16. See Ross Shepard Kraemer, *Her Share of the Blessings: Women's Religions among Pagans, Jews, and Christians in the Greco-Roman World* (Oxford: Oxford University Press, 1992), 137. For a comprehensive treatment of marriage and Judaism see especially Michael Satlow, *Jewish Marriage in Antiquity* (Princeton: Princeton University Press, 2001).

17. In discussing the limited possibilities for freed female slaves Gillian Clark ("Roman Women," *Greece and Rome* [ser. 2] 28 [1981]: 193–212) has noted that "it was not respectable to marry a *libertina*, though it had been known to happen before Augustus allowed it for non-senators" (198). Economic reasons, such as inability to produce a dowry, and restrictions between certain categories of people, meant that some women became concubines and not wives. Concubinages were associated especially with freedpersons, but there was a tendency for the men to be of a higher status than the women. A significant number of freeborn men were involved in such arrangements. See also Gardner, *Women in Roman Law and Society*, 56–58. Note that on the basis of Phil. 4:22 and other texts, Wayne Meeks has argued that the presence of freedpersons among Pauline Christians was very likely. See *The First Urban Christians: The Social World of the Apostle Paul* (New Haven: Yale University Press, 1983), 21–23, 63–72.

18. See Beryl Rawson, "Roman Concubinage and Other De Facto Marriages," in *TAPA* 104 (1974): 288.

19. On the "new woman," including detailed treatment of ancient sources, see especially Bruce W. Winter, *Roman Wives, Roman Widows: The Appearance of New Women and the Pauline Communities* (Grand Rapids: Eerdmans, 2003). Winter concentrates more on the public roles of women and their new social mores and less specifically on the household setting than the present study. His focus is especially on how an understanding of new attitudes toward dress and comportment among women can shed light on various texts in the Pauline corpus such as 1 Cor. 11:2-16 and 1 Tim. 2:9-15. Particularly relevant for the present study, however, is his argument that by the first century, Roman imperial marriage values had spread rapidly to centers in the East such as Ephesus and the presence of the "new woman" was significant (32–37).

20. On the terms of marriage and the rights of the *paterfamilias* in relation to his married children see Suzanne Dixon, *The Roman Mother* (London: Croom Helm, 1988), 26–27. See also Nathan, *The Family in Late Antiquity*, 16–17.

21. On women and household management see also chapters 6 and 7.

22. Dixon, *Roman Mother*, 44. For a discussion of the system of *tutela* (often translated as "guardianship") and its consequences for the lives of women, see 43–47.

23. Ibid., 62–63. Dixon notes that the mother's permission was eventually recognized in law by the *Codex Theodosianus* (9.24).

24. See *Acts of [Paul and] Thecla*, 7–10, 21, in Ross S. Kraemer, *Women's Religions in the Greco-Roman World: A Sourcebook* (Oxford: Oxford University Press, 204), 299–302. Andrew S. Jacobs ("A Family Affair: Marriage, Class, and Ethics in the Apocryphal Acts of the Apostles," *JECS* 7 [1999]: 104–38) has attached special significance to the absence of a focus on paternal *potestas* in this work as a sign of a more direct focus on marital *concordia* and implied critique of the conjugal family associated with upper-class ethics (108). In light of Dixon's analysis, however, it seems just as likely that the mother's strong reactions (and lack of reference to Thecla's father's authority) reflect the influence of mothers in making arrangements for their daughters.

25. Dixon, *Roman Mother*, 63–66. She notes that by 390 the law gave the right of the mother to become *tutrix* of her children, but only if she swore that she would not remarry.

26. This has been argued, for example, by Dennis R. MacDonald in *There Is No Male and Female: The Fate of a Dominical Saying in Paul and Gnosticism* (Philadelphia: Fortress, 1987). In contrast, Bruce W. Winter has recently argued that these women were married and that they were identifying themselves with the "new women" of the Roman Empire who "behaved loosely at banquets which were often held in private homes" (*Roman Wives, Roman Widows*, 91).

27. See Clement of Alexandria (*Miscellanies* 3.6.53.3), who also understands the partnership to be one of "spiritual marriage." On the meaning of 1 Cor. 9:5 see Mary Rose D'Angelo, "Women Partners in the New Testament," *JFSR* 6 (1990): 65–86.

28. In discussing 1 Cor. 9:5 John Dominic Crossan, for example, has suggested that the missionary pairings of men and women in the Pauline mission were inspired by the necessity of giving the appearance of marriage in a world of male power and violence (*The Historical Jesus: The Life of a Mediterranean Jewish Peasant* [San Francisco: HarperSanFrancisco, 1991], 335). On the issue of spiritual marriage in the Pauline letters more generally see Antoinette Clark Wire, *The Corinthian Women Prophets: A Reconstruction through Paul's Rhetoric* (Minneapolis: Fortress, 1990), 224–25; J. Duncan M. Derrett, "The Disposal of Virgins," in *Studies in the New Testament*, vol. 1: *Glimpses of the Legal and Social Presuppositions of the Authors* (Leiden: Brill, 1977), 184–91. For a broader discussion of the phenomenon throughout early Christianity see Elizabeth A. Castelli, "Virginity and Its Meaning for Women's Sexuality in Early Christianity," *JFSR* 2 (1986): 61–88, esp. 80.

29. For a full discussion of how Roman definitions of licit marriage related to the various categories and classes of people in the Roman Empire see Gardner, *Women in Roman Law and Society*, 31–44.

30. See Kraemer, *Her Share of the Blessings*, 136–38, esp. 136.

31. Meeks, *The First Urban Christians*, 57.

32. Such arrangements may have grown out of engagements that were considered binding according to Jewish tradition. See discussion in Wire, *Corinthian Women Prophets*, 224.

33. Note, however, that Prisc(ill)a and Aquila combined aspects of an itinerant existence with the more settled existence of hosting a house church. Wire may be exaggerating the distinction between itinerant existence and local existence somewhat. See further discussion below.

34. Wire, *Corinthian Women Prophets*, 102–3.

35. Ibid., 92. This is noted by Wire, but her interpretation differs somewhat from the one being offered here. On widows caring for children in early Christianity see chapter 4 of this volume.

36. See Clarice J. Martin, "The Acts of the Apostles," in *Searching the Scriptures*, vol. 2: *A Feminist Commentary*, ed. Elisabeth Schüssler Fiorenza (New York: Crossroad, 1994), 763–99. On women in Luke-Acts see also Mary Rose D'Angelo, "Women in Luke-Acts: A Redactional View," *JBL* 109/3 (1990): 441–61.

37. See especially L. Michael White, "Visualizing the 'Real' World of Acts 16: Toward Construction of a Social Index," in *The Social World of the First Christians: Essays in Honor of Wayne A. Meeks*, ed. L. Michael White and O. Larry Yarbrough (Minneapolis: Fortress, 1995), 234–61. On the difficulties of drawing historical conclusions about real women underlying Acts see also Judith Lieu, "The Attraction of Women in/to Early Judaism and Christianity: Gender and the Politics of Conversion," *JSNT* 72 (1998): 5–22.

38. See Martin, "The Acts of the Apostles," 785–86.

39. David Noy, *Foreigners at Rome: Citizens and Strangers* (London: Duckworth with the Classical Press of Wales, 2000), 259.

40. For textual reasons and reasons related to the manuscript tradition, some have viewed Romans 16 as a later addition to the Epistle to the Romans, perhaps originally intended for Ephesus. But many today see the long list of greetings as fitting well with the situation of the letter to the Romans. See a summary of the issues and discussion of current scholarly opinion in Brendan Byrne, S.J., *Romans*, ed. Daniel J. Harrington, S.J. (SP 6; Collegeville, Minn.: Liturgical, 1996), 29.

41. Noy, *Foreigners at Rome*, 149–50.

42. Ibid., 149, 155. See also A. Scobie, "Slums, Sanitation, and Mortality in the Roman World," *Klio* 68 (1986): 399–433.

43. On early Christian hospitality's following patterns already established by Diaspora Jews see Meeks, *The First Urban Christians*, 109.

44. Ibid., 59. On the significance of women being named first see Marleen Boudreau Flory, "Where Women Precede Men: Factors Influencing the Placement of Names in Roman Epitaphs," *Classical Journal* 79/2 (1983-84): 216–24.

45. If this is the case, Paul's relationship with Prisc(ill)a would be similar to his relationship with Phoebe (see Rom. 16:1-2).

46. See chapter 1 of this volume. On early Christians and *insulae* see Robert Jewett, "Tenement Churches and Communal Meals in the Early Church: The Implications of a Form-Critical Analysis of 2 Thessalonians 3:10," *BR* 38 (1993): 23–43.

47. The most important Roman author presenting differences in the segregation of women between East and West is Vitruvius (for example, *Architecture* 6.10.1-5). But, as Carolyn Osiek and David L. Balch have noted, even in Pompeii (where one would not have expected segregation) some houses have two dining rooms side by side, suggesting the possibility of separate dining for men and women (*Families in the New Testament World: Households and House Churches* [Louisville: Westminster John Knox, 1997], 16–17).

48. See, for example, Tacitus, *Dialogue* 28.4–5, trans. Forster and Heffner in LCL. See also discussions in Kathleen E. Corley, *Private Women, Public Meals: Social Conflict in the Synoptic Tradition* (Peabody, Mass.: Hendrickson, 1993), 25; Karen Jo Torjesen, *When Women Were Priests: Women's Leadership in the Early Church and the Scandal of Their Subordination in the Rise of Christianity* (San Francisco: HarperSanFrancisco, 1993), 113.

49. See Jill Dubisch, *Gender and Power in Rural Greece* (Princeton: Princeton University Press), 18.

50. For some discussion of such a relationship among Jewish mothers and daughters, see Ross S. Kraemer, "Jewish Mothers and Daughters in the Greco-Roman World," in *The Jewish Family in Antiquity*, ed. Shaye J. D. Cohen (Brown Judaic Studies 289; Atlanta: Scholars, 1993), 89–112.

51. In 1 Cor. 7:12-16 Paul applies the case of marriage between believers and unbelievers equally to men and women, but the case of marriage between believing men and nonbelieving women is virtually unheard of in the literature. See further discussion below.

52. As noted previously, the historical reliability of details found in Acts are subject to considerable debate. We cannot be certain that Ananias and Sapphira were real historical persons. There is a strong resemblance between Luke's account and the story of Achan in the book of Joshua (Josh. 7:1-26). Part of Luke's literary artistry involves the use of "pairing." It is interesting to note here that the negative picture involving Ananias and Sapphira is contrasted with the positive actions of Barnabas (Acts 4:36-37). Barnabas's submission to the Twelve prepares the way for his subsequent defense of Paul (9:27). See Luke Timothy Johnson, *The Acts of the Apostles*, ed. Daniel J. Harrington, S.J. (SP 5; Collegeville, Minn.: Liturgical, 1992), 91–92.

53. Polycarp, *Phil.* 11.4; trans. Lake, LCL.

54. Johnson, *The Acts of Apostles*, 87.

55. On the importance of the house-church setting for understanding the leadership structures revealed by the writings of the Apostolic Fathers, see especially Harry O. Maier, *The Social Setting of the Ministry as Reflected in the Writings of Hermas, Clement, and Ignatius* (Dissertations SR 1; Waterloo, Ont.: Wilfrid Laurier, 1991).

56. Literary and epigraphic evidence from the third and fourth centuries suggests that the use of this title for women cannot be ruled out. See, for example, Cyprian, *Epistle* 75.10.5, and other evidence cited by Karen Jo Torjesen in *When Women Were Priests*, 10–11, 115; Kevin Madigan and Carolyn Osiek, *Ordained Women in the Early Church* (Baltimore: Johns Hopkins University Press, 2005), chapter 8. It should also be noted that Carolyn Osiek has argued that no firm conclusions may be drawn about the sex of the presbyters mentioned in the second-century work *The Shepherd of Hermas* (Herm. *Vis.* 2.4.3). See Carolyn Osiek, *The Shepherd of Hermas: A Commentary* (Hermeneia; Minneapolis: Fortress, 1999), 18, 58–59.

57. While Rome has generally been accepted for the setting of this work, there has been considerable debate about dating, literary sources, and historical reliability. See detailed discussion of these issues in Osiek, *Shepherd of Hermas*, 18–28. All references below are to Osiek's translation.

58. Ibid., 24.

59. Ibid., 49. On marriage "without *manus*" see above.

60. This seems to reflect a general attitude about the inclination of women to lack restraint in speaking—well attested in early Christian literature (see 1 Tim. 3:11; 5:13; Titus 2:3; Polycarp, *Phil.* 4.3; *Didascalia* 15 = *Apostolic Constitutions* 3.6.4.)—rather than a specific episode involving the wife speaking out in church as in the case of 1 Cor. 14:34-35 (compare 1 Tim. 2:11-16).

61. See, for example, Juliet du Boulay, *Portrait of a Greek Mountain Village* (Oxford: Clarendon, 1974), 130–33; Jill Dubisch, *Gender and Power in Rural Greece* (Princeton: Princeton University Press, 1986), 207–11. For a full discussion of the relevance of these anthropological insights for studying the context of early Christianity, including points of contact with Greco-Roman ideals, see MacDonald, *Early Christian Women*, 67–73, 240–42.

62. See Osiek, *The Shepherd of Hermas*, 228–29.

63. Dubisch, *Gender and Power*, 211. That the description of the sin of Hermas's wife has important symbolic value for the community as a whole is supported by the widespread use of female symbolism in the work, including the revelatory symbol of the woman church. See Osiek, *The Shepherd of Hermas*, 16–18.

64. Osiek, *The Shepherd of Hermas*, 42.

65. Ibid., 42–43.

66. Ibid., citing P. R. C. Weaver, "Children of Freedmen [and Freedwomen]," in *Marriage, Divorce, and Children in Ancient Rome*, ed. Beryl Rawson (Oxford: Clarendon, 1991), 166–90. Osiek also notes Clement of Alexandria's comments directed against Alexandrian women who strip before their male slaves at the baths (*Educator* 3.5.32.3).

67. Osiek, *The Shepherd of Hermas*, 46–47.

68. There are interesting similarities between Justin's presentation of the Roman matron and Jerome's late fourth-century presentation of the Christian

matron Fabiola, who not only divorced a disreputable husband, but also remarried. See Jerome, *Letter* 77 (see also *Letters* 64–78).

69. Marriage is actually a common theme of the second-century Christian apologists. See, for example, Aristides, *Apology* 15; Justin 1 *Apology* 15, 29; Athenagoras, *A Plea for the Christians* 33. Scholars have tended to understand Justin's description as historical, and this is supported especially by the details that are offered; yet his apologetic interests more than likely also shape the account, and the possibility that the Roman matron is a construct based on what was rumored or known to happen in a few instances cannot be ruled out entirely.

70. Apology 2.2; trans. ANF 1.188.

71. R. M. Grant (*Greek Apologists of the Second Century* [Philadelphia: Westminster, 1988], 72) has examined the legal issues involved here in detail. See also "A Woman of Rome: Justin, Apol 2,2" *CH* 54 (1985): 461–72.

72. See MacDonald, *Early Christian Women*, 211–12.

73. Nathan (*The Family in Late Antiquity*, 49–50; 205 n.288) has argued that the terminology used to describe the legal measures undertaken by the husband and wife argues for Roman citizenship.

74. Initiating divorce was possible for both men and women in the empire, but according to ancient historian Gillian Clark ("Roman Women") true independence in such matters for women was actually quite rare.

75. The ANF translates the expression as "friends." But the Greek text refers literally to the "ones belonging to her" (*hypō tōn autēs*) and is best understood as a reference to the members of her household. The same Greek construction occurs in 1 Cor. 1:11 to refer to the members of the household of Chloe (literally, the ones belonging to her).

76. All references to this work are to the translation by H. Musurillo, *The Acts of the Christian Martyrs* (Oxford: Oxford University Press, 1972). Because it offers the earliest evidence we have of authorship of an early Christian text by a woman, this work has been of great interest to scholars. See Maureen A. Tilley, "The Passion of Perpetua and Felicity," in *Searching the Scriptures*, vol. 2: *A Critical Commentary*, ed. Elisabeth Schüssler Fiorenza (New York: Crossroad, 1994), 830–58, esp. 833. It should be noted, however, that Ross S. Kraemer and Shira L. Lander ("Perpetua and Felicitas," in *The Early Christian World*, ed. Philip F. Esler, vol. 2 [London: Routledge, 2000], 1051–58) have expressed reservations about the document's historicity (including its value for recovering real female experience) and claims of female authorship. Strong references to intensely female experiences, such as the physical consequences of nursing babies, would nevertheless suggest that at the very least the document has been strongly influenced by a feminine point of view.

77. Note, however, that while it is not made explicit in the narrative, the husband and father of the child may be Saturus. See Carolyn Osiek, "Perpetua's Husband," *JECS* 10/2 (2002): 287–90.

78. There have been other theories with respect to the absence of a mention of a husband. The document has frequently been seen as reflecting Montanist elements and, therefore, may reflect the connections between Montanism and sexual renunciation; see Kraemer, *Her Share of the Blessings*, 160–61. For a critical evaluation of the association of the work with Montanism see Tilley, "The Passion of Perpetua and Felicity," 833–36. Among the most controversial theories about the relationships in the narrative is that by Mary R. Lefkowitz, who has argued that the emotional relationship between Perpetua and her father is in keeping with what is known of modern incestuous relationships ("The Motivations for St. Perpetua's Martyrdom," *JAAR* 44 [1976]: 417–21).

79. The following phrase suggests that of Perpetua's family only her father is a non-Christian: "he alone of all my kin would be unhappy to see me suffer" (5).

80. See Nathan, *The Family in Late Antiquity*, 51.

81. Tilley, "The Passion of Perpetua and Felicity," 831.

82. The same may well be true of the wife of Epitropos, who is greeted along with her whole household and children in Ignatius's letter to Polycarp (Ignatius, *Pol.* 8.2). This woman may in fact have been the wife of a relatively well-to-do pagan official, as is suggested by the alternate translation of *epitropos* as "procurator" (a term that covered a wide range of administrators with potentially varying social status). See William R. Schoedel, *Ignatius of Antioch: A Commentary on the Letters of Ignatius of Antioch* (Philadelphia: Fortress, 1985), 280n.14.

3. Giving Birth:
Labor, Nursing, and Care of Infants in House-Church Communities

1. See Beryl Rawson, *Children and Childhood in Roman Italy* (Oxford: Oxford University Press, 2003), 114–16. See also Keith M. Hopkins, "Contraception in the Roman Empire," *Comparative Studies in the Society and History* 8 (1965): 124–51.

2. For other negative views of abortion and contraception in antiquity see Aristotle, *Politics* 7.14.10, 1335b (but allowable if fetus is still unformed); Plautus, *Truculentus* 201–2; Cicero, *In Defense of Cluentius* 2.32; Ovid, *Amores* 2.13–14.

3. Philo's position seems somewhat more complex. See Philo, *The Special Laws* 3.108–15, where there is a distinction drawn in penalties for causing a woman to miscarry when the fetus is yet unformed and for causing a woman to miscarry when the fetus is fully formed (in this latter case, the penalty is death). He relates the practice of abortion to infanticide, which he treats in much more detail. On the relationship between abortion and infanticide see also the *Sentences of Pseudo-Phocylides*, 184–85. On abortion, infanticide, and exposure in Jewish texts and the relationship to early Christian teaching see O. M. Bakke, *When Children Became People: The Birth of Childhood in Early Christianity*, trans. Brian McNeil (Minneapolis: Fortress, 2005), 110–39.

4. Although there is great uncertainty with respect to the dating and provenance of the text, abortion and exposure are also condemned along with various sexual vices in the *Sibylline Oracles* 2.279–82.

5. Note, for example, that W. A. Strange has argued that Judaism and Christianity brought different estimations of infant life into the ancient world (*Children in the Early Church: Children in the Ancient World, the New Testament, and the Early Church* [Carlisle, Cumbria: Paternoster, 1996], 22). But recent work on Roman families suggests that this may be an overstatement. On Judaism see note 8 below.

6. Rawson, *Children and Childhood*, 105. See also B. D. Shaw, "Raising and Killing Children: Two Roman Myths," *Mnemosyne* 54 (2001): 33–77. The role of the midwife in decisions about the rearing of infants has been emphasized by Valerie French in "Midwives and Maternity Care in the Roman World," *Helios*, New Series 13/2 (1986): 69–84.

7. See E. Scott, "Unpacking a Myth: The Infanticide of Females and Disabled Infants in Antiquity," in *Proceedings of the Tenth Annual Theoretical Roman Archaeology Conference: London 2000*, ed. G. Davies, A. Gardner, and K. Lockyear (Oxford: Oxbow, 2000), 143–51. See also Rawson, *Children and Childhood*, 117.

8. That presentations of Jewish life should not be taken literally even with respect to such issues as abandonment of children has been stressed by John Boswell, *The Kindness of Strangers: The Abandonment of Children in Western Europe from Late Antiquity to the Renaissance* (New York: Pantheon, 1988), 139–52. See also Adele Reinhartz, "Philo's Exposition of the Law and Social History," in *SBL Annual Meeting 1993 Seminar Papers*, ed. Eugene H. Lowering Jr. (Atlanta: Scholars, 1993), 6–21.

9. See Jennifer A. Glancy, *Slavery in Early Christianity* (Oxford: Oxford University Press, 2002), 76.

10. Ibid., 7–8; Rawson, *Children and Childhood*, 118.

11. Cited in Rawson, *Children and Childhood*, 100. See also Soranus, *Gynecology* 98.

12. For evidence of female doctors see S. Treggiari, "Jobs for Women," *American Journal of Ancient History* 1 (1976): 76–104; R. Flemming, *Medicine and the Making of Roman Women: Gender, Nature, and Authority from Celsus to Galen* (Oxford: Oxford University Press, 2000).

13. Midwives in the East seem to have enjoyed a higher status, with some advancing to the profession of physician obstetrician. See French, "Midwives and Maternity Care."

14. See Margaret Y. MacDonald, *Early Christian Women and Pagan Opinion: The Power of the Hysterical Woman* (Cambridge: Cambridge University Press, 1996), 1–5.

15. Rawson, *Children and Childhood*, 98–105.

16. Ibid., 120–21, citing R. Jackson, *Doctors and Diseases in the Roman Empire* (London: British Museum, 1988).

17. See French, "Midwives and Maternity Care," citing *Natural History* 30.44.129–30. Although the rate of maternal mortality is very difficult to determine. For estimates, see *Civilization of the Ancient Mediterranean*, vol. 3, ed. Michael Grant and Rachel Kitzinger (New York: Scribner's, 1988), 1357. On the mortality of infants see note 38 below.

18. See D. J. Harrington, S.J., *The Gospel of Matthew* (SP 1; Collegeville, Minn.: Liturgical, 1991), 11; Luke Timothy Johnson, *The Gospel of Luke* (SP 3; Collegeville, Minn.: Liturgical, 1991), 50.

19. Jane Schaberg, "The Infancy of Mary of Nazareth," in *Searching the Scriptures*, vol. 2: *A Feminist Commentary*, ed. Elisabeth Schüssler Fiorenza (New York: Crossroad, 1994), 717; on questions of date, authorship, and provenance, see 717–18.

20. References are to the translation of the work (also known as the *Protoevangelium of James*) in *The Apocryphal New Testament*, ed. J. K. Elliott (Oxford: Oxford University Press, 1993).

21. Mary's childbirth is not really associated with the lives of female ascetics until the fourth century. Schaberg notes that the retelling of the story that occurs in the closely related sixth-century *Pseudo-Matthew* offers indications that Mary is being presented as a model for female ascetics. See "Infancy of Mary of Nazareth," 727.

22. MacDonald, *Early Christian Women and Pagan Opinion*, 94–120. See also chapter 10 of this book.

23. Schaberg, "Infancy of Mary of Nazareth," 720. See Origen, *Against Celsus*, 1.28–39, 69–70. All references are to the translation by Henry Chadwick: Origen, *Contra Celsum* (Cambridge: Cambridge University Press, 1953).

24. See chapter 2.

25. Schaberg, "Infancy of Mary of Nazareth," 725.

26. Among the historical complexities that have occupied the attention of scholars is the possible association of *The Martyrdom of Perpetua and Felicitas* with Montanism. Although it has often been understood as reflecting the theology of Montanism, which idealized asceticism, the text assumes the normalcy of marriage and pregnancy.

27. From the translation by H. Musurillo in *The Acts of the Christian Martyrs* (Oxford: Oxford University Press, 1972), 123–24.

28. Ibid., 127.

29. That the baby's father was actually Revocatus (2.1) cannot be ruled out completely. He is described as Felicitas's "companion in service" (*conserua*), which could mean that she was his wife (though not legally recognized) or his slave but most likely means simply that they were the fellow slaves of the same owner. See Maureen A. Tilley, "The Passion of Perpetua and Felicity," in Schüssler Fiorenza, *Searching the Scriptures*, 2:847.

30. Ibid., 849.

31. Trans. Colson and Whitaker, LCL.

32. On the use of infancy as a metaphor in the New Testament see Strange, *Children in the Early Church*, 68–69.

33. Rawson, *Children and Childhood*, 106.

34. Ibid., 106–8.

35. This refers to Plutarch's wife, Timoxena, and her nursing of a now-deceased son. The correspondence in question was, however, primarily intended to comfort his wife upon the death of their two-year old daughter, Timoxena the younger. He seems to accept that his wife used a wet nurse in the case of this younger child (*A Consolation to His Wife* 5). See discussion of this text in the next chapter.

36. See Rawson, *Children and Childhood*, 123.

37. Trans. Babbitt, LCL.

38. See Rawson, *Children and Childhood*, 103–4, where she compares the most important recent studies and discusses expectations concerning the mourning of very young children.

39. Gillian Clark, "Roman Women," *Greece and Rome* (ser. 2) 28 (1981): 198.

40. See Glancy, *Slavery in Early Christianity*, 34–38. She analyzes the complex use of slavery, kinship, and adoption imagery in Galatians 3–4 in light of their social setting.

41. For a thorough discussion of the use of these Greek terms in the New Testament see especially Peter Müller, *In der Mitte der Gemeinde: Kinder im Neuen Testament* (Neukirchen-Vluyn: Neukirchener, 1992), 304–8.

42. Johnson, *The Gospel of Luke*, 280.

43. Rawson, *Children and Childhood*, 104. That such ideas were also prevalent in Eastern regions of the empire is suggested by Plutarch's letter to his wife after the death of their two-year-old daughter. See note 35 and discussion in next chapter.

4. Growing Up in House-Church Communities

1. Beryl Rawson, *Children and Childhood in Roman Italy* (Oxford: Oxford University Press, 2003). Rawson published several shorter studies in anticipation of this major work. Also worthy of note among earlier works is T. Weidemann, *Adults and Children in the Roman Empire* (London: Routledge, 1989).

2. Rawson, *Children and Childhood*, 11.

3. Given the great interest in the early Christian family in recent years, we are surprised by the scarcity of works on early Christian children. With the exception of David L. Balch and Carolyn Osiek, eds., *Early Christian Families in Context: An Interdisciplinary Dialogue*, Religion, Marriage, and Family (Grand Rapids: Eerdmans, 2003), which includes a separate section on children (though not dealing with specifically Christian evidence), recent works on the early Christian family have not concentrated on the lives of children to any significant degree. There

have been many studies on related topics such as the use of fatherhood language and sibling terminology in early Christianity (see, for example, Halvor Moxnes, ed., *Constructing Early Christian Families: Family as Social Reality and Metaphor* [London: Routledge, 1997]). There have also been some essays (cited below) on children in early Christianity, but few monographs. Notable exceptions include O. M. Bakke, *When Children Became People: The Birth of Childhood in Early Christianity*, trans. Brian McNeil (Minneapolis: Fortress, 2005); W. A. Strange, *Children in the Early Church: Children in the Ancient World, the New Testament, and the Early Church* (Carlisle, Cumbria: Paternoster, 1996); Peter Müller, *In der Mitte der Gemeinde: Kinder im Neuen Testament* (Neukirchen-Vluyn: Neukirchener, 1992). With a somewhat more narrow focus see also Peter Balla, *The Child-Parent Relationship in the New Testament and Its Environment* (WUNT 155; Tübingen: Mohr Siebeck, 2003).

4. It is important to note that Herodias's daughter may have been as young as twelve. The term for young woman (*korasion*) used in Mark 6:22, 28 is also used to refer to Jairus's daughter in Mark 5:42, who is explicitly described as being twelve years old. As Donahue and Harrington have noted, "the narrative could conceivably depict a child's performance rather than the sensuous and seductive dance of later art and literature—and imagined by many commentators on this text." See John R. Donahue, S.J., and Daniel J. Harrington, S.J., *The Gospel of Mark* (SP 2; Collegeville, Minn.: Liturgical, 2002), 198–99.

5. One might also include the slave girl in the high-priest's household (Matt. 26:69, 71; Mark 14:66, 69; Luke 22:56; John 18:16-17) and the female slave with the spirit of divinization in Philippi (Acts 16:16-19). The Greek term for slave in these texts is *paidiskē*. But there is overlap in the terminology for slaves and children, and we cannot be absolutely sure that these female slaves were young. See further discussion below and in chapter 5.

6. See especially Rawson, *Children and Childhood*, 203–7. With respect to Jewish sources from our period, interesting evidence from the Dead Sea Scrolls concerning the education of both boys and girls has been highlighted by Cecilia Wassen. She discusses a reference in the Damascus Document in one of the copies from Cave 4 (4Q266 9 iii 1-10/CD XIII 15–19) as well as a segment from the Rule of the Congregation (1QSa I 4–9). See *Women in the Damascus Document*, Society of Biblical Literature Academia Biblica Series 21 (Leiden: Brill, 2005), 164–68. We are grateful to Dr. Wassen for allowing us to read a portion of her manuscript prior to publication.

7. While there were certainly sometimes service areas of Roman houses, Michele George has recently argued that there is very limited evidence for specific slave quarters in the Roman period. She points especially to the remarks of the historian Tacitus (*Germany* 25), who finds the custom of the northern tribe of Germani to have separate slave quarters remarkable. See Michele George, "Domestic Architecture and Household Relations: Pompeii and Roman Ephesos," *JSNT* 21 (2004): 13.

8. All references are to translation by Henry Chadwick in Origen, *Contra Celsum* (Cambridge University Press, 1953). See Rawson, *Children and Childhood*, 216. On Celsus see also chapters 3 and 10 of this book.

9. For discussion of the terminology used to refer to children see James Francis, "Children and Childhood in the New Testament," in *The Family in Theological Perspective*, ed. Stephen Barton (Edinburgh: T & T Clark, 1996), 67–68.

10. Trans. Babbitt, LCL.

11. It is certainly not beyond the realm of possibility that the audience of Colossians included slaves and slave families who had been kidnapped or captured in war as well as slaves born in households or adopted as foundlings. On how children figured in this experience see Josephus, *B.J.* 7.379–86, cited in Jennifer Glancy, *Slavery in Early Christianity* (Oxford: Oxford University Press), 77–78. Glancy notes that Rome's great wars of expansion had slowed down by the first century, "but occasional wars throughout the provinces and at the edges of the Empire meant a continuing, if episodic, supply of captives as slaves" (77). She also notes that after the Jewish War the slave markets of the empire were flooded with captives. Many have dated Colossians to approximately this time period, about the year 70. Glancy speculates that at least a small number of these slaves would have been members of the emerging Christian cult (78).

12. Rawson, *Children and Childhood*, 53.

13. While the scope of Martin's study was limited and some of the material is difficult to interpret (he examined 115 funerary inscriptions with seventy-four showing evidence of family structure), he nevertheless substantially challenges modern assumptions about the uniform nature of a slave's life. See Dale B. Martin, "Slave Families and Slaves in Families," in Balch and Osiek, *Early Christian Families in Context*, 207–8.

14. Ibid., 227, citing Hermann Dessau, *ILS* 7479; see also discussion of slaves being taken up as foundlings or bought as children and raised in someone else's home, 221–26.

15. Ibid., 230.

16. For relevant references to Celsus see note 8 above. See Lucian of Samosata, *The Passing of Perigrinus*, 12–13. Both texts are discussed extensively in Margaret Y. MacDonald, *Early Christian Women and Pagan Opinion: The Power of the Hysterical Woman* (Cambridge: Cambridge University Press, 1996).

17. See discussion in Harry O. Maier, *The Social Setting of the Ministry as Reflected in the Writings of Hermas, Clement, and Ignatius* (Dissertations SR 1; Waterloo, Ont.: Wilfrid Laurier, 1991), 154–55.

18. See Carolyn Osiek, *The Shepherd of Hermas: A Commentary* (Hermeneia; Minneapolis: Fortress, 1999), 59, citing Heikki Solin, *Die griechische Personennamen in Rom: ein Namenbuch* (Berlin: de Gruyter, 1982), 3.1171–73.

19. Osiek (*Shepherd of Hermas*, 59) has suggested on the basis of this text and 1 Tim. 3:11 (which may be taken as a reference to women deacons of this same

period) that Grapte may actually be a deacon (see also 249). On the role of Grapte as a patron see chapter 9 in this book.

20. Note also that on the basis of 1 Tim. 5:4, 8, it is clear that the grown children and grandchildren of needy widows were expected to support them.

21. William R. Shoedel, *Ignatius of Antioch: A Commentary on the Letters of Ignatius of Antioch* (Hermeneia; Philadelphia: Fortress, 1985), 252.

22. Technically, Roman law recognized a child to be an orphan (*pupillus/ pupilla*) upon the death of the father. See Rawson, *Children and Childhood*, 71. The law stipulated measures, including the appointment of a guardian (*tutor*) to protect fatherless children. But much must surely have depended on the particular circumstances of families.

23. Ibid., 211.

24. The author of 1 Timothy is clearly trying to restrict the activities of younger widows in particular; see discussion in chapter 10.

25. Trans. J. K. Elliott, *The Apocryphal New Testament* (Oxford: Oxford University Press, 1993).

26. Keith Bradley, "Images of Childhood," in *Plutarch's Advice to the Bride and Groom and A Consolation to His Wife*, ed. Sarah B. Pomeroy (New York: Oxford University Press, 1999), 184. Bradley cites various demographic studies of Roman antiquity.

27. Scholars now have serious reservations about earlier theories that ascribed a certain indifference to the death of children among the Romans. See ibid., 191–92. It has sometimes been suggested also that Plutarch's era reflected a new sensibility with respect to children. Bradley has questioned this assumption. His analysis includes an interesting comparison of the art of Pompeii to Plutarch's ideas (193–95).

28. See Sarah B. Pomeroy, "Reflections on Plutarch, *A Consolation to His Wife*," in Pomeroy, *Plutarch's Advice*, 76–77.

29. Trans. Donald Russell, in Pomeroy, *Plutarch's Advice*, 59. With this brief vignette, Plutarch indirectly offers evidence about the importance of the nurse in a child's life and about a nursery-style approach to childrearing: the other babies most likely are slaves.

30. Pomeroy, "Reflections on Plutarch, *A Consolation to His Wife*," 76. On the pervasive experience of mothers in mourning in the Roman world see Mark Golden, "Mortality, Mourning and Mothers," in *Naissance et petite enfance dans l'Antiquité*, Actes du colloque de Fribourg, 28 novembre–1 décembre 2001, ed. Véronique Dasen (Fribourg: Academic Press, 2004), 145–57.

31. Pomeroy, "Reflections on Plutarch, *A Consolation to His Wife*," 76. Pomeroy cites extensive evidence concerning women's participation in funerals. Rituals of mourning are also widely attested among Jews (see Jer. 9:17-20). Mourning practices continued in the early church (Acts 8:2), but the expulsion of the loud mourners present after the death of Jairus's daughter may reflect the rejection of

more elaborate pagan mourning practices in Mark's community (Mark 5:38-40). See Donahue and Harrington, *The Gospel of Mark*, 177.

32. We must also consider the possibility, however, that since he probably wrote the work with a broader audience in mind, Plutarch's advice to his wife concerning restraint may well have been strongly influenced by his desire to communicate his particular philosophies with respect to death.

33. On Gregory of Nyssa's *Life of Macrina* see also chapter 3.

34. On these texts see especially Judith M. Gundry-Volf, "The Least and the Greatest: Children in the New Testament," in *The Child in Christian Thought*, ed. Marcia J. Bunge (Grand Rapids: Eerdmans, 2001), 29–60.

35. On this question see, for example, John Dominic Crossan, *The Historical Jesus: The Life of a Mediterranean Jewish Peasant* (San Francisco: HarperSanFrancisco, 1992), 265–302.

36. On the views concerning the inherent deficiencies of children in the Roman world see Müller, *In der Mitte der Gemeinde*, 89–90, 161–64.

37. See also *Targum Yerushalmi* Exod. 15:2 cited in Francis, "Children and Childhood," 73. See also his comparison of the various versions of Jesus' teaching on children found in the Gospels, 72–73.

38. Ibid.

39. Ibid.

40. Ibid., 82.

41. Ibid.

42. Note that Francis (76–77) senses a radical edge with respect to the patriarchal tradition of the teachers, especially in Matthew's Gospel. He discusses the focus on humility in Matthew's presentation of Jesus and children (Matt. 18:4) and various texts in Matthew that question the authority of teachers and deference to the received tradition. See esp. Matt. 23:9.

43. For other examples and discussion of the relationship between Jewish traditions and early Christian teaching on the education of children, see Bakke, *When Children Became People*, 174-77.

44. See John M. G. Barclay, "The Family as the Bearer of Religion," in Moxnes, *Constructing Early Christian Families*, 77.

45. On these women see Rawson, *Children and Childhood*, 197n.115. On the influence of mothers on the education of their children see also Tacitus, *Dialogue on Orators* 28.5–6. Here an older woman relative is given a kind of supervisory role that recalls the instructions in Titus 2:4-5.

46. Rawson, *Children and Childhood*, 154–56; on the education of slave children see also 187–91.

47. Ibid., 155. Similarly, the home has been stressed as specially important for the instruction of Jewish girls in contrast to the "public" education of boys in schools. See Shoshana Pantel Zolty, *"And All Your Children Shall Be Learned": Women and the Study of Torah in Jewish Law and History* (Northvale, N.J.: Aronson, 1993), 114–17.

48. Rawson, *Children and Childhood*, 203–5. On educated Jewish women see Zolty, *"And All Your Children Shall Be Learned,"* 106–13, with a list of women mentioned in the Talmud who studied Torah in depth, 125. See also detailed discussion of the Torah scholar from the second century CE, Beruriah, 117–24, and the learned woman from the fourth century, Yalta, 126–29.

49. See *CIL* 6.21846, cited and discussed in Rawson, *Children and Childhood*, 47–48.

50. On the various technical terms for teachers and levels of schooling in the Roman world, see ibid., 164–65. See also Carolyn Osiek and David L. Balch, *Families in the New Testament World: Households and House Churches* (Louisville: Westminster John Knox, 1997), 68–74; Mary Ann Beavis, "'Pluck the Rose but Shun the Thorns': The Ancient School and Christian Origins," *SR* 29 (2000): 411–23.

51. Rawson notes the existence of a special training establishment for male imperial slave children founded in the early second century CE that operated for at least a century, the *paedagogium Caesaris*, on the Caelian Hill in Rome. See *Children and Childhood*, 190–91.

52. See summary of evidence in ibid., 198–99.

53. Ibid., 199. Rawson refers to inscription evidence for two freedwomen (*CIL* 6.6331, 9754) and two slaves (4459, 9758); see also ibid., 166.

54. Trans. Melmoth (revised by Hutchinson), LCL.

55. See Beavis, "'Pluck the Rose,'" 411–23. Specifically Christian schools seem to have begun in the East as monastic schools. But an early example of a Christian school dates from about 372 CE: Valens exiles two priests from Edessa to Antinoe in the Thebaid as punishment for resisting his authority. They start an elementary school like what they know back home (Theodoret, *Church History* 4.18.7–14). See Henri I. Marrou, *A History of Education in Antiquity*, trans. George Lamb (Madison: University of Wisconsin Press, 1956), 314–29. The situation among Christians is apparently in contrast to the situation among Jews, in which the separate schooling of children seems to have existed by the first century CE. See discussion in Strange, *Children in the Early Church*, 12–15, 79–81; Zolty, *"And All Your Children Shall Be Learned,"* 107–8; 113–14. There is little evidence that Christians attended Jewish schools as an alternative to pagan education (see Beavis, "'Pluck the Rose,'" 412–13). See also L. Millar, *Christian Education in the First Four Centuries* (London: Faith, 1946).

56. This story of the boy Jesus in the Temple here as well as the Lukan version stresses Jesus' independence, wisdom, and transition into manhood. It is interesting to compare the story of the raising of Mary in the Temple in *The Proto-Gospel of James*. As a three-year-old child who is left to grow up among the priests of the Temple, Mary displays a level of composure and independence that far exceeds the normal capabilities for this age. But in contrast to the events in Jesus' life, her twelfth birthday brings a reminder that menstruation will soon cause her to defile

the Temple, and rather than marking the beginning of her independence, it leads to a search for an appropriate husband. We find no direct references to Mary's education in the Temple; rather, the focus is on her purity and her display of traditional female talents. She is chosen to weave the veil of the Temple.

57. See Horace, *Epistles* 2.1.70–71; Ovid, *Amores* 1.13.17–18; Seneca, *Letters* 94–99; on bad teachers and the avoidance of corporal punishment (though viewed as acceptable for slaves) see Pseudo-Plutarch, *Moralia* 4D, 8F–9A; *On the Education of Children*; Quintillian, *The Orator's Education*, 1.3.13–17.

58. Even nurses were involved in storytelling; see Rawson, *Children and Childhood*, 167. Note that Tertullian (*On Idolatry* 10) actually forbade Christians to be schoolteachers, but encouraged Christian children to attend school as a matter of necessity for the sake of their education. See Beavis, "'Pluck the rose,'" 416.

59. Ibid., citing Gregory Nazianzen, *Carmen 8, To Seleucus.*

60. Osiek, *Shepherd of Hermas*, 54.

61. For translation and commentary on this text, see M. L. W. Laistner, *Christianity and Pagan Culture in the Later Roman Empire* (Ithaca, N.Y.: Cornell University Press, 1951). Note that while he acknowledges that Chrysostom expressed similar views to Pseudo-Plutarch and Quintillian on education, he does not believe that Chrysostom was dependent on these two writers (77–78).

62. On the age of girls at marriage in the Roman world, see chapter 2. This was a topic of considerable interest among ancient authors, including medical writers. According to some, it was better for girls to marry a little later, with one author from the mid-first century suggesting that moderate food, exercise, and work could delay puberty (Athenaeus of Attalia 21.5; cited in Peter Garnsey, *Food and Society in Classical Antiquity* [Cambridge: Cambridge University Press, 1999], 2).

63. For more detail, see chapter 7.

64. For more on female teachers of women, see Osiek and Balch, *Families in the New Testament World*, 167–73; for more on women deacons, see Kevin Madigan and Carolyn Osiek, *Ordained Women in the Early Church* (Baltimore: Johns Hopkins University Press, 2005).

65. Trans. Russell, LCL.

66. On children being exposed early to the realities of sexual life see Rawson, *Children and Childhood*, 214. Rawson notes the presence of children at banquets and celebrations (including wedding celebrations, which were often sexually explicit), but points also to "the very nature of domestic space—the openness of the architectural plan, wall-paintings, the comparative lack of privacy, and children's frequent presence in the slave quarters." See also Christian Laes, "Desperately Different? *Delicia* Children in the Roman Household," in Balch and Osiek, *Early Christian Families in Context*, 298–324; John R. Clarke, *Looking at Lovemaking: Constructions of Sexuality in Roman Art 100 B.C.—A.D. 250* (Berkeley: University of California Press, 1998).

5. Female Slaves: Twice Vulnerable

1. Elizabeth Spelman, *Inessential Woman: Problems of Exclusion in Feminist Thought* (Boston: Beacon, 1988), 52–55; William G. Thalman, "Female Slaves in the Odyssey," in *Women and Slaves in Greco-Roman Culture: Differential Equations*, ed. Sandra R. Joshel and Sheila Murnaghan (London: Routledge, 1998), 25.

2. Marilyn B. Skinner, "Introduction: Quod multo fit aliter in Graecia...," in *Roman Sexualities*, ed. Judith P. Hallett and Marilyn B. Skinner (Princeton: Prince-ton University Press, 1997), 14, quoted in Jennifer A. Glancy, "Three-fifths of a Man: Slavery and Masculinity in Galatians" (unpublished paper, Society of Biblical Literature Annual Meeting, 1999), 2. For a helpful recent collection on (mostly male) slavery, see *Slavery in Text and Interpretation*, ed. Allen D. Callahan, Richard A. Horsley, and Abraham Smith (Semeia 83/84; Atlanta: Society of Biblical Literature, 1998).

3. It is to be expected, however, that there was a replication of the honor system in the slave subculture, based on status and personal characteristics, but this system is no longer accessible to us except through chance allusions. See Carlin A. Barton, *Roman Honor: The Fire in the Bones* (Berkeley: University of California Press, 2001), 11–13.

4. An interesting verification of this notion is the legislation that a female slave cannot be prosecuted for adultery because chastity is not required or expected of her (Paul 2.26.11; *Digest* 23.2.44; *Cod. theod.* 9.7.1). This idea was extended in later legislation to a slave or hired woman working in a tavern. The exemption did not apply to the mistress of a tavern (*ministra cauponae*) but to female workers and slaves employed there and to women merchants. See Thomas A. J. McGinn, "The Legal Definition of Prostitute in Late Antiquity," in *Memoirs of the American Academy in Rome*, vol. 42, ed. Malcolm Bell III and Caroline Bruzelius (Washington, D.C.: American Academy in Rome, 1997), 90–91, 94–96; idem, *Prostitution, Sexuality, and the Law in Ancient Rome* (New York: Oxford University Press, 1998), 196.

5. T. Crisafulli, "Representations of the Feminine: The Prostitute in Roman Comedy," in *Ancient History in a Modern University: Proceedings of a Conference Held at Macquarie University, 8-13 July 1993: to Mark Twenty-five Years of the Teaching of Ancient History and the Retirement from the Chair of Professor Edwin Judge*, ed. T. W. Hillard et al. (New South Wales, Australia: Ancient History Documentary Research Centre, 1998), 1.225–26; Jennifer A. Glancy, "Obstacles to Slaves' Participation in the Corinthian Church," *JBL* 117 (1998): 481–501; idem, *Slavery in Early Christianity* (Oxford: Oxford University Press, 2002).

6. Orlando Patterson, *Slavery and Social Death: A Comparative Study* (Cambridge: Harvard University Press, 1982), 293–94, 453n.1.

7. "Owner," though more brutal a word than "master," is preferable, since many women also owned slaves. The habitual use of "master" in both ancient and modern discussion is another way of marginalizing women, in this case, slaveholding women.

8. William L. Westermann, *The Slave Systems of Greek and Roman Antiquity* (Philadelphia: American Philosophical Society, 1955), 96.

9. See Dale B. Martin, "Slave Families and Slaves in Families," in *Early Christian Families in Context: An Interdisciplinary Dialogue*, ed. David L. Balch and Carolyn Osiek (Religion, Marriage, and Family; Grand Rapids: Eerdmans, 2003).

10. Keith R. Bradley, *Slaves and Masters in the Roman Empire: A Study in Social Control* (New York: Oxford University Press, 1987), 53; Keith Hopkins, *Conquerors and Slaves* (Cambridge: Cambridge University Press, 1978), 159, quoted in Patterson, *Slavery and Social Death*, 167.

11. Westermann, *Slave Systems*, 102n.4; Suzanne Dixon, *The Roman Mother* (London: Routledge, 1988), 17–18, 70–71.

12. Dixon, *Roman Mother*, 146.

13. Holger Thesleff, ed., *The Pythagorean Texts of the Hellenistic Period*, Acta Academiae Aboensis, Series A; Humanistika Vetenskaper, Socialvetenskaper, Teologi, 30.1 (Abo: Abo Akademi, 1965), 123–24; French translation in Mario Meunier, ed., *Femmes Pythagoriciennes: Fragments et Lettres de Théano, Périctioné, Phintys, Mélissa et Myia* (Paris: L'Artisan du Livre, 1932), 113–15. For more on the nursing of infants, see chapter 3.

14. William V. Harris, "Towards a Study of the Roman Slave Trade," in *Memoirs of the American Academy in Rome* 36, ed. John H. D'Arms and E. C. Kopff (Rome: American Academy in Rome, 1980), 119–20; John Madden, "Slavery in the Roman Empire: Numbers and Origins," *Classics Ireland* 3 (1996): 109–28. Online: http://www.ucd.ie/classics/96/Madden96.html.

15. Beryl Rawson, *Children and Childhood in Roman Italy* (Oxford: Oxford University Press, 2003), 117–18, cites discussion that questions this assumption. It does correlate, however, with the evidence for lower numbers of adult female slaves.

16. Madden, "Slavery," 4; Susan Treggiari, "Family Life among the Staff of the Volusii," *TAPA* 105 (1975): 393–401; Susan Treggiari, "Jobs in the Household of Livia," *PBSR* 43 (1975): 48–77.

17. This question is very much discussed currently. See, for example, Walter Scheidel, "Quantifying the Sources of Slaves in the Early Roman Empire," *JRS* 87 (1997): 156–69; William V. Harris, "Demography, Geography and the Sources of Roman Slaves," *JRS* 89 (1999): 62–75.

18. Patterson, *Slavery and Social Death*; Madden, "Slavery," 4.

19. Martin, "Slave Families."

20. E.g., *CIL* 6.14014; 14462; 1516; 23915. See also Judith Evans Grubbs, "'Marriage More Shameful Than Adultery': Slave-Mistress Relationships, 'Mixed Marriages,' and Late Roman Law," *Phoenix* 47 (1993): 130–34.

21. Published by L. Bove in *Labeo* 13 (1967): 43–48; *AE* 1971 no. 88; translation in Jane F. Gardner and Thomas Wiedemann, *The Roman Household: A Sourcebook* (London: Routledge, 1991), 24–27.

22. M. I. Finley, *Ancient Slavery and Modern Ideology* (New York: Viking, 1980), 94–96.

23. Susan Treggiari, *Roman Marriage: Iusti Coniuges from the Time of Cicero to the Time of Ulpian* (Oxford: Clarendon, 1991), 301.

24. See McGinn, "Legal Definition of Prostitute," 313–14.

25. Treggiari, *Roman Marriage*, 263.

26. Diana C. Moses, "Livy's Lucretia and the Validity of Coerced Consent in Roman Law," in *Consent and Coercion to Sex and Marriage in Ancient and Medieval Societies*, ed. Angeliki E. Laiou (Washington, D.C.: Dumbarton Oaks Research Library & Collection, 1993), 46.

27. References given in Westermann, *Slave Systems*, 74nn.112–14; other examples in Glancy, "Obstacles to Slaves' Participation," 483–90.

28. See LSJ s.v.; Diodorus Siculus 34.12: what revolting slaves did to women; Athenagoras, *On the Resurrection* 19.7.

29. For a good introduction to Jewish slaveholding in the Roman period, see Dale B. Martin, "Slavery and the Ancient Jewish Family," in *The Jewish Family in Antiquity*, ed. Shaye J. D. Cohen (Brown Judaic Studies 289; Atlanta: Scholars, 1993), 113–29.

30. *The Wisdom of Ben Sira*, trans. and notes by Patrick W. Skehan, intro. and commentary by Alexander A. di Lella (AB 39; Garden City, N.Y.: Doubleday, 1987), 479.

31. *Genesis Rabbah* 15.7, ed. Theodor-Albeck, 140; Tal Ilan, *Jewish Women in Greco-Roman Palestine: An Inquiry into Image and Status* (Peabody, Mass.: Hendrickson, 1996), 205–10, with further examples.

32. In Luke, Peter addresses her as *gynai* (woman), an unusual form of address for a slave, but probably her slave status is not at issue here.

33. For more on Felicitas's childbirth, see chapter 3.

34. The manuscript tradition of the various pieces of the Andrew legends is complex. The text probably originated in the late second century. For this story, see the translation by Wilhelm Schneemelcher, *NTA* 2.139–41.

35. Bruce J. Malina, "Does *Porneia* Mean Fornication?" *NovT* 14 (1972): 10–17.

36. Discussion in Glancy, "Obstacles to Slaves' Participation," 492–93; idem, *Slavery*, 65–67.

37. Glancy, "Obstacles to Slaves' Participation," 496; idem, *Slavery*, 67–69.

38. Glancy suggests that here Paul is sanctioning the use of slaves for male Christians' sexual needs as "morally neutral" (*Slavery*, 59–62).

39. Translation by C. Detlef G. Müller, *NTA* 2.632.

40. A cache of jewelry discovered at Pompeii contained a gold bracelet inscribed *dominus ancillae suae* ("the master to his female slave"), testimony that such relationships could be deeply affectionate. Bruce Johnston, "Pompeii Dig Reveals Gift to Ex-Slave Girl," *Daily Telegraph*, December 9, 2000. The girl may or may not have been an "ex-slave." *Ancilla* is a normal designation for a female slave, not a freedwoman.

41. Earlier, Justin had used the same argument against the common practice of abandoning unwanted newborns (*Apol.* 1.27).

42. Beryl Rawson, "Roman Concubinage and Other *De Facto* Marriages," *TAPA* 104 (1974): 279–305, makes the helpful clarification, against some earlier scholarship, that Roman concubinage carried no moral connotations but was only a factor of disparate or servile social status between the partners.

43. Glancy, "Obstacles to Slaves' Participation," 482; idem, *Slavery*, 50–51.

44. Glancy, "Obstacles to Slaves' Participation," 482–83.

45. Angeliki Laiou, "Sex, Consent, and Coercion in Byzantium," in Laiou, *Consent and Coercion*, 128–32.

46. See Peter Garnsey, *Ideas of Slavery from Aristotle to Augustine* (Cambridge: Cambridge University Press, 1996), 240, 243.

47. *CIL* 15.7186: Joyce Reynolds, "Roman Inscriptions 1971-5," *JRS* 66 (1976): 196. It has been debated whether putting a collar on a runaway was more humane than the alternative branding on the face: see Glancy, *Slavery in Early Christianity*, 9, 158n.1.

48. *CIL* 15.7192. Both collars contain a Christogram, and both are discussed in Giovanna Sotgiu, "Un collare di schiavo rinvenuto in Sardegna," *Archeologia classica: Rivista dell'Istituto di archeologia dell'Università di Roma* 25–26 (1973–74): 688–97.

49. Denis Feissel, *Recueil des Inscriptions Chrétiennes de Macédoine du IIIe au Ve Siècle* (Athens: French School of Athens, 1983), 150.

50. *Cod. justin.* 9.11.1, in Mary R. Lefkowitz and Maureen B. Fant, eds., *Women's Life in Greece and Rome: A Sourcebook in Translation* (Baltimore: Johns Hopkins University Press, 1992), #144.

51. *Cod. theod.* 9.12.1; Richard Saller, "The Hierarchical Household in Roman Society: A Study of Domestic Slavery," in *Serfdom and Slavery: Studies in Legal Bondage*, ed. M. L. Bush (London: Longman, 1996), 119.

52. Richard Saller, *Patriarchy, Property, and Death in the Roman Family* (Cambridge: Cambridge University Press, 1994), 152–53. See also Theodore S. de Bruyn, "Flogging a Son: The Emergence of the *pater flagellans* in Latin Christian Discourse," *JECS* 7/2 (1999): 249–90.

53. See Robert E. Winn, "The Church of Virgins and Martyrs: Ecclesiastical Identity in the Sermons of Eusebius of Emesa," *JECS* 11/3 (2003): 336.

54. Discussion and more references in Antti Arjava, *Women and Law in Late Antiquity* (Oxford: Clarendon, 1998), 202–20.

55. Laiou, "Sex, Consent, and Coercion," 132.

6. Ephesians 5 and the Politics of Marriage

1. The seminal work on the topic is David L. Balch, *Let Wives Be Submissive: The Domestic Code in 1 Peter* (SBLMS 26; Chico, Calif.: Scholars, 1981). On the

consensus among scholars see James D. G. Dunn, *The Epistles to the Colossians and to Philemon: A Commentary on the Greek Text* (NIGTC; Grand Rapids: Eerdmans, 1996), 243.

2. Sampley's study provides the clearest example of understanding Eph. 5:21-33 as key to unlocking the purpose of Ephesians (J. Paul Sampley, *"And the Two Shall Become One Flesh": A Study of the Traditions in Eph 5:21-33* [SNTSMS 16; Cambridge: Cambridge University Press, 1971], 158–63). Few scholars have gone as far Sampley in their assertions, but many have understood the text as a central means by which the author conveys and brings together theological arguments and ethical teachings found throughout the letter. See Andrew T. Lincoln, *Ephesians* (WBC 42; Dallas: Word, 1990), 388.

3. Despite the lack of manuscript evidence for such a claim, it has sometimes been argued that the household code was a later addition to the letter. See Winsome Munro, "Col. III.18—IV.1 and Eph. V.21—VI.9: Evidence of a Late Literary Stratum?" *NTS* 18 (1972): 434–47, and more recently Sarah Tanzer, "Ephesians," in *Searching the Scriptures*, vol. 2: *A Feminist Commentary*, ed. Elisabeth Schüssler Fiorenza (New York: Crossroad, 1994), 325–47. Problems with such a theory include the fact that the treatment of marriage in Ephesians is in keeping with the author's interest in defining the identity of the church. See detailed response to Munro in Ernest Best, *Ephesians* (ICC; Edinburgh: T & T Clark, 1998), 522–23.

4. On imperial ideology and Ephesians see especially Eberhard Faust, *Pax Christi et Pax Caesaris: Religionsgeschichtliche, traditions-geschichtliche und sozialgeschichtliche Studien zum Epheserbrief* (NTOA 24; Göttingen: Vandenhoeck & Ruprecht, 1993). See also Carmen Bernabé Ubieta, "'Neither *Xenoi* nor *paroikoi, sympolitai* and *oikeioi tou theou*' (Eph 2:19) Pauline Christian Communities: Defining a New Territoriality," in *Social-Scientific Models for Interpreting the Bible*, ed. John J. Pilch (Leiden: Brill, 2001), 260–80; Margaret Y. MacDonald, "The Politics of Identity in Ephesians," *JSNT* 26/4 (2004): 419–44.

5. See Bruce W. Winter, *Roman Wives, Roman Widows: The Appearance of the New Women and Pauline Communities* (Grand Rapids: Eerdmans, 2003), 35.

6. See Suzanne Dixon, "The Sentimental Ideal of the Roman Family," in *Marriage, Divorce, and Children in Ancient Rome*, ed. Beryl Rawson (Oxford: Clarendon, 1991), 99–113, esp. 99.

7. Ibid., 105–7.

8. Peter Brown, *The Body and Society: Men, Women and Sexual Renunciation in Early Christianity* (London: Faber and Faber, 1988), 57. Dixon ("The Sentimental Ideal of the Roman Family," 107–8) notes the association of the concept of *concordia* with relations within the imperial family, drawing special attention to Livia's dedication of a shrine to Concord in gratitude for marriage to Augustus (Ovid, *Calendar* 6.637–40). She also points to second-century coin issues celebrating the harmony of imperial couples and families more generally, the use of *concordia* and

its cognates in legal writings (e.g., Paulus, *Opinions* 5.15), and the tendency for tombstones and literature to describe marriages as "without discord" (e.g., Pliny, *Letters* 3.16.10).

9. Lincoln, *Ephesians*, 432–34. He cites Quintillian 6.1.1 and Aristotle, *Rhetoric* 3.19.

10. Note that there has been extensive scholarly work on the identity and role of "the powers" in Ephesians, and whether these powers should really be viewed as hostile remains a subject of debate in New Testament scholarship. For example, Pheme Perkins believes that Eph. 1:21 displays a positive understanding of angelic powers (*Ephesians* [ANTC; Nashville: Abingdon, 1997]), 51. In contrast, Clinton E. Arnold has highlighted the association of the terminology with angels in Jewish literature and has argued that the powers are both angelic and evil (*Ephesians, Power and Magic: The Concept of Power in Ephesians in the Light of Its Historical Setting* [SNTMS 63; Cambridge: Cambridge University Press, 1989], 52–54). The "spiritual" nature of the battle in Eph. 6:10-20 should not be overstated. Although clearly depicted as not ultimately against human enemies (6:12), these ruling spiritual powers shape the present order and still clearly affect society (2:2).

11. On the political associations of the term "gospel" see Richard A. Horsley, "Rhetoric and Empire—and 1 Corinthians," in *Paul and Politics*, ed. Richard A. Horsley (Harrisburg, Pa.: Trinity Press International, 2000), 91–92.

12. Commentators often highlight this sentiment in their discussions of the parallels between Ephesians and the Qumran literature. Recent work on Ephesians has drawn attention to the extensive nature of these parallels. See Nils Alstrup Dahl, "Ephesians and Qumran," in *Studies in Ephesians: Introductory Questions, Text- and Edition-Critical Issues, Interpretation of Texts and Themes*, ed. David Hellholm, Vemund Blomkvist, and Tord Fornberg (Tübingen: Mohr Siebeck, 2000), 115–44. See also Perkins, *Ephesians*. With specific reference to Eph. 2:12 (which describes the Gentile recipients of Ephesians as once alienated from the commonwealth of Israel and having no hope without God in the world), Terence L. Donaldson has compared Ephesians to texts from Second Temple Judaism that display the most negative characterization of the Gentiles (*Paul and the Gentiles: Remapping the Apostle's Convictional World* [Minneapolis: Fortress, 1997], 52–54). In addition to the Qumran literature, Donaldson draws special attention to *Jubilees*, *Fourth Ezra*, the *Testament of Moses*, and *Pseudo-Philo*, among others. See also Margaret Y. MacDonald, *Colossians and Ephesians*, ed. Daniel J. Harrington, S.J. (SP 17; Collegeville, Minn.: Liturgical, 2000), 222–25, 268–69, 283–84.

13. Scholars are divided in viewing Eph. 5:21 ("Be subject to one another out of reverence for Christ") as linked more closely either to Eph. 4:17—5:20 or to the household code of Eph. 5:22—6:9 (and consequently functioning as an introduction to the code). Compare, for example, Lincoln (*Ephesians*, 352), who argues that Eph. 5:21-33 can be seen as a unit (understanding Eph. 5:15—6:9 as a

broader textual unit that includes the household code [*Ephesians*, 338]), with Tanzer ("Ephesians," 333), who does not believe that Eph. 5:21 should be included as part of the household code. For discussion of the matter see MacDonald, *Colossians and Ephesians*, 325–26.

14. See Tanzer, "Ephesians," 330.

15. Ibid., 336.

16. Ibid.

17. On the sexual nuances within Eph. 5:22-33, see Carolyn Osiek, "The Bride of Christ (Eph. 5:22-33): A Problematic Wedding," *BTB* 32 (2002): 29–39.

18. Ibid., 35.

19. Sampley, *'And the Two Shall Become One Flesh,'* 68–69. In contrast, the term for "wrinkle" (*rutis*) occurs nowhere else in the New Testament. See also Osiek, "The Bride of Christ."

20. Note that there are interesting textual similarities between Eph. 5:21-33 and 2 Cor. 11:2-3. Both Eph. 5:27 and 2 Cor. 11:2 use the verb "present" (*paristēmi*). In 1 Cor. 11:2 the term for "chaste" is *hagnos*, which is closely related to the term *hagios* in Eph. 5:27. Both Paul (2 Cor. 11:3; see Gen. 3:4) and the author of Ephesians (Eph. 5:31; see Gen. 5:31) appeal to the story of Adam and Eve. See Sampley, *'And the Two Shall Become One Flesh,'* 82.

21. See Turid Karlsen Seim ("A Superior Minority: The Problem of Men's Headship in Ephesians 5," in *Mighty Minorities? Minorities in Early Christianity—Positions and Strategies*, ed. David Hellholm, Halvor Moxnes, and Turid Karlsen Seim [Oslo: Scandinavian University Press, 1995], 167–81).

22. It is impossible to determine whether Ignatius knows the text of Eph. 5:21-33 or simply shares with its author a traditional theme. See Margaret Y. MacDonald, "The Ideal of the Christian Couple: Ign. *Pol.* 5.1-2 Looking Back to Paul," *NTS* 40 (1994): 105–25.

23. See Martin Goodman, "Josephus' Treatise *Against Apion*," in *Apologetics in the Roman Empire: Pagans, Jews, and Christians*, ed. Mark Edwards, Martin Goodman, and Simon Price (Oxford: Oxford University Press, 1999), 45–58. Goodman argues that the situation in Rome in the nineties CE offers the most likely background for the shape, tone, and structure of Josephus's apologetic response. The only thing that can be determined with any certainty with respect to the dating of the work, however, is that it was composed after the publication of the *Antiquities* in 93 CE ("Josephus' Treatise *Against Apion*," 50–51). Ephesians is commonly dated to about 90 CE.

24. *Against Apion* 2.181, trans. Thackeray, LCL.

25. With respect to an apologetic function for the Ephesian household code in particular, some scholars have expressed reservations. See especially Tanzer, "Ephesians," 330.

26. In assessing the degree of apologetic interest of a given early Christian text, it is useful to consider the following remark by L. Michael White: "Most

apologetic literature was really addressed to insiders who were looking toward that margin with the larger society as the arena of acculturation and self-definition" ("Visualizing the 'Real World' of Acts 16: Toward Construction of a Social Index," in *The Social World of the First Christians: Essays in Honor of Wayne A. Meeks*, ed. L. Michael White and O. Larry Yarbrough [Philadelphia: Fortress, 1995], 159–69).

27. MacDonald, *Colossians and Ephesians*, 222–27, 234–40, 295–300.

28. Osiek, "The Bride of Christ."

29. Josephus, *Against Apion* 2.179–81, trans. Thackeray, LCL.

30. See also MacDonald, "The Politics of Identity," 440–41.

31. Ibid., 439–40.

32. In Gnostic circles in particular such language could be associated with sexual asceticism and a return to a perfect androgynous state (e.g., *Gospel of Thomas* 22). See full discussion in MacDonald, *Colossians and Ephesians*, 246.

33. See also MacDonald, "The Politics of Identity," 441–42.

34. Perkins (citing Faust, *Pax Christi et Pax Caesaris*) has noted that the cities of Asia Minor sought to secure imperial favor by competing with one another to build a temple to Augustus (*Ephesians*, 75).

35. The focus on the chastity of woman in Ephesians is in keeping with the Mediterranean values of honor and shame that have been extensively discussed by anthropologists and New Testament scholars engaged in social-scientific criticism of the New Testament. See, for example, David D. Gilmore, ed., *Honor and Shame and the Unity of the Mediterranean* (American Anthropological Association Special Publication 22; Washington, D.C.: American Anthropological Association, 1987).

36. Plutarch, *Advice to the Bride and Groom* 142F–43A, trans. Babbitt, LCL 2:324; cited in Andrew Jacobs, "A Family Affair: Marriage, Class, and Ethics in the Apocryphal Acts of the Apostles," *JECS* 7 [1999]: 116. According to Jacobs (citing Susan Treggiari, *Roman Marriage*: Iusti Coniuges *from the Time of Cicero to the Time of Ulpian* [Oxford: Clarendon, 1991], 224–26), Plutarch retains a notion of hierarchy within his understanding of marriage as symbiosis.

37. See Geoffrey S. Nathan, *The Family in Late Antiquity: The Rise of Christianity and the Endurance of Tradition* (London: Routledge, 2000), 19, citing Pliny, *Letters* 4.19.

38. Suzanne Dixon, *The Roman Mother* (London: Croom Helm, 1988), 233.

39. Nathan, *The Family in Late Antiquity*, 17, citing Valerius Maximus, *Memorable Sayings and Doings* 2.1.6.

40. Plutarch, *Advice to the Bride and Groom* 144C, trans. Babbitt, LCL 2:332.

41. Craig A. Williams, *Roman Homosexuality: Ideologies of Masculinity in Classical Antiquity* (Oxford: Oxford University Press, 1999), 141.

42. Ibid., 142.

43. Origen, *Against Celsus* 3.50., trans. Henry Chadwick, Origen, *Contra Celsum* (Cambridge: Cambridge University Press, 1953).

44. Origen, *Against Celsus* 3.55; see also 3.44.

45. See, for example, David D. Gilmore, "Introduction: The Shame of Dishonor," in Gilmore, *Honor and Shame*, 14; see also 8–16. See discussion in MacDonald, *Early Christian Women*, 29–30, 110–12.

46. Williams, *Roman Homosexuality*, 139.

47. See discussion of the remarks concerning the involvement of women in early Christianity by Pliny, Marcus Cornelius Fronto, Lucius Apuleius, Lucian of Samosata, Galen of Pergamum, and Celsus in MacDonald, *Early Christian Women*, 49–126.

48. Valerius Maximus, *Memorable Sayings and Doings* 9.1.ext.7, cited and translated by Williams, *Roman Homosexuality* 137; see also 136–37.

49. Ibid., 137.

50. Pliny's label for early Christianity was in keeping with assessments of oriental religions, including Judaism, in the first and second centuries that often included accusations of indiscriminate defilement of women and immodest relations between men and women. Pliny's language is similar to and may in fact be dependent upon the Roman historian Livy's presentation of the suppression of the Bacchic (Dionysian) rites in Italy, which was written during the reign of Augustus (27 BCE–14 CE). Livy highlights promiscuity in the group and inappropriate mingling of men and women. See Livy, *Annals* 39.8–19.

51. See Pliny, *Letters* 10.96–97. It is generally held that the Latin term *ministra* corresponds to the Greek term *diakonos* (deacon), which occurs in other early Christian texts, but this is not certain. It seems clear, however, that *ministra* refers to some kind of widely acknowledged and defined leadership role. See Kevin Madigan and Carolyn Osiek, *Ordained Women in the Early Church* (Baltimore: Johns Hopkins University Press, 2005), 26–27.

52. Williams (*Roman Homosexuality*, 137) writes, "Masculinity meant being in control, both of oneself and of others, and femininity meant ceding control."

53. In addition to the notion of *imperium* discussed above, *virtus* (which might be translated roughly as "virtue" or "valor") was a second central concept in Roman conceptualization of masculinity. On women exceptionally attaining it, see Williams, *Roman Homosexuality*, 132–33. Women are also portrayed as displaying manly valor in early Christian martyrological accounts such as *The Martyrdom of Perpetua and Felicitas*, which is discussed at length in chapter 2.

54. According to David Hunter (*Marriage in the Early Church*, ed. William G. Rusch [Sources of Early Christian Thought; Minneapolis: Fortress, 1992], 14–15), Clement of Alexandria gave the fullest defense of marriage of his era against Gnostics and Marcionite and Encratite Christians.

55. Clement of Alexandria, *Educator* 2.96. All references are to translation by David G. Hunter in *Marriage in the Early Church*.

56. Ibid., 2.10.97.

57. Clement of Alexandria, *Miscellanies* 2. 23.140–41.

58. Ibid., 3.12.79. Clement's treatment of marriage is much more positive than that of Tertullian, who wrote at approximately the same time. However, it should

be noted that Tertullian implies some association of marriage with ministry in his address to his wife as his "beloved fellow servant in the Lord"; see Tertullian, *To His Wife* 1.1.

59. Clement, *Miscellanies* 2.23.140.

60. Ibid., 2.23.146. Clement's description of the lives of wives is very similar to the first-century description of appropriate behavior for women by Philo of Alexandria (*Spec. leg.* 3.31.169).

61. See Nathan, *The Family in Late Antiquity*, 45. Tertullian treated the issue of remarriage in two other treatises, *An Exhortation to Chastity* (208–10) and *On Monogamy* (217). In keeping with a growing interest in Montanism, these works reflect a progressive association of second marriage with sin. In the latter work he rejects the possibility of remarriage altogether. See discussion in Hunter, *Marriage in the Early Church*, 10–11.

62. Tertullian, *To His Wife* 1.3. All references are to translation by David G. Hunter in *Marriage in the Early Church*.

63. Ibid., 2.1.

64. Ibid., 2.4.; see also 2.3–4.

65. See further discussion in chapter 10.

66. See Osiek, "The Bride of Christ," 36–38.

7. Women Leaders of Households and Christian Assemblies

1. So Christine Roy Yoder, *Wisdom as a Woman of Substance: A Socioeconomic Reading of Proverbs 1–9 and 31:10-31* (Berlin: de Gruyter, 2001), 38. See also Claudia Camp, "Woman Wisdom and the Strange Woman: Where Is Power to Be Found?" in *Reading Bibles, Writing Bodies: Identity and the Book*, ed. Timothy K. Beal and David M. Gunn (London: Routledge, 1997), 85–112.

2. Al Wolters, "Sōpiyyā (Prov 31:27) as Hymnic Participle and Play on *Sophia*," *JBL* 104 (1985): 577–87, argues that there is a deliberate wordplay in v. 27 on the Greek word *Sophia*. This would necessitate a later date, in the Hellenistic period.

3. Yoder's name for this figure, whom she insists, against other interpretations, represents "a composite figure of real—albeit exceptional—women in the Persian period" (*Wisdom as a Woman of Substance*, 90).

4. Joseph Blenkinsopp, "The Family in First Temple Israel," in *Families in Ancient Israel*, ed. Leo G. Perdue, Joseph Blenkinsopp, John J. Collins, and Carol Meyers (Louisville: Westminster John Knox, 1997), 48–103; 84. Patty Bandy, one of Carolyn Osiek's students, refers to her as "the empowered home-based CEO."

5. Aspasia of Miletus (c. 470–410 BCE), legendary mistress and power behind the throne of Pericles, influence on Athenian statesmen and possibly on Socrates, is consultant to Socrates elsewhere as well (Plato, *Menexenus* 235–36) and is mentioned in other ancient sources as Socrates' teacher and Pericles' instructor in rhetoric and politics (Athenaeus, *Deipnosophists* 5.219b-e, 220e; Plutarch, *Life of*

Pericles 24–25; Philostratus, *Epistle* 73). She was known not only for her states-
manship but for her philosophical dialogues as well (fragment cited in Cicero *de
Inventione* 51–52). She is considered in the tradition both a philosopher and one
who can speak for women's experience, even though the legends about her do not
suggest that she spent much time in household management. See Cheryl Glenn,
Rhetoric Retold: Regendering the Tradition from Antiquity through the Renaissance
(Carbondale: Southern Illinois University Press, 1997), 37–42.

6. Keith Hopkins, "The Age of Roman Girls at Marriage," *Population Studies*
18 (1965): 309–27; "Men's Age at Marriage and Its Consequences in the Roman
Family," *Classical Philology* 82/1 (1987): 21–34. In the surviving Christian inscriptions of the fourth and following centuries, median age at marriage for both girls
and boys is slightly older than in the previous population: Carlo Carletti, "Aspetti
biometrici del matrimonio nelle iscrizioni christiane di Roma," *Augustianum* 17
(1977): 39–51.

7. Book Two is a collection of advice and stories about political leadership,
an independent source that is not relevant here. Book Three is preserved only in
Latin.

8. Sarah B. Pomeroy, *Women in Hellenistic Egypt from Alexander to Cleopatra*
(New York: Schocken, 1984), 61–71. Texts of the Pythagorean letters in Hol-
ger Thesleff, ed., *The Pythagorean Texts of the Hellenistic Period*, Acta Academiae
Aboensis, Series A; Humanistika Vetenskaper, Socialvetenskaper, Teologi, 30.1
(Abo: Abo Akademi, 1965). French translation of the letters from women with
introduction by Mario Meunier, *Femmes Pythagoriciennes, Fragments et Lettres de
Théano, Périctioné, Phintys, Mélissa et Myia* (Paris: L'Artisan du Livre, 1932). Eng-
lish translations given here are by Carolyn Osiek.

9. E.g., Pseudo-Aristotle, *Oeconomica* 1.1344a; 3.2 (LCL 332–34, 408–9);
Iamblichus, *Life of Pythagoras* 28; Seneca, *Ep.* 94.26; Musonius Rufus 12 (Cora
Lutz, *Musonius Rufus, The "Roman Socrates,"* Yale Classical Studies [New Haven:
Yale University Press, 1947], 86–89).

10. Jerome, *Ep.* 77.3; Augustine, *Sermon on the Mount* 1.16.49; *Sermon* 9.3.3;
Adulterous Marriages 2.7.8; see Elizabeth A. Clark, *Reading Renunciation: Asceticism and Scripture in Early Christianity* (Princeton: Princeton University Press,
1999), 237. For acknowledgment of the double standard, Basil *Ep.* 199.21.

11. Thesleff, *Pythagorean Texts*, 144; Meunier, *Fragments et Lettres*, 53–60.

12. Thesleff, *Pythagorean Texts*, 198–200; Meunier, *Fragments et Lettres*, 87–93.
Plutarch (*Advice to the Bride and Groom* 144A) gives a further circuitous motivation for a cheated wife to remain faithful: what would make her husband's mistress
happier than for her to abandon the marriage? Therefore, so as not to appease the
mistress, the wife should remain faithful.

13. See further chapter 4.

14. Thesleff, *Pythagorean Texts*, 152–53; Meunier, *Fragments et Lettres*, 64–66.

15. Thesleff, *Pythagorean Texts*, 197–98; Meunier, *Fragments et Lettres*, 95–98.

16. Lutz, *Musonius Rufus*, 40–43.

17. T. E. V. Pearce, "The Role of the Wife as *Custos* in Ancient Rome," *Eranos* 72 (1974): 16–33.

18. Cited in Peter Garnsey, *Food and Society in Classical Antiquity* (Cambridge: Cambridge University Press, 1999), 102.

19. Lutz, *Musonius Rufus*, 40–43.

20. John Chrysostom, "Sermons on City Life," trans. Blake Leyerle, in *Religions of Late Antiquity in Practice*, ed. Richard Valantasis (Princeton: Princeton University Press, 2000), 257.

21. For reflections on similar relationships in the Hebrew Bible, see Jennifer A. Glancy, "The Mistress-Slave Dialectic: Paradoxes of Slavery in Three LXX Narratives," *Journal for the Study of the Old Testament* 72 (1996): 71–87.

22. Richard Saller, "*Pater Familias, Mater Familias*, and the Gendered Semantics of the Roman Household," *Classical Philology* 94 (1999): 194–95.

23 Ibid., 194.

24. Ibid., 184, 187.

25. Pliny's grandson later inherited two-thirds of her estate, including the *domus*, his sister the other third. This is probably the same Ummidia Quadratilla, originally from Cassinum, who dedicated an amphitheater and temple there (*CIL* 10.5183).

26. See Roger W. Gehring, *House Church and Mission: The Importance of Household Structures in Early Christianity* (Peabody, Mass.: Hendrickson, 2004), 99 n.201, 219 n.563.

27. *NewDocs* 1.5–9. The editor notes that it is rare for a woman to do so, and concludes that she must be head of her household (p. 8).

28. H. C. Youtie, *Zeitschrift für Papyrologie und Epigraphik* 14 (1974): 261–62; see also *NewDocs* 2.31.

29. *As[pas]ai pantes tous sous ka[i t]ous en tō oikō sou pantas. New Docs* 2.30–32; *The Wisconsin Papyri*, 2 vols., ed. P. J. Sijpesteijn, Studia Amstelodamensia ad epigraphicam (Leiden: Brill, 1967–77). Caution should be exercised in the assumption that every woman who builds a tomb for herself and her *familia* is an independent householder. Wives' property and dependents could be administered separately. The same must be said for Christian women benefactors or recipients of teaching, e.g., Chrysophera, "a most faithful sister," to whom Dionysius of Corinth wrote spiritual instruction (Eusebius, *Hist. eccl.* 4.22.1, 12).

30. Some examples are given in Roger S. Bagnall and Bruce W. Frier, *The Demography of Roman Egypt* (Cambridge: Cambridge University Press, 1994), 11–13; others in *NewDocs* 2.29–31. The payment of property taxes, however, is not definitive evidence for women's independent households, since wives' and husbands' property remained distinct.

31. The social status and relative affluence of Lydia has been much disputed, from successful freedwoman entrepreneur who caters to the elite to wretched

worker in a smelly business. It is hardly likely that her house was a center of an egalitarian "contrast society" (Ivoni Richter Reimer, *Women in the Acts of the Apostles: A Feminist Liberation Perspective* [Minneapolis: Fortress, 1995], 125–26; cited but not with approval by Jennifer A. Glancy, *Slavery in Early Christianity* [Oxford: Oxford University Press, 2002], 47). It is probable that she both dyed and sold her fabrics, and that the dye business was located in her house, situated near the river both because of the need for water and because the inhabitants of the city would not want such industry in their midst. Thus Paul and Silas's acceptance of hospitality may not have placed them at the Ritz. See Theresa Bednarz, "Lydia Speaks: Examining the Life of Lydia through Her Social and Theological Context" (MA thesis, Catholic Theological Union, 2002), for insertion of Lydia into the dye industry of the day; Luise Schottroff, *Let the Oppressed Go Free: Feminist Perspectives on the New Testament* (Louisville: Westminster John Knox, 1993); idem, *Lydia's Impatient Sisters: A Feminist Social History of Early Christianity* (Louisville: Westminster John Knox, 1995), which, while it has little to say about Lydia herself, sets the framework for feminist analysis.

32. See below, chapter 11, on the negative effects on women. On the freedom of slaves to practice their own forms of religion, within limits, see J. Albert Harrill, "The Domestic Enemy: A Moral Polarity of Household Slaves in Early Christian Apologies and Martyrdoms," in Balch and Osiek, *Early Christian Families in Context*, 236–39. The stories in Acts, of course, may not be historical, and in the case of Philippi there is Paul's puzzling silence about Lydia in his letter to that community. But the stories in Acts must be taken to be credible descriptions of life in Roman cities at the time, even if some of the characters are fictitious.

33. On the place of Nympha in Colossians and the historicity of the reference to her, see Margaret MacDonald, "Can Nympha Rule This House? The Rhetoric of Domesticity in Colossians," in *Rhetorics and Realities in Early Christianities*, ed. Willi Braun (Studies in Christianity and Judaism; Waterloo, Ont.: Wilfrid Laurier University Press, 2005).

34. For further discussion on Phoebe and her patronage, see chapter 9.

35. Harnack saw them as founders of the church of Philippi: Roger W. Gehring, *House Church and Mission: The Importance of Household Structures in Early Christianity* (Peabody, Mass.: Hendrickson, 2004), 211.

36. More references to women and meal customs in Kathleen E. Corley, *Private Women, Public Meals: Social Conflict in the Synoptic Tradition* (Peabody, Mass.: Hendrickson, 1993), 24–34.

37. E.g., the well-known house of the Vettii; see further discussion in Carolyn Osiek and David L. Balch, *Families in the New Testament World: Households and House Churches* (Louisville: Westminster John Knox, 1997), 16, 228n.29.

38. Matthew Roller, "Horizontal Women: Posture and Sex in the Roman *Convivium*," *American Journal of Philology* 124/3 (2003): 377–422.

39. Dennis E. Smith, *From Symposium to Eucharist: The Banquet in the Early Christian World* (Minneapolis: Fortress, 2003), 14–18; Katherine Dunbabin, *The*

Roman Banquet: Images of Conviviality (Cambridge: Cambridge University Press, 2003), 11–35, 80–83.

40. L. Michael White, *The Social Origins of Christian Architecture*, HTS 42 (Valley Forge, Pa.: Trinity Press International, 1990), 1:102–39.

41. See above, chapter 4.

42. Kyria in Egypt (*NewDocs* 1.121; 4.240); Theodora in fourth-century Rome; another Theodora of fifth- and sixth-century Beroea: see Ute E. Eisen, *Women Officeholders in Early Christianity: Epigraphical and Literary Studies*, trans. Linda M. Moloney (Collegeville, Minn.: Liturgical, 2000), 89–115.

43. See discussion in chapter 9.

44. For a helpful history of scholarship on the question of women's leadership in early Christianity, see Gehring, *House Church and Mission*, 211–25.

8. Women Leaders in Family Funerary Banquets

1. For an excellent account of these positions and their nuanced variations, see Peter Dückers, "Agape und Irene: Die Frauengestalten der Sigmamahlszenen mit antiken Inschriften in der Katakombe der Heiligen Marcellinus und Petrus" (Agape and Irene: The female figures in the scenes of a sigma meal with ancient inscriptions in the catacomb of the saints Marcellinus and Peter in Rome), *JAC* 35 (1992): 147–67.

2. Norbert Zimmerman, personal communication with the author (June 29, 2004). See also Norbert Zimmerman, *Werkstattgruppen römischer Katakomben-malerei, JAC* 35 (Munich: Aschendorff, 2002), 169–74, plates 25–26.

3. Some research supporting this argument is currently available in Janet H. Tulloch, "Image as Artifact: A Social-Historical Analysis of Female Figures with Cups in the Banquet Scenes from the Catacomb of SS. Marcellino e Pietro, Rome" (PhD dissertation, University of Ottawa, Canada, 2001). A full presentation of this data will be published in *Speaking about Agape and Irene: Women and Hospitality in Roman Christian Funerary Art* (Waterloo, Ont.: Wilfrid Laurier University Press, forthcoming).

4. Zimmerman, *Werkstattgruppen*, 170.

5. Jas Elsner, *Imperial Rome and Christian Triumph: The Art of the Roman Empire AD 100-450* (Oxford: Oxford University Press, 1998), 91.

6. Katherine M. D. Dunbabin, *The Roman Banquet: Images of Conviviality* (Cambridge: Cambridge University Press, 2003), 6–7.

7. For a discussion of Roman aristocratic funerals as public spectacle, see John Bodel, "Death on Display: Looking at Roman Funerals," in *The Art of Ancient Spectacle*, ed. Bettina Bergman and Christine Kondoleon (Studies in the History of Art 56; Washington, D.C.: National Gallery of Art, 1999), 259–81.

8. *Refrigerium* is the Latin name by which funeral banquets are known in the ancient literature. For a review of its origin and where it is used in early Christian literature, see G. van der Leeuw, "Refrigerium," *Mnemosyne* 3/3 (1935–36): 125–48.

9. See Mary Beard, John North, and Simon Price, *Religions of Rome*, vol. 2: *A Sourcebook* (Cambridge: Cambridge University Press, 1998), 104–5.

10. Ibid., 2:102.

11. J. M. C. Toynbee, *Death and Burial in the Roman World* (London: Thames & Hudson, 1971), 63–64. A race run on February 15 during the *Parentalia* called the *Lupercalia* involved near-naked runners circling the city of Rome. The race was believed by some to be a ritual of purification whereby the inhabitants of the city were purified from the pollution of the dead who "inundated" the capital at this time of year. It wasn't until the end of the fifth century that the bishop of Rome prevented Christians from participating in it. See also Beard, North, and Price, *Religions of Rome*, 2:120–23.

12. Heikki Kotila, *Memoria Mortuorum: Commemoration of the Departed in Augustine* (Rome: Institutum Patristicum Augustinianum, 1992), 33.

13. Toynbee, *Death and Burial*, 61–63.

14. Matthew Roller describes these positions as "head of the couch" for the male figure and "foot of the couch" for the female figure. See Matthew Roller, "Horizontal Women: Posture and Sex in the Roman Convivium," *American Journal of Philology* 124 (2003): 407.

15. Rita Amedick, "Klinen-Mahl," *Die Sarcophage mit Darstellungen aus dem Menschenleben: Vita Privata* (Berlin: Gebr. Mann, 1991), 11–24.

16. See Elisabeth Jastrzebowska, "Les scènes de banquet dans les peintures et sculptures chrétiennes des IIIe et IVe siècles," *Recherches Augustiniennes* 14 (1979): fig. 16.

17. Katherine M. D. Dunbabin, "Triclinium and Stibadium," in *Dining in a Classical Context*, ed. William J. Slater (Ann Arbor: University of Michigan Press, 1991), 134. According to Dunbabin, the Greek word *stibades* literally means the foliage on which people reclined.

18. Ibid., figs. 21, 22, 24, 25.

19. See "House-Tomb at Isola Sacra—Interior," in Beard, North, and Price, *Religions of Rome*, 2:105, 4.13b.

20. For a list of female patrons see J.-P. Waltzing, *Étude historique sur les corporations*, 4 vols. (Rome: L'Erma di Bretschneider, 1968 [1895–1900]), 4:369–70, 373; for a list of funerary clubs in Rome, see 3:345–48. Apparently some colleges were made up of family members only (see 3:348–49). See further this book's chapter 5 on women patrons.

21. *CIL* 6.10234; *ILS* 7213. See also see Waltzing, *Étude historique*, vol. 3, inscription no. 1083:268–69, lines 1–4 only. The author would like to extend her gratitude to John Bodel, Brown University, and Carolyn Osiek, Brite Divinity School, for their kind assistance with this translation.

22. Waltzing, *Étude historique*, vol. 4, inscription nos. 544 and 564 (*CIL* 5.5295; 5.5869).

23. Ibid., vol. 4, inscription no. 1921 (*CIL* 12.6310).

24. Here they are referred to as "*matres*." See ibid., vol. 4, inscription no. 1826 (*CIL* 11.1355B).

25. According to Roller, there are two moral issues at stake here. One is the orderly conduct of respectable women at banquets, which corresponds to the seated convivial posture. The second is the overall moral decline of Roman society as signified by the acceptance of respectable women's changed banquet posture from sitting to reclining within the family setting. See Roller, "Horizontal Women," 378.

26. There are, of course, exceptions to this convention. See, for example, Guntram Koch and K. Wight, "Front of the Sarcophagus of Titus Aelius Euangelus and Gaudenia Nicene," in *Roman Funerary Sculpture: Catalogue of the Collections* (Malibu: J. P. Getty Museum, 1988), 24–27.

27. See Roller, "Horizontal Women," 393–404. Roller argues that the visualization of gender-differentiated postures relating to eating and drinking practices in the funerary monument is a distortion of actual elite practice in which upwardly mobile men and women did recline and drink together on the couch, according to the literary evidence. See his analysis of a couple reclining in a second-century relief on a funerary altar, 407–10. Others argue that there was a change in Roman custom in this regard in the late first century CE: see Kathleen E. Corley, *Private Women, Public Meals: Social Conflict in the Synoptic Tradition* (Peabody, Mass.: Hendrickson, 1993), 28–34; Carolyn Osiek and David L. Balch, *Families in the New Testament World: Households and House Churches*, Family, Religion, and Culture (Louisville: Westminster John Knox, 1997), 59–60; and chapter 7 above.

28. Roller, "Horizontal Women," 409–10.

29. Dunbabin, *The Roman Banquet*, 114.

30. Roller argues that in some of the Pompeian paintings of banqueting, e.g., "House of Chaste Lovers" (see plate I in Dunbabin, *The Roman Banquet*), the reclining clothed female figure may actually share a licit sexual connection with her male partner. Roller, "Horizontal Women," 411.

31. See, for example, Eve d'Ambra, "The Cult of Virtues and the Funerary Relief of Ulpia Epigone," in *Roman Art in Context: An Anthology*, ed. Eve d'Ambra (Englewood Cliffs, N.J.: Prentice Hall, 1993), 104–14.

32. The idea that death conferred the status of deification on the deceased is much older than the classical period of Greece and Rome. See Jon Davies, *Death, Burial and Rebirth in the Religions of Antiquity* (London: Routledge, 1999), 55.

33. Richard Lattimore, *Themes in Greek and Latin Epitaphs* (Urbana: University of Illinois Press, 1962), 100–106. His inscriptional evidence demonstrates that the process of deification of ordinary Roman citizens occurred in at least three different ways, including: (1) the identification of the deceased with a specific god or goddess; (2) the dedication of the deceased to a specific deity; or (3) the direct invocation of the deceased as himself or herself. In this last case Lattimore

states that "the dead person is invoked in his own personality and character and name; these are not merged in the plural of *Manes*, or in any way confused with the totality of the dead."

34. This new status could also apply to children: "No longer, my daughter, shall I make sacrifice to you with lamentation, now that I know you have become divine." Ibid., 100–101.

35. See Diana E. E. Kleiner and Susan B. Matheson, eds., *I, Claudia: Women in Ancient Rome* (Austin: University of Texas Press, 1996).

36. See Jean Guyon, *Le Cimetière aux deux Lauriers: Recherches sur les catacombes romaines* (Paris: École Française de Rome, 1987), 336–37.

37. On the popularity of private funeral celebrations among Christians in the late fourth century, see Kotila, *Memoria Mortuorum*, 65.

38. For a history of the early Christian practices based on the literature, see ibid., 35–53. For the development of these practices in the western church, see Frederick S. Paxton, *Christianizing Death: The Creation of a Ritual Process in Early Medieval Europe* (Ithaca, N.Y.: Cornell University Press, 1990).

39. Ibid., 33. According to Paxton, the reception of the Eucharist before death as a necessity for all Christians was passed by the Council of Nicaea in 325 CE. The issue for the North African Council was that some Christians were being given the Eucharist after they had already died.

40. Kotila, *Memoria Mortuorum*, 53.

41. Louis Duchesne, *Liber pontificalis* (Paris: École Française de Rome, 1995), 1:10–12; Theodore Mommsen, *Chronica minora* (Berlin: Weidmannschen, 1892), 1:71–72, as excerpted in Beard, North, and Price, *Religions of Rome*, 2:76.

42. Beard, North, and Price, *Religions of Rome*, 2:75.

43. Another fresco depicting a male figure holding his hands above a plate set on a *mensa* can be found on the adjacent wall to the banquet scene (fig. 8.2) in chamber 45, Marcellino and Pietro. See J. G. Deckers, H. R. Seeliger, and G. Mietke, *Die Katacombe "Santi Marcellino e Pietro" Repertorium der Malereien = La catacomba dei Santi Marcellino e Pietro, Repertorio delle pitture*, Roma Sotterranea Cristiana 6 (Vatican City: Pontificio Istituto di Archeologia Cristiana, 1987), color plate 21 a, Nr. 45, Wand 3. See fig. 8.1 in this chapter.

44. Guyon, *Le Cimetière aux deux Lauriers*, 330–35.

45. In this section the art and archaeological data to be discussed were originally collected by two teams of archaeologists, one headed by Jean Guyon on behalf of the École française de Rome and the other led by Johannes Deckers and Hans Seeliger on behalf of the Institut für Christliche Archäologie, Kunstgeschichte der Universität Freiburg in Breisgau. Both reports were published in association with the Pontificio Istituto di Archeologia Cristiana in Rome, 1987. The author has used both of these reports extensively in her research on the frescoes as well as evidence gathered from private tours of the catacombs of Priscilla on the Salaria Nuova, Callixtus on the via Appia Antica, and the catacomb of Domitilla on the via Ardeatine.

46. This number can very according to the condition and iconography of the fresco. Jean Guyon lists the number of banquet scenes in Marcellino and Pietro as fifteen. See fig. 95D, "Les peintures des sujets des classes 4 à 6 dans les cimetières de Rome," in *Le Cimetière aux deux Lauriers*, 164. In order to distinguish the banquet scenes from other types of meal scenes identified as "Cana" or "Multiplication of the loaves," Guyon classified the fifteen banquet scenes in Marcellino and Pietro as *"Agape* et Assimilés" (*"Agape* and scenes comparable to *Agapes*).

47. For the relationship between burial space and living space between the fourth and ninth centuries and the church's role in making them interdependent, see Anna Campese Simone, *I cimiteri tardoantichi e altomedievali della Puglia settentrionale: Valle del basso Ofanto, Tavoliere, Gargano* (Vatican City: Pontificio Istituto di Archeologia Cristiana, 2003).

48. "Lau" is the common term used to designate a site within the Catacomb of Marcellino and Pietro, probably because the original name of the cemetery was *ad duas lauros* (at the two laurel trees). See Deckers, Seeliger, and Mietke, *Die Katacombe "Santi Marcellino e Pietro,"* Lau 45, 266–70, plates 30a-b, 31a-b, color plates 19 a-b, 20 a-b, 21; Lau 47, 271–73, plate 33c, color plates 22a-b, 23a-b; Lau 78, 343–48, plates 57, 58a-b, 59a-b, 60a-b, 61a-b, 62a-b, 63, 64a-b, 65, color plates 59a, 60a-b, 61a-c, 62a-b, 63a-d.

49. Guyon, *Le Cimetière aux deux Lauriers*, 340.

50. See note 2 above.

51. Zimmerman, *Werkstattgruppen*, 284.

52. See ibid., fig. 12, Plan Katacombe Marcellino e Pietro mit Daterungen der Malerei.

53. An examination of artifacts represented in a work of art allows a comparison of the actual object with the item represented. It can help identify which visual elements in an image are historical or how historical elements were added, combined, or omitted within a scene to create a visual rhetoric intended to communicate a particular message to the viewer about something in the image. Representational strategies such as visual narrative or the multilayering of scenes through registers or by the presentation of altered points in a single view may provide insights into ancient perception.

54. There are a number of scholars working in this area. Key texts include Mieke Bal, *Reading Rembrandt: Beyond the Word-Image Opposition* (Cambridge: Cambridge University Press, 1991); W. J. T. Mitchell, *Picture Theory: Essays on Verbal and Visual Representation* (Chicago: University of Chicago Press, 1994); David Freedberg, *The Power of Images: Studies in the History and Theory of Response* (Chicago: University of Chicago Press, 1989); Norman Bryson, *Looking at the Overlooked* (Cambridge: Harvard University Press, 1990); and John A. Walker and Sarah Chaplin, *Visual Culture: An Introduction* (Manchester: Manchester University Press, 1997).

55. For discussions of visual rhetoric theory see Sonja K. Foss, "Theory of Visual Rhetoric" in Ken Smith et al., eds., *Handbook of Visual Communication:*

Theory, Methods, and Media (Mahwah, N.J.: Lawrence Erlbaum Associates, 2005), 141–52; Charles A. Hill and Marguerite Helmers, eds., *Defining Visual Rhetorics* (Mahwah, N.J.: Lawrence Erlbaum Associates, 2004); Bal, *Reading Rembrandt*, 60–90.

56. There seems to have been particular dining clothes for women. See A. T. Croom, *Roman Clothing and Fashion* (Stroud, U.K.: Tempus, 2002), 89.

57. This oratorical gesture in Roman art is for use during exhortation. See Gregory S. Aldrete, *Gestures and Acclamations in Ancient Rome* (Baltimore: Johns Hopkins University Press, 1999), fig. 1.

58. See Deckers, Seeliger, and Mietke, *Die Katacombe "Santi Marcellino e Pietro,"* Lau 39, 255–57, plates 24a-b, 25, color plates 12 a-b, 13; Lau 50, 278–81, plates 36a-c, 42a-b, color plates 27a-c, 28a-b; Lau 76, 338–40, color plates 56, 57a-b, 58a-c. The banquet scene in Lau 75 shows a young girl bringing a cup to participants in an all-male banquet. See Lau 75, 336–38, plates 55a-b, 56a-b, color plate 55a-b.

59. See ibid., Lau 13, 213–14, plates 5a-b, 6b-d and Lau 14, 214–17, plates 7a-b, 8a-b, color plate 7a-b.

60. See ibid., Lau 62, 304–9, plates 43b, 44b-c, color plate 40.

61. See Amedick, "Klinen-Mahl," cat. 186 plate 28.1; cat. 260 plate 26.1; cat. 78 plate 34.5.

62. Even Christians considered themselves to be dining with the deceased at the funerary banquet. See Tertullian, *On the Testimony of the Soul*, 4.5.

63. According to Josef Engemann, third- and fourth-century Roman examples of banquets in the sigma formation (e.g., funerary scenes of Vibia and Vincentius from the tomb of Vibia, Rome) show the most important person reclining in the middle. Engemann states that this same pattern is also suggested for some of the Marcellino and Pietro banquet scenes (i.e., Lau 39, 45, 50, and 78). See J. Engemann, "Der Ehrenplatz beim antiken Sigmamahl," in *Jenseitsvorstellungen in Antike und Christentum, JAC* 9 (Munich: JAC, 1982), 239–50; Dunbabin suggests that by the late empire, it is the guest of honor and not the host who reclines *in cornu dextro* (in the right corner). See Dunbabin, "Triclinium and Stibadium," 135. See also Dunbabin, "Place Settings," in *The Roman Banquet*, 36–71. The clearest discussion of seating arrangements for the guest of honor and host at the Roman banquet can be found in John R. Clarke, *Art in the Lives of Ordinary Romans: Visual Representation and Non-Elite Viewers in Italy, 100 BC–AD 315* (Berkeley: University of California Press, 2003), 223–27. For banquets in the *triclinium* (or three-couch) formation, which accommodated up to nine banqueters (three on each couch), Clarke argues that the guest of honor reclined at "the place at the right on the middle couch (as seen by someone sitting on the couch)—he or she was *imus in medio* . . . [also known as] the *locus consularis*. The host reclined at the top of the low couch (*summus in imo*), at the right hand of the guest of honor." This arrangement might explain how the host ended up *in cornu*

dextro in the sigma meal formation. When dining practices shifted from the formal *triclinium* to the intimate sigma-couch formation, the *imus* (low) and *medius* (middle) positions on the low couch were lost, leaving the *summus in imo*, or host's position, exposed.

64. See Joan R. Mertens, "Pair of Drinking Cups," *Metropolitan Museum of Art Bulletin* 50 (fall 1992): 11, for an example of a pair of Roman silver drinking cups from Pompeii. See Catherine Johns, M. J. Hughes, and R. Holmes, "The Roman Silver Cups from Hockwold, Norfolk," *Archaeologia* 108 (1986): 8–9, plate 5, for a pair of silver *kantharoi* found in England. See also Dunbabin, *The Roman Banquet*, 66, plates 6, 7.

65. See Ulrich Friedhoff, *Der römische Friedhof an der Jakobstraße zu Köln* (Mainz am Rhein: Philipp von Zabern, 1991), 233–34, plates 12 and 74. See also Fritz Fremersdorf, "Nordafrikanische Terra Sigillata aus Köln," *Kölner Jahrbuch für Vor- und Frühgeschichte* 3 (1958): 11–19.

66. These individuals include the emperor Balbinus and his wife. See fig. 70 in Dunbabin, *The Roman Banquet*, 123.

67. Due to the number of times this image has been restored (at least twice since 1952), the visual information for each section of this scene needs to be carefully retraced. Pre-restoration images of this fresco from before 1952, held by the Pontificia Commissione di Archeologia Sacra, show that a cup is clearly in front of the second and third banqueter to the viewer's left (slightly closer to the third banqueter). The female figure with the veil (third figure from the viewer's right) appears to be holding something in her right hand (her elbow is bent—unlike the other figures); however, it is extremely difficult to determine what the object might be. Restored images of this banquet scene still show this figure's arm in the same position, but the object she is holding, if any, is not any clearer.

68. *Saint Augustine: Confessions*, trans. R. S. Pine-Coffin (New York: Penguin, 1961), 112–13.

69. See figures 1 and 2 depicting the remains of a late antique tunic with stripes and shoulder patches in Christopher Jones, "Processional Colors," in Bergmann and Kondoleon, *The Art of Ancient Spectacle*, 246, 253.

70. The author's interpretation of *Agape* as "Love-Affection" is based on Tertullian's *Apology* 39, which describes the name of the Christian banquet as the Greek word for affection.

71. Similar Latin inscriptions are typically found on both terra-cotta and glass cups from this time period. Inscriptions with the expressions *"Da caldam," "Misce," "Misce mi,"* and *"Misce nobis"* can be found on terra-cotta cups and vases throughout the Latin-speaking empire. For studies on these cups, see Susanna Künzl, *Die Trierer Spruchbecherkeramik: Dekorierte Schwarzfirniskeramik des 3. und 4. Jahrhunderts n. Chr.* (Trier: Rheinischen Landesmuseums, 1997); R. P. Symonds, *Rhenish Wares: Fine Dark Coloured Pottery from Gaul and Germany* (Oxford: Oxford University Committee for Archaeology, 1992); for information on patterns of

distribution, see Anne C. Anderson, *A Guide to Roman Fine Wares* (Highworth, Wiltshire, U.K.: Vorda, 1980).

72. See Künzl, *Die Trierer Spruchbecherkeramik,* 165 plate 59c; 255–56; Symonds, *Rhenish Wares,* 116–17.

73. Full inscription reads: [*Vin*]*vmnob*[*isda*]. See Künzl, *Die Trierer Spruch-becherkeramik,* 247 plate 47 a-b; Symonds, *Rhenish Wares,* 121 fig. 44 no. 768.

74. See Künzl, *Die Trierer Spruchbecherkeramik,* 172; 183 plate 68 c-d; 218; 230 plate 32a-b; Symonds, *Rhenish Wares,* 56 plate 41; 114 fig. 42 no. 736; 117 fig. 41 no.725, fig. 53 no. 896.

75. See Künzl, *Die Trierer Spruchbecherkeramik,* 98; 172 plate 68a-b; Symonds, *Rhenish Wares,* 113–15; 118 fig. 52 no. 891. The wine amphora with the Latin inscription *Copo* inscribed around the base of the neck, is from a Roman camp in Dormagen, between Cologne and Neuss. The author is deeply grateful to Dr. Ursula Heimberg, Curator of Roman Artifacts, Rheinisches Landesmuseum in Bonn, for sharing her extensive knowledge on inscribed pots from the Rhine Valley. On this particular find see G. Müller, "Ausgrabungen in Dormagen, 1963–1977," *Rheinische Ausgrabungen* 20 (1979): 125–26.

76. See Künzl, *Die Trierer Spruchbecherkeramik,* 141; 209 plate 3b-c; Symonds, *Rhenish Wares,* 115 fig. 48 no.824.

77. Matthias Bös, "Aufschriften auf Rheinischen Trinkgefässen der Römerzeit," *Kölner Jahrbuch für Vor- und Frühgeschichte* 3 (1958): 21.

78. See Deckers, Seeliger, and Mietke, *Die Katacombe "Santi Marcellino e Pietro,"* Lau 76, color plates 56, 57a-b, 58a-c. The top line reads, "*Misce mi.*" The following line reads, "*Irene.*"

79. According to a list of "Vetri dorati con espressioni riconducibili al refrigerium" (gold-glass with expressions recalling the *refrigerium*), provided to the author by the Department of Decorative Arts, Vatican Museums, there are twenty-three surviving examples of early Christian gold-glass in their collection inscribed with the words "*Pie Zeses*" either as part of a larger inscription in Latin (fourteen examples) or as a stand-alone inscription (nine examples). For a catalogue of the Vatican's collection, see Guy Ferrari, ed., *The Gold-Glass Collection of the Vatican Library: With Additional Catalogues of Other Gold-Glass Collections* (Vatican City: Vatican Library, 1959).

9. Women Patrons in the Life of House Churches

1. Ernest Gellner and John Waterbury, eds., *Patrons and Clients in Mediterranean Societies* (London: Duckworth, 1977); S. N. Eisenstadt and L. Roniger, *Patrons, Clients, and Friends: Interpersonal Relations and the Structure of Trust in Society* (Cambridge: Cambridge University Press, 1984); John H. Elliott, "Patronage and Clientage," in *The Social Sciences and New Testament Interpretation*, ed. Richard Rohrbaugh (Peabody, Mass.: Hendrickson, 1996), 144–56, with extensive further bibliography.

2. Richard P. Saller, *Personal Patronage under the Early Empire* (Cambridge: Cambridge University Press, 1982); Andrew Wallace-Hadrill, ed., *Patronage in Ancient Society* (London: Routledge, 1989); Jens-Uwe Krause, *Spätantike Patronatsformen im Westen des Römischen Reiches* (Munich: C. H. Beck, 1987).

3. Frederick W. Danker, *Benefactor: Epigraphic Study of a Graeco-Roman and New Testament Semantic Field* (St. Louis: Clayton, 1982); more recently, John K. Chow, *Patronage and Power: A Study of Social Networks in Corinth*, JSNTSup 75 (Sheffield: Sheffield Academic Press, 1992); David A. DeSilva, *Honor, Patronage, Kinship and Purity: Unlocking New Testament Culture* (Downers Grove, Ill.: InterVarsity Press, 2000); Zeba A. Crook, *Reconceptualizing Conversion: Patronage, Loyalty, and Conversion in the Religions of the Ancient Mediterranean* (Berlin: de Gruyter, 2004). Stephan J. Joubert, "One Form of Social Exchange or Two? 'Euergetism,' Patronage, and Testament Studies," *BTB* 31 (2001): 17–25, places public or group patronage ("euergetism") in the Greek world and personal patronage in the Roman world. The difference is not so simple. Public and personal patronage are indeed two different aspects of the same social phenomenon, and there is far less evidence in the *earlier* Greek world for personal patronage, but public patronage was common in both worlds.

4. E. A. Judge, *The Social Pattern of Christian Groups in the First Century* (London: Tyndale, 1960); "The Early Christians as a Scholastic Community," *Journal of Religious History* (1960): 4–15; (1961): 125–37; "Paul as a Radical Critic of Society," *Interchange* 16 (1974): 191–203; "Cultural Conformity and Innovation in Paul: Some Clues from Contemporary Documents," *Tyndale Bulletin* 35 (1984): 3–24.

5. Eisenstadt and Roniger, *Patrons, Clients, and Friends*, 48–49.

6. Elliot, "Patronage and Clientage," 148.

7. Saller, *Personal Patronage*, 1.

8. Wallace-Hadrill, *Patronage in Ancient Society*, 3.

9. Saller, *Personal Patronage*, 191–92.

10. Peter White, "*Amicitia* and the Profession of Poetry in Early Imperial Rome," *JRS* 68 (1978): 90–92.

11. Saller, *Personal Patronage*, 127–28.

12. Paul Millett, "Patronage and Its Avoidance in Classical Athens," in Wallace-Hadrill, *Patronage in Ancient Society*, 15–47.

13. Ibid., 33–34.

14. Saller, *Personal Patronage*, 2–3; Andrew Wallace-Hadrill, "Patronage in Roman Society: From Republic to Empire," in Wallace-Hadrill, *Patronage in Ancient Society*, 63–87, esp. 74, 79–81; Terry Johnson and Chris Dandeker, "Patronage: Relation and System," in *Patronage in Ancient Society*, 219–42, esp. 237–38.

15. Saller, *Personal Patronage*, 11–15; P. A. Brunt, "'Amicitia' in the Late Roman Republic," *Proceedings of the Cambridge Philological Society* n.s. 11 (1965): 1–20; reprinted in Robin Seager, ed., *The Crisis of the Roman Republic: Studies in Political and Social History* (Cambridge: Heffer, 1969), 199–218.

16. Saller, *Personal Patronage*, 12; White, *Amicitia*, 81.

17. Joubert, "One Form of Social Exchange," 20; White, *Amicitia*, 79; see also Barbara K. Gold, ed., *Literary and Artistic Patronage in Ancient Rome* (Austin: University of Texas Press, 1982).

18. White, *"Amicitia,"* 80–81.

19. Saller, *Personal Patronage*, 12–22.

20. Richard P. Saller, "Patronage and Friendship in Early Imperial Rome: Drawing the Distinction," in Wallace-Hadrill, *Patronage in Ancient Society*, 53–54.

21. Jennifer Glancy, *Slavery in Early Christianity* (Oxford: Oxford University Press, 2002), 124–26.

22. Louis Harmand, *Le patronat sur les collectivités publiques, des origines au bas-Empire: Un aspect social et politique du monde romain* (Paris: Presses Universitaires de France, 1957); A. R. Hands, *Charities and Social Aid in Greece and Rome* (Ithaca, N.Y.: Cornell University Press, 1968); Joubert, "One Form of Social Exchange," whose attempt to draw sharp distinctions between Roman patronage and Greek euergetism is not convincing.

23. Hands, *Charities and Social Aid*, 49.

24. Jane F. Gardner, *Women in Roman Law and Society* (Bloomington: Indiana University Press, 1986), 233–36.

25. Marcus Cornelius Fronto, trans. C. R. Haines (LCL; Cambridge: Harvard University Press, 1962), 1:145–51; Edward Champlin, *Fronto and Antonine Rome* (Cambridge: Harvard University Press, 1980), 25.

26. Alan K. Bowman and J. David Thomas, eds., *"Per Lepidinam": The Vindolanda Writing-Tablets (Tabulae Vindolandenses II)* (London: British Museum, 1994), no. 257 (inv. 85.117), 230–31. The tablet is dated to period 3 of the fort, 97–102/3 CE.

27. *NewDocs* 2.55–56.

28. Champlin, *Fronto and Antonine Rome*, 109, 171n.87; Richard A. Bauman, *Women and Politics in Ancient Rome* (London: Routledge, 1992); Suzanne Dixon, "A Family Business: Women's Role in Patronage and Politics at Rome 80–44 B.C.," *Classica et Mediaevalia* 34 (1983): 91.

29. Dixon, "Family Business," 100.

30. Ibid., 94, with other examples.

31. Other imperial women who were benefactors to the Herodians, according to Josephus, were Antonia and Agrippina the Younger. Poppaea Sabina, wife of Nero, was also said to be mediator for Jewish causes (*Ant.* 18.143, 164; 20.135–36; 20.189–96; *Life* 13–16). In a typical patronage maneuver, Josephus records that at Puteoli he met an actor named Aliturus and, through him, was introduced to Poppaea. Domitia, wife of Domitian, was also a personal benefactor and defender of Josephus, toward whom she was *euergetousa*, benefactor (*Life* 429). See Shelly Matthews, *First Converts: Rich Pagan Women and the Rhetoric of Mission in Early Judaism and Christianity* (Stanford: Stanford University Press, 2001), 30–36.

32. Bauman, *Women in Politics*, 124–29. Livia's power was derivative of that of Augustus, but, like many queens and empresses, while she had it, she exercised it quite independently.

33. Ibid., 146–98.

34. See Suzanne Dixon, *Reading Roman Women: Sources, Genres, and Real Life* (London: Duckworth, 2001), 101.

35. Roy Bowen Ward, "Women in Pompeii: Work in Progress" (unpublished paper), 10–11.

36. Other examples in Mary R. Lefkowitz and Maureen Fant, *Women's Life in Greece and Rome: A Source Book in Translation*, 2nd ed. (Baltimore: Johns Hopkins University Press, 1992), 152–53.

37. For a discussion of women landowners in Hellenistic Egypt, see Sarah B. Pomeroy, *Women in Hellenistic Egypt: From Alexander to Cleopatra* (New York: Schocken, 1984), 148–60, 171–73.

38. Translation by Ward, "Women in Pompeii," 9.

39. *NewDocs* 2.60–61.

40. John R. Clarke, *Art in the Lives of Ordinary Romans* (Berkeley: University of California Press, 2003), 184–85.

41. This was a bit restricted by the Papian Law of the Augustan period: *patronae* acquired more inheritance rights if they had two or three children (see Susan Treggiari, "Jobs in the Household of Livia," *PBSR* 43 [1975]: 74–75).

42. Dixon, *Reading Roman Women*, 106–7.

43. Riet Van Bremen, "Women and Wealth," in *Images of Women in Antiquity*, ed. Averil Cameron and Amélie Kuhrt, rev. ed. (Detroit: Wayne State University Press, 1993), 223.

44. *NewDocs* 1.69, p. 111.

45. L. Michael White, ed., *Social Networks in the Early Christian Environment: Issues and Methods for Social History*, Semeia 56 (Atlanta: Scholars, 1992), 18–19.

46. See Roy Bowen Ward, "The Public Priestesses of Pompeii," in *The Early Church in Its Context: Essays in Honor of Everett Ferguson*, ed. Abraham J. Malherbe, Frederick W. Norris, and James W. Thompson (Leiden: Brill, 1998), 323–27. Eumachia's tomb outside the Nucerian Gate is one of the largest funerary monuments in the area, stating simply her name and filiation on one side, *Evmachia L F*, and on the other side, *Sibi et Svis*, for herself and those who belong to her *familia*.

47. Dixon, *Reading Roman Women*, 108.

48. Van Bremen, "Women and Wealth," 223.

49. See Mary Taliaferro Boatwright, "Plancia Magna of Perge: Women's Roles and Status in Roman Asia Minor," in *Women's History and Ancient History*, ed. Sarah B. Pomeroy (Chapel Hill: University of North Carolina Press, 1991), 249–72. Other female gymnasiarchs are known: L. Casarico, "Donne ginnasiarco," *Zeitschrift für Papyrologie und Epigraphik* 48 (1982): 118–22. There is even one in Egypt, and a female tax collector: *NewDocs* 8.49.

50. *NewDocs* 6.26.

51. Ross Shepard Kraemer, *Her Share of the Blessings: Women's Religions among Pagans, Jews, and Christians in the Greco-Roman World* (New York: Oxford University Press, 1992), 84; idem, ed., *Women's Religions in the Greco-Roman World: A Sourcebook* (New York: Oxford University Press, 2004), 249. Another *stephanephora*, the first woman in her city, was Philo of Priene, who in the first century BCE erected by herself a cistern and water system (H. W. Pleket, *Epigraphica II: Texts on the Social History of the Greek World* [Leiden: Brill, 1969], 16 #5); James Rives, "Civic and Religious Life," in *Epigraphic Evidence: Ancient History from Inscriptions*, ed. John Bodel (London: Routledge, 2001), 136.

52. Roz Kearsley, "Women in Public Life in the Roman East: Junia Theodora, Claudia Metrodora, and Phoibe, Benefactress of Paul," *Ancient Society: Resources for Teachers* 15 (1985): 124–28, translation of documents, 132–34; also in *Tyndale Bulletin* 50:2 (1999): 189–211; *NewDocs* 6.24–25. See long discussion in Bruce W. Winter, *Roman Wives, Roman Widows: The Appearance of New Women and the Pauline Communities* (Grand Rapids: Eerdmans, 2003), 183–93.

53. Kearsley, "Women in Public Life," 128–30; translation of fragments of inscription, 135–36.

54. Chow, *Patronage and Power*, 68n.2.

55. Evidence and discussion in Bernadette J. Brooten, *Women Leaders in the Ancient Synagogue*, Brown Judaic Studies 36 (Chico, Calif.: Scholars, 1982), 57–72.

56. John H. D'Arms, "Memory, Money, and Status at Misenum: Three New Inscriptions from the Collegium of the Augustales," *JRS* 90 (2000): 143.

57. J.-P. Waltzing, *Étude historique sur les corporations professionelles chez les Romains depuis les origines jusqu'à la chute de l'Empire d'Occident* (Rome: L'Erma di Bretschneider, 1968 [1895–1900]), 4.254–57.

58. Dixon, *Reading Roman Women*, 109 and n. 109, p. 188.

59. Harmand, *Le patronat*, 282, 301, 241; Dixon, *Reading Roman Women*, 109.

60. Giuseppina Cerulli Irelli, "Archaeological Research in the Area of Vesuvius: Portraits from Herculaneum," in *Pompeii and the Vesuvian Landscape* (Washington, D.C.: Archaeological Institute of America and the Smithsonian Institution, 1979), 16–24; Caroline Dexter, "The Epigraphic Evidence of Pompeiian Women" (unpublished paper), 23n.18.

61. Tessa Rajak and David Noy, "*Archisynagogoi*: Office, Title and Social Status in the Greco-Jewish Synagogue," *JRS* 83 (1993): 75–93.

62. Judge, *Social Pattern*, iii.

63. See Chow, *Patronage and Power*; White, *Social Networks*.

64. John T. Fitzgerald, ed., *Friendship, Flattery, and Frankness of Speech: Studies on Friendship in the New Testament* (Leiden: Brill, 1996).

65. A good exposition of *charis* as language of patronage is in DeSilva, *Honor, Patronage, Kinship and Purity*, 95–156. Elliott, "Patronage and Clientage," 152, lists seventeen New Testament terms associated with patronage.

66. Jerome Murphy-O'Connor, *Paul: A Critical Life* (Oxford: Clarendon, 1996), 305–7.

67. Chow, *Patronage and Power*, 88–90.

68. Murphy-O'Connor, *Paul*, 367.

69. See discussion of women's participation in family funerary rites in chapter 8.

70. Charles A. Bobertz, "The Role of Patron in the *Cena Dominica* of Hippolytus' *Apostolic Tradition*," *JTS* 44 (1993): 170–84.

71. Brian Daley, "Position and Patronage in the Early Church: The Original Meaning of the 'Primacy of Honour,'" *JTS* 44 (1993): 529–53, carries the expectations of honor through episcopal relationships among the great centers in the fourth and fifth centuries, showing that the language of primacy and honor cannot be separated from the expectations of the patronage system.

72. On the various readings of Lydia's social status, see Matthews, *First Converts*, 85–89.

73. On the topos of the rich female convert in many ancient religious traditions, see ibid., 51–71.

74. But for discussion of the difficulties for husbands and wives caused by such "mixed" marriages, see chapter 2 of this book.

75. "Service rendered in an intermediary capacity, *mediation, assignment*," BDAG 230.

76. However, Ignatius also uses the term "deacon" in a triple-tiered leadership structure, as he does in the next paragraph, saying that other churches have sent on the same mission bishops, presbyters, and deacons. See William R. Schoedel, *Ignatius of Antioch: A Commentary on the Letters of Ignatius of Antioch*, Hermeneia (Philadelphia: Fortress, 1985), 213–14, 248.

77. Margaret M. Mitchell, "New Testament Envoys in the Context of Greco-Roman Diplomatic and Epistolary Conventions: The Example of Timothy and Titus," *JBL* 111 (1992): 641–62.

78. A mother is *prostatis* for her son in an inscription of 142 BCE (probably a guardian), and another named Zmyrna is *prostatis* of the god Anubis (probably a benefactor); *NewDocs* 4.243.

79. As suggested by Marco Zappella, "A proposito di Febe *Prostatis* (Rm 16,2)," *RivB* 37 (1989): 167–71.

80. Robert Jewett, "Paul, Phoebe and the Spanish Mission," in *The Social World of Formative Christianity: Essays in Tribute of Howard Clark Kee*, ed. Jacob Neusner et al. (Philadelphia: Fortress, 1988), 153.

81. Caroline F. Whelan, "Amica Pauli: The Role of Phoebe in the Early Church," *JSNT* 49 (1993): 84.

82. *NewDocs* 4.241.

83. For further discussion, see Margaret Y. MacDonald, "Reading Real Women through the Undisputed Letters of Paul," in *Women and Christian Origins*, ed. Ross Shepard Kraemer and Mary Rose D'Angelo (New York: Oxford University Press, 1999), 200–202.

84. On this issue, see also chapter 10.

85. Some manuscripts read *pistos ē pistē* (believing man or believing woman), but the majority and better witness is that only women are referred to here.

86. See discussion in chapter 10; Bonnie Bowman Thurston, *The Widows: A Women's Ministry in the Early Church* (Minneapolis: Fortress, 1989), 96–104.

87. See Carolyn Osiek, "The Widow as Altar: The Rise and Fall of a Symbol," *SecCent* 3/3 (1983): 159–69.

88. See Carolyn Osiek, "The Patronage of Women and Roman and Christian Burial Practices," forthcoming.

89. Texts and discussion in Ute E. Eisen, *Women Officeholders in Early Christianity: Epigraphical and Literary Studies*, trans. Linda M. Maloney (Collegeville, Minn.: Liturgical, 2000), 164–67, 175–76. Matrona and Maria also in *NewDocs* 2.193–95; Agrippiane in Kraemer, *Women's Religions in the Greco-Roman World*, 259; see also Kevin Madigan and Carolyn Osiek, *Ordained Women in the Early Church: A Documentary History* (Baltimore: Johns Hopkins University Press, 2005), 70, 82–85.

10. Women as Agents of Expansion

1. Origen, *Against Celsus* 3.44. See also 3.50. Trans. Henry Chadwick, *Origen: Contra Celsum* (Cambridge: Cambridge University Press, 1953).

2. Origen, *Against Celsus* 3.55.

3. On Celsus and women see Margaret Y. MacDonald, *Early Christian Women and Pagan Opinion: The Power of the Hysterical Woman* (Cambridge: Cambridge University Press, 1996), 94–126.

4. See, for example, Juvenal, *Satire* 6. On women in Greco-Roman criticism of various Eastern religions, see David L. Balch, *Let Wives Be Submissive: The Domestic Code in 1 Peter* (Chico, Calif.: Scholars, 1981), 65–80.

5. See, for example, the anti-Christian oration by Marcus Cornelius Fronto recorded in Marcus Minucius Felix, *Octavius* 8–9; Apuleius, *Metamorphoses* 9.14 (note, however, that this text could refer to either a Jewish proselyte or a Christian woman).

6. R. Joseph Hoffmann, *Celsus on the True Doctrine* (Oxford: Oxford University Press, 1987), 36. See also Harold Remus, *Pagan-Christian Conflict over Miracle in the Second Century* (Cambridge, Mass.: Philadelphia Patristics Foundation, 1983), 270n.68; Pierre de Labriolle, *La réaction païenne: Étude sur la polémique antichrétienne du 1er au VIe siècle* (Paris: L'Artisan du livre, 1948), 124–27.

7. See MacDonald, *Early Christian Women*. On early Christianity generally, Robert L. Wilken, *The Christians as the Romans Saw Them* (New Haven: Yale University Press, 1984).

8. Robin Lane Fox, *Pagans and Christians* (New York: Knopf, 1986), 308. See Adolf von Harnack, *The Mission and Expansion of Christianity in the First Three*

Centuries, trans. James Moffat (New York: Harper, 1961 [1908]), 368; see also 393–98; also Peter Brown, "Aspects of the Christianization of the Roman Aristocracy," *JRS* 51 (1961): 1–11. See discussion by Elizabeth A. Castelli, "Gender, Theory, and the Rise of Christianity: A Response to Rodney Stark," *JECS* 6/2 (1998): 242.

9. See Rodney Stark, *The Rise of Christianity: A Sociologist Reconsiders History* (Princeton: Princeton University Press, 1996); also R. Stark and W. S. Bainbridge, "Networks of Faith: Interpersonal Bonds and Recruitment in Cults and Sects," *American Journal of Sociology* 85 (1980): 1376–95. For an evaluation of this theoretical perspective for understanding conversion, among other theories, see Brock Kilbourne and James T. Richardson, "Paradigm Conflict, Types of Conversion, and Conversion Theories," *Sociological Analysis* 50 (1988): 1–21.

10. Kate Cooper, "Insinuations of Womanly Influence: An Aspect of the Christianization of the Roman Aristocracy," *JRS* 82 (1992): 150–64.

11. Ibid.,155.

12. Judith Lieu, "The 'Attraction of Women' in/to Early Judaism and Christianity: Gender and the Politics of Conversion," *JSNT* 72 (1998): 16–19. Similar ideas about Josephus and Acts are found in Shelley Matthews, *First Converts: Rich Pagan Women and the Rhetoric of Mission in Early Judaism and Christianity* (Stanford: Stanford University Press, 2001). She makes the interesting point that texts implying that women's involvement with foreign religions led to widespread disapproval must be balanced against the tendency to highlight the involvement of high-standing women in order to enhance the profile of certain suspicious groups. With respect to early Christian evidence, Matthews concentrates especially on the status of Lydia as a rhetorical strategy in Acts. She argues (99) that the juxtaposition of Lydia and the slave girl who had the gift of divination in Acts 16 "serves to deflect attention from lower class female adherents/converts."

13. Lieu, "The 'Attraction of Women,'" 20.

14. The numerical estimates of the sex ratio of early Christianity are of necessity so tangential as to be of questionable use. Archaeological remains and epigraphic evidence are a potential source of information here, but to date the findings are not conclusive. See, for example, the prosopographical and epigraphical evidence discussed by Michele Renée Salzman in "Aristocratic Women: Conductors of Christianity in the Fourth Century," *Helios* 16 (1989): 207–20. While her results offer reasons to be cautious with respect to women's playing a major role in Christian expansion, in the end her pool of cases is simply too small to be really conclusive. See also her similar discussion in "How the West Was Won: The Christianization of the Roman Aristocracy in the West in the Years after Constantine," *Studies in Latin Literature and Roman History, Collection Latomus* 217 (1992): 451–79. Similarly, as noted by Castelli, Rodney Stark probably puts too much weight upon limited evidence to come to conclusions opposite to that of Salzman in dealing with the evidence from a fourth-century house church in North African Cirta, where a

disproportionately large number of women's articles of clothing were listed in an inventory: *Gesta apud Zenophilum*, CSEL 26:185–97, at 187.4–10; cited in Castelli, "Gender, Theory, and the Rise of Christianity," 242n.29. See Stark, *The Rise of Christianity*, 98; also Fox, *Pagans and Christians*, 310.

15. On ordinary women see Harold Remus, "Unknown and Yet Well-Known: The Multiform Formation of Early Christianity," in *A Multiform Heritage: Studies on Early Judaism and Christianity in Honor of Robert A. Kraft*, ed. Benjamin G. Wright (Atlanta: Scholars, 1999), 79–93.

16. Particularly relevant for the present study, however, is the treatment of Pauline material in Roger W. Gehring, *House Church and Mission: The Importance of Household Structures in Early Christianity* (Peabody, Mass.: Hendrickson, 2004). See esp. "The House in the Pauline Mission," 179–90.

17. See Elisabeth Schüssler Fiorenza, *In Memory of Her: A Feminist Theological Reconstruction of Christian Origins* (London: SCM, 1983). On missionary activities of women in the Pauline churches, see, for example, 167, 183. On the leadership of women in general in Pauline circles, see Ross Shepard Kraemer, *Her Share of the Blessings: Women's Religions among Pagans, Jews, and Christians in the Greco-Roman world* (New York: Oxford University Press, 1992), 65–86, 136–38, 174–76.

18. On the nature of these partnerships and the issues involved in interpreting references to them, see chapter 2.

19. It is possible that the Greek text should be taken to mean that Andronicus and Junia were prominent among the apostles in the sense that they were valued by apostles without being apostles themselves. For example, Daniel B. Wallace and Michael H. Burer, "Was Junia Really an Apostle?" (*Journal for Biblical Manhood and Womanhood* 6/2 [2001]: 4–11), argue on the basis of a grammatical search that *episēmos en* + dative, the construction used here, is used only for impersonal objects, whereas *episēmos* + genitive is used for personal objects modified by the adjective. However, they never mention that John Chrysostom, the earliest commentator on the text and a native Greek speaker, specifically remarks in his commentary on this passage that Paul calls Junia an apostle (Homily on Romans 31.2, Migne, *Patrologia Graeca* 60.669–70). The most straightforward reading accepts that they are actually being called apostles; so Joseph A. Fitzmyer, *Romans*, AB 33 (New York: Doubleday, 1993), 739. For a very recent study responding to Wallace and Burer and arguing that Junia is indeed an apostle, see Linda Belleville, "Iounian…episēmois en tois apostolois: A Re-examination of Romans 16.7 in Light of Primary Source Materials," *NTS* 51 (2005): 231–49. Note also that Junia has sometimes been understood to be a man. See discussion in Margaret Y. MacDonald, "Reading Real Women through the Undisputed Letters of Paul," in *Women and Christian Origins*, ed. Ross Shepard Kraemer and Mary Rose D'Angelo (Oxford: Oxford University Press, 1999), 209–10.

20. See chapter 2 for detailed discussion of all of the texts in which Prisc(ill)a and Aquila are mentioned.

21. See Francis X. Malinowski, "The Brave Women of Philippi," *BTB* 15 (1985): 62.

22. Robert Jewett, "Paul, Phoebe and the Spanish Mission," in *The Social World of Formative Christianity and Judaism: Essays in Tribute to Howard Clark Kee*, ed. Jacob Neusner et al. (Philadelphia: Fortress, 1988), 142–61.

23. On Phoebe see Caroline F. Whelan, "Amica Pauli: The Role of Phoebe in the Early Church," *JSNT* 49 (1993): 67–85; Roman Garrison, "Phoebe, the Servant-Benefactor and Gospel Traditions," in *Text and Artifact in the Religions of Mediterranean Antiquity: Essays in Honour of Peter Richardson*, ed. Stephen G. Wilson and Michel Desjardins (Waterloo, Ont.: Wilfrid Laurier University Press, 2000), 63–73.

24. The use of the term must be distinguished both from its usage to describe an office that formed part of the threefold organizational framework of bishop, presbyter, and deacon that emerged in some circles at the beginning of the second century and from the female office of "deaconess" that developed considerably later. Paul's use of the term is in fact quite flexible, being employed in the plural along with "overseers" to refer to local leaders of a community, or perhaps even to refer to believers in general, in Phil. 1:1.

25. Schüssler Fiorenza has argued vigorously for the missionary connotations of the term *diakonos* and its cognates. See *In Memory of Her*, 171.

26. Clement of Alexandria, *Miscellanies* 3.6.53.3.

27. *Apostolic Constitutions* 3.15. See MacDonald, "Reading Real Women," 203.

28. Kraemer, *Her Share*, 191–98; Bernadette J. Brooten, *Women Leaders in the Ancient Synagogue*, Brown Judaic Studies 36 (Chico, Calif.: Scholars, 1982); Valerie Abrahamsen, "Women at Philippi: The Pagan and Christian Evidence," *JFSR* 3 (1987): 17–30.

29. Bonnie Bowman Thurston, *The Widows: A Women's Ministry in the Early Church* (Minneapolis: Fortress, 1989), 32–35.

30. On the importance of healings and exorcisms for the expansion of Christianity, see especially Ramsay MacMullen, *Christianizing the Roman Empire (A.D. 100–400)* (New Haven: Yale University Press, 1984).

31. MacDonald, *Early Christian Women*, 227–29.

32. On the relationship between the treatment of women and communal relations with society at large in the Pastoral Epistles, see ibid., 154–82.

33. Lucian, *The Passing of Peregrinus*, 12–13. On the historical reliability of Lucian's satirical account and its use in the study of early Christianity, see MacDonald, *Early Christian Women*, 73–82.

34. R. Hugh Connoly, ed., *Didascalia Apostolorum* (Oxford: Clarendon, 1929), 132–33 (chapter 15).

35. The text here is based on an Arabic source translated and edited by Richard Walzer, from his *Galen on Jews and Christians* (London: Oxford University Press,

1949), 15. For a full discussion of the meaning of this text, including textual issues, see MacDonald, *Early Christian Women*, 82–94.

36. Philo, *On the Contemplative Life* 12, 32–33, 68–69, 83–88. See Justin, *First Apology* 15 (*ANF* 1.167).

37. Lieu, "The 'Attraction of Women,'" 9.

38. Origen, *Against Celsus* 5.62. See discussion in Hoffmann, *Celsus on the True Doctrine*, 42. Unfortunately, much of Celsus's text concerning these women has been lost.

39. Origen, *Against Celsus* 6.34; on the Sybil, Herm. *Vis.* 2.4.1.

40. Christine Trevett, *Montanism: Gender, Authority, and the New Prophecy* (Cambridge: Cambridge University Press, 1996), 154. See also Kraemer, *Her Share of the Blessings*, 157–59.

41. See Ross S. Kraemer and Shira L. Lander, "Perpetua and Felicitas," in *The Early Christian World*, ed. Philip F. Esler (London: Routledge, 2000), 2.1061–62.

42. Ibid.

43. *The Martyrdom of Perpetua and Felicitas* 16; trans. H. Musurillo, *Acts of the Christian Martyrs* (Oxford: Clarendon, 1972), 106–31.

44. *The Martyrdom of Perpetua and Felicitas* 17.

45. John M. G. Barclay, "The Family as the Bearer of Religion," in *Constructing Early Christian Families: Family as Social Reality and Metaphor*, ed. Halvor Moxnes (London: Routledge, 1997), 77.

46. Ibid., 76.

47. See Balch, *Let Wives Be Submissive*, 54–55, 73–76. Balch draws parallels between the New Testament use of the code and the apologetic function of the topos of household management in other ancient texts. See also Margaret Y. MacDonald, *Colossians and Ephesians*, ed. Daniel J. Harrington, S.J., SP 17 (Collegeville, Minn.: Liturgical, 2000), 159–69, 336–41; E. Elizabeth Johnson, "Ephesians," in *The Women's Bible Commentary*, ed. Carol A. Newsom and Sharon H. Ringe (Louisville: Westminster/John Knox, 1992), 340–41.

48. MacMullen, *Christianizing the Roman Empire*, 33–42. Note the similar observation made by Martin Goodman: "It is a separate question how many Christians believed a proselytizing mission to be desirable after the eschatological fervor of the first generations. Against any view that such a mission was generally seen by Christians as applicable in later times is the treatment of the texts of Jesus' commission to the apostles (Matt. 28:19-20; Mark 16:15-16) in patristic writings of the second to fourth centuries." See Martin Goodman, *Mission and Conversion: Proselytizing in the Religious History of the Roman Empire* (Oxford: Clarendon, 1994), 106.

49. MacDonald, *Early Christian Women*, 240–43.

50. Note that Gehring (*House Church and Mission*, 185–87) has argued that the descriptions of household conversions in Acts offer important confirmation that

the intentional recruitment of householders was an important Pauline missionary strategy.

51. David Lertis Matson, *Household Conversion Narratives in Acts: Pattern and Interpretation*, JSNTSup 123 (Sheffield: Sheffield Academic, 1996), 87–88.

52. See L. Michael White, "Visualizing the 'Real' World of Acts 16: Toward Construction of a Social Index," in *The Social World of the First Christians*, ed. L. Michael White and O. Larry Yarbrough (Minneapolis: Fortress, 1995), 259.

53. On this tendency see detailed discussion by Matthews, *First Converts*, 85–89.

54. Matson, *Household Conversion*, 140–41.

55. Lieu, "The 'Attraction of Women,'" 16.

56. Ibid., 17.

57. For example, see Ramsay MacMullen, "Women in Public in the Roman Empire," *Historia* 29 (1980): 208–18; idem, "Women's Power in the Principate," in *Changes in the Roman Empire: Essays on the Ordinary* (Princeton: Princeton University Press, 1990), 169–76.

58. For an illustration of how the religious activities of women could be viewed as an assault upon the head of the household, see Apuleius, *Metamorphoses* 9.14. See full discussion of this text in MacDonald, *Early Christian Women*, 67–73.

59. Stark, *The Rise of Christianity*, 115.

60. Reported in Hippolytus, *Philosophumena (refutatio omnium haeresium)* 9.12.24, cited in Marie-Thérèse Raepsaet-Charlier, "Tertullien et la législation des mariages inégaux," *Revue internationale des droits de l'antiquité* 29 (1982): 262. Note that Michele Renée Salzman has pointed out that this was not a problem unique to the Christian community and Roman legislation was drawn up to respond to it. See Salzman, "Aristocratic Women," 213.

61. Stark, *The Rise of Christianity*, 112.

62. Ibid., 112–13.

63. See Justin *2 Apology* 2.

64. Tertullian, *To His Wife* 2.3 (*ANF* 4).

65. Ibid., 2.8. See discussion of this in Raepsaet-Charlier, "Tertullien et la législation," 254–63.

66. MacDonald, *Early Christian Women*, 195–204.

67. See, for example, *Acts of Peter* 34, in E. Hennecke and W. Schneemelcher, eds., *New Testament Apocrypha*, vol. 2, trans. Robert McL. Wilson (Philadelphia: Westminster, 1965), 317. Compare Justin, *2 Apology* 2.

68. See Ross S. Kraemer, "The Conversion of Women to Ascetic Forms of Christianity," *Signs* 6 (1980): 298–307. Kraemer offers the following examples: Andronicus in the *Acts of John* 63 and Misdaeus in the *Acts of Thomas* 170 (300).

69. Barclay, "The Family as the Bearer of Religion," 77.

70. On the importance of Christian teaching being absorbed at the mother's side, see Jean Delumeau, *La religion de ma mère: Les femmes dans la transmission de la foi* (Paris: Cerf, 1992).

71. On the relationship between the Roman mother and her adolescent son, see Suzanne Dixon, *The Roman Mother* (London: Croom Helm, 1988), 168–203.

72. Ibid., 220–28.

73. For a full discussion of this complicated text, see MacDonald, *Early Christian Women*, 189–95.

74. Dixon, *The Roman Mother*, 159–61.

75. Letter 107, *Jerome to Laeta*, excerpt from Ross Shepard Kraemer, ed., *Women's Religions in the Greco-Roman World: A Sourcebook* (New York: Oxford University Press, 2004), 171.

76. References are to the translation by W. Schneemelcher in Hennecke and Schneemelcher, *New Testament Apocrypha*, 2.353–64.

77. See Kate Cooper, *The Virgin and the Bride: Idealized Womanhood in Late Antiquity* (Cambridge: Harvard University Press, 1996). See especially pp. 62–63, where she questions these earlier theories.

78. Ibid., 54–55.

79. For a somewhat similar argument and valuable discussion of the relationship between "fiction and reality" in the *Acts of [Paul and] Thecla* (including response to Cooper), see Stephen J. Davis, *The Cult of Saint Thecla: A Tradition of Women's Piety* (Oxford: Oxford University Press, 2001), 12–13, 18–19. Davis makes the following important point: "Tertullian provides solid external evidence indicating that the *ATh* did in fact have an early audience among women for whom the work had a very different public function" (12). See Tertullian, *On Baptism* 17.

80. See MacDonald, *Early Christian Women*, 240–43.

81. For fuller discussion see ibid., 172–78.

82. Note, however, that with a special focus on the identity of Thecla as a "stranger" in the work, Davis has presented an interesting case for viewing Thecla as a "social type" for itinerant, charismatic teachers. See Davis, *The Cult of Saint Thecla*, 22–35.

11. Conclusion: Discovering a Woman's Place

1. See Elizabeth Clark, "The Lady Vanishes: Dilemmas of a Feminist Historian after the 'Linguistic Turn,'" *CH* 67/1 (1998): 1–31.

2. Judith Lieu, "The 'Attraction of Women' in/to Early Judaism and Christianity: Gender and the Politics of Conversion," *JSNT* 72 (1998): 20.

BIBLIOGRAPHY

Abrahamsen, Valerie. "Women at Philippi: The Pagan and Christian Evidence." *JFSR* 3 (1987): 17–30.

Abu-Lughod, Lila. *Veiled Sentiments: Honor and Poetry in a Bedouin Society.* Berkeley: University of California Press, 1986.

Aldrete, Gregory S. *Gestures and Acclamations in Ancient Rome.* Baltimore: Johns Hopkins University Press, 1999.

Amedick, Rita. "Klinen-Mahl." In *Die Sarcophage mit Darstellungen aus dem Menschenleben: Vita Privata.* Berlin: Mann, 1991.

Anderson Anne C. *A Guide to Roman Fine Wares.* Highworth, Wiltshire, U.K.: Vorda, 1980.

Arjava, Antti. *Women and Law in Late Antiquity.* Oxford: Clarendon, 1998.

Arnold, Clinton E. *Ephesians, Power and Magic: The Concept of Power in Ephesians in the Light of Its Historical Setting.* SNTSMS 63. Cambridge: Cambridge University Press, 1989.

Aspegren, Kerstin. *The Male Woman: A Feminine Ideal in the Early Church.* Uppsala Women's Studies. Women in Religion 4. Uppsala: Almqvist & Wiksell, 1990.

Bagnall, Roger S., and Bruce W. Frier. *The Demography of Roman Egypt.* Cambridge: Cambridge University Press, 1994.

Bakke, O. M. *When Children Became People: The Birth of Childhood in Early Christianity.* Translated by Brian McNeil. Minneapolis: Fortress, 2005.

Bal, Mieke. *Reading Rembrandt: Beyond the Word-Image Opposition.* Cambridge New Art History and Criticism. Cambridge: Cambridge University Press, 1991.

Balch, David L. *Let Wives Be Submissive: The Domestic Code in 1 Peter.* SBLMS 26. Chico, Calif.: Scholars, 1981.

Balch, David L., and Carolyn Osiek, editors. *Early Christian Families in Context: An Interdisciplinary Dialogue.* Religion, Marriage, and Family. Grand Rapids: Eerdmans, 2003.

Balla, Peter. *The Child-Parent Relationship in the New Testament and Its Environment.* WUNT 155. Tübingen: Mohr/Siebeck, 2003.

Barclay, John M. G. "The Family as the Bearer of Religion in Judaism and Early Christianity." In *Constructing Early Christian Families: Family as Social Reality and Metaphor,* edited by Halvor Moxnes, 66–80. London: Routledge, 1997.

Barth, Markus, and Helmut Blanke. *Colossians: A New Translation with Introduction and Commentary.* Translated by Astrid B. Beck. AB 34B. New York: Doubleday, 1994.

Barton, Carlin A. *Roman Honor: The Fire in the Bones.* Berkeley: University of California Press, 2001.

Barton, Stephen C. "Paul's Sense of Place: An Anthropological Approach to Community Formation in Corinth." *NTS* 32 (1986): 225–46.

Bauer, Walter, F. W. Danker, W. F. Arndt, and F. W. Gringrich. *A Greek-English Lexicon of the New Testament and Other Early Christian Literature.* 3rd ed. Chicago: University of Chicago Press, 2000.

Bauman, Richard A. *Women and Politics in Ancient Rome.* London: Routledge, 1992.

Beal, Timothy K., and David M. Gunn, editors. *Reading Bibles, Writing Bodies: Identity and the Book.* London: Routledge, 1997.

Beard, Mary, John North, and Simon Price. *Religions of Rome.* 2 vols. Cambridge: Cambridge University Press, 1998.

Beavis, Mary Ann. "'Pluck the Rose, but Shun the Thorns': The Ancient School and Christian Origins." *SR* 29/4 (2000): 411–23.

Bednarz, Theresa. "Lydia Speaks: Examining the Life of Lydia through Her Social and Theological Context." MA thesis. Catholic Theological Union in Chicago, 2002.

Belleville, Linda. "*Iounian…episēmoi en tois apostolois*: A Re-examination of Romans 16.7 in Light of Primary Source Materials." *NTS* 51 (2005): 231–49.

Benko, Stephen. "Pagan Criticism of Christianity during the First Two Centuries AD." In *ANRW*, edited by H. Temporini and W. Haase, 23.2, 1055–118. Berlin: de Gruyter, 1980.

Bernabé Ubieta, Carmen. "'Neither *Xenoi* nor *paroikoi, sympolitai* and *oikeioi tou theou*' (Eph 2:19): Pauline Christian Communities: Defining a New Territoriality." In *Social-Scientific Models for Interpreting the Bible: Essays by the Context Group in Honor of Bruce J. Malina,* edited by John J. Pilch, 260–80. Biblical Interpretation Series 53. Leiden: Brill, 2001.

Best, Ernest. *Ephesians.* ICC. Edinburgh: T & T Clark, 1998.

Bisconti, F. "L'ipogeo degli Aureli in viale Manzoni: Un esempio di sincresi privata." *Augustinianum* 25 (1985): 889–903.

Blenkinsopp, Joseph. "The Family in First Temple Israel." In Perdue et al., *Families in Ancient Israel*, 48–103.

Boatwright, Mary Taliaferro. "Plancia Magna of Perge: Women's Roles and Status in Roman Asia Minor." In Pomeroy, *Women's History and Ancient History*, 249–72.

Bobertz, Charles A. "Almsgiving as Patronage: The Role of Patroness in Early Christianity." Unpublished paper. American Academy of Religion annual meeting, 1992.

———. "The Role of Patron in the *Cena Dominica* of Hippolytus' *Apostolic Tradition*." *JTS* 44 (1993): 170–84.

Bodel, John. "Death on Display: Looking at Roman Funerals." In *The Art of Ancient Spectacle*, edited by Bettina Bergmann and Christine Kondoleon, 259–81. Studies in the History of Art 56. Washington, D.C.: National Gallery of Art, 1999.

———, editor. *Epigraphic Evidence: Ancient History from Inscriptions*. London: Routledge, 2001.

Boswell, John. *The Kindness of Strangers: The Abandonment of Children in Western Europe from Late Antiquity to the Renaissance*. New York: Vintage, 1988.

Bowman, Alan K., and J. David Thomas, editors. *The Vindolanda Writing-Tablets (Tabulae Vindolandenses II)*. London: British Museum Press, 1994.

Bradley, Keith R. *Discovering the Roman Family*. Oxford: Oxford University Press, 1991.

———. "Images of Childhood: The Evidence of Plutarch." In *Plutarch's Advice to the Bride and Groom and A Consolation to His Wife*, edited by Sarah B. Pomeroy, 183–196. New Oxford: Oxford University Press, 1999.

———. *Slaves and Masters in the Roman Empire: A Study in Social Control*. New York: Oxford University Press, 1987.

Braun, Willi, editor. *Rhetorics and Realities in Early Christianities*. Studies in Christianity and Judaism. Waterloo, Ont.: Wilfrid Laurier University Press, 2005.

Brilliant, Richard. *Gesture and Rank in Roman Art: The Use of Gestures to Denote Status in Roman Sculpture and Coinage*. Memoirs of the Connecticut Academy of Arts & Sciences 14. New Haven: The Academy, 1963.

Brooten, Bernadette J. "Jewish Women's History in the Roman Period: A Task for Christian Theology." *HTR* 79 (1986): 22–30.

———. *Women Leaders in the Ancient Synagogue: Inscriptional Evidence and Background Issues*. Brown Judaic Studies 36. Chico, Calif.: Scholars, 1982.

Brown, Peter. "Aspects of the Christianization of the Roman Aristocracy." *JRS* 51 (1961): 1–11.

———. *The Body and Society: Men, Women and Sexual Renunciation in Early Christianity*. London: Faber and Faber, 1988.

Brunt, P. A. "'Amicitia' in the Late Roman Republic." *Proceedings of the Cambridge Philological Society* 11 (1965) 1–20. Reprinted in *The Crisis of the Roman Republic: Studies in Political and Social History*, edited by Robin Seager, 199–218. Cambridge: Heffer, 1969.

Bryson, Norman. *Looking at the Overlooked: Four Essays on Still Life Painting*. Cambridge: Harvard University Press, 1990.

Burns, J. Patout. "Death and Burial in Christian Africa: The Literary Evidence." Paper presented to North American Patristics Society, May 1997.

Bush, M. L., editor. *Serfdom and Slavery: Studies in Legal Bondage*. London: Longman, 1996.

Byrne, Brendan S.J. *Romans*. SP 6. Collegeville, Minn.: Liturgical, 1996.

Callahan, Allen Dwight, Richard A. Horsley, and Abraham Smith, editors. *Slavery in Text and Interpretation*. Semeia 83/84. Atlanta: Society of Biblical Literature, 1998.

Cameron, Averil, and Amélie Kuhrt, editors. *Images of Women in Antiquity*. Revised edition. Detroit: Wayne State University Press, 1983.

Camp, Claudia. "Woman Wisdom and the Strange Woman: Where Is Power to Be Found?" In Beal and Gunn, *Reading Bibles, Writing Bodies*, 85–112. London: Routledge, 1997.

Campese Simone, Anna. *I cimiteri tardoantichi e altomedievali della Puglia settentrionale: Valle del basso Ofanto, Tavoliere, Gargano*. Rome: Città del Vaticano, 2003.

Carletti, Carlo. "Aspetti biometrici del matrimonio nelle iscrizioni chritiane di Roma." *Augustianum* 17 (1977): 39–51.

Casarico, L. "Donne ginnasiarco." *Zeitschrift für Papyrologie und Epigraphik* 48 (1982): 118–22.

Castelli, Elizabeth A. "Gender, Theory, and the Rise of Christianity: A Response to Rodney Stark." *JECS* 6/2 (1998): 227–57.

———. "Paul on Women and Gender." In Kraemer and D'Angelo, *Women and Christian Origins*, 221–35.

———. "Virginity and Its Meaning for Women's Sexuality in Early Christianity." *JFSR* 2 (1986): 61–88.

Castelli, Elizabeth A., and Hal Taussig, editors. *Reimagining Christian Origins: A Colloquium Honoring Burton L. Mack*. Valley Forge, Pa.: Trinity Press International, 1996.

Cerulli Irelli, Giuseppina. "Archaeological Research in the Area of Vesuvius: Portraits from Herculaneum." In *Pompeii and the Vesuvian Landscape: Papers of a Symposium*, 16–24. Washington, D.C.: Archaeological Institute of America and the Smithsonian Institution, 1979.

Chadwick, Henry, translator. *Origen: Contra Celsum*. Cambridge: Cambridge University Press, 1953.

Champlin, Edward. *Fronto and Antonine Rome*. Cambridge: Harvard University Press, 1980.

Chow, John K. *Patronage and Power: A Study of Social Networks in Corinth*. JSNT-Sup 75. Sheffield: Sheffield Academic, 1992.

Clark, Elizabeth. *Reading Renunciation: Asceticism and Scripture in Early Christianity*. Princeton: Princeton University Press, 1999.

Clark, Gillian. "Roman Women." *Greece and Rome* 28 (1981): 193–212.

Clarke, John R. *Art in the Lives of Ordinary Romans: Visual Representation and Non-elite Viewers in Italy, 100 BC–AD 315*. Berkeley: University of California Press, 2003.

————. *Looking at Lovemaking: Constructions of Sexuality in Roman Art 100 B.C.–A.D. 250*. Berkeley: University of California Press, 1998.

Cohen, Shaye J. D., editor. *The Jewish Family in Antiquity*. Brown Judaic Studies 289. Atlanta: Scholars, 1993.

Cole, Sally. *Women of the Praia: Work and Lives in a Portuguese Coastal Community*. Princeton: Princeton University Press, 1991.

Connolly, Hugh, editor. *Didascalia Apostolorum*. Oxford: Clarendon, 1929.

Cooper, Kate. "Insinuations of Womanly Influence: An Aspect of the Christianization of the Roman Aristocracy." *JRS* 82 (1992): 150–64.

————. *The Virgin and the Bride: Idealized Womanhood in Late Antiquity*. Cambridge: Harvard University Press, 1996.

Corley, Kathleen E. "Feminist Myths of Christian Origins." In Castelli and Taussig, *Reimagining Christian Origins*, 51–67.

————. *Private Women, Public Meals: Social Conflict in the Synoptic Tradition*. Peabody, Mass.: Hendrickson, 1993.

————. *Women and the Historical Jesus: Feminist Myths of Christian Origins*. Santa Rosa, Calif.: Polebridge, 2002.

Countryman, L. William. *The Rich Christian in the Church of the Early Empire: Contradictions and Accommodations*. Texts and Studies in Religion. New York: Mellen, 1980.

Crisafulli, T. "Representations of the Feminine: The Prostitute in Roman Comedy." In *Ancient History in a Modern University: Proceedings of a Conference held at Macquarie University, 8–13 July 1993: To Mark Twenty-five Years of the Teaching of Ancient History at Macquarie University and the Retirement from the Chair of Professor Edwin Judge*, edited by T. W. Hillard et al., 1:222–29. N.S.W. Australia: Ancient History Documentary Research Centre, 1998.

Crook, Zeba A. *Reconceptualizing Conversion: Patronage, Loyalty, and Conversion in the Religions of the Ancient Mediterranean*. Berlin: de Gruyter, 2004.

Croom, A. T. *Roman Clothing and Fashion*. Stroud, U.K.: Tempus, 2002.

Crossan, John Dominic. *The Historical Jesus: The Life of a Mediterranean Jewish Peasant*. San Francisco: HarperSanFrancisco, 1992.

Dahl, Nils Alstrup. "Ephesians and Qumran." In *Nils Alstrup Dahl, Studies in Ephesians: Introductory Questions, Text- and Edition-Critical Issues, Interpretation of Texts and Themes*, edited by David Hellholm, Vemund Blomkvist, and Tord Fornberg, 115–44. Tübingen: Mohr/Siebeck, 2000.

Daley, Brian. "Position and Patronage in the Early Church: The Original Meaning of the 'Primacy of Honour.'" *JTS* 44 (1993): 529–53.

d'Ambra, Eve. "The Cult of Virtues and the Funerary Relief of Ulpia Epigone." In *Roman Art in Context: An Anthology*, edited by Eve d'Ambra, 104–14. Englewood Cliffs, N.J.: Prentice Hall, 1993.

D'Angelo, Mary Rose. "Colossians." In *Searching the Scriptures*, vol. 2: *A Feminist Commentary*, edited by Elisabeth Schüssler Fiorenza, 313–24. New York: Crossroad, 1994.

———. "Women in Luke-Acts: A Redactional View." *JBL* 109 (1990): 441–61.

———. "Women Partners in the New Testament." *JFSR* 6 (1990): 65–86.

D'Arms, John H. "Memory, Money, and Status at Misenum: Three New Inscriptions from the Collegium of the Augustales." *JRS* 90 (2000): 126–44.

Dasen, Véronique, editor. *Naissance et petite enfance dans l'Antiquité*. Actes du colloque de Fribourg, 28 novembre–1 décembre 2001. Fribourg: Academic Press, 2004.

Danker, Frederick W. *Benefactor: Epigraphic Study of a Graeco-Roman and New Testament Semantic Field*. St. Louis: Clayton, 1982.

Davies, Jon. *Death, Burial and Rebirth in the Religions of Antiquity*. Religion in the First Christian Centuries. London: Routledge, 1999.

Davies, Stevan L. *Revolt of the Widows: The Social World of the Apocryphal Acts*. Carbondale: Southern Illinois University Press, 1980.

Davis, Stephen J. *The Cult of Saint Thecla: A Tradition of Women's Piety*. Oxford Early Christian Studies. Oxford: Oxford University Press, 2001.

De Bruyn, Theodore S. "Flogging a Son: The Emergence of the *pater flagellans* in Latin Christian Discourse." *JECS* 7 (1999): 249–90.

Deckers, Johannes Georg, H. R. Seeliger, and Gabriele Mietke. *Die Katacombe "Santi Marcellino e Pietro" Repertorium der Malereien = La catacomba dei Santi Marcellino e Pietro: Repertorio delle pitture*. 3 vols. Roma Sotterranea Cristiana 6. Vatican City: Pontificio istituto di archeologia cristiana, 1987.

De Labriolle, Pierre. *La réaction païenne: Étude sur la polémique antichrétienne du 1er au VIe siècle*. Paris: L'Artisan du livre, 1948.

Delumeau, Jean. *La religion de ma mère: Les femmes et la transmission de la foi*. Paris: Cerf, 1992.

Derrett, J. Duncan M. "The Disposal of Virgins." In *Studies in the New Testament*, 1:184–91. Leiden: Brill, 1977.

DeSilva, David A. *Honor, Patronage, Kinship and Purity: Unlocking New Testament Culture*. Downers Grove, Ill.: InterVarsity, 2000.

Dexter, Caroline. "The Epigraphic Evidence of Pompeiian Women." Unpublished paper.

Dixon, Suzanne. "A Family Business: Women's Role in Patronage and Politics at Rome 80–44 B.C." *Classica et Mediaevalia* 34 (1983): 91–112.

———. *Reading Roman Women: Sources, Genres, and Real Life.* London: Duckworth, 2001.

———. *The Roman Mother.* London: Croom Helm, 1988.

———. "The Sentimental Ideal of the Roman Family." In *Marriage, Divorce, and Children in Ancient Rome,* edited by Beryl Rawson, 99–113. Oxford: Clarendon, 1991.

Donahue, John R., S. J., and Daniel J. Harrington, S. J. *The Gospel of Mark.* SP 2. Collegeville, Minn.: Liturgical, 2002.

Donaldson, Terence L. *Paul and the Gentiles: Remapping the Apostle's Convictional World.* Minneapolis: Fortress, 1997.

Donfried, Karl P. "A Short Note on Romans 16." In *The Romans Debate,* edited by Karl P. Donfried, 44–52. Revised edition. Peabody, Mass.: Hendrickson, 1991.

Dubisch, Jill. *Gender and Power in Rural Greece.* Princeton: Princeton University Press, 1986.

Du Boulay, Juliet. *Portrait of a Greek Mountain Village.* Oxford Monographs on Social Anthropology. Oxford: Clarendon, 1974.

Dückers, Peter. "Agape und Irene. Die Frauengestalten der Sigmamahlszenen mit antiken Inschriften in der Katakombe der Heiligen Marcellinus und Petrus." *Jahrbuch für Antike und Christentum* 35 (1992): 147–67.

Dunbabin, Katherine M. D. *The Roman Banquet: Images of Conviviality.* Cambridge: Cambridge University Press, 2003.

———. "Triclinium and Stibadium." In Slater, *Dining in a Classical Context,* 212–48.

———. "The Waiting Servant in Later Roman Art." *American Journal of Philology* 124 (fall 2003): 443–67.

———. "Water and Wine at the Roman Convivium." *Journal of Roman Archaeology* 6 (1993): 116–41.

Dunn, James D. G. *The Epistles to the Colossians and to Philemon: A Commentary on the Greek Text.* NIGTC. Grand Rapids: Eerdmans, 1996.

Eisen, Ute E. *Women Officeholders in Early Christianity: Epigraphical and Literary Studies.* Translated by Linda M. Maloney. Collegeville, Minn.: Liturgical, 2000.

Eisenstadt, S. N., and L. Roniger. *Patrons, Clients, and Friends: Interpersonal Relations and the Structure of Trust in Society.* Themes in the Social Sciences. Cambridge: Cambridge University Press, 1984.

Elliott, J. K., editor. *The Apocryphal New Testament: A Collection of Apocryphal Christian Literature in an English Translation.* Oxford: Clarendon, 1993.

Elliott, John H. "Patronage and Clientage." In Rohrbaugh, *The Social Sciences and New Testament Interpretation*, 144–56.

Elsner, Jas. *Imperial Rome and Christian Triumph: The Art of the Roman Empire AD 100–450.* Oxford: Oxford University Press, 1998.

Engemann, J. "Der Ehrenplatz beim antiken Sigmamahl." In *Jenseitsvorstellungen in Antike und Christentum*, 239–50. *JAC* expanded vol. 9. Münster: Aschendorff, 1982.

Esler, Philip F. "1 Thessalonians." In *The Oxford Bible Commentary*, edited by John Barton and John Muddiman, 1199–212. Oxford: Oxford University Press, 2001.

Faust, Eberhard. *Pax Christi et Pax Caesaris: Religionsgeschichtliche, traditionsgeschichtliche und sozialgeschichtliche Studien zum Ephesebrief.* NTOA 24. Göttingen: Vandenhoeck & Ruprecht, 1993.

Feissel, Denis. *Recueil des Inscriptions Chrétiennes de Macédoine du IIIe au VIe Siècle.* Athens: French School of Athens, 1983.

Ferrari, Guy, editor. *The Gold-Glass Collection of the Vatican Library: With Additional Catalogues of Other Gold-Glass Collections.* Vatican City: Vatican Library, 1959.

Finley, M. I. *Ancient Slavery and Modern Ideology.* New York: Viking, 1980.

Finney, Paul Corby. *The Invisible God: The Earliest Christians on Art.* New York: Oxford University Press, 1994.

Fisher, Karl Martin. *Tendenz und Absicht des Epheserbriefes.* FRLANT 111. Göttingen: Vandenhoeck & Ruprecht, 1973.

Fitzgerald, John T., editor. *Friendship, Flattery, and Frankness of Speech: Studies on Friendship in the New Testament World.* NovTSup 82. Leiden: Brill, 1996.

Fitzmyer, Joseph A. *Romans: A New Translation with Introduction and Commentary.* AB 33. New York: Doubleday, 1993.

Flemming, Rebecca. *Medicine and the Making of Roman Women: Gender, Nature, and Authority from Celsus to Galen.* Oxford: Oxford University Press, 2000.

Flory, Marleen Boudreau. "Where Women Precede Men: Factors Influencing the Placement of Names in Roman Epitaphs." *Classical Journal* 79 (1983–84): 216–24.

Fox, Robin Lane. *Pagans and Christians.* New York: Knopf, 1986.

Francis, James. "Children and Childhood in the New Testament." In *The Family in Theological Perspective*, edited by Stephen Barton, 65–85. Edinburgh: T. & T. Clark, 1996.

Freedberg, David. *The Power of Images: Studies in the History and Theory of Response.* Chicago: University of Chicago Press, 1989.

Fremersdorf, Fritz. "Nordafrikanische Terra Sigillata aus Köln." *Kölner Jahrbuch für Vor- und Frühgeschichte* 3 (1958): 11–19.

French, Valerie. "Midwives and Maternity Care in the Roman World." *Helios*, New Series 13/2 (1986): 69–84.

Friedhoff, Ulrich. *Der römische Friedhof an der Jakobstraße zu Köln.* Mainz: von Zabern, 1991.

Gallagher, Eugene. "Conversion and Community in Late Antiquity." *JR* 73 (1993): 1–15.

Gardner, Jane F. *Women in Roman Law and Society.* London: Croom Helm, 1986.

Gardner, Jane F., and Thomas Wiedemann, editors. *The Roman Household: A Sourcebook.* London: Routledge, 1991.

Garnsey, Peter. *Food and Society in Classical Antiquity.* Cambridge: Cambridge University Press, 1999.

———. *Ideas of Slavery from Aristotle to Augustine.* Cambridge: Cambridge University Press, 1996.

Garrison, Roman. "Phoebe, the Servant-Benefactor and Gospel Traditions." In *Text and Artifact in the Religions of Mediterranean Antiquity: Essays in Honour of Peter Richardson,* edited by Stephen G. Wilson and Michel Desjardins, 63–73. Waterloo, Ont.: Wilfrid Laurier University Press, 2000.

Gehring, Roger W. *House Church and Mission: The Importance of Household Structures in Early Christianity.* Peabody, Mass.: Hendrickson, 2004.

Gellner, Ernest, and John Waterbury, editors. *Patrons and Clients in Mediterranean Societies.* London: Duckworth, 1977.

George, Michele. "Domestic Architecture and Household Relations: Pompeii and Roman Ephesos." *JSNT* 21 (2004): 7–25.

Gilmore, David D., editor. *Honor and Shame and the Unity of the Mediterranean.* American Anthropological Association Special Publication 22. Washington, D.C.: American Anthropological Association, 1987.

Glancy, Jennifer A. "The Mistress-Slave Dialectic: Paradoxes of Slavery in Three LXX Narratives." *Journal for the Study of the Old Testament* 72 (1996): 71–87.

———. "Obstacles to Slaves' Participation in the Corinthian Church." *JBL* 117 (1998): 481–501.

———. *Slavery in Early Christianity.* Oxford: Oxford University Press, 2002.

———. "Three-fifths of a Man: Slavery and Masculinity in Galatians." Paper presented at Society of Biblical Literature Annual Meeting, 1999.

Glenn, Cheryl. *Rhetoric Retold: Regendering the Tradition from Antiquity through the Renaissance.* Carbondale: Southern Illinois University Press, 1997.

Gold, Barbara K., editor. *Literary and Artistic Patronage in Ancient Rome.* Austin: University of Texas Press, 1982.

Goodman, Martin. "Josephus' Treatise against Apion." In *Apologetics in the Roman Empire: Pagans, Jews, and Christians,* edited by Mark Edwards, Martin Goodman, and Simon Price in association with Christopher Rowland, 45–58. Oxford: Oxford University Press, 1999.

———. *Mission and Conversion: Proselytizing in the Religious History of the Roman Empire.* Oxford: Clarendon, 1994.

Grant, Michael, and Rachel Kitzinger, editors. *Civilization of the Ancient Mediterranean: Greece and Rome.* 3 vols. New York: Scribner's, 1988.

Grant, Robert M. *Greek Apologists of the Second Century.* Philadelphia: Westminster, 1988.

———. "A Woman of Rome: Justin, Apology 2,2." *CH* 54 (1985): 461–72.

Grubbs, Judith Evans. *Law and Family in Late Antiquity: The Emperor Constantine's Marriage Legislation.* Oxford: Clarendon, 1995.

———. "'Marriage More Shameful Than Adultery': Slave-Mistress Relationships, 'Mixed Marriages,' and Late Roman Law." *Phoenix* 47 (1993): 125–54.

Gundry-Volf, Judith M. "The Least and the Greatest: Children in the New Testament." In *The Child in Christian Thought,* edited by Marcia J. Bunge, 29–60. Grand Rapids: Eerdmans, 2001.

Guyon, Jean. *Le Cimetière aux Deux Lauriers: Recherches sur les catacombes romaines.* Palais Farnèse: École Francaise de Rome, 1987.

Hallett, Judith P., and Marilyn B. Skinner, editors. *Roman Sexualities.* Princeton: Princeton University Press, 1997.

Hands, A. R. *Charities and Social Aid in Greece and Rome.* Ithaca, N.Y.: Cornell University Press, 1968.

Harmand, Louis. *Le patronat sur les collectivités publiques, des origines au bas-Empire: Un aspect social et politique du monde romain.* Paris: Presses Universitaires de France, 1957.

Harnack, Adolf von. *The Mission and Expansion of Christianity in the First Three Centuries.* 2 vols. Translated by James Moffatt. Theological Translation Library 19, 20. New York: Putman, 1904.

Harrill, J. Albert. "The Domestic Enemy: A Moral Polarity of Household Slaves in Early Christian Apologies and Martyrdoms." In Balch and Osiek, *Early Christian Families in Context,* 231–54.

Harrington, D. J., S.J., *The Gospel of Matthew.* SP 1. Collegeville, Minn.: Liturgical, 1991.

Harris, William V. "Demography, Geography and the Sources of Roman Slaves." *JRS* 89 (1999): 62–75.

———. "Towards a Study of the Roman Slave Trade." In *Memoirs of the American Academy in Rome* 36, edited by John H. D'Arms and E. C. Kopff, 117–40. Rome: American Academy in Rome, 1980.

Hennecke, E., and W. Schneemelcher, editors. *New Testament Apocrypha.* Translated by R. McL. Wilson. 2 vols. Louisville: Westminster John Knox, 1991–92.

Hobson, Deborah. "The Role of Women in the Economic Life of Roman Egypt." *Echos du monde classique/Classical Views* 28 n.s. 3 (1984): 373–90.

Hoffmann, R. Joseph, translator. *Celsus on the True Doctrine: A Discourse against the Christians.* Oxford: Oxford University Press, 1987.

Hopkins, Keith M. "The Age of Roman Girls at Marriage." *Population Studies* 18 (1965): 309–27.

———. *Conquerors and Slaves*. Sociological Studies in Roman History 1. Cambridge: Cambridge University Press, 1978.

———. "Contraception in the Roman Empire." *Comparative Studies in Society and History* 8 (1965): 124–51.

———. "Men's Age at Marriage and Its Consequences in the Roman Family." *CP* 82 (1987): 21–34.

Horsley, Richard A. "1 Corinthians: A Case Study of Paul's Assembly as an Alternative Society." In *Paul and Empire: Religion and Power in Roman Imperial Society*, edited by Richard A. Horsley, 242–52. Harrisburg, Pa.: Trinity Press International, 1997.

Hunter, David G., editor and translator. *Marriage in the Early Church*. Sources of Early Christian Thought. Minneapolis: Fortress, 1992.

Ilan, Tal. *Jewish Women in Greco-Roman Palestine*. Peabody, Mass.: Hendrickson, 1996.

Jackson, Ralph. *Doctors and Diseases in the Roman Empire*. Norman: University of Oklahoma Press, 1988.

Jacobs, Andrew S. "A Family Affair: Marriage, Class, and Ethics in the Apocryphal Acts of the Apostles." *JECS* 7 (1999): 104–38.

Jameson, Michael H. "Domestic Space in the Greek City-State." In Kent, *Domestic Architecture and the Use of Space*, 92–113.

Jastrzebowska, Elisabeth. "Les scènes de banquet dans les peintures et sculptures chrétiennes des IIIe et IVe siècles." *Recherches Augustiniennes* 14 (1979): 3–90.

Jensen, Robin Margaret. *Understanding Early Christian Art*. London: Routledge, 2000.

Jewett, Robert. "Paul, Phoebe and the Spanish Mission." In Neusner et al., *The Social World of Formative Christianity and Judaism*, 142–61.

———. "Tenement Churches and Communal Meals in the Early Church: The Implications of a Form-Critical Analysis of 2 Thessalonians 3:10." *BR* 38 (1993): 23–43.

Johns, Catherine, M. J. Hughes, and R. Holmes. "The Roman Silver Cups from Hockwold, Norfolk." *Archaeologia* 108 (1986): 1–13.

Johnson, Elizabeth E. "Ephesians." In *The Women's Bible Commentary*, edited by Carol A. Newsom and Sharon H. Ringe, 340–41. Louisville: Westminster John Knox, 1992.

Johnson, Luke Timothy. *The Acts of the Apostles*. SP 5. Collegeville, Minn.: Liturgical, 1992.

———. *The Gospel of Luke*. SP 3. Collegeville, Minn.: Liturgical, 1991.

Johnson, Terry, and Chris Dandeker. "Patronage: Relation and System." In Wallace-Hadrill, *Patronage in Ancient Society*, 219–42.

Jones, Christopher. "Processional Colors." In *The Art of Ancient Spectacle*, edited by Bettina Bergmann and Christine Kondoleon, 247–57. Studies in the History of Art 56. Washington, D.C.: National Gallery of Art, 1999.

Joshel, Sandra R., and Sheila Murnaghan, editors. *Women and Slaves in Greco-Roman Culture: Differential Equations*. London: Routledge, 1998.

Joubert, Stephan J. "One Form of Social Exchange or Two? 'Euergetism,' Patronage, and Testament Studies." *BTB* 31 (2001): 17–25.

Judge, E. A. "Cultural Conformity and Innovation in Paul: Some Clues from Contemporary Documents." *Tyndale Bulletin* 35 (1984): 3–24.

———. "The Early Christians as a Scholastic Community." *Journal of Religious History* 1 (1960): 4–15; 2 (1961): 125–37.

———. "Paul as a Radical Critic of Society." *Interchange* 16 (1974): 191–203.

———. *The Social Pattern of Christian Groups in the First Century*. London: Tyndale, 1960.

Kaimio, J. *The Romans and the Greek Language*. Helsinki: Societas Scientiarum Fennica, 1979.

Kampen, Natalie. *Image and Status: Roman Working Women in Ostia*. Gebr.-Mann Studio Reihe. Berlin: Mann, 1981.

Kearsley, Roz. "Women in Public Life in the Roman East: Junia Theodora, Claudia Metrodora, and Phoibe, Benefactress of Paul." *Ancient Society: Resources for Teachers* 15 (1985): 124–37. Reprinted in *Tyndale Bulletin* 50 (1999): 189–211.

Kent, Susan, editor. *Domestic Architecture and the Use of Space: An Interdisciplinary Cross-Cultural Study*. New Directions in Archaeology. Cambridge: Cambridge University Press, 1990.

Kilbourne, Brock, and James T. Richardson. "Paradigm Conflict, Types of Conversion, and Conversion Theories." *Sociological Analysis* 50 (1988): 1–21.

Kleiner, Diana E. E. *Roman Group Portraiture: The Funerary Reliefs of the Late Republic and Early Empire*. Outstanding Dissertations in the Fine Arts. New York: Garland, 1977.

Kleiner, Diana E. E., and Susan B. Matheson, editors. *I, Claudia: Women in Ancient Rome*. New Haven: Yale University Art Gallery, 1996.

Kloppenborg, John S., and Stephen G. Wilson, editors. *Voluntary Associations in the Greco-Roman World*. London: Routledge, 1996.

Koch, Guntram, and K. Wight. "Front of the Sarcophagus of Titus Aelius Euangelus and Gaudenia Nicene." In *Roman Funerary Sculpture: Catalogue of the Collections*, 24–27. Malibu: J. Paul Getty Museum, 1988.

Kotila, Heikki. *Memoria Mortuorum: Commemoration of the Departed in Augustine*. Rome: Institutum Patristicum Augustinianum, 1992.

Kraemer, Ross S. "The Conversion of Women to Ascetic Forms of Christianity." *Signs* 6 (1980): 298–307.

———. *Her Share of the Blessings: Women's Religions among Pagans, Jews, and Christians in the Greco-Roman World.* New York: Oxford University Press, 1992.

———. *Women's Religions in the Greco-Roman World: A Sourcebook.* Oxford: Oxford University Press, 2004.

Kraemer, Ross S., and Mary Rose D'Angelo, editors. *Women and Christian Origins.* New York: Oxford University Press, 1999.

Kraemer, Ross S., and Shira L. Lander. "Perpetua and Felicitas." In *The Early Christian World,* edited by Philip F. Esler, 2:1051–58. London: Routledge, 2000.

Krause, Jens-Uwe. *Spätantike Patronatsformen im Westen des Römischen Reiches.* Vestigia 38. Munich: Beck, 1987.

Kunzl, Susanna. *Die Trierer Spruchbecherkeramik: Dekorierte Schwarzfirniskeramik des 3. und 4. Jahrhunderts n. Chr.* Beihefte zur Trierer Zeitschrift für Geschichte und Kunst des Trierer Landes und seiner Nachbargebiete. Trier: Rheinischen Landesmuseums Trier, 1997.

Laes, Christian. "Desperately Different? *Delicia* Children in the Roman Household." In Balch and Osiek, *Early Christian Families in Context,* 298–324.

Laiou, Angeliki E. "Sex, Consent, and Coercion in Byzantium." In Laiou, *Consent and Coercion to Sex and Marriage,* 109–221.

Laiou, Angeliki E., editor. *Consent and Coercion to Sex and Marriage in Ancient and Medieval Societies.* Washington, D.C.: Dumbarton Oaks Research Library and Collection, 1993.

Laistner, M. L. W. *Christianity and Pagan Culture in the Later Roman Empire.* Ithaca, N.Y.: Cornell University Press, 1951.

Lattimore, Richard. *Themes in Greek and Latin Epitaphs.* Illini Books. Urbana: University of Illinois Press, 1962.

Lefkowitz, Mary R. "The Motivations for St. Perpetua's Martyrdom." *JAAR* 44 (1976): 417–21.

Lefkowitz, Mary R., and Maureen Fant. *Women's Life in Greece and Rome: A Source Book in Translation.* 2nd ed. Baltimore: Johns Hopkins University Press, 1992.

Leyerle, Blake. "John Chrysostom Sermons on City Life." In *Religions of Late Antiquity in Practice,* edited by Richard Valantasis, 247–60. Princeton: Princeton University Press, 2000.

Lieu, Judith. "The 'Attraction of Women' in/to Early Judaism and Christianity: Gender and the Politics of Conversion." *JSNT* 72 (1998): 5–22.

Lincoln, Andrew T. *Ephesians.* WBC 42. Dallas: Word, 1990.

Lutz, Cora E. "Musonius Rufus 'The Roman Socrates.'" *Yale Classical Studies* 10 (1947): 3–147.

MacDonald, Dennis R. *The Legend and the Apostle: The Battle for Paul in Story and Canon.* Philadelphia: Westminster, 1983.

———. *There Is No Male and Female: The Fate of a Dominical Saying in Paul and Gnosticism.* Philadelphia: Fortress, 1987.

MacDonald, Margaret Y. "Can Nympha Rule This House? The Rhetoric of Domesticity in Colossians." In Braun, *Rhetorics and Realities in Early Christianities.*

———. *Colossians and Ephesians.* SP 17. Collegeville, Minn.: Liturgical, 2000.

———. *Early Christian Women and Pagan Opinion: The Power of the Hysterical Woman.* Cambridge: Cambridge University Press, 1996.

———. "The Ideal of the Christian Couple: Ign. *Pol* 5.1–2 Looking Back to Paul." *NTS* 40 (1994): 105–25.

———. "The Politics of Identity in Ephesians." *JSNT* 26 (2004): 419–44.

———. "Reading Real Women through the Undisputed Letters of Paul." In Kraemer and D'Angelo, *Women and Christian Origins,* 199–220.

———. "Rereading Paul: Early Interpreters of Paul on Women and Gender." In Kraemer and D'Angelo, *Women and Christian Origins,* 236–53.

———. "Was Celsus Right? The Role of Women in the Expansion of Early Christianity." In Balch and Osiek, *Early Christian Families in Context,* 157–84.

———. "Women Holy in Body and Spirit: The Social Setting of 1 Corinthians 7." *NTS* 36 (1990): 161–81.

MacMullen, Ramsay. *Christianizing the Roman Empire (A.D. 100–400).* New Haven: Yale University Press, 1984.

———. "Women in Public in the Roman Empire." *Historia* 29 (1980): 208–18.

———. "Women's Power in the Principate." In *Changes in the Roman Empire: Essays on the Ordinary,* 169–76. Princeton: Princeton University Press, 1990.

Madden, John. "Slavery in the Roman Empire: Numbers and Origins." *Classics Ireland* 3 (1996): 109–28.

Madigan, Kevin, and Carolyn Osiek. *Ordained Women in the Early Church: A Documentary History.* Baltimore: Johns Hopkins University Press, 2005.

Maier, Harry O. *The Social Setting of the Ministry as Reflected in the Writings of Hermas, Clement and Ignatius.* Dissertations SR1. Waterloo, Ont.: Wilfrid Laurier University Press, 1991.

Malherbe, Abraham J., Frederick W. Norris, and James W. Thompson, editors. *The Early Church in Its Context: Essays in Honor of Everett Ferguson.* NovTSup 90. Leiden: Brill, 1998.

Malina, Bruce J. "Does *Porneia* Mean Fornication?" *NovT* 14 (1972): 10–17.

———. *The New Testament World: Insights from Cultural Anthropology.* 3rd ed. Louisville: Westminster John Knox, 2001.

Malinowski, Francis X. "The Brave Women of Philippi." *BTB* 15 (1985): 60–64.

Marrou, Henri I. *A History of Education in Antiquity.* Translated by George Lamb. Madison: University of Wisconsin Press, 1956.

Martin, Clarice J. "The Acts of the Apostles." In *Searching the Scriptures,* vol. 2: *A Feminist Commentary,* edited by Elisabeth Schüssler Fiorenza, 763–99. New York: Crossroad, 1994.

Martin, Dale B. "Slave Families and Slaves in Families." In Balch and Osiek, *Early Christian Families in Context*, 207–30.

———. "Slavery and the Ancient Jewish Family." In Cohen, *The Jewish Family in Antiquity*, 113–29.

———. *Slavery as Salvation: The Metaphor of Slavery in Pauline Christianity*. New Haven: Yale University Press, 1990.

Matson, David Lertis. *Household Conversion Narratives in Acts: Pattern and Interpretation*. JSNTSup 123. Sheffield: Sheffield Academic, 1996.

Matthews, Shelly. *First Converts: Rich Pagan Women and the Rhetoric of Mission in Early Judaism and Christianity*. Contraversions. Stanford: Stanford University Press, 2001.

Matthews, Thomas F. *The Clash of Gods: A Reinterpretation of Early Christian Art*. Rev. ed. Princeton: Princeton University Press, 1999.

Mattila, Sharon Lee. "Where Women Sat in Ancient Synagogues: The Archaeological Evidence in Context." In *Voluntary Associations in the Greco-Roman World*, edited by John S. Kloppenborg and Stephen G. Wilson, 266–86. London: Routledge, 1996.

McGinn, Thomas A. J. "The Legal Definition of Prostitute in Late Antiquity." In *Memoirs of the American Academy in Rome*, vol. 42, edited by Malcolm Bell III and Caroline Bruzelius, 73–116. Washington, D.C.: American Academy in Rome, 1997.

———. *Prostitution, Sexuality, and the Law in Ancient Rome*. New York: Oxford University Press, 1998.

McKay, Alexander G. *Houses, Villas, and Palaces in the Roman World*. Baltimore: Johns Hopkins University Press, 1998.

Meeks, Wayne A. *The First Urban Christian: The Social World of the Apostle Paul*. New Haven: Yale University Press, 1983.

Mertens, Joan R. "Pair of Drinking Cups." *Metropolitan Museum of Art Bulletin* 50 (fall 1992): 11.

Metzger, Bruce M. *A Textual Commentary on the Greek New Testament*. 2nd ed. New York: United Bible Societies, 1994.

Meunier, Mario, editor. *Femmes Pythagoriciennes: Fragments et Lettres de Théano, Périctioné, Phintys, Mélissa et Myia*. Paris: L'Artisan du livre, 1932.

Millar, L. *Christian Education in the First Four Centuries*. London: Faith, 1946.

Millett, Paul. "Patronage and Its Avoidance in Classical Athens." In Wallace-Hadrill, *Patronage in Ancient Society*, 15–47.

Mitchell, Margaret M. "New Testament Envoys in the Context of Greco-Roman Diplomatic and Epistolary Conventions: The Example of Timothy and Titus." *JBL* 111 (1992): 641–62.

Mitchell, W. J. Thomas. *Picture Theory: Essays on Verbal and Visual Representation*. Chicago: University of Chicago Press, 1994.

Moses, Diana C. "Livy's Lucretia and the Validity of Coerced Consent in Roman Law." In Laiou, *Consent and Coercion to Sex and Marriage*, 39–82.

Moxnes, Halvor, editor. *Constructing Early Christian Families: Family as Social Reality and Metaphor.* London: Routledge, 1997.

———. "Honor and Shame." In Rohrbaugh, *The Social Sciences and New Testament Interpretation*, 19–40.

Müller, G. "Ausgrabungen in Dormagen, 1963–1977." *Rheinische Ausgrabungen* 20 (1979): 125–26.

Müller, Peter. *In der Mitte der Gemeinde: Kinder im Neuen Testament.* Neukirchen Vluyn: Neukirchener, 1992.

Munro, Winsome. "Col. III.18—IV.1 and Eph. V.21—VI.9: Evidence of a Late Literary Stratum?" *NTS* 18 (1972): 434–47.

Murphy-O'Connor, J. *Paul: A Critical Life.* Oxford: Clarendon, 1996.

Musurillo, H. *The Acts of the Christian Martyrs: Introduction, Texts and Translations.* Oxford Early Christian Texts. Oxford: Oxford University Press, 1972.

Nathan, Geoffrey S. *The Family in Late Antiquity: The Rise of Christianity and the Endurance of Tradition.* London: Routledge, 2000.

Neusner, Jacob, et al., editors. *The Social World of Formative Christianity and Judaism: Essays in Tribute to Howard Clark Kee.* Philadelphia: Fortress, 1988.

Noy, David. *Foreigners at Rome: Citizens and Strangers.* London: Duckworth, 2000.

Osiek, Carolyn. "The Bride of Christ (Eph 5:22-33): A Problematic Wedding." *BTB* 32 (2002): 29–39.

———. "Perpetua's Husband." *JECS* 10 (2002): 287–90.

———. *The Shepherd of Hermas: A Commentary.* Hermeneia. Minneapolis: Fortress, 1999.

———. "The Widow as Altar: The Rise and Fall of a Symbol." *SecCent* 3/3 (1983): 159–69.

Osiek, Carolyn, and David L. Balch. *Families in the New Testament World: Households and House Churches.* Family, Religion, and Culture. Louisville: Westminster John Knox, 1997.

Patterson, Orlando. *Slavery and Social Death: A Comparative Study.* Cambridge: Harvard University Press, 1982.

Paxton, Frederick S. *Christianizing Death: The Creation of a Ritual Process in Early Medieval Europe.* Ithaca, N.Y.: Cornell University Press, 1990.

Pearce, T. E. V. "The Role of the Wife as CUSTOS in Ancient Rome." *Eranos* 72 (1974): 16–33.

Perdue, Leo G., Joseph Blenkinsopp, John J. Collins, and Carol Meyers, editors. *Families in Ancient Israel.* Family, Religion, and Culture. Louisville: Westminster John Knox, 1997.

Peristiany, John G., editor. *Mediterranean Family Structures.* Cambridge: Cambridge University Press, 1976.

Peristiany, John G., and Julian Pitt-Rivers, editors. *Honor and Grace in Anthropology*. Cambridge Studies in Social and Cultural Anthropology 76. Cambridge: Cambridge University Press, 1992.

Perkins, Pheme. *Ephesians*. ANTC. Nashville: Abingdon, 1997.

Plaskow, Judith. "Christian Feminism and Anti-Judaism." *Cross Currents* 28 (1978): 306–9.

Pleket, H. W. *Texts on the Social History of the Greek World*. Epigraphica 2. Leiden: Brill, 1969.

Pomeroy, Sarah B. "Reflections on Plutarch, A Consolation to His Wife." In *Plutarch's Advice to the Bride and Groom and A Consolation to His Wife*, edited by Sarah B. Pomeroy, 75–81. Oxford: Oxford University Press, 1999.

———. *Women in Hellenistic Egypt: From Alexander to Cleopatra*. New York: Schocken, 1984.

———, editor. *Women's History and Ancient History*. Chapel Hill: University of North Carolina Press, 1991.

Praet, Danny. "Explaining the Christianization of the Roman Empire: Older Theories and Recent Developments." In *Sacris Erudiri: Jaarboek voor Godsdienstwetenschappen* 33 (1992–93): 7–119.

Raepsaet-Charlier, Marie-Thérèse. "Tertullien et la législation des mariages inégaux." *Revue internationale des droits de l'antiquité* 29 (1982): 253–63.

Rajak, Tessa, and David Noy. "*Archisynagogoi*: Office, Title and Social Status in the Greco-Jewish Synagogue." *JRS* 83 (1993): 75–93.

Rawson, Beryl. *Children and Childhood in Roman Italy*. Oxford: Oxford University Press, 2003.

———. "Roman Concubinage and Other De Facto Marriages." *TAPA* 104 (1974): 279–305.

———. "The Roman Family." In *The Family in Ancient Rome: New Perspectives*, edited by Beryl Rawson, 1–57. Ithaca, N.Y.: Cornell University Press, 1986.

Reimer, Ivoni Richter. *Women in the Acts of the Apostles: A Feminist Liberation Perspective*. Translated by Linda M. Maloney. Minneapolis: Fortress, 1995.

Reinhartz, Adele. "Philo's Exposition of the Law and Social History." In *SBL Annual Meeting 1993 Seminar Papers*, edited by Eugene H. Lowering Jr., 6–21. Atlanta: Scholars, 1993.

Remus, Harold. *Pagan-Christian Conflict over Miracle in the Second Century*. Cambridge, Mass.: Philadelphia Patristic Foundation, 1983.

———. "Unknown and Yet Well-Known: The Multiform Formation of Early Christianity." In *A Multiform Heritage: Studies on Early Judaism and Christianity in Honor of Robert A. Kraft*, edited by Benjamin G. Wright, 79–93. Atlanta: Scholars, 1999.

Reynolds, Joyce. "Roman Inscriptions 1971–75." *JRS* 66 (1976): 174–99.

Rives, James. "Civic and Religious Life." In *Epigraphic Evidence: Ancient History from Inscriptions*, edited by John Bodel, 118–36. London: Routledge, 2001.

Rohrbaugh, Richard L., editor. *The Social Sciences and New Testament Interpretation*. Peabody, Mass.: Hendrickson, 1996.

Roller, Matthew. "Horizontal Women: Posture and Sex in the Roman *Convivium*." *American Journal of Philology* 124 (2003): 377–422.

Saller, Richard P. "The Hierarchical Household in Roman Society: A Study of Domestic Slavery." In *Serfdom and Slavery: Studies in Legal Bondage*, edited by M. L. Bush, 112–29. London: Longman, 1996.

———. "Men's Age at Marriage and Its Consequences in the Roman Family." *CP* 82 (1987): 21–34.

———. "*Pater Familias, Mater Familias*, and the Gendered Semantics of the Roman Household." *CP* 94 (1999): 182–97.

———. *Patriarchy, Property, and Death in the Roman Family*. Cambridge: Cambridge University Press, 1994.

———. "Patronage and Friendship in Early Imperial Rome: Drawing the Distinction." In Wallace-Hadrill, *Patronage in Ancient Society*, 49–62.

———. *Personal Patronage under the Early Empire*. Cambridge: Cambridge University Press, 1982.

Salvadori, Sharon Marie. "*Per Feminam Mors, Per Feminam Vita*: Images of Women in the Early Christian Funerary Art of Rome." Ph.D. dissertation. New York University, 2002.

Salzman, Michele Renée. "Aristocratic Women: Conductors of Christianity in the Fourth Century." *Helios* 16 (1989): 207–20.

———. "How the West Was Won: The Christianization of the Roman Aristocracy in the West in the Years after Constantine." *Studies in Latin Literature and Roman History, Collection Latomus* 217 (1992): 6.451–79.

Sampley, J. Paul. *"And the Two Shall Become One Flesh": A Study of the Traditions in Eph 5:21–33*. SNTSMS 16. Cambridge: Cambridge University Press, 1971.

Satlow, Michael. *Jewish Marriage in Antiquity*. Princeton: Princeton University Press, 2001.

Schaberg, Jane. "The Infancy of Mary of Nazareth." In *Searching the Scriptures*, vol. 2: *A Feminist Commentary*, edited by Elisabeth Schüssler Fiorenza, 708–27. New York: Crossroad, 1994.

Scheidel, Walter. "Quantifying the Sources of Slaves in the Early Roman Empire." *JRS* 87 (1997): 156–69.

Schlier, Heinrich. *Der Brief an die Epheser: Ein Kommentar*. Düsseldorf: Patmos, 1957.

Schoedel, William R. *Ignatius of Antioch: A Commentary on the Letters of Ignatius of Antioch*. Hermeneia. Philadelphia: Fortress, 1985.

Schottroff, Luise. *Let the Oppressed Go Free: Feminist Perspectives on the New Testament*. Translated by Annemarie S. Kidder. Louisville: Westminster John Knox, 1993.

————. *Lydia's Impatient Sisters: A Feminist Social History of Early Christianity.* Translated by Barbara and Martin Rumscheidt. Louisville: Westminster John Knox, 1995.

Schüssler Fiorenza, Elisabeth. *In Memory of Her: A Feminist Theological Reconstruction of Christian Origins.* New York: Crossroad, 1983.

Scobie, A. "Slums, Sanitation, and Mortality in the Roman World." *Klio* 68 (1986): 399–433.

Scott, E. "Unpacking a Myth: The Infanticide of Females and Disabled Infants in Antiquity." In *Proceedings of the Tenth Annual Theoretical Roman Archaeology Conference, London 2000,* edited by G. Davies, A. Gardner, and K. Lockyear, 143–51. Oxford: Oxbow, 2000.

Seim, Truid Karlsen. "A Superior Minority: The Problem of Men's Headship in Ephesians 5." In *Mighty Minorities? Minorities in Early Christianity—Positions and Strategies: Essays in Honor of Jacob Jervell on His 70th Birthday, 21 May 1995,* edited by David Hellholm, Halvor Moxnes, and Turid Karlsen Seim, 167–81. Oslo: Scandinavian University Press, 1995.

Shaw, Brent D. "Raising and Killing Children: Two Roman Myths." *Mnemosyne* 54 (2001): 31–77.

Sijpesteijn, P. J., editor. *The Wisconsin Papyri II.* Zutphen, Holland: Terra, 1977.

Skehan, Patrick W. *The Wisdom of Ben Sira: A New Translation with Notes.* Introduction and commentary by Alexander A. di Lella. AB 39. Garden City, N.Y.: Doubleday, 1987.

Skinner, Marilyn B. "Introduction: Quod multo fit in graecia." In *Roman Sexualities,* edited by Judith P. Hallett and Marilyn B. Skinner, 3–28. Princeton: Princeton University Press, 1997.

Slater, William J., editor. *Dining in a Classical Context.* Ann Arbor: University of Michigan Press, 1991.

Smith, Dennis E. *From Symposium to Eucharist: The Banquet in the Early Christian World.* Minneapolis: Fortress, 2003.

Solin, Heikki. *Die griechische Personennamen in Rom: Ein Namenbuch.* Berlin: de Gruyter, 1982.

Sotgiu, Giovanna. "Un collare di schiavo rinvenuto in Sardegna." *Archeologia classica: Rivista dell'Istituto di archeologia dell'Università di Roma* 25–26 (1973–74): 688–97.

Spelman, Elizabeth V. *Inessential Woman: Problems of Exclusion in Feminist Thought.* Boston: Beacon, 1988.

Stark, Rodney. *The Rise of Christianity: A Sociologist Reconsiders History.* Princeton: Princeton University Press, 1996.

Stark, Rodney, and William S. Bainbridge. "Networks of Faith: Interpersonal Bonds and Recruitment to Cults and Sects." *American Journal of Sociology* 85 (1980): 1376–95.

Stewart, Frank Henderson. *Honor.* Chicago: University of Chicago Press, 1994.

Strange, W. A. *Children in the Early Church: Children in the Ancient World, the New Testament, and the Early Church.* Carlisle: Paternoster, 1996.

Symonds, R. P. *Rhenish Wares: Fine Dark Coloured Pottery from Gaul and Germany.* Oxford: Oxford University Committee for Archaeology, 1992.

Tanzer, Sarah. "Ephesians." In *Searching the Scriptures,* vol. 2: *A Feminist Commentary,* edited by Elisabeth Schüssler Fiorenza, 325–48. New York: Crossroad, 1994.

Thalman, William G. "Female Slaves in the Odyssey." In *Women and Slaves in Greco-Roman Culture: Differential Equations,* edited by Sandra R. Joshel and Sheila Murnaghan, 22–34. London: Routledge, 1998.

Thesleff, Holger, editor. *The Pythagorean Texts of the Hellenistic Period.* Acta Academiae Aboensis, Series A. Humanistika Vetenskaper, Socialvetenskaper, Teologi, 30.1. Abo: Abo Akademi, 1965.

Thurston, Bonnie Bowman. *The Widows: A Women's Ministry in the Early Church.* Minneapolis: Fortress, 1989.

Tilley, Maureen E. "The Passion of Perpetua and Felicity." In *Searching the Scriptures,* vol. 2: *A Feminist Commentary,* edited by Elisabeth Schüssler Fiorenza, 829–58. New York: Crossroad, 1994.

Torjesen, Karen Jo. *When Women Were Priests: Women's Leadership in the Early Church and the Scandal of Their Subordination in the Rise of Christianity.* San Francisco: HarperSanFrancisco, 1993.

Toynbee, J. M. C. *Death and Burial in the Roman World.* London: Thames and Hudson, 1971.

Treggiari, Susan. "Family Life among the Staff of the Volusii." *TAPA* 105 (1975): 393–401.

———. "Jobs for Women." *American Journal of Ancient History* 1:2 (1976): 76–104.

———. "Jobs in the Household of Livia." *PBSR* 43 (1975): 48–77.

———. *Roman Marriage: Iusti Coniuges from the Time of Cicero to the Time of Ulpian.* Oxford: Clarendon, 1991.

Trevett, Christine. *Montanism: Gender, Authority, and the New Prophecy.* Cambridge: Cambridge University Press, 1996.

Tulloch, Janet H. "Art and Archaeology as a Historical Resource for the Study of Women in Early Christianity: An Approach for Analyzing Visual Data." *Journal of Feminist Theology* 12/3 (May 2004): 277–304.

———. "Gender." In *Encyclopedia of Early Christian Art and Archaeology,* edited by Paul Corby Finney. Grand Rapids: Eerdmans, forthcoming.

———. "Image as Artifact: A Social-Historical Analysis of Female Figures with Cups in the Banquet Scenes from the Catacomb of SS. Marcellino e Pietro, Rome." PhD dissertation, University of Ottawa, 2001.

————. *Speaking about Agape and Irene: Women and Hospitality in Roman Christian Funerary Art.* Waterloo, Ont.: Wilfrid Laurier University Press, forthcoming.

Valantasis, Richard, editor. *Religions of Late Antiquity in Practice.* Princeton: Prince-ton University Press, 2000.

Van Bremen, Riet. "Women and Wealth." In *Images of Women in Antiquity*, edited by Averil Cameron and Amélie Kuhrt, 223–42. Rev. ed. Detroit: Wayne State University Press, 1993.

Van der Leeuw, G. "Refrigerium." *Mnemosyne* 3 (1935–36): 125–48.

Walker, John A., and Sarah Chaplin. *Visual Culture: An Introduction.* Manchester: Manchester University Press, 1997.

Wallace-Hadrill, Andrew. *Houses and Society in Pompeii and Herculaneum.* Prince-ton: Princeton University Press, 1994.

————, editor. *Patronage in Ancient Society.* Leicester-Nottingham Studies in Ancient Society 1. London: Routledge, 1989.

Walters, J. C. "Romans, Jews, and Christians: The Impact of the Romans on Jewish/Christian Relations in First-Century Rome." In *Judaism and Christianity in First-Century Rome*, edited by Karl P. Donfried and Peter Richardson, 175–95. Grand Rapids: Eerdmans, 1998.

Waltzing, J. P. *Étude historique sur les corporations professionelles chez les Romains depuis les origines jusqu'à la chute de l'Empire d'Occident.* 4 vols. Louvain, 1895–1900; Rome: L'Erma di Bretschneider, 1968.

Walzer, Richard. *Galen on Jews and Christians.* London: Oxford University Press, 1949.

Ward, Roy Bowen. "The Public Priestesses of Pompeii." In Malherbe, Norris, and Thompson, *The Early Church in Its Context*, 318–34.

————. "Women in Pompeii: Work in Progress." Unpublished paper.

Wassen, Cecilia. *Women in the Damascus Document.* Society of Biblical Literature Academia Biblica Series 21. Leiden: Brill, 2005.

Weaver, P. R. C. "Children of Freedmen (and Freedwomen)." In *Marriage, Divorce, and Children in Ancient Rome*, edited by Beryl Rawson, 166–90. Oxford: Clarendon, 1991.

Westermann, William L. *The Slave Systems of Greek and Roman Antiquity.* Philadelphia: American Philosophical Society, 1955.

Whelan, Caroline F. *"Amica Pauli*: The Role of Phoebe in the Early Church." *JSNT* 49 (1993): 67–85.

Wiedemann, Thomas E. J. *Adults and Children in the Roman Empire.* New Haven: Yale University Press, 1989.

White, L. Michael. "Adolf Harnack and the Expansion of Early Christianity: A Reappraisal of Social History." *SecCent* 5 (1985/86): 97–127.

————. *The Social Origins of Christian Architecture.* HTS 42. 2 vols. Valley Forge, Pa.: Trinity Press International, 1996–97.

————. "Visualizing the 'Real' World of Acts 16: Toward Construction of a Social Index." In *The Social World of the First Christians: Essays in Honor of Wayne A. Meeks*, edited by L. Michael White and O. Larry Yarbrough, 234–61. Minneapolis: Fortress, 1995.

————, editor. *Social Networks in the Early Christian Environment: Issues and Methods for Social History*. Semeia 56. Atlanta: Scholars, 1992.

White, Peter. "*Amicitia* and the Profession of Poetry in Early Imperial Rome." *JRS* 68 (1978): 74–92.

Wikan, Unni. "Shame and Honor: A Contestable Pair." *Man* 19 (1984): 635–52.

Wilken, Robert L. *The Christians as the Romans Saw Them*. New Haven: Yale University Press, 1984.

Williams, Craig A. *Roman Homosexuality: Ideologies of Masculinity in Classical Antiquity*. Oxford: Oxford University Press, 1999.

Winn, Robert E. "The Church of Virgins and Martyrs: Ecclesiastical Identity in the Sermons of Eusebius of Emesa." *JECS* 11 (2003): 309–38.

Winter, Bruce W. *Roman Wives, Roman Widows: The Appearance of New Women and the Pauline Communities*. Grand Rapids: Eerdmans, 2003.

Wire, Antoinette Clark. *The Corinthian Women Prophets: A Reconstruction through Paul's Rhetoric*. Minneapolis: Fortress, 1990.

Wolters, Al. "Sôpiyyâ" (Prov 31:27) as Hymnic Participle and Play on *Sophia*." *JBL* 104 (1985): 577–87.

Yarbrough, O. Larry. *Not Like the Gentiles: Marriage Rules in the Letters of Paul*. SBLDS 80. Atlanta: Scholars, 1985.

Yoder, Christine Roy. *Wisdom as a Woman of Substance: A Socioeconomic Reading of Proverbs 1–9 and 31:10–31*. Berlin: de Gruyter, 2001.

Zanker, Paul. *Pompeii: Public and Private Life*. Cambridge: Harvard University Press, 1998.

Zappella, Marco. "A proposito di Febe PROSTATIS (Rm 16,2)." *Rivista biblica italiana* 37 (1989): 167–71.

Zimmerman, Norbert. "Werkstattgruppen römischer Katakombenmalerei." In *Jahrbuch für Antike und Christentum* Expanded vol. 35. Münster: Aschendorff, 2002.

Zolty, Shoshana Pantel. *"And All Your Children Shall Be Learned": Women and the Study of Torah in Jewish Law and History*. Northvale, N.J.: Aronson, 1993.

⧉ ⧉ ⧉

INDEX OF MODERN AUTHORS

INDEX OF SUBJECTS

ABOUT THE AUTHORS

◻◻ ◻◻ ◻◻

Carolyn Osiek
is Professor of New Testament at Brite Divinity School, Fort Worth, Texas. Her other books include, with Kevin Madigan, *Ordained Women in the Early Church: A Documentary History* (2005); *The Shepherd of Hermas*, Hermeneia (Fortress, 1999); and, with David L. Balch, *Families in the New Testament World: Households and House Churches* (1997).

Margaret Y. MacDonald
is Professor of New Testament at St. Francis Xavier University (Nova Scotia, Canada). Her other books include *Early Christian Women and Pagan Opinion* (1996) and *The Pauline Churches: A Socio-Historical Study of Institutionalization* (1988).

Janet H. Tulloch
received her Ph.D. in Religious Studies from the University of Ottawa.